MW00813442

American Women in Amateur
Wrestling, 2000–2022

ALSO BY JASON NORMAN
AND FROM McFARLAND

New Jack: Memoir of a Pro Wrestling Extremist
(New Jack and Jason Norman, 2020)

*Welcome to Our Nightmares: Behind the Scene
with Today's Horror Actors* (2015)

American Women in Amateur Wrestling, 2000–2022

Jason Norman

LIBRARY OF
CONGRESS
SURPLUS
DUPLICATE

McFarland & Company, Inc., Publishers
Jefferson, North Carolina

Library of Congress Cataloguing-in-Publication Data

Names: Norman, Jason, 1979– author.
Title: American women in amateur wrestling, 2000-2022 / Jason Norman.
Description: Jefferson, North Carolina : McFarland & Company, Inc., Publishers, 2023.
| Includes bibliographical references and index.
Identifiers: LCCN 2023026867 | ISBN 9781476684864 (paperback : acid free paper) ∞
| ISBN 9781476649078 (ebook)
Subjects: LCSH: Women wrestlers—United States—Biography. |
Women Olympic athletes—United States—Biography. | Greco-Roman wrestling—United States.
Classification: LCC GV1196.A1 N67 2023 | DDC 796.812082—dc23/eng/20230627
LC record available at https://lccn.loc.gov/2023026867

British Library cataloguing data are available

ISBN (print) 978-1-4766-8486-4
ISBN (ebook) 978-1-4766-4907-8

© 2023 Jason Norman. All rights reserved

*No part of this book may be reproduced or transmitted in any form
or by any means, electronic or mechanical, including photocopying
or recording, or by any information storage and retrieval system,
without permission in writing from the publisher.*

Front cover image: Kayla Miracle (left) and Helen Maroulis (right) battle it out
for U.S. Open supremacy. Photograph provided by AJ Grieves/MatFocus.

Printed in the United States of America

*McFarland & Company, Inc., Publishers
Box 611, Jefferson, North Carolina 28640
www.mcfarlandpub.com*

Contents

Preface

Right around the start of the new millennium, the fuse that so many had been trying to light under female wrestling for so long finally caught fire. It had started low—and then it started to grow! Wrestling for women just blew up like crazy over the past few decades. Women had all sorts of new reasons to try this game—and not to give up if things didn't go well. More and more people would be there for them if things didn't start off right. That kind of teamwork extends far off the mat.

By this time, women had won world titles in wrestling. Ladies were showing up on high school and college teams. The University of Minnesota–Morris had become the first such school to start a female team for the 1993–94 season, and others had quickly followed. In Arizona's 1992 event, Miyuu Yamamoto had become the first gal to finish in the top six in a state tournament. Alaska's Melina Hutchison would be the first state titlist in 2001. Hawaii's public school system had sanctioned the sport in 1998, and Texas had followed the next year.

It had taken far too long to reach certain marks, and it would take time to reach many more. But it would happen, and maybe not all that far in the distance.

Over the nearly two years it took to write this book, one of the most amazing things that I kept seeing was just how resourceful, how brave the female wrestling community was. When the Covid virus, which kicked off literally just as I got to work, threw a roadblock right into the path of wrestling, as it did with all sports, the community barely hesitated, altering workout schedules, staying in shape, doing what needed to be done to keep moving up, even at a much slower pace. It's all you can do, and so many of them did.

We'll talk about that. We're going to be jumping back and forth to the 2020 Olympics—which, as we all know, weren't the 2020 Games at all. We'll go over the ways that female wrestling is starting to branch all over American culture, extending, for the first time, past the sports world. And the competitors we discuss near the end of this book, well, let's hope we keep hearing those same names for a very, very long time.

Yes, it's been incredibly educational and quite inspiring over the past few years to become a part of this community. And as the group moves forward, it's going to keep going!

Generations of women wrestlers have fought for legitimacy. Now it's time for normalcy. Maybe the greatest gift these ladies could get—and I know, because many of them told me themselves!—is to get gender out of the equation. Don't see them as lady wrestlers. Don't see them as women of the mat.

Just great athletes. Just dedicated wrestlers.

They deserve more than that. But it's a hell of a start.

Now let us begin…

1

Will the Trials Begin?

"Women's wrestling is freaking taking off, and I think all of us carry ourselves with that in mind. We're very aware that the steps in us chasing our dream is creating a bigger platform for the women coming behind us, and that can really fire you up, knowing that this is planting a seed for the people coming after you. To have that extra purpose and knowing that you're growing a sport is just really cool. It's creating a domino effect that I think will continue to explode after the Olympics."

—Sarah Hildebrandt

You think hell hath no fury like a woman scorned?

Try explaining to one exactly why something she worked herself half to death and back again for the past four years (if not longer!) might suddenly never happen!

Then find a nice bed to hide under for a couple of weeks.

Getting caught out of nowhere with a takedown, and then overpowered while trying to get back up. Knowing that you're only down by two, or even one, as those last seconds tick away, unable to fight back, to get up, to do whatever to score. Battling the same person for the dozenth time, and still not finding that eternally elusive way to win.

Every wrestler goes through these once in a while. This was so much worse.

Women of the mat have long been tired of hearing the word *no*. *No*, you can't wrestle, because no girl ever has. *No*, you can't wrestle my wrestlers because *I* think it's inappropriate. *No*, I won't wrestle you because it's just, I don't know, *wrong* to do that! *No*, women can't wrestle in high school/college/club teams/the Olympics because wrestling's a *guys' game*! That's been going on for decades, and still happens too often today.

Women have been through court battles, school board suppressions, and, of course, sexism, that common enemy that for so long and probably much longer has held down so many lady wrestlers (and women in about every other co-ed sport). They've got every right and more to be royally pissed.

This, however, was something else. Those extra sessions in practice after the rest of the team had gone home, that new set of workouts in the gym, that move that looked so impossible when she first tried it and worked and worked until it became routine, none of that could get the wrestlers past this issue.

Nothing personal or anything. This nemesis wasn't singling out any particular participant, regardless of gender or particular sport. Everyone had been hurt by this, and those who had only lost practice and playing time could consider themselves luckier than most.

But that gave them as much consolation as, well, a consolation match.

All those years of work, on a quest that, for many, had been going since childhood.

It had already taken them all over America, and many around the globe. Now the dream of every wrestler—male or female—who'd ever strapped on a singlet was right *there*. A few wins away from a shot at immortality.

A place in American sports history. Forget that—*world* history.

It was supposed to have started in early April 2020. Dozens of ladies would gather at Penn State to battle it out, warming up on each other to take on the world. Many of them had squared off before, but when the Olympics are on the line, people focus on the present.

This was the final chance for some of them, and not just for the 2020 Games. Four years is an eternity for any top-level athlete, particularly in a sport as physical as wrestling, and a whole new, much younger and maybe more enthusiastic crowd would be around by the time 2024 rolled around. A win in these trials could be their final push to the top; a loss might be a sad farewell to a dream that many had come *this* close to.

By early March 2020, murmurs were starting to roll across America about this troublesome virus. Corona? Covid? Covid-19? Whatever anyone wanted to call it, it was getting people sick.

Months before, everyone had hoped it would stay in Asia, where it had originated. People were sure that the few cases in America would be isolated and healed fast. Hey, even those infected could feel better fast by just laying around for a few days, right? The flu's no picnic, but there are vaccines for it, and a simple shot could take care of this, right?

No. Sadly, tragically, not even close. On January 31, the World Health Organization had declared Covid just its sixth global health emergency in world history. Four days later, the Trump administration declared a public health emergency, halting and limiting most America-China travel. After spending the next few weeks claiming that Covid was "very under control in the USA," and that, "one day—it's like a miracle—it will disappear," our then-president finally called it a national emergency, and tons of time and money were dumped into our newest invisible enemy.

But it didn't help enough. Over the next weeks and months, millions were sickened. Thousands, then hundreds of thousands died. Even today in the summer of 2023, Covid still victimizes far too many all over the world.

Even as legally imposed quarantines and the infamous term "social distancing" started popping up all over the nation, our hopeful Olympians did what they could to stay in shape, hoping that that "miracle" would occur, that this would go away, and their Olympic dreams would stay within reach.

But we all know what happened. On March 13, USA Wrestling announced that its sports trials wouldn't happen—not on their original April 4–5 date at Penn, or maybe ever. Eleven days after that, the International Olympic Committee and the Tokyo Organizing Committee told a sad sports world that the 2020 Tokyo Games wouldn't be in 2020 after all. If anyone was lucky, the Games might happen the next year—perhaps sounding like cockeyed optimism at the time.

> "I was against postponing the Olympics. I thought it was dramatic and would place so many in a difficult situation. I was hurt by athletes who were so forthright with their support of postponement; they weren't thinking about athletes with families, those planning to start families, or the financial hardships of waiting a year."
> —Katherine Shai, four-time Olympic trial qualifier

Again, though, no athlete or sport was being singled out. Major League Baseball flirted with cancelling its whole season before reverting to a shortened one in July.

The NHL halted its action in March, spent a few months debating and rescheduling, then came back in June and didn't finish until late September (hockey season normally ends in early May). The NBA paused operations for a while before playing in front of near-empty arenas for the remainder of the season. Pro football, lucky enough to finish up the 2019–20 season just weeks before the pandemic hit, had to postpone several contests as the next season drew near, some a few times over. NASCAR postponed, cancelled, and shortened many of its races. Golf and tennis each postponed their respective U.S. Open events, and Wimbledon found its courts empty for the first time since World War II. All three of horse racing's Triple Crown events were delayed. Even the matsters' sports entertainment counterparts were afflicted, with virtually every major pro wrestling promotion forced to run in near or fully empty arenas—if they ran at all.

Never had the sports world been so disrupted. Now, already handicapped by laws against physical contact, the mat men and women of the world could *only* do their best to stay sharp with a goal that had just been yanked away. The fact that it was out of their control was the smallest of comforts.

Still, wrestlers had come back before. In February 2013, the IOC had informed a stunned athletic community that all of its hard work was going for naught; wrestling was being removed from the Olympics. It just wasn't important enough.

Then the wrestling community responded (like anyone could have predicted otherwise) in ways that few other groups in sport ever could. Displaying the family-level connections that wrestling boasts probably more than any other sport, athletes— past, present, and future, male and female, from across the globe—had done everything but a worldwide revolution against the IOC. Just over seven months after declaring that a sport around since the first Olympics was no more, the committee was beaten back worse than a thousand majority decisions, reversing itself—not just the right thing to do, but the only thing.

But a committee decision couldn't resolve this matter. A time that seemed to go slower every day would be the only teller.

Her mat opponents at the Pan American Games hadn't kept Kayla Miracle from winning a gold there the year before in Lima. They hadn't stopped her from winning two U.S. Open titles, three University National Championships, and four Women's Collegiate Wrestling Association national events back at Kentucky's Campbellsville University.

Yes, four years before, in Iowa City, Alli Ragan had prevented Miracle from representing in front of the world at the 2016 trials—but don't think that hadn't been running all over Miracle's mind as she'd won match after match, title after title since.

And then, just as every sense of redemption was within grasp of her bruised hands and arms, Miracle felt herself nearly be taken out by an opponent tougher than Ragan, Helen Maroulis, Mallory Velte, or anyone else on the short list of those who'd found a way past her during her career.

Never one to discriminate on grounds of age, gender, or physical fitness, the goddamn virus had grabbed her. To be fair, most people infected with Covid do recover, but no one bounces right back the next moment, and Miracle wasn't certain this enemy could or even should be battled off in time for the "event."

"Is this even worth it?" Miracle wondered around the time the trials were postponed. "We've put so much into it. This sport is rough. But we've hit those low lows. I've lost in finals matches. I've lost in World Championship matches. It's the core system that you have around you that gets you through. Wrestling is no game; it's my life."

It wouldn't be the first time that Tamyra Mensah-Stock had seen fate intervene in her trip to the Games. Four years before, she'd taken tops in the 69-kilogram trials, only to be victimized by the Olympics' long-controversial (read: ridiculous) quota spot rule that requires competitors to win a certain number of matches overall to make the Games. Without enough victories, the probable medalist was confined to the sidelines (Kelsey Campbell, who'd defeated Ragan for the 58-kilogram spot, was rooked for the same reason).

"I learned that I was more capable than what I was letting myself be," Mensah-Stock said, "and that's why now I've been learning to leave it on the mat. I've learned I shouldn't hold back. I can't lose focus."

With the same combination of positivity and tenacity that kept lifting her throughout her career, Mensah-Stock bounced back, heading to Argentina for a Pan Am title in April 2019 and Kazakhstan for a World Title five months later, scoring another Pam Am title early in 2020, then opening 2021 by winning tournaments in France and Rome.

Winning the World event would give Mensah-Stock (and fellow champ Adeline Gray, a record five-time World gold medalist) a bye round in the trials, the right to watch the lower seeds fight it out in the first round before going into battle. Then the IOC hit the pause button, and all they could do was wait and hope.

After stepping into the Rio Games as all but a sure thing to finish somewhere on the medal stand, if not at its top, Gray's shoulder went down and took her dream with it. Now she'd have to wait four long years for, almost literally, the only empty entry on her resume.

And now that might not even occur.

Adeline Gray: "I don't want to blame [2016] solely on the injuries because it really does just kind of feel like a loss, and losses are part of wrestling. But I also know that there were some contributing factors physically and mentally that were very wearing leading up to the 2016 Olympic Games. I was a great wrestler back in 2016, and I'm a great wrestler now, and I don't really think that loss means that much. It's disappointing. I was disappointed that the timing of that loss happened at the 2016 Olympic Games. But at the same time, that is part of the sport: having those losses and moving forward."

As her teammates stayed in shape just a few feet outside its doors, Gray dejectedly sprawled across a sauna at the Olympic Training Center in Colorado Springs, itself only opened sporadically because of the virus. The moisture running down her intensely bright face was more than sweat.

No athlete wants to end her occupation without it being her choice, but every career stops, and after spending over two-thirds of her 30 years on the mat, maybe that time had come. She'd done more than almost all, but no one escapes fate, and forces beyond her control were threatening to deliver the final blow to her career.

"I definitely had some moments where I did want to step away from the sport," she admitted. "I went through highs and lows where I thought, 'Maybe this is the right year to stop.' This is the rockiest road that I've ever been on."

Four years after advancing female wrestling farther than any of her countrywomen ever had before, Maroulis figured she just didn't need to listen anymore, and Covid wasn't the only culprit. Months before it had hit, her second serious concussion in as many years—one of so many issues she'd faced since that glorious day back in Rio de Janeiro—became everything but the knockout punch to Maroulis's career.

Dizziness, headaches, vision issues, anxiety attacks … she didn't need this anymore. No one does.

But just before 2020 and all its infamy arrived, the love of the game brought her back to a wrestling club in Maryland. Her workouts went from minutes to hours. Her symptoms went from torture to tolerable.

"I remember crying to my mom," Maroulis remembers. "And she said, 'You can't go out there and worry that someone's going to touch your head, because you're going to lose every time, or you're going to get hurt again.' She said she thought I could win again, and that kind of broke me, because I didn't want to stop too soon. There's just been a lot that happened, and I'm still that little girl that fell in love with this sport, and I'll love it until the day I die. But I had to do a lot of stuff within myself, with healing, with forgiveness."

With the pandemic's dark claws slowly approaching from the distance, she headed up to Ottawa in March 2020 for the Olympic Wrestling Pan American Qualification Tournament. Her 50-kilogram colleague, Sarah Hildebrandt, fresh off a tournament in Rome, dominated her way through two shutout blowouts, and Jacarra Winchester won at 53-kgs. Maroulis went undefeated at 57kgs and Kayla Miracle stamped her trial spot with a 62-kg victory.

"I started studying my old matches, and reliving stuff," Maroulis said. "Everything just came back. It was like riding a bicycle. The wrestling needed work, but the feeling and contentment [were there]."

A few weeks later, the IOC lurched forward, proclaiming (praying) that the Games would absolutely be held—same place, same months. Just a year later.

Assuming again, that someone, or someones, would find a way to stop, if not reverse, the wildfire-esque spread of Covid.

Moving (mentally) to track, cross country, swimming, or one of the other endurance-focused sports in which many school-level wrestlers participate when the mats are out of season, imagine being in a long race. One does not sprint for the entire time, instead maintaining a steady pace, still making sure that there's always going to be enough left in the tank to slam the hammer down in the closing moments. The uncertain period was the gap between postponement and action; acceleration would rise when that elusive trial date was announced.

Left with a finish line and no way to reach—let alone cross—it, the wrestlers did what they could to stay in shape. Every great wrestler learns to pace herself, and we're not just talking about one three-minute period to another. With so much time left, it was time to take their feet off the gas and go into a holding pattern.

As in, staying in sufficient enough shape to find a quick way to morph all the way back into wrestling character when the date came about.

Sarah Hildebrandt: "It was really difficult, because the year before the Olympics, being told to full-on stop or even slow down when you are moving forward with the Olympics in sight is a very huge shift. I worked into coming down a little, putting on some weight, letting my body recover. There's a lot to be gained in recovery for all that time, and knowing that I would have time to come back up again and train to where I need to be, because my body and mind are feeling better. You're coming to it a lot more refreshed. It meant a lot to me, to avoid that burnout, when there's no reason to train like a madman all summer. When the time came to turn it up, that's what I was doing."

"It feels it took forever, and it feels like it flew by [the Olympic postponement]. I've made great use of the year. My body feels really great. I'm not trying to look at the trials or put any extra pressure, like it's some greater event than anything I've participated in before. I don't have to wrestle more or be bigger or better than I actually am. Training can be a little nitpicky and redundant, and that can be hard on anybody. I love when it's time to go live, when it's time to compete."

Nearly a year after seeing their Olympic dreams put on hold, with the pandemic showing its first semblances of landing under control, American women of the mat finally got a clear glimpse forward. On February 10, 2021, USA Wrestling finally announced that the trials that had once been a few days away were now back.

Rather than the state that had housed the Constitutional Convention, things were heading way down south to the first continental state, and second overall, to sanction female wrestling. In the first days of April 2021, athletes would be tried deep in the heart of Texas. Nearly 80 women would fight it out to represent their country in six weight classes.

Adeline Gray: "Women's wrestling didn't get put into the Olympics and get adequate weight classes until halfway through my career. I believe I would have made an Olympic team in 2012 if they had had my weight classes. Women's wrestling is growing and getting opportunity, and you have great athletes like myself who haven't had as many chances as some of the men have had to be able to go out and make an Olympic team. If there had been six or seven weight classes, this is something I might have accomplished in 2008. I have figured out how to win world titles, but I just need to put that together on that one day that happens every four years."

Emily Shilson: "For me, it helped, having it postponed a year. I had another year to get bigger and stronger, to keep working. Others in my bracket were late 20s, early 30s, so they were already physically mature [she turned 20 in early 2021]. I was lucky, able to compete a lot before the trials. A lot of women didn't have the opportunities to compete, but being a college wrestler [at Minnesota's Augsburg University, where she won a national title], I had a lot of opportunities."

Tamyra Mensah-Stock (April 2020): "I wasn't really bummed [about the postponement]. The way I look at it is that this gives me another year to get better. I'm down for that. It's not like I wasn't ready to go wrestle. I'm like a bull in the pen ready to be released. However, I can take this time to get better. This [postponement] is only helping me."

The rules about qualifying for the trials can be complicated on the best of days, but having to move some tournaments and cancel others, having chances stolen from so many eligible ladies, USA Wrestling had to do its best to help out Covid victims. One desperate shot in the dark came just days before the trials in the aptly named Last Chance Olympic Qualifier at Texas Wesleyan University, less than seven miles and 10 minutes from the Dickies Arena that would house the trials. With the previous qualifiers left to sit out, the top two Chance catchers would make it to the last round before the Olympics.

"I was mad that I had to be there, because I thought I should have qualified sooner, in different areas," said Lauren Louive. "But it was my fault that I hadn't qualified in the previous ones. It was like, here are the circumstances, here's what you have to do, so go get it done." The New Yorker got things started with a 10–0 shutout over Wisconsin's Sophia Smith in 57-kilogram competition, then took a similar win from Payton Stroud of Washington. Pennsylvania's Samantha Klingel didn't give her much trouble either, as Louive roared to a 12–1 victory.

Now it was Louive and Xochitl Mota-Pettis for the final. Equipped with Texas homeland advantage, Mota-Pettis was out for revenge as well, as Louive had taken her, 10–8, in the finals of the Senior Nationals the previous October in Iowa.

And she got it big, charging off to a 14–2 win to get to the trials. Now Louive had to tackle California's Lauren Mason for second—*True* Second, that is!

Up 1–0, Louive kept grabbing Mason in a front headlock for the first 90 seconds, but couldn't get behind her. Then Mason overtook her momentum and nearly planted her on her back before Louive rolled away, Mason slipping behind her for a 2–1 lead to start the second period.

Louive went back to the front facelock, Mason's strong arms and low balance still keeping her from getting to the back. Then Louive pushed forward, Mason falling to her back and nearly over before rolling to her stomach, handing Louive two takedown points and a 3–2 lead. Mason went to the dive a few times, but Louive managed to catch her and take her down again, nearly pinning her and going up 5–2 with less than a minute left.

One restart later, Mason grabbed a page from her opponent's book, snatching Louive in her own front lock before moving around for a takedown. With 30 seconds left, the match stayed at 5–4.

After another restart, Mason went back for Louive's legs, with Louive stepping back and trying to grab her, locking on a front headlock as the clock hit single digits. She went to go behind again, and Mason caught her, but time ran out, and Louive was going to the next level.

"Not to sound cocky," Louive said, "but if you look at it like, 'I'm going to be going up against the best in the world,' you're not going to do well. You have to recognize that you deserve to be there, that you're one of the best as well, and that people fear you."

Now it was time. Time to leave a pandemic as far behind, or outside, as possible. Time to grab that last chance as America's best, and maybe, just a few months later, the world's. As the doors to Dickies opened, dozens of women finally walked toward their future…

CHAPTER 2

The Olympics Are Coming!

"FILA, which is the governing body for wrestling, is really behind making it an Olympic sport, but the U.S. Wrestling Federation just seems to have a wait-and-see attitude. Part of my goal is to get more women involved in it and strength the U.S. role in women's wrestling."
—Two-time World silver medalist Marie Ziegler, July 1990

"We are trying to get women's wrestling to be an Olympic sport."
—Six-time national champ Lauren Wolfe, May 1992

"Women's wrestling is here to stay and people who think it's not are still in the Dark Ages. About 47 countries are now competing. We're going to be [a demonstration sport] in the Olympics by the year 2000."
—Wrestling pioneer Afsoon Johnston, January 1995

"I'm sure it will be in the Olympics someday. The international organizations are considering it right now."
—Tricia Saunders, July 1996

As women's numbers started to grow in wrestling throughout the 1990s, so did certain rumblings. People had been discussing lady participation in grade school. Then in college. And then came something else.

Few other sports had a longer Olympic life than wrestling. Since centuries back into B.C. life, people had been competing in the Ancient Olympic Games, albeit in a slightly less structured atmosphere than today's athletes enjoy.

Like, say, wrestling naked! And people whine about co-ed mat action being sexualized.

When the modern Olympics, hardly a semblance of the 2021 competitions, started off in Athens in 1896, wrestling was there.

Well, for men. It's tough to comprehend how so many people could have such different opinions of a sport based solely on its competitors, but many did. Per usual with female wrestling, nothing happened too quickly.

In the 1990s, a push finally grew to allow women to compete at the Olympics. Well, not compete exactly, but exhibit. For decades, the Games allowed demonstration sports as something of a team tryout. Like an opening act for a band or the preseason of a pro sport, demonstration sports were held on a smaller scale than the regular ones and not counted in the team standings or medal count. If enough people showed up to participate and even more to cheer, the contest might just become a new Olympic addition. Everything from baseball to tennis to badminton began as a demonstration sport, and women had used the technique to grab Olympic spots in judo.

Unfortunately, the practice ended after the 1992 events, and now women had to look for another way.

And they did. With the same guts and brute force that took so many to success on the mat, a growing and driving force pushed forward. More numbers, more appeals, more movements, more persistence. As more and more women rocked the mats in the late 1990s, more and more officials paid attention.

Just over a week after the 9/11 attacks shook the world, a shaken International Olympic Committee sat down in the Swiss land of Romandy to discuss the future. Spurred on by IOC president Jacques Rogge, who'd been chosen as its leader just the month before, the committee gave its OK to add women's mat action to the 2004 Games. Suddenly, women around the globe had a new reason to try a little harder, or to start something new.

Now it was about forming a unit. Someone to do the physical work, and some others to show them how. Less than three years is scarcely enough time to put together a title-winning team in any sport. Finding triers-out probably wouldn't be a problem, but thinning the herd and molding the leftovers into a title squad … miracle workers would have trouble with that one.

Still, someone had to do it.

"I was an assistant coach at the University of Wisconsin," remembers Terry Steiner, who'd won an NCAA title wrestling at Iowa University before starting his coaching career at Oregon State. "I was really getting antsy to get into my own program. I always thought my path was to be a Division I head coach."

Then it appeared to appear. Just a few weeks after the IOC decree arrived from Switzerland, a job at Cal State Fullerton popped open, and Steiner called a pal at USA Wrestling to ask for a recommendation.

The friend quickly agreed. Then he asked if Steiner might go where no American coach had gone (or, to be fair, could have gone) before. USA Wrestling would be kicking off a program for women at the U.S. Olympic Training Center in Colorado. Now they needed a leader.

Steiner had never thought too much of or about women's wrestling; Wisconsin wouldn't be sanctioning the sport for about two more decades.Now he was being asked to lead a new squad in a new sport into new prominence.

Not surprisingly, he didn't exactly lunge at the chance. Not right away. Would coaching gals be radically different than guys? Would his peers, many of whom had seen their male programs crippled or removed by the Title IX athletic gender equality bill, see him as a turncoat?

Or would he find success in a place he'd never even thought to look? Might this be a road to rocking not just the country but the globe?

"At the time, my daughter was a year and a half," Steiner recalls. "What if she wants to follow in your footsteps? I think right there I knew it was the right thing to do. The one thing I want to give my daughter is opportunity."

Just three weeks after the call, Steiner stepped into the wrestling room at Colorado Springs. For one of the first times in his wrestling career, he felt out of place.

"I didn't know names," he says. "I didn't know opponents. I didn't know accomplishments. I left the practice feeling really disappointed in myself. I thought I had known everything."

Time to change. And in many ways, to stay exactly the same.

"At that point, I just said that I'm gonna coach the way I coach with the athletes in front of me," he says. "Wrestling is wrestling. I may have to learn some things, and I'm going to stick my foot in my mouth, but that's gonna happen without wrestling too. I went through some growing pains with the athletes, but for the most part it was a pretty smooth ride."

Like most new rides, such as in the amusement park sense, a few bugs needed working out.

"My first month on the job, I had more individual one-on-one meetings than I did in six years of coaching boys," Steiner says. "It was about their need for communication. The main thing with female athletes is that they want details: what we're doing, how we're doing, why we're doing it. Guys just follow; when I was wrestling, a coach said to do something and I just did it. I didn't ask a lot of questions. Females aren't like that. I have to have things laid out. If I'm on the phone with my twin brother and I ask what we're up to for Christmas, we can go over the whole thing in 30 seconds. My wife and my brother's wife will get on the phone and talk about the same thing, and they'll be on there for an hour. It's not bad or good; it's just a difference between men and women."

As she became one of Steiner's first charges, Jenny Wong was in the midst of studying biology at the nearby University of Colorado.

"I was pretty terrible when I started wrestling when I was a freshman in high school," says the Minnesota native. "I didn't start winning until halfway through my junior year." Before graduation, she was wrestling in international competition.

"It taught me persistence," she says. "It made me feel powerful, able to do whatever I set my mind to. I loved the physicality. It scared me and excited me at the same time. It became my life for a while. At that time, it was an obsession. It wasn't a sacrifice so much as an investment. It wasn't a thing to miss some college parties and some social events."

Before finishing high school, Toccara Montgomery had won a national title. Then she'd scored a sliver at the World Championships in Bulgaria, and helped her homeland to the top of her sport's debut at the 2003 Pan American Games in the Dominican Republic.

Now Montgomery was stepping into Colorado and hoping to leave with a new medal.

"Everything about wrestling was tough," remembers Montgomery, who attended Cleveland's East Technical High. "I didn't choose the easy route as a student either, because the first two years I did basketball and wrestling in the same season. It was tough to leave basketball practice and go straight to wrestling. I won't say I was a natural talent at wrestling either. At first, it was a lot of dedication and hard work to the sport, which I think is where a lot of wrestlers fail. It was about going to practices, go[ing] to open mats, going up to Canada and wrestling in the off season, in freestyle tournaments, getting in as much mat time as possible."

Disclosure notice: As her high school wrestling career was kicking off, Montgomery's father, Paul, pled guilty to double murder, and was sentenced to 30 years in prison in Ohio.

"That's not something I really care to talk about," Montgomery asserts, "but my dad has always been a huge supporter of everything I do, and wrestling was no different in that regard."

"I knew that, anything I did, I wanted to be the best at," she says. "I wanted to be a competitor. It didn't matter to me that some girls had been wrestling since they were five or six, and I had just started. It was something that I wanted to get good at. When my coach told me, 'We're going to a tournament and entering you in two divisions,' I entered two divisions. I didn't think twice about it. I knew it would help me to my ulti-mate goal, which was to be the number one person in the weight class."

As her East Technical career moved toward graduation, Montgomery saw a few col-lege doors start to open for her. What few there were back then, sadly.

"I didn't know that there were even schools that offered scholarships for girls wres-tling," she says. "I think there were three at the time. I decided to visit them if I could. A big factor was that I wanted to be part of a women's team. In high school, I had almost always been the only girl there. We'd go to tournaments or wherever, and there wasn't a locker room full of girls. I had to get changed in a bathroom. That wouldn't be my expe-rience if I was on a women's team."

Over the past few years, the University of the Cumberlands has become almost syn-onymous with female wrestling. Montgomery would become one of the first reasons why. Her perfect 29–0 career dual record helped spread the word about the school, as did her 158-pound national collegiate title of 2004.

But that would come later. Just like every other mat woman in a certain age and experience window of the time, Montgomery felt her life change the moment the IOC's decision came through.

"My goal when I went onto the senior circuit was to make a World team," says Montgomery. "From [the announcement] on, I worked toward making that team for the next two years."

Mere weeks after becoming a team for the first time, the squad plied its collective trade at the 2002 World Championships in Greece. Results were not promising. Tina George managed a silver, Kristie Marano a bronze. The team finished behind 10 other teams in the standings.

"After that, we were doing a drill session," Steiner says. "I didn't see the intensity. They were being lackadaisical."

Time to have at least one last meeting. Time to make those communication issues a little more one-sided. Steiner called his women into a room.

One simple message.

"We're done."

What did he mean? They had a chance to make it into the world's spotlight, and now he was ditching them, and their dreams?

Maybe. Or a tough reminder that dreams don't happen without some serious hard work behind the scenes.

"You're wasting your own time today," Steiner asserted, "and you're wasting my time. See you tomorrow." He left, a shocked group staying behind.

The next day, no one was sure who, if anyone, would show up, and what, if any-thing, would be accomplished.

Everyone did, including the coaches. And a hell of a lot was.

"I came in and I didn't have to say a word," Steiner says. "All day, I kept hearing that they were crying, very upset. I could tell that they wanted what I wanted. They were ready to go, and when we started our practice, they were laser-focused. So intense. At the end of the day, I said that if we have that kind of work ethic, we'll be fine. It really hit me. I could tell that they really wanted to do what I wanted to do, but maybe I wasn't explaining it enough."

Things moved up—fast. In front of their homeland fans for the 2003 Worlds, the Americans medaled in all seven classes, with Marano scoring a gold in 67-kilogram competition. Wong got bronze at 48-kilograms, Montgomery a silver at 72-kilograms.

Now it was time for the big games. At the Olympic trials in Indianapolis the next May, just two consecutive wins were all that would be necessary to grab a spot on the Olympic squad. Patricia Miranda (105.5), Sara McMann (138¾), and Tela O'Donnell (121) won out to take it home.

Marano's misfortune happened to become both McMann's and Montgomery's luck; scheduled to be the top seed in the 138 class, Marano walked in a single pound overweight, pushing her to 158.5.

Without her main competition, McMann breezed through her division. Equipped with a sizable weight advantage, Montgomery took Marano out.

"My real goal, if you put it down in medals like the Olympic gold, is to be proud of myself," said Miranda, who wrestled guys for four years at Stanford before taking home her first co-ed victory in her senior year. "Proud of how I left it all out there, committing to something and training like no one has ever trained. Inherent in that is that I do hope there will be other people who are proud to see that in their country."

When she first got into the sport in middle school, Miranda's own father had threatened to sue the school … if they *allowed* her to wrestle! He'd personally appear at events to try to get her removed. It took a guarantee of serious academic improvement to get her on the squad.

"What I apply myself to is a reflection of me," she says. "So I stayed up that extra hour, I understood that math problem."

Patricia Miranda: "It's like when you see a car wreck. Are you the one who's freaking out? Are you the one who gives help? It's one of those moments where you get to say, 'Hey, who am I, deep down?' For me, wrestling provides that. When it gets hard, are you going to run or are you going to fight? Mental toughness is something that's trainable.

In the moment, you're the one who feels privileged. When you're training, you're dripping sweat, you've got a black eye, and you've got that burning in your lungs. But you love it. You love the fact that you get to push yourself that far. You love the fact you get to see how good you can be at something you love to do.

One quote I love is that anybody can sing in the shower. It's about whether you can do it when everybody's watching. Wrestling is more of a raw, grinding thing—you can make plenty of mistakes and still come out on top. But in order to be the best of the best, there's a point in the match where you have to dig deep. You remember that one sprint workout that just killed you. You were scared to death that you wouldn't measure up, but you reached down deep and pulled it out."

McMann warmed up for the Olympics on national TV—and didn't even need sanctioning to do it; she took down Katie Couric on the *Today* show.

Steiner would have some help running things; female wrestling pioneer Tricia Saunders and her husband, Townsend, were assisting with the squad.

"We have four people who we can look at," Tricia said, "and say we have the potential for four golds."

Right up the continent, another mat icon could see her own finish line in the short sight. Eight World titles, six of them gold, would be more than anyone could have hoped for. Christine Nordhagen had done it for the Great White North, and she was almost finished.

"I was 33, and near the end," Nordhagen admits. "My body was starting to shut down, but I kept training. I loved the life of an athlete. I'd get up, go to university, train with my friends, go teach a couple classes at the high school, then go back and train. I traveled to international competitions, making friends all over the world." After winning Canada's inaugural title in 1992, she'd medaled in every World meet from 1993 to 2001, except for 1995. From the start of her career until she'd quit right after the Games, Canada's female wrestling numbers went from less than 200 to more than 4,000.

Nordhagen had campaigned as hard as anyone for her sport to get to the Games, but it making it in time for her to compete didn't look likely.

"I'd had knee surgery, when they'd scraped around under my kneecap," she says. "They were trying to get scar tissue to grow under the patella. But it didn't help; the cushioning was gone. I couldn't go running, but I'd do biking or the ellipticals."

Then she'd learned that her efforts, and everyone else's, were paying off.

"I was like, I *gotta* go to the Olympics!" she says. "I knew I wouldn't be able to wait four more years. No one cared about the Worlds except the wrestling community. The Olympics had way more attention."

Imagine arriving at college for your freshman year. New surroundings, new classes, new textbooks, new … entire life.

However, you're there for a purpose, and you're going to make it happen.

So you try. For four long years, give or take a term, you work as hard as anything you've ever tried before. This is a personal goal, a chance to really say you've accomplished something. A chance to see that hard work pays off. You avoid the party scene (mostly!). You stay in touch with your professors, impressing them all with your work ethic. You and your classmates work together, pulling each other through. Things go steadily upward, albeit with a drawback here and there, for four years.

But there's one major difference between this school and the typical college grounds. Before that glorious day of diploma awarding can occur, you've got to pass a test.

Just one. Not one for each class, like with most colleges. You take this one, and that's it. If you pass, great. But if anything goes wrong—you get sick, have a brain freeze, maybe forget just enough answers— you fail.

And then you get nothing. No diploma, no degree, no retakes, nothing whatsoever. All those years with nothing to show.

That wonderful analogy actually came from national titlist Jennifer Page, who competed at the 2012, 2016, and 2021 Olympic trials. But that's how things work for Olympic-caliber athletes in every sport. They work their tails off for years, getting better, winning one qualifying tournament after another (the warmup exams) to make it to the big game, that last step up to the pedestal, in a few senses.

Then, as invariably happens for *someone*, both in the trials and each Olympics, something goes wrong. A rare bad day happens. A favorite falls short. Someone else gets the medal (the Games diploma) despite everyone knowing that the first person could out-talent him or her any day of the millennium. No matter what, someone's going to be disappointed.

American women would feel a great deal of this at the first Games. O'Donnell started things off with a pin of Russia's Olga Smirnova, but got whaled 11–1 by Tonya Verbeek of Canada, who herself would drop the final match to Japan's Saori Yoshida.

A few years before, McMann had broken the gender mold on McDowell High's wrestling team in Maryland, then battled mat men at Lock Haven University. Now she'd score another first on a quite larger scale; two minutes into the first women's wrestling match in Olympic history, she pinned China's Meng Lili.

The next day, she took less than a minute to make it past Stavroula Zygouri of Greece, and on to a chance at history. One more win, and the Americans would come out with a gold in their first-ever foray. Not only that, but McMann could avenge the loss that Japan's Kaori Icho—ironically, a longtime training partner of McMann—had handed her the year before in the World Championships.

At first, it looked like it was going to happen. McMann scored two quick takedowns and held to a 2–0 lead for over half the match. Then Icho took back over. Early in the third period, she tied the score. With about 30 seconds left, McMann went for a headlock, but Icho slipped away, then snared a takedown for the deciding point in a 3–2 victory.

"I don't think there's anything more painful in the world," McMann sighed afterward. A few weeks later, she'd sadly be proven wrong.

Christine Nordhagen: "Going into my first match, I'm feeling good. It's on a stage.

In our first scramble, [future golden gal China's Xu Wang] shoots in on my legs, and we go out of bounds. I'm sprawling and pushing. Then I reached back, and the floor was gone. I fell off the stage. Everyone runs over, saying, 'Are you OK?' I said I thought so. Adrenaline was going through my body so much, I could have been missing a leg, and I wouldn't have felt it. Then she shot in and took me down, I wasn't there mentally. She took me out. I remember watching the clock tick down. I was crushed. I knew my dream of a medal was gone. I wanted to go home.

The next morning, in the warmup area, I started crying. My coach told my training partner to beat the crap out of me to snap [me] out of my negative attitude. It was hard for her to do it, because she was my friend. I was about to go out of the warmup area to fight Toccara Montgomery, who had beaten me a few months prior.

Right before I left the warmup area, there was this girl, Anna Gomis, from France, getting ready for the [55-kilogram] bronze medal match. She must have seen that I was having a really hard time. She grabbed me by the arm, looked me in the eye, and said three words: "Don't give up." Why did she leave her warmup just to say that? She had been to Canada and trained with me, and I'd been to France and trained with her.

I walked out into the stadium, and looked up into the stands. In the Canadian section, 17 people of my family had stayed to cheer for me. I was fighting for fifth place, and they were still there and excited. A lady in the stands was screaming my name. She was a mother from Germany. I used to train her in Germany, and stayed at her house. Just having them there, I was so excited to wrestle one match. Something snapped and made me realize how grateful I was to be at the Olympics. It was not just about winning, but about competing your best in the moment. I ended up competing well. [She got fifth in the event, with Montgomery, who lost to eventual bronze medalist Kyoko Hamaguchi of Japan, taking seventh.]"

Toccara Montgomery: "Losing to Christine, an amazing competitor, I knew that my dreams of being an Olympic champion were done. Everyone was like, 'Oh, what a great experience!' But nobody trains to be seventh at the Olympics. I trained to be a champion, and to fall short of that was devastating in a sense.

I blew out my knee after the Olympics. I told myself I was going to take time off. I think I took a week off. I didn't stay for the closing ceremonies. I didn't want to fall behind classes at Cumberlands. I think I took a week off. Wrestling is one of those sports that you can't get away from. It's just a part of you. It's a lifestyle.

At a wrestling practice with high school kids, we were just finishing up, and they said, 'Hey, can you do a couple more drills?' I think they were trying to cut weight. Whatever move it was, it didn't go right, I basically destroyed everything inside: my ACL, MCL, and meniscus. I didn't have insurance at the time, only school insurance, so I had to go to the doctor they provided. It wasn't the best choice for me. The doctor told me I would be out up to a year recovering from the surgery.

I went through physical therapy, and everything seemed to be going great. But somewhere along the lines, the graft didn't take or loosened up and sent me back even farther. Nothing healed correctly. I tried to come back and wrestle in the middle of 2005, but I could never get back to the level I was. I could never get my knee to function the way I wanted to. Later on, I went in for a second opinion, and I found out my ACL had been torn again."

Miranda charged off, defeating China's Li Hui, Russia's Lorisa Oorzhak, and Mayelis Caripá of Venezuela to solidify her shot at a medal. Then she hit a concrete barrier known as Irina Merlini of Ukraine, who tossed her around the mat from start to finish in a 9–0 victory, arguably an even worse beating that Merlini had handed her in the finals of the 2003 World Championships.

While Merlini continued her dominance in a gold medal win over Japan's Chiharu Icho, a seemingly shell-shocked Miranda let France's Angélique Berthenet get out to a 4–0 lead in the bronze match. But she recovered in time, rattling off 12 consecutive points for a 12–4 win and the first medal in American history (her victory came before McMann's silver win).

"That six hours between the semifinals and my bronze-medal match were six of the hardest I've had in my sport," Miranda said. "Every time you thought and dreamed about the Olympics, it was all about gold. I told myself I had a chance to go out and get the best placement I can for my sport and all women, that I could bounce back and win a medal. This was step one in legitimizing our sport. The triumph and tragedy proved today will show that everyone in the world can wrestle."

Patricia Miranda: "I'm the lucky one who gets to come in and take the stage for the first time. But I owe it to the pioneers that came before me that fought this fight for decades and got us there. You're going to see the pain in people's faces, the triumph that says, yes, I spent 10 years of my life and I finally did it."

Tricia Saunders: "When you say you're an Olympic athlete, you don't have to explain that to anybody."

Just a few days after returning from Athens, McMann and her boyfriend, three-time NCAA All-American Steven Blackford, left the Olympic Training Center in Colorado Springs on the way to Washington, D.C., where Blackford was attending law school.

At about 1:20 p.m. on September 3, McMann was driving her 1997 Jeep Cherokee on Interstate 76 in northeastern Colorado, about 90 miles northeast of Denver.

As the vehicle drifted toward the center lane, McMann turned the wheel. But she overcorrected, and the Jeep went off the shoulder, and rolled over. Seatbelts unfastened, Blackford and McMann were ejected from the vehicle.

Just a month past his 27th birthday, Blackford died at the scene. McMann, who suffered a broken arm and other less serious injuries, was charged with careless driving causing death, but competed for the 2005 World Championship team the next summer.

Ironically, just a month after the accident, Fabian Desmond Smart was convicted in the 1999 murder of McMann's brother Jason, a crime that had gone unsolved until 2001. Smart was sentenced to life in prison.

McMann would eventually step into cagefighting, scoring the dubious distinction of losing to Ronda Rousey, Miesha Tate, and Amanda Nunes. At press time, she owned a 14–6 overall record, her last fight a unanimous decision over Arlene Blencowe in April 2023.

It's strange to consider this sometimes, but even winning can bring a certain sense of disappointment. Winning a tournament means denying so many others who worked as hard as you and wanted it just as badly. Being the reason for someone's dream dying can be tough to handle.

Especially if they helped move yours up in the past.

Ali Bernard had a few strong obstacles in her way at the 2008 trials in Las Vegas, and some were coming from the inside.

She was used to battling alongside Katie Downing; Downing had trained her in the past, mentored her, guided her on and off the mat for years.

Now the two had to square off—with a bid at stake. As tough as the four national college titles she'd scored up at Saskatchewan's University of Regina had been, wrestling had never been this personal for Bernard.

"It was hard," Bernard says. "She'd stayed at my house. She was a great person who'd put in all the work, but you have to put that aside. A lot of wrestlers get in that position: they help mentor younger ones, and then they go into competition."

The student defeated the teacher in two straight at 72-kilograms. Now it was on to Beijing.

Same place, same trials—Randi Miller kept McMann from another medal shot, and prepped to make her Olympic debut at 63-kilograms.

"It was amazing coming out of the tunnel and hearing people chant 'USA! USA!'" says the Texas native, who took up the sport in high school after getting cut from the basketball team. "After a few workouts, I was addicted."

Miller got off to a hot streak in the Games, taking her first few matches before falling short against eventual golden girl Kaori Icho of Japan.

"Wrestling her was quite an experience," Miller remembers. "I felt that I wasn't at a 100 percent when wrestling her. I learned a lot."

In the bronze medal match, Canada's Martine Dugrenier jumped out ahead of Miller as the last minutes ticked away.

"I knew I had time to score points, so that was the main thing on my mind," Miller says. "I don't think about what [my opponents] are going to do to me, so that's what makes it fun. If you want to keep going and get that point at the last second, you have to be in shape yourself to do it."

She did, as it turned out, and it would be her country's only medal that year, though the first ever by an African American; Bernard beat Amarachi Obiajunwa of Nigeria, then fell to China's Wang Jiao. She rebounded by defeating Sweden's Jenny Fransson, but lost the bronze medal match to Kyoko Hamaguchi of Japan.

"It was stressful," she says. "Obviously, I really wanted to get a medal, but it was about leaving it all out on the mat. It's the pinnacle of the biggest event I could ever be at, a lot of excitement, a lot of disappointment, but who could ask to be in a better position for your country?" Undaunted, she went back up over the border and scored a fifth national title at Regina (Canadian laws allow athletes five years of eligibility).

Later that year, Miller scored a U.S. Senior National Championship, a feat she repeated in 2014, along with a Military World Championship. In August 2021, just days after her colleagues tore it up at the Games, Miller was named the first ever coach of the Texas Woman's University wrestling program.

Kelsey Campbell: "I was born in Alaska, but I grew up in Oregon. I started wrestling in my senior year of high school. I had some friends on the team, and they challenged me to join. I figured out early on that this was a sport that I could really become great at. You didn't have to have any extraordinary talent. I was a decent athlete, not super great. You didn't have to have anything spectacular to be really good. You just had to work hard.

I had coaches around me that supported me. They would include me. If there were tournaments, they would bring me. Everyone says they support women's wrestling, but support is a 'do' word. It's an action. You don't just say it. I finished up that season in high school, and a coach gave me a flyer for a girls' tournament. I didn't even know that there were other girls that did it. I wouldn't have started wrestling girls if he hadn't given me that flyer.

In the spring of 2003, I went to the tournament. I was terrified. I thought, it'll suck, but I'll do it and go on with my life. I pinned my way to the finals, where I lost in overtime. That showed me I was good against my peers. I could complete against people like me.

People asked me to come train with them. Why not? It was kind of incredible that I ever went; not even that I competed, but that I showed up. That blows my mind. You don't know how showing up can really change your entire life.

At Arizona State, I joined the grappling club. I was going to tournament on and off. For fundraisers, I'd knock on doors and wash cars. It was this weird thing I did. Most people aren't dropping $500 on a tournament that they're not even playing in. I was training with the grappling club, wherever they'd let me come.

I went to the trials in 2004, but I didn't qualify. It seemed like a Cinderella story when I look back, but it was so far from that. If I went back in time, I don't think I could go through that again.

I wrestled one year at ASU, the first girl there. The second year, the team was dropped. Lots of people tried to blame Title IX, but that wasn't the issue. The issue is, does the athletic department want to invest in this sport? Not *can* they, but do they want to? Two days after the wrestling team got cut, I saw them building the football dome. It was nauseating at the time.

I thought it was it when the team was cut. I took second at the World Team Trials, and it broke my heart in a way I hadn't expected. I thought, 'I am not done with this.' Then I won the 2009 and 2010 U.S. Open. I thought, "Maybe I should quit on a high note." I wanted to pursue music. I wanted to pursue the ministry.

Then I moved to Colorado to put my dreams on hold for the 2012 Olympic trials. I put all my eggs in the basket."

Now back to yet another perspective on that disappointment we keep touching. Sometimes it hits even before the Games begin. We actually see it quite often in the trials beforehand—which, sadly, is as close as many of the competitors will ever come.

As the 2012 London Games drew near, competitors gathered in April at Iowa City's Carver-Hawkeye Arena—and not just them, as spectatorship at the trials zoomed to almost 14,000 for the first time. Clarissa Chun and Bernard had been on the 2008 squad, and now looked forward to getting back, and scoring higher.

> "I was going to kiss that medal if I got that gold. Everyone bites it. I was going to make out with mine."
>
> —Clarissa Chun, after falling short at the 2008 Games

Helen Maroulis had blasted through three U.S. Open titles to the top seed at 55-kilograms, and she chugged through the competition, soon facing Campbell in the finals. She had reason to brim with confidence; she was 2–0 against Campbell, including during Maroulis's Outstanding Wrestler performance at the U.S. Open the previous December. Campbell had also had to drop a few quick pounds to get to 55 kilograms, as her normal competition weight was 59, which didn't have its own weight class.

Then things got started; winners must take two best-of-three contests.

In the first match, Maroulis got the first fall, but Campbell rallied for two straight, finishing with a 2–1 victory.

She followed it up with a win in the second match's opener, but Maroulis held her off to tie things up, 1–0, in the second.

As the clock ticked down in the third, neither wrestler could score. Then, with double-digits left, Campbell notched a takedown for a 1–0 lead. Maroulis got up and lunged at her, but couldn't get Campbell off her feet for the loss.

Kelsey Campbell: "I had been winning nationals, a steady rise. Going into the World Championships in 2011, I was favored to win. I was the most picked athlete at 59-kg. Then in the first round, I lost. I'd had setbacks, but this was the most heart-wrenching thing in my life. I cried my brains out. I was eight months from the Olympic trials, and no way was I the top pick.

At the U.S. Open, I took third. I did everything as perfect as I could. The selfishness that it takes to do that, I really held myself to a high standard.

Four or five weeks before trials, I was walking around the Olympic Training Center praying, 'You know, God, I don't even know If I'm meant to be here. I don't know if I'm meant to win this.' It had broken my heart, but I was OK with this. Maybe I'd done everything I could and was just not good enough. In the trials, the headspace I was in, finally I just let it go.

I had my first match, and I won. In my mind, I didn't know if it was my day, so I had to let it go. I zoned out. I don't remember much. Victoria Anthony told me, 'I'll never forget seeing you back then. You were in the back room, meditating.' I was praying, listening to music, not caught up on hype.

Then I had to wrestle Helen. I had never beat her. I am not a historically offensive wrestler, but I won the first match with a takedown with 16 seconds left. In the last one, I scored with 46 seconds left. I still remember the takedown, getting busy on top. The ref called us up, and it was the longest 18 seconds of my life.

I couldn't believe it. I just kept crying. The next few days, I thought I was in an alternate world that I'd wake up from, like a whirlwind. A lot of people didn't expect me to win. This was in April, and I flew out to the Olympics in July."

Chun had even more trouble in her 48-kg final, as Alyssa Lampe took the first fall before she was able to take two in a row.

A few months before, Adeline Gray had debuted at World competition with a bronze in Istanbul. Now she wanted a medal of similar or different shade—but standing in her way was Elena Pirozhkova, herself arriving with three Pan American Games titles.

And Pirozhkova creamed Gray for the 63-kilogram title, winning two straight while giving up just one point.

It appeared that Bernard would be staying home as well, as Stephany Lee rocked her for the 72-kilogram title.

Lee celebrated her trial victory with a walk down the marriage aisle just a few days later. Bernard prepped to take the next step in her own wrestling career, off the mat and toward becoming a colleague of Steiner.

"This is a time all athletes go through," Bernard says. "Who am I if I am not a wrestler? Especially with defeat at the end of it, going out on a low note. It took time for me to wrap my mind around my accomplishments, to be proud of what I have done. Then you get the phone call: hold on, and stop eating those cookies!"

Things had twisted like a high-speed takedown.

On June 28, the U.S. Anti-Doping Agency announced that a drug sample Lee had provided at the trials had been explored—and dirt was there.

Marijuana traces were located. It was the second test she'd failed in three years.

She was out. And not long after, Bernard was in.

"There was some limbo," Bernard says. "They were not the ideal circumstances. You want to win. You don't want to get in because someone got kicked out. But at the same time, you want to represent the United States. It was a weird time. It wasn't yet time to move on and figure out the rest of my life. Once I got the green light, there was a time to be stressful. It took a lot of mental self-talk to get into the mindset for the Games." That, along with an ankle surgery that ended with a plate being inserted and a neck disc that slowly became herniated, returning her to surgery right after getting back from China.

Unfortunately, 2012's team could hardly duplicate America's tough showing of four years before. Pirozhkova didn't even make the top 10 in her division, while Bernard lost early—ironically, to Fransson!—putting her medal chances away soon.

Kelsey Campbell: "My first match, I lost to the lady who won the gold [Saori Yoshida of Japan]. Then lost to the lady who won the bronze [Yuliya Ratkevich of Belarus].

It's taken me a lot of years to have those feelings about it. Until 2016, I couldn't talk about it, and I didn't want people to ask me about it. I remember it was so painful to lose. People would ask me about it, and I would say, 'Do you celebrate a great wedding if you divorce two years later? You're heartbroken that it didn't work out.' I went through a really low time. Everyone assumes that medaling is the same as going. It's not. I'm honored to be able to have that forever, but when you're the one who falls short, you don't justify it because it's the Olympics. You don't justify it because of what it is.

I'd like to go again, but I'd be lying if I said I'm just glad I went. I also had to educate myself. I used to get an attitude about it. It's something that a lot of people won't understand. But if everyone understood it, it wouldn't be special. An aspect of it is trying to be the best in the world at something you just go through alone.

I appreciate the experience. It's exciting to tell people about it, but it doesn't make losing any easier. Watching the matches, my heart breaks all over again.

It took a lot of time and counseling to get there. I had a serious collarbone surgery right after the Olympics. Once I was healthy, I was so ready to get back, I needed to heal all of those wounds. I wasn't going to end up this way. Coming back from the injury was pretty big. If I hadn't gotten surgery, my career would have been over. I had thought about rehab and cortisone shots, but I knew that wouldn't work.

It was a turning point in my career, realized that no one else has to live with my body, my decisions. A lot of people want to tell you what to do, but they're not the ones out on the mat competing, if I had listened to those experts, I wouldn't be on the mat today."

But there was one small (literally, if not figuratively) bright spot. Chun got things rolling with a shutout of China's Zhao Shasha, then was shut out by Azerbaijan's Mariya Stadnik. Her consolation foray got off to a rough start, as Poland's Iwona Matkowska took the first in a best-of-three. But Chun pinned her in the second and eventually made her way to the title contest.

Now she had her own shot at redemption against Merlini, who'd denied her a bronze at the previous Games.

Chun came out at full force and Merlini was there to meet her, no one giving an inch for the first period. Well, almost: with two seconds to go, Chun notched a takedown and the deciding point.

Merlini grabbed her for a near-takedown in the second, but Chun countered with an arm throw to put her down, then held on for a 3–0 victory. The 4'11" mat woman had earned the right to stand as one of the tallest at the Games.

"This time I learned from Beijing that I didn't get caught in the emotional roller-coaster ride," said Chun, who actually shared third place with Canada's Carol Huynh. "I just stayed calm, cool, and collected for the opportunity. [Bronze] is not the color I imagined, but I'm happy. For me, it was about finishing strong. That's the difference I made from Beijing when I lost in the semis."

Now America had two tough Games to come back from. Running out of chances to be seen as a pretender, hardly an afterthought. But four years to regroup and…

No. No, suddenly they didn't, and they wouldn't. Not them, not their counterparts, not the men or the women, from any country.

This wasn't discrimination. Far worse than that. Certain people were about to plant a bigger roadblock in the Olympic wrestling community than ever before, and they had the juice and the numbers to do it.

The wrestling community was about to find out how fast everything could disappear.

Everything.

CHAPTER 3

Wrestling's Sudden Death
... and Resurrection

Maybe they were adding weight classes to the Olympics, giving more ladies a place to compete. Perhaps the message was exactly where the 2020 Games would take place; Istanbul and Madrid had been pushing hard, but the wrestling world might have actually been hoping that dark-horse Azerbaijan would find an inside track, as the ladies had fared well in a couple of World Championships in that neck of the woods.

The wrestling community had been notified that a major announcement was coming. No one was sure what, but all expected, or certainly hoped for, a new building block, an assisting step forward on a journey that had just recently gotten a little easier.

If only. This was much worse. They were done. The dream of every wrestler was going to disappear with the votes of a few people—too few people to even form a full wrestling team—without the first damned clue of how hard every Olympic wrestler worked.

That February day of 2013 would live in wrestling infamy. Hell, in sports infamy.

From a meeting in Switzerland, the International Olympic Committee decided to be judge, jury, and, without any kind of trial, executioner. It told everyone already looking past 2016 and on to 2020 that they just didn't matter to the right people.

Too few people were watching from home. Not enough articles had been written or read. They'd failed to sell out the year before in the London Games (which couldn't have had *anything* to do with the hometown crowd having little to cheer for; Britain's sole wrestling rep was Olga Butkevych, who lost her only match and was eliminated in the round of 16).

Wrestling had been around since the Olympics were around. And after the 2016 Games, it wouldn't be around anymore.

Erica Wiebe, Canadian competitor: "I was shocked. My world was rocked. But I also had a belief in my heart that this wouldn't be the end for women's wrestling."

In a decision made by secret vote, without giving wrestling's insiders the slightest chance to defend it, a 15-member board chose to omit the mat game.

"In the view of the executive board, this was the best program for the Olympic Games in 2020," claimed IOC spokesman Mark Adams. "It's not a case of what's wrong with wrestling; it is what's right with the 25 core sports."

Translation: "Nothing personal. We just know what you want and what's best for you better than you do." Politics (not democracy, but politics) to the extreme. Table tennis, badminton, handball, and the rest of the core contests were safe, but wrestling was gone.

To be fair, wrestling's leading groups hadn't been doing as much leading as they could. FILA, which legislates the sport all over the world, had established its own decision-making boards without any medical officials or even a single athlete in the groups. After three Olympics with women in battle, the organization hadn't bothered to create a commission for the ladies. Not taking much initiative didn't show a hell of a lot in the way of non-stagnation.

But that didn't lessen the shock.

"We will use all of our strength to persuade the IOC not to exclude wrestling from the Olympic program," vowed Russian Olympic Committee president Alexander Zhukov, whose country had brought home 77 mat golds in Olympic history, including an event-leading five in the 2012 contests.

Five years before, Carol Huynh had become the first Canadian woman to win a gold, scoring tops in 48-kilogram competition. In 2012, she became the second lady from northernmost North America to win two Olympic medals (Tonya Verbeek scored her third 55-kilogram medal at the same Games). Now it looked like the two would be the last ones ever to do so.

"If the IOC recommendation goes through," she claimed, "our federal funding will be reduced drastically and this will affect our entire program…. It is important to have female role models in sports and careers that are traditionally seen as masculine. Raising awareness that women can accomplish what they set out to do, regardless of constricting social expectations, is so important for all youth to see, male and female." Along with the federal funding, the sport might lose millions in Olympic financial output.

All over the sports world, and even outside it, people went berserk, mainly through the blaring and screaming and cursing and ranting all over social media and everywhere else. Shock, fear, anger, heartbreak, depression, and every other negative emotion smashed together for a tornado.

This, however, is normal. The rule-makers could have expected it. Sadly, whiny social media posts and online petitions and everything else are like fireworks at times like this; they go up, blow up (even the most viral ones), and vanish. As destructive as they can be, tornadoes tend to die out fairly quickly, especially when water is around. With problems like this, people tend to let their words, and *only* their words, do the speaking. Action is too difficult for most; too many come across with, "This is a huge problem … and I really hope that *someone else does something*!"

Everyone obviously wanted wrestling to be allowed back. But a few tough-to-answer questions became quickly apparent.

First, what exactly to do? Were they going to grab some IOC members and threaten them with throws and takedowns unless some minds were changed? With such a large community all over the world being affected, and so many ideas as to how to solve a problem, how could enough unity and mobility be found, especially in time to make a difference in time for Olympics that were just three years away?

And even assuming this could happen, what difference *might* it make? Even if the entire community could come together to make a movement, a plea, the IOC might just choose not to listen. They made the choice, and didn't *have* to explain it to anyone. How could so many different people be persuaded to change their minds?

Large groups are tough to create, let alone maintain, if their chances of success aren't good, or even clear. From the moment they had decided to kick wrestling out, the

IOC was already talking about its replacement; before the shock had even finishing passing through the wrestling community, the higher-ups had moved on to discussing roller sports, wakeboarding, and other possibilities. Could a group so quick—and so determined—to brush wrestling aside and move on be brought back?

Well, it was time to go to battle. And the first step in doing so was to fix an issue within.

As tough as it was to admit, maybe the IOC had a point about FILA not doing enough to help itself. Addressing it could send a quick message to the community that a movement, some sort of counterattack, was already under way.

After beginning as the International Amateur Wrestling Federation in 1921 and keeping wrestling on the Olympic ballot after World War II endangered it, FILA had slowed down in recent years. Mere days after the dark call came down from above, FILA sat down for a meeting in Thailand. By the time the chats were done, president Raphaël Martinetti was finished.

A driving force behind wrestling in his native Serbia, Nenad Lalović took over.

"We have only one goal: to be back on the Olympics," Lalović said. "Lobbying is very important, but it's not something that you can determine in advance. We have to prepare a serious presentation that must be prepared by professionals to present the real picture of our sport. This sport has been practiced by millions of people. We will use this fact in order to promote our sport." Just over a year later, FILA would become United World Wrestling.

"We have to tell the world that there is no other sport that is more of a meritocracy than wrestling," explained FILA vice president Stan Dziedzic, himself a former World Champion and Olympic medalist. "No bats, no balls, no gloves; it's not how fast, how far, how high—but how much better. Two equal-size wrestlers ground on the mat to determine who the best is, with the wits and the will to win. Nothing could be more fundamental." The organization added more women, including Russian Vice President Natalia Yariguina, and threw together a directive to bring in more female participation. Eventually, the best-of-three periods format would shrink to two, and the sport ditched the ball-draw format to start overtime.

To its credit, and perhaps predicting the inevitable, the IOC quickly gave wrestling a chance to appeal, inviting its people a chance to chat with its executive board as soon as the following May. They also agreed to reconsider the decision the September after that.

Not much time, but something.

Adding women to the Olympic wrestling program three Games before had energized the overall sport, and the Games as a whole. It was time to do the same thing women had been doing since the fight for Olympic wrestling had begun, only faster and in a slightly different direction: time to re-convince, not convince.

Just as they had for the years of effort it took to get their sport to the Olympics to begin with, lady matsters across the Earth formed a global squad to battle everyone's common enemy. With an extra reason to celebrate World Wrestling Month that May, female teams from Canada, Ukraine, and the United States joined up at Niagara Falls on the Canadian border for the Battle of the Falls. Katherine Shai, Afsoon Johnston, Erica Wiebe, and others helped prove that a mini-worldwide event could come together fast, that people could work as a team in a short while. Johnston had been here before; after her U.C. Davis alma mater tried to get rid of the mat sport in 1991, she and the rest of Davis's squad had gone on a media tour to convince the right people to keep it there.

Around the same time, Lalović, Huynh, and French medalist Lisa Legrand were part of a team that appealed to the IOC in a meeting in Russia, telling the committee what had already been done and how they believed, how they hoped, how they downright knew, that things would keep moving up.

The IOC was convinced, up to a point. Wrestling, along with squash and baseball/softball, was shortlisted to a group that would get another shot in September.

"It's not finished," Lalović said afterward, "but I think we impressed them because we have changed in such a short time." The next month, Olympic-level squads from Canada and Russia arrived in Los Angeles for the United 4 Wrestling event.

Soon after, they went back to where it had all begun.

That June, Helen Maroulis, whose last name is so Greek it sounds like she's a descendent of Persephone (come to think of it, it *would* be appropriate for a *wrestler* to be related to the goddess of destruction!), led a group of American women to the site of the first Olympics. For the first time ever, women would do battle at the Olympia site that had spawned the Games' name.

She, Tamyra Mensah-Stock, Elena Pirozhkova, and others wrestled it out, but Alyssa Lampe was the only American to take home a gold; Russia won everything else. That wasn't the point. The point was that women had shown that they cared, and that they were ready and willing to keep fighting, in every sense of the phrase. Wherever, whenever, they would show up and fight—because that's what wrestling meant to them. And how much they hoped it would mean to others. Even Vladimir Putin and Iran, not exactly allies of the United States, joined the fight to save wrestling.

In early August, as the new vote drew near, FILA announced that its lady numbers had grown enough for weight class numbers to expand. Two extra groups of women would compete at the next Olympics, while men's freestyle and Greco-Roman would each have one fewer weight class. Both genders would have six in each competition.

On August 15, FILA sent each IOC member a brochure explaining just how much of an evolutionary difference women's wrestling had made, especially over the last few months. The sport, claimed the announcement, is "a trend we're committed to increasing."

It started to rub off. "[FILA] is now here with a new president, new program, and new ideas for the sport," IOC vice president Thomas Bach said soon afterward. "That is why I personally believe that wrestling has a good chance to come through the vote in September."

Now all there was left to do was hope. Every wrestler at some point is faced with the sad reality that doing everything she could wasn't enough to come out on top in a match, and now FILA was against the same dark possibility.

Carol Huynh: "There have been quite a few great changes over the last six months. It's been very exciting. We have a strong voice as women in the FILA bureau, and FILA is strongly encouraging national federations to encourage women to be in higher positions within their national federations."

Early in September, the IOC gathered in Buenos Aires to make a few important decisions. On September 7, as anyone reading this is well aware, Tokyo became the runaway winner as host of the 2020 Games, whomping Istanbul 60–36 on the final ballot.

As tough as it is to believe, now and then, for many, that was secondary. The following day, a Sunday, wrestlers across America and around the world crowded around TVs, computers, and every other potential news source. The USA Wrestling headquarters in Colorado Springs filled with female wrestlers, their coaches, their friends, families, everyone else, hoping that they'd have a new reason to go back out and practice soon.

As IOC president Jacques Rogge stepped to the podium, the room suddenly became dead silent.

A new round of secret ballots had been cast. Twenty-four members had voted to keep baseball and softball, two more than had wanted squash.

Wrestling? Only *forty-nine* marks! The mat game was back, and by a wide margin.

The community released a collective breath it had been holding for exactly 208 long days.

"Normally, this is done in a few years," Lalović gleefully glowed. "We did it in a few months. It was a question of our survival."

Afsoon Johnston: "It was a very difficult and trying year for a lot of people in wrestling, but it was also a very exciting year as well. The sport became considerably better, the leadership improved tremendously on the international level, and there became even more opportunities for women in wrestling. There are still ways that the sport of women's wrestling can advance and evolve, but we have come so far when you consider what it was like in 1989."

The story of Helen Maroulis's wrestling career begins much the same as, oh, about *ninety-eight percent* of females of the mat. It's the tale of a young lady with an older brother whom she found a reason to follow into the epitome of a guy's sport. Who faced danger and discrimination as she made her way through a man's sport, even as she kept winning. And someone who found a new reason to try and believe when word came that ladies would be allowed to hit Olympic mats.

Where it ends, well, that's yet to be written. Yes, even in this book. After medaling at the bronze level at the 2021 Olympics and then taking gold a few months later at the Worlds, there was no indication that Maroulis was done. By the time these words are published, or soon after, she may have hit it even bigger.

But now let's walk right through the six minutes she took to become a legend.

Maroulis didn't have a snowball's prayer that August 2016 day in Rio de Janeiro.

Just as the sun had risen that day and would set that night, just as Christmas falls in December, just like death and taxes, and just like traffic jams happening only when we're in a rush, it was a certainty. Saori Yoshida was walking out of the Carioca Arena 2 with a 53-kilogram gold.

She'd done so in every Olympics since ladies had been allowed onto the mat in 2004, including the 2012 event in which she'd been Japan's flagbearer. She'd done it in 13 World Championship events. She'd come out ahead in 207 consecutive matches, twice holding down the gal who stood across from her that very day.

Yoshida losing? Life would be found on Neptune first!

Even her opponent had started to believe it.

"I'm thinking, silver is good enough," Maroulis admits. "Then I said: No, Helen. Go for it."

Helen Maroulis (left, battling Kayla Miracle) became the first American woman to win an Olympic gold medal in the 2016 games, then snared a bronze in 2021. Photograph provided by A.J. Grieves.

But Yoshida was, after all, Yoshida. The same Yoshida who'd walloped three opponents by a combined 19–0 on her way to the finals. Yeah, some people had already started to blither about her skills rusting a bit (after over a decade in the game, someone's going to pull that one), but a performance like this shuts people up quickly. These opponents had had all the time they needed to prepare for her, and either they hadn't done so or, more likely, she was just that good. The greatest always come through in the big contests, and Yoshida looked to be adding one more golden neck decoration soon enough.

Maroulis had rolled off with a 12–1 walloping of Yuliya Khalvadzhy of Ukraine and *fed it* to China's Zhong Xuechun, 10–0. Then North Korea's Jong Myong-suk had given her a pretty good fight before Maroulis escaped with a 7–4 win.

Maroulis appeared to have regrouped in the semis, building an 8–0 lead over Sweden's Sofia Mattsson before scoring her first pin of the tournament. But five matches in one day is tough for any wrestler, let alone against the *greatest of their countries!* Walking in as the top seed, Yoshida had only had to battle four. Yeah, many believed that Maroulis would have better luck flapping her arms and flying back up to her Maryland homeland than beating Yoshida.

Look, it wasn't as though any of this was going for naught. Those four long years she'd waited for another shot at the Games after being edged by Campbell in the 2012 tryouts. All that time she'd spent walking a pencil-thin line between greens and protein on her diet or all the isolative training or everything else that every great wrestler undergoes ... wouldn't be a waste. Even if she lost to Yoshida—again!—she'd at least

A few months after Helen Maroulis took her second Olympic medal, Illinois middle-schooler Piper Sandell (above) herself an up-and-coming lady of the mat, paid a special tribute to her at Sandell's school event (for more information, see p. 240). Photograph provided by Kelly Staver.

wind up with a silver, which only fellow American Sara McMann had managed since women had started competing 12 years ago.

Disappointment had become common for American wrestlers at these Games. After waiting over a week since the ceremonies had opened, the U.S.A.-ers hadn't exactly made up for lost time. Since wrestling had started four days before, nine tournaments had finished—and not a single American had managed so much as a bronze.

And Maroulis's past bouts with Yoshida weren't exactly reasons for optimism; seven years before, a newly adulted Maroulis had roared into battle with the already gold medalist and World winner, and Yoshida had squelched that youthful optimism *real* fast. In less than 70 seconds, Maroulis had been left with a pinfall loss and torn elbow ligament. A few years later, Yoshida had pinned her again.

In 2014, Maroulis had been part of a group of Americans that went to Japan for some training. Yoshida and her teammates had tossed them around like rag dolls.

But even when Maroulis was winning the 2015 World title, even as she'd qualified to make this team, and, to a much smaller degree, as she'd made her way to Yoshida that very day, her mind was on her final opponent. She'd been watching Yoshida's matches, turning into Sherlock Holmes's female form, searching everywhere for that elusive vulnerability (weakness would be far too strong a word) that no one had been able to successfully exploit for over a decade.

And she might just have found it. It came down to paying attention to something that requires looking well below the surface to see.

"From what I saw, she's better at being patient [during matches]," Maroulis says. "When you're used to being patient, knowing someone panics, what happens when you're patient and someone matches you in that? Then you'll be the one to panic."

But who's to say it would work? If it were that easy, how come no one else had pulled it off? How could she know that Yoshida wouldn't catch on to her ploy, adapt as a champion does, and find some other way to victory?

Well, she couldn't. Sometimes everything a wrestler can possibly do isn't enough. You just hope.

Time for things to come to a head.

It becomes obvious pretty fast that Maroulis is a crowd favorite, as "U-S-A! U-S-A!" chants ring through Carioca about a minute into the match.

That patience that Maroulis was looking for suddenly ends, as Yoshida suddenly goes for Maroulis's right leg. She twists it every which way, and it's amazing that nothing from Maroulis's right hip down to her toes gets sprained or strained or shattered or at least dislocated, or maybe it does and she just doesn't notice. This kind of focus and adrenalin can help someone shove that pain away for a later hour.

Yoshida's got her right arm draped over Maroulis, and it's just one source of brute strength against another here. But even holding her opponent's leg and over her arm, Yoshida can't roll her opponent over or get atop her, and the ref stops the action.

Then things go all the way around. Maroulis's patience gets too excessive for the official, who decides she's got 30 seconds to score or Yoshida gets a freebie. Not surprisingly, that decision gets some heavy boos. When Yoshida indeed is handed that 1–0 lead, it's tough to swallow.

With a bit of time left, especially against Yoshida, many would have used it to go for a quick point. Maroulis doesn't, and things reach the halfway point with her still behind.

"Do nothing. Be patient," Maroulis reminds herself. "I can be down 1–0 and that's OK. I'm going to show her, even being down 1–0, I'm still not going to get out of my game plan, I'm not going to get out of my stance, I'm not going to react to her movement. I'm going to set the pace." After a bit more face to face, things suddenly get haywire.

Yoshida goes in high. About four nanoseconds later, Maroulis leaps low. She jerks back up, then rushes Yoshida backward. The Japanese woman grabs her in a headlock, but Maroulis yanks free and plants Yoshida to her stomach. Now she's ahead, and the place is going insane.

Yoshida nearly rolls her to her back, but Maroulis pushes back and goes back upstairs.

They fall out of bounds. Maroulis is back up and to the circle much faster than her opponent.

There's a minute to go now, and the crowd's switched to "Helen! Helen!" Yoshida, still a takedown from the lead, nearly wrenches Maroulis down, but the pair falls out of bounds again.

And just as they land, Maroulis manages behind her opponent. Her lead has increased to 4–1. Surrealism has rarely felt so real.

"I was in a zone," Maroulis says. "All I was thinking was, Christ is in me. I am enough."

Patience isn't going to work for Yoshida anymore. She suddenly gets offensive, grabbing Maroulis in a headlock. But Maroulis stays standing, and the action stops again.

Then Yoshida takes one of her first shots in a while, grabbing at Maroulis's left leg. And just as before, Maroulis power-matches her, not allowing her to take either of the American's limbs.

"That scared me so much!" Maroulis admits. "I was like, I'm just going to fight, no matter what it takes. I'm trying to feel where she's putting the pressure and trying to calculate what she's going to attempt."

With 10 seconds left, there's one more stoppage.

Yoshida fakes one shot, then another. Maroulis doubles back. She looks just a bit off-balance. But when Yoshida grabs at her left again, this time she just needs to step back a step, and time runs out on Yoshida's record and blasts Maroulis into history.

Both wrestlers hit their knees and bury their faces in the mat, albeit for opposite reasons. But Yoshida is gracious in her rare defeat, shaking Maroulis's hand and hugging her (she retires not long afterward). In one of the strongest Olympic images in American history, Maroulis charges around the mat, the flag adorning her shoulders.

"In that moment, I was seven-year-old Helen again," Maroulis says. "I was this little shy girl who just started wrestling and just loved the sport. I remember thinking, I've been saying I was going to be an Olympic champion for 17 years, and when it happens, I was like, 'Really, God? Me? Is it really me?' I've been chasing something I put on this pedestal. There must be some level that I have to reach, there must be some elite club."

Over the next two days, two of her countrymen join the club, as Kyle Snyder notches his own gold in 97-kilogram competition and J'den Cox a bronze in 86-kilogram.

"I had to accept that I'm not the fastest, I'm not the most technical, I'm definitely not in the running game with Yoshida on medal counts," Maroulis says. "But I'm enough, and you can be an Olympic champion by being enough. You don't have to be extraordinary or superior. You can be enough, and that's what it felt like."

By the time she'd make it back to the Olympics four years later, however, other feelings would be ringing through … and they'd be as far opposite as the ones of that day could reach.

Terry Steiner: "Helen winning the Olympic gold was so important to us. We'd been to four Olympics already and I thought we should have had one before. I wasn't match-side; she had a personal coach who asked if they could be there. I said it was fine. I was up on the second-tier balcony, and I ran down in the second period. The reason the Olympics are so great is because they're so hard to attain. I saw the struggle she had.

Before we left for overseas, we went out for a run one day. She said, 'Coach, I don't know if I can do it anymore. I don't know if I can put anything into it anymore.' In sports, you can do all the right things and nothing is ever guaranteed. But if you're gonna do this, you're gonna have to find a way to go all in. Otherwise, it's not going to happen. That's what she did. She started making changes. When she started making all the little decisions right and really dug in, that's how you know as a coach that we're on the right track. It's a professional integrity. They're doing it because they're doing it, not because someone wants them to do it. You need those moments, as hard as they are. If Helen had never had that moment, she may not have been the champion. The Olympic champion may not be the most talented; it's often the person that just stays the course and gives herself enough chances. They keep putting themselves in the fire enough times."

As we'll see now, though, sadly sometimes not even the combination of the community's strength, the help of teammates, and the support of one's friends and family can fix every issue.

CHAPTER 4

Body Issues—and Bullies

"As a result of the sometimes insane demands wrestlers place on their time, mind, and body, I'd be willing to bet there's not another sport out there that requires a fraction of the discipline that wrestling does. And for the most part, that discipline is great. Before a wrestling tournament, you're dialed in. Your vision is so narrow, and everything you do is based around one thing: to win. You're going to bed early, eating exactly how much you need to, getting those extra reps in after practice, and staying in when your friends go out and party on a Friday night."
—Emma Bruntil, U.S. Open and national collegiate champ

When a few pounds here and there can mean the difference between a win and a loss, and sometimes even whether a competition happens, you take the extra measures to hold them off for those few precious hours before a match.

And yes, there are ways to do that. Diet and exercise are part of the everyday routine (hell, every minute of the season!) for some of the most dedicated and disciplined athletes in sports history!

Emma Bruntil: "Hell, some of us would probably eat dirt if it made us more likely to win. So, you grind. You're so dialed in on your next tournament, the next chance you have to prove yourself. And every day you look in the mirror and see your body shrinking. Every day you see yourself become more lean, more muscular looking, and one step closer to your next goal. You feel so great, because in that space of time, you have so much purpose. And that feeling of control, of having everything in your life together in one neat little package, correlates to how you see yourself when you look in the mirror."

But this can go too far, too fast for us to control, or even realize. Again, when our weight plays a role in how or if we get to participate in a match, we do things to ourselves that seem justified at the time. A worthy sacrifice for our record, our team, our school. We're doing what we must to show that these points for the team are more important to us than our individual greater good.

Hey, maybe it's for us as well! What makes a great athlete is the willingness to push oneself as far as everyone else, and then a few steps farther! Where the pushing comes from, and in what direction, though, are issues we don't always consider.

And sometimes that means a little pain, even self-inflicted, along the way. After all, the season won't last forever, right? We'll be able to step out of this mindset and these practices as easily as we got into them when the pressure's off, right?

Right?

No. Not always. Eating disorders and their effects can hit us as hard in the mind as in the body.

Kaylee McFadden, Wisconsin champ: "What hurts wrestling the most for me is cutting weight. I have problems with my metabolism. I don't have the right mindset when it comes to cutting weight. I was cutting weight when I was 10, and a 10-year-old shouldn't be cutting weight. I was with my friends, and they wanted me to go to McDonald's. I had state or regionals the next weekend, so my friends had to promise me that they wouldn't tell my dad I got a cheeseburger instead of a wrap!

In October 2020, I cut 12 pounds for a tournament; in March 2021, I cut seven for one tournament and 10 for another. It's from not eating at all, a lot of running, sleeping in garbage bags. It's miserable when you try to sweat it off. Lots of laxatives, too. I've had eating disorders because of it. Since sixth grade, when I started to cut weight and not eat, I started to crave the feeling of being hungry. For days or even weeks after a tournament, I won't eat; I'll feel like crap. I get over it because I'm skinny, but I know that's not good. I've passed out before, and gotten really sick from it. The older I get, the more cutting weight I have to do, I go from eating normally to not eating for, it seems, like a month at a time. Then I'd start eating again, and it destroys my metabolism."

Shania Villalba, two-time Texas champ: "I did everything from eating right to not eating at all to taking laxatives and diet pills to wearing trash bags to wearing five layers of shirts and three levels of pants. Two days before a tournament, I would take three water pills; two days before, I'd take a laxative to empty out everything. I was completely dead, no energy. At weigh-ins, I took a Gatorade into the locker room to hydrate myself. There I am in the locker room at 6 a.m., right before a tournament, with everyone's jackets and shirts on, running to lose weight, wrapping myself up in the mats to make me sweat.

Wrestling gave me an eating disorder that's still in my life now. I go from not wanting to eat at all, and then the next morning, my stomach wants to throw up acid, because there's nothing there. You pig out after wrestling because you can eat anything, and then you're eating five nuts and five pieces of ham a day to be careful. I still feel afraid to eat, because I think I'll eat until I throw up."

Emma Bruntil: "When you're in your offseason and you finally have a much-needed break? You would think you would enjoy that time, that you would appreciate having a break and stepping back (just a little) from the strict structure you're used to. But the realityis, that's not often the case. And how you look physically during that time is often a perfect representation of how you might feel internally. You feel undisciplined, lazy, and out of shape because you don't have that immediate focus wrestling provides. And, your beliefs are all the more confirmed when you look in the mirror and don't like what you see, or better yet, when what you see isn't what you remember seeing when you felt your best."

As male wrestling has been around for much longer than women's wars, the issue of eating disorders amongst men from the mats has been studied for quite some time. How successful these academic exploits have been is another question.

Men, by their pseudo-manly nature, don't like to admit their issues, their addictions, their disorders to anyone, especially in a sport like wrestling, where open vulnerability is an invitation for opponent exploitation. If the guy on the other side of the mat learns that you've got a weakness, he's going to jump all over it, physically or psychologically, and you know damn well you'd do the same thing.

And many people with eating disorders don't realize it, not for a while. Do you think anyone right off the bat thinks, "Hey, it would be a great idea to try bulimia!"? They don't see it as a problem, just a difficult and necessary step. One more example of doing what the other guy doesn't have the guts to, and getting ahead in the bargain!

So when studies throughout the late 1990s and early 2000s started popping up to really show the impact that the eating disorder epidemic was having, people took notice. Studies have shown that between 30 and 50 percent of males—depending on the source—in weight classification sports (wrestling, rowing, boxing, cagefighting, to name a few) were afflicted with one eating disorder, or maybe more.

Emma Bruntil: "Making weight takes an already demanding sport to new heights. Now you not only have to go to practice, you have to stay after to do a half-hour of cardio. You don't just have to eat healthy—you sometimes have to track every single thing that goes into your mouth. For wrestlers, this is normally not a problem. Day of weigh-ins, you see yourself at your absolute leanest. Maybe you have abs, or ripped arms, or maybe you can see all sorts of muscles that you have never seen on yourself before. Your concept of what a lean physique is will forever be changed after this point, and every time you look in the mirror thereafter, you'll compare yourself to how you look on competition day. Finally, all your discipline and hard work with your nutrition, cardio, and your weight cut comes to a head. And man, does it feel good."

Eating disorders are difficult for *anyone* to face, and to openly discuss. Men especially don't like to talk about having them. First of all, because it's an insult to that *manliness* they wear like a medal. Second of all, eating disorders are a *girls'* thing! Anorexia? Bulimia? Fasting that can shove one into unconsciousness? Guys just don't *do* that! Hell, we don't even like to admit we're on a diet.

So consider this—if so many men were willing to admit that they just *might* have a problem, how many still held it away, for one reason or another? Chances are, quite a few more. It's a sad truth that wrestlers have many "incentives" to fall into the trap of eating issues.

And while female wrestling still doesn't have the numbers that the men's game does, it's going up. And there are a few sad reasons why.

Clearly, the more competitors, the more likelihood for these issues. And with women more likely to develop eating disorders than men in general, it's a dark, but legitimate prediction that body dysmorphia will be happening more and more amongst those in a sport dominated by weight classification. It's estimated that up to 30 percent of female athletes (not just wrestlers) suffer from these troubles—and, again, we're talking only about those willing to stand up and openly say, "Yes, I have (or had) a problem."

In the early stages of her wrestling career back at Washington's Mount Baker Senior High, Emma Bruntil didn't see an issue.

Emma Bruntil: "I need to get in shape again. 'I feel fat.' 'I only like how I look when I'm cutting weight.'

How many times have you heard wrestlers saying these seemingly harmless phrases? I know I have heard them a lot, even from myself. In the offseason, when you might look different than you did when you were competing week in and week out, this way of thinking becomes especially relevant. Why? Because it's easy to glamorize the process of cutting weight and the demands of elite wrestling. It's easy to remember how ripped you looked when you were cutting weight, but you don't often remember how tired, overworked, or burnt out you felt. It's easy to remember how much you loved 'the grind' when you are no longer in it, but it is hard to remember how overwhelming it was when you were going through it."

"I was always very competitive, and I wanted to be good at wrestling," Bruntil remembers. "I got really strict with my diet, but I didn't have a lot of understanding of nutrition." She remembered a middle school project in which she'd reported on the paleo diet, and been her own test subject in the process.

"When I tried wrestling, I tried what I thought was healthy, since I'd already done it," she says of the diet, which eschews processed food, dairy products, salts, and grains in favor of hardcore lean meats, veggies, fruits, and even roots. "I thought [paleo] would work again. You see it a lot among wrestlers."

Over the next few years, so much looked to go right for Bruntil at Mount Baker. After not taking up wrestling until just before high school, she ended up with two state titles, national championships, even a gold medal at Peru's Pan American Games in the summer of 2017. Everyone probably knew she was on some kind of diet—every great wrestler watches closely what she eats—but it was working.

Or so they thought.

"I didn't have my monthly cycles for three years," she remembers. "I had trouble with osteoporosis. I broke several bones, and I was super anemic. One time, my mom put a spot of regular milk in my eggs instead of almond milk. I freaked out and tried to spit it up." Almost every week, she was cutting up to four pounds. That's just what champions do.

"Once, I went to the doctor, and he asked me what I was eating," she says. "My skin had this greenish tone. I was bruising easily, and my hair was super thin. He was majorly concerned. He said that if I kept going down that path, I was going to have serious problems." This kind of self-treatment can lead to faster or irregular heartbeat, edema, and other issues that can affect us in the long term, or can end things in a second.

Like many in her situation, she brushed it off. What did this guy, degrees or otherwise, know about what it took to make it on the mat?

"He wasn't a female and he wasn't a wrestler, so he didn't understand," Bruntil recalls. "I figured that he just saw me as a girl that was hyper-focused on being perfect. Food was soothing to me; it was the one thing I had control over, like a coping mechanism."

But there is much more to weight issues than just poor dieting. Those afflicted are often found to sit in saunas, or even hot cars, sometimes wearing layers of heavy clothes or rubber suits. Others sneak down laxatives and diuretics to make sure that whatever does find a way inside gets right back out as soon as possible (this puts users in greater danger of colon and bladder cancer). Many walk around spitting like human sprinklers, a different and obscene way to rid oneself of water weight. Legal or otherwise, these things happen.

Fortunately, Bruntil realized that, as tough as dieting can be for most wrestlers, there are ways to do it right, and her way wasn't working. She learned that it is possible to have a great relationship with food and still tear it up and down on the mat. Now at McKendree University, she continued winning national titles—and even qualified to try out for the Olympic team that Covid pushed back to 2021.

"I had to figure out how to wrestle at a high level and not have this borderline disorder relationship with food," she says. "You can eat anything in moderation, as long as you hit certain targets. In my freshman year, I wrestled at 120. My sophomore year, I was up to 130. I wrestle at 143, but I don't weigh 143. It's nice not to have to cut weight every week."

Here's where the true team aspect of a sport that combines individual and group performance can come in. Wrestlers may not recognize their issues. Maybe because they don't want to, maybe because they're too busy to care, or anything else. Self-care can't always be a one-person job. Those who have seen it, even been there themselves, must step in once in a while.

Like, say, coaches who faced their own eating disorders, or saw a teammate go through one. Looking past the regular injuries seen on a too-regular basis in the wrestling room, there are quite a few more symptoms that come from a place worse than throws and takedowns:

- Extreme weight changes, up or down
- Frequent bathroom breaks, especially after eating
- Increased focus on weight and/or shape
- Bloodshot eyes
- Disappearances during meals, or avoidance of social issues where food is involved
- Clear, sudden reduction in strength and/or energy
- Consistent smell of vomit. Don't cover your nose and run away; this matters more.

If coaches can't give enough help themselves, they can certainly get the process going. Referring athletes to guidance counselors, support groups, or wellness centers (or contacting such places to ask them to take the first move) can start things off. Sometimes, seeing that someone else might have seen a problem is all wrestlers need to *want* to get better.

In order to coach at USA Wrestling, and other prestigious mat organizations, coaches need certification and renewal. If looking out for issues such as this were made a part of requirements to obtain either, it could shine a new light on this matter, Bruntil asserts.

"It's important for coaches to know what to look for and handle it in a delicate way that doesn't accuse anybody," she says. "I've heard coaches tell girls they look fat or that their thighs jiggle when they run. Having an open, honest, private conversation can help. Take weight out of the conversation. Help athletes learn about a healthy relationship with food."

Emma Bruntil: "First and foremost, to the athletes: recognize that there are different seasons of life. It's okay to not look like you do when you're cutting weight; hell, you probably shouldn't. This isn't an excuse to go off the rails or eat an entire box of Twinkies; it's just a way of saying you shouldn't feel bad for being human.

Ask yourself—truly ask yourself—do I tie my worth to wrestling? And, most importantly, do I tie my worth to winning? If you answered 'yes' to either of those questions, work on it, and don't be afraid to seek help. Most of us love wrestling so much it's easy to confuse what we do with who we are. But your worth as a person doesn't correlate to how many takedowns you can score, no matter how much some parents and coaches may think so. Your value as a person wouldn't change even if you never won another match in your life. So, love you for YOU, and love wrestling for wrestling.

As a coach, there will be times when you will inevitably have to talk to an athlete about their weight, which begs the question: How do you talk to an athlete about their weight without doing unintended harm? Simple: Keep it objective. Instead of telling an athlete she "looks fat" (and yes, this does happen), or using subjective adjectives, focus on objective facts.

'Hey Sally, on your last weight check you were 10 pounds over your weight class. Let's talk about some proactive steps you can take so that you can compete at your best.'

And, if you are constantly having to talk to an athlete about their weight, it may be time to consider that they have outgrown a weight class.

And lastly, to the parents out there: be parents. It may be hard if you have younger kids in the sport who don't know how to 'cut weight' or be healthy, so support the hell of them. Don't have your kids cutting 10 pounds every week; instead, lead by example. Cook healthy meals with your athletes, work out together, and be a listening ear when they need one. Most of the time, athletes get enough coaching from their coaches at practices, and what they need from you is encouragement."

A Monthly Issue

OK, let's go ahead and explore this topic.

Yes, female and male wrestlers face many of the same issues when it comes to health. Cutting those last few pounds before a match can cause trouble for anyone, especially those still in the midst of a growth spurt. Cuts and scrapes and strains and even cauliflower ear show up on either gender, and expected though they might be, they're certainly not welcome. Knee, neck, and back pain can hang out long after anyone's match, and sometimes even beyond a career.

But there's another issue, another inconvenience that men are *so* lucky not to have to handle, and that doesn't just apply to wrestlers, either. For a few days every single month, often at unpredictable and often inopportune of times, women are forced through a tough cycle that would have men bedridden for at least a week at a time were it to occur to them.

Yes, the cramps that can cause one hell of a distraction during a match. Retaining of water (and poundage) that one can't always sweat or diet off. Pain sensitivity and fatigue that can wear down even the toughest lady matster.

And, of course, the bleeding. Now that everyone's sadly clear as to where we're going with this, let's hear from some ladies who had to accept that this would always be just one more problem, and get used to toughing out just one more, cough cough, *inconvenience*.

Warry Bonney (Woodward), Virginia: "One of the biggest things was that I felt really exposed. You're not going to want to leak all over your singlet. Tampons can be really bulky and uncomfortable. If you want to be consistent on your weight, being on your period can throw you off, but athletes training hard and cutting weight, sometimes don't get their period. In high school, I often didn't get my period, because I trained so hard, with cross country on Saturday, wrestling on a Monday, and track the next day."

Emma Bruntil, Washington: "If you're weighing in, and it happens to be your time of the month, you can gain anywhere from a pound to [three] depending on your size. There's not really anything you can do about it. You have to suck it up and cut the weight. I've had to cut almost six pounds before a match. When I didn't have [a period], bones can be brittle, so I broke my nose three times in three years, and I broke my collarbone."

Jessica Medina, California: "It was awkward, being at a camp and having to ask someone to take me to the store [for feminine products]. But you adapt to the situations. I'd never talk about it with my coaches. I never brought up anything feminine; anything that had to do with femininity didn't belong in the room. It was unspoken, or taken care of ahead of time. I wouldn't even wear anything pink. There's no sign of femininity or fear."

Jill Remiticado, Hawaii: "[As a coach], a lot of it is just making sure the communication lines are open. We ask our athletes, 'Have you had your period yet? Do you need anything? Make sure you've packed extra supplies if you need. Make sure to wear bike shorts in practice.' If girls aren't feeling well, sometimes they need to take Ibuprofen."

Diana Wesendunk, California: "I came from a very conservative family where we didn't really talk about that stuff, so I'm not going to talk about it with a wrestling coach. Every month, at a certain time, I was five or six pounds over, and it's water weight. Dad would take me to the gym, and I'd run to get the weight off. Missing weight was not an option. Missing weight would be bad enough, but you don't want to be the girl that doesn't make weight. Once, I was seven and a half pounds over from my period, and I told my coach I didn't know if I was going to make weight tomorrow. He thought about it, then he moved me to the next weight up. We were having this conversation while another wrestler was eavesdropping. When he realized that he didn't have to make weight the next day, he told everybody that I was getting bumped up, so nobody had to make weight. The next day, only me and three other people made weight, and our coach had to forfeit all the other matches."

Ashley Iliff, New Jersey: "Not having a coach to go to, it can be [a problem]. When I first started coaching women, they were all around men, and had male coaches. It's hard when cutting weight, especially for the high school girls, because you hold a lot of water. It's hard for them, as a comfort level, to reach out. Coming from women's teams, I had a female coach to go to. My wrestlers can reach out to me. It was hard in the weight-cutting aspect. A girl has to weigh in the next day, and she can be lightheaded with low iron, and pass out. I passed out once in college from cutting weight, when I was 99 pounds."

Bullying

> "Most coaches that coached against me were OK with it, but with that being said, through my wrestling career, other coaches said that, "You need to rip her shoulder out of her socket,' 'Drop her right on her head so she knows she doesn't belong here,' 'You wrestle good for having a vagina,' 'Maybe come back next year and try to beat my kid.' The last one, I did do, and it felt amazing."
>
> —Allicyn Schuster, Nebraska, wrestler

Bullies don't act with rationale or logic, just a demented sense of self-gratification. With a mindset like that, they don't need much of an excuse to do the dirtiest of work.

And some keep doing it long after that maturity stuff is supposed to kick in.

As with any who have attempted to lead their gender into a new sport, female wrestlers have been prime harassment targets since the first ones stepped onto the mat. It stopped several careers before they had a chance to move forward. It's still doing so.

The classmates and pseudo-friends who can't comprehend how important this can be to someone with enough guts to try it out. The men, and still too many women, still so damned sure that women don't belong in a sport full of physical contact and exertion. The guys (and if not the wrestlers, their dads usually) all too ready to be the messengers that this is *our* mat and *you're* not going to be here.

Maya Nelson, Colorado: "As a child, I overheard grown male adults tell their sons to hurt me. I've had an article in a newspaper written about how I shouldn't be wrestling with the boys, where if I had the option to wrestle with girls, I would have gladly taken it. I've been called manly. I've been in gyms that many people believed that I didn't belong, nor did I deserve to be there. The only reason I got through a lot of that is the work ethic I learned from my dad and the will to continue moving forward no matter what that my mom instilled in me. I said this before, but I'll say it again: being a girl in this sport, especially around the time I was coming up, there was no room for any mental weakness. Anything can be used against you to prove their point that girls shouldn't wrestle. You have to work 10 times as hard for none of the recognition and be okay with it."

"I wrestled a match once and got off the mat and this kid walked up to me specifically and just said, 'Get out of here,'" remembers Lisa Whitsett, who started her career in Iowa in the 1980s and made it all the way to the national ranks. "I couldn't believe someone could be so ignorant of the determination it takes to walk into a room and start wrestling, period, whether you're a guy or a girl."

In the summer of 1991, wrestling camp officials refused to allow her to attend because no girls were allowed.

"When I called to get housing, it was a question as to what my relationship to the other wrestlers was when I was there," she says. "They ended up telling me I couldn't come. They tried to tell me it was because of my age, but the year before that, there had been a wrestler there my same age and they let him go. This stuff gets to you. When you have to practically beg your way in sometimes, it hurts your pride a little bit."

Getting this sort of grief from the outside is a realistically sad expectation. You don't want it, but you're not really surprised. It's happened to every woman who's ever crossed any kind of athletic gender lines.

"Fathers would warn their sons, 'You'd better not lose to that girl. Break her arm,'" says pioneer Tricia Saunders of her own early days. "Mothers would warn me, 'You'd better stay off the mat. Girls can't wrestle.'"

And yes, it's probably most from opposing fans. Opposing parents. Coaches and opponents. Once in a while, even your own classmates and teammates.

But from your own coach? The guy (a male in this case) who's not only supposed to be showing you the fundamentals of the sport, but setting an example as an adult, both as a coach and a teacher at your school? Especially since he had a good enough set of leaders to himself wrestle all four years of high school?

It's tough to imagine any coach worth his salt openly badmouthing his own athletes, especially on the high school level. Sadly, that's what a few Alaskan gals were forced into in early 1993.

"What I want to teach, to me," declared Mount Edgecumbe High rookie coach Rod Eakin, "is not what a woman should be taught. I have a problem with them wrestling." Apparently setting a record for world's oldest 24-year-old, Eakin asserted that women couldn't understand what it meant to lead a household, to make decisions for themselves and others.

"There are a lot of things about the team that I'd like to teach that have to do with being a man in our society," claimed the impromptu pulpit pontificator, ironically speaking to a female sportswriter, another field that's been slow to accept women.

Basically, Eakin announced his open intent to discriminate. That one really boosted morale amongst his squad, especially its females.

"I would rather die than give in to him," asserted junior Tracy Lundahl, in the mat game since elementary school.

But for one of the first times, Lundahl and her teammates didn't have to stand alone. Not even just with their teammates, friends, and families. Community readers responded, letters pouring in from everywhere to stand up for the athletic minority.

On February 8, the school announced an investigation into gender discrimination, hardly a matter of debate by this point. The next day, four days after his comments were originally published, Eakin resigned.

But the story didn't end there.

Along with the entire school faculty, Eakin underwent sexual harassment and gender equality training, along with an individual three-month crash course in communication for just him. In mid–January 1994, the school gave him another shot. Lundahl made it to regional competition, and Eakin helped her grab a spot in the Women's National Freestyle Tournament that April in Vegas, where she finished fifth.

Whitney Conder, Washington: "Lots of parents would pull their sons from wrestling me. They'd tell me I didn't belong on the mat, telling me to get back in the kitchen and go make a sandwich. I had one father, when I beat his son in a finals match, come up and ask me if I was sure I was a girl. I said, 'Yes, last time I checked. Would you like to find a doctor and find out?' Parents would tell their sons they would pay them if they would beat me or make me cry. Parents would call my parents and discriminate against them, trying to say that my mom wore the pants. They were threatening my family because they were letting me wrestle."

As Brianna Staebler started to tear through the no-longer-all-male high school wrestling ranks, she and her family started to hear similar rumblings from across the Wisconsin community.

"In her freshman year, the mental side of wrestling we learned more than anything else," Keith Staebler recalls of his daughter's career. "You can do all the work, but you have to be mentally ready for it. We had some issues with some coaches that were saying some really mean things, and weren't supportive. People were telling her that I was using her for my personal gains. It was from one of the top coaches in the Wisconsin Wrestling Federation. They were telling that to a 14-, 15-year-old girl. She didn't tell me about that for about six months. We're sitting there in the truck, both of us started crying."

It might have been because she was a girl. It might have been because she was part Native American. It might have been that the wrong people just got in the mood to act like assholes for the sheer reason of having nothing else to do. That's typically how and why this sort of thing starts.

It was in her genes. It was in her blood. If she didn't know it, if she and her family couldn't see it or feel it, someone else sure as hell could, and did.

Belief in something much higher than the mere and puny mortal has *long* been a staple of almost every Native American culture.

"I wasn't the same as everybody else," says Cheyenne Atwater. "I wore darker clothes, different styles. I had different music tastes. I was not one of the skinny, preppy girls." So many prime targets all over her back.

She and her family members were constantly getting hit. Things were always being thrown at them. Her sister was thrown into some mud and stomped on.

The teachers and principal at her first high school stood around. No one did anything. Students who take matters into their own hands with this often end up getting punished worse than the ones who provoked them.

So what was she to do? Go to town in the hallways? Being just over five feet might not have intimidated anyone, but a woman that size doesn't bounce around 150 pounds without some staunch bodily artillery. Turning to the closest thing that a schoolgirl can locate to legalized ass-whipping, she turned to the wrestling team.

"I couldn't do this anymore," she says. "I didn't have anger outside anymore. I saved all my energy for wrestling." Boys kept messing with her, but this time Atwater could hand back one hell of an ultimatum.

Want to see if you can kick my ass? Hell, maybe you can, even right in front of everyone, and get away with it! Just do me the honor of showing up and wrestling and doing it on the mat.

Guy after guy chickened out. Many never bothered her again.

But as one problem was solved, another took its place. Atwater's teammates and even her coach told her to get the hell off the mat and quit wasting their time and her own.

When that didn't work, the measures intensified in their drastic-ness. Atwater was paired with a teammate who just *happened* to be well ahead of her in both size and experience. And even with all that experience, he just *happened* to toss legality off the mat and smash down on her ankle with his knee. Teammates crowded around, dousing her in taunts.

Atwater jumped up and ran up, down, and around the bleachers. The next day, she won a tournament. Then she learned that she had five torn ligaments.

She powered through. Native Americans are known for being about the toughest to ever walk the Earth, and many of her ancestors had been through a hell of a lot worse than this.

And while she would never remember it, something had happened in her infancy. Something that just may have gifted her from beyond.

In another battle, this one at least against a fellow female, albeit one well above in poundage terms, Atwater came out well on top.

Soon after, she was freshening up in the restroom. Turning to leave, Atwater found herself face to face with her opponent.

"She kept trying to touch me," she says. "She was grabbing me sexually. I had bruises on my breasts."

Surely, something would finally be done at this point, right? What else had to happen?

More, as it turned out. Atwater's coaches snickered off the assault.

Another girl chopped off her hair. An opponent poked her in the eye. When Atwater's mother attempted to intervene, she herself was reported to the school board and banned for the season.

Enough was enough. The Atwaters were only human.

Braving an extra three-minute drive in the mornings, Atwater switched over to Bauxite High for her junior season. She started off with a win. She placed near the top of her first tournament. It was time to make a new first impression and one hell of an impact on those who had thrown her away the previous years.

Her coaches weren't easy on her. No great wrestling coach ever is. Then again, they were just as tough on everyone else. Difficulty's acceptable and even positive, as long as it's equal.

Before, during, and after her first year at Bauxite, she led the rest of the squad through powerwashes, football concession stands, booster club work, and other fundraising. Her win total kept going up, her skills rising even faster. Moving toward her senior year in the fall of 2020, Atwater had a shot at becoming the first lady to captain her school's wrestling team.

Then came something else. A moment that, had certain results occurred, might have halted more than her sports career.

Trying to remember where she'd parked in front of a Walmart, Atwater chatted with one friend and texted with another at the same time. Finally locating her vehicle, she stepped toward it.

Almost out of nowhere, a man appeared. Thinking that a short lady might make an easy target (clearly unaware of her athletic background), he grabbed her wrists.

"Why don't you come with me?" he leeringly snarled. He started dragging her down the lot, going into all kinds of disgusting detail about what he was going to do to her. With no time limit, no official to break it up, no teammates to have her back, no rules at all, Atwater was in a new kind of fight, and her safety and virtue, if not her life, were the prize in this one.

Suddenly, she felt something new. A strength far past the typical adrenalin rush. One that had come from (or been instilled in her from) elsewhere so long ago.

Late in the summer of 2003, Atwater's mom had held her family's recent arrival, watching her fellow tribe members at a pow-wow.

One of the group's medicine men noticed her. He stepped forward, and asked if her might hold her.

"May I give her a naming ceremony?" asked the elder. Her family said sure.

Calling the hundreds in attendance to attention, the gentleman and his new friend walked into the middle of a huge ring. Clearly, he and they were waiting for a message from somewhere far above.

Then a sound echoed from within. He was calling out the child's name.

It meant Iron Woman. She was destined for something great.

By that 2020 night, her family, her friends, her teammates, even her opponents, might have been convinced of this prophecy. But perhaps not Atwater herself.

Until now.

"I pulled away, trying to get away," she says. "I finally punched him in the face."

Falling back, the shocked assailant showed the colors that shine in so many of his kind when the playing field levels, scurrying away. Unfortunately, to anyone's knowledge, as of this book's publication, he hadn't been apprehended.

"My strength helped me through it," Atwater says. "I walk now with my finger on the trigger of pepper spray."

And she absolutely did make captain at Bauxite. She kept collecting donations. She was up at 5 a.m. to work out. When the Covid virus hit, she jogged around her yard and lifted heavy branches. She started helping area youth improve their own mat skills.

"I'm expected to be there for everybody," says Atwater, who hopes to become a lawyer, "driving people to practice, taking people home, showing them how to do everything. I know I'm strong enough to handle it."

Christen Marie Dierken, California: "I wrestled on a boys' high school team, and everyone I encountered did everything they could to try to get me to quit wrestling because, to them, girls didn't belong in a man's sport. I was demonized by my peers and even by one of my teachers. I was called a dyke and slut, because the only reason I would join the wrestling team is because I was either a lesbian or wanting to have sex with the guys on the team.

If I wanted to have a college wrestling career, then I was forced to deal with coaches without integrity, sexual predators, and manipulation. I cannot tell you how many times we would be traveling as a team and a bystander would ask me if I 'wrassled in mud or jello?' The sexualization of women in this country and in sports specifically is very troubling.

As a coach, I have been told that some of my standards are a little bit over the top. For example, I do not allow my athletes to pull down their singlet straps, walk around in just a sports bra, or hike up their singlets. I also encourage our athletes to represent themselves as respectable young women—as professionals and with confidence. It's sad that I have to set our social media to private because of the perverts out there and that I have to always be on my toes to protect our young women from predators.

Another thing that's troubling as a coach is that while women's wrestling is growing at a rapid speed, we are still not being given equal opportunities. Without getting into too much detail, there is a trend of some universities adding a women's program and not giving them a complete coaching staff. The universities feel it is sufficient to just take the men's assistant coach and have him also be over the women's program. In my opinion, that is giving the women's team sloppy seconds."

Karissa Avallone, Oklahoma: "I started wrestling living in Oklahoma when I was four. You were called butch or you were told you didn't belong on the map because you're a girl. It's a boys' sport. Back then in Oklahoma, women were supposed to stay home and clean the house. I had a boy shake my hand and then say, 'Why don't you go home and bake me some cookies?' Then I beat him and said, 'Why don't you go home and bake *me* some cookies?'"

Ally Fitzgerald, New York: "When I was a freshman and a sophomore, I would be in a sports bra and thong weighing in with three middle-aged men. My parents weren't allowed in. Everyone else used one scale, and I had to use a different one. Being a 13-, 14-, 15-year-old girl, half naked in a closed room with a group of men, was very uncomfortable. This was every tournament and match from my freshman and sophomore year. It was traumatizing. It was only my junior year that I started getting weighed by females."

Bella Hoffman, state champ of South Carolina: "When I'm in the middle of a match, I tune out everything except my coaches. There have been many times where I come off the mat and I find out that my team is ready to kill a kid who was yelling at me. I don't hear it because I'm focused on the match, the guy in front of me, and what my coaches are saying. I get a bunch of crap just walking down the hallway. It used to bother me a lot. Kids used to cuss at me and call me a dyke."

Catherine Mullis, Georgia: "Georgia wrestling has multiplied about 20 times since when I started. Everywhere I went, I was the only girl, and I would hear that there shouldn't be females on the mat. I got called a dyke one time. Once I was wrestling a boy, and his dad starts yelling from the stands, 'You better get this!' and pointing to his bicep. I pinned him. His dad got quiet. I've had people talk trash, and then I've lost to them. It's just something you have to take."

Cassandra Herkelman, Iowa: "A lot of people's doubt was always a motivation my first few days of practice. A lot of guys were like, 'She's just going to get her picture taken and then quit.' That happened a lot of times."

Brittany Delgado, Oklahoma: "There was so much background noise, every day, all day. Every time I faced a new team, every time I faced a new opponent, I'd hear that wrestling's not a girls' sport. This was a man's sport. 'What are you doing here, little girl?' Then, when I kicked the kid's ass, everybody would say, 'Ooh, you got beat by a girl!' It was never, 'You got beat by someone who's been wrestling since age four.' We lost a lot of good guy wrestlers because they lost to me."

CHAPTER 5

Back to the Trials!

At its outset, the female wrestling community is basically a sizable community—not quite metropolitan level, but pretty close and on its way. Hey, maybe a sorority would be a more appropriate analogy.

Because one of the main trademarks, maybe offerings, of a sorority is its tight-knit nature. Everyone knows everyone else. And most everyone helps. Sometimes these colossal teams stretch up and down a state, all over the country, everywhere.

Wrestling's not that far off. Stay in the sport for a good while, and chances are you'll almost run out of surprises. After some time, you look over the brackets for your next tournament, and if you haven't personally gotten down with your opponents, you know someone who does.

If the sport were a sorority, Tricia Saunders would undoubtedly be the president, the house mom, the one who manages the organization, keeps things in line and running smoothly. There's no one to look farther up to in female wrestling than arguably its first driving force, who started in elementary school and rolled all the way to World titles and the Hall of Fame.

The accomplished members, the Big Sisters, would be the ones we're about to discuss. The ones who stuck it out, who braved the toughest treks of sports to make it to the top. These are the ones who finish in the first class on a regular basis. Either they win or they almost do, but these names have certainly reached household level, and most are closer to the end than to the beginning of their careers.

The incoming class is pretty big, and gets larger all the time. It's made up of those who dream of making it to the top, and have taken the first couple of steps. These are those in high school, middle school, even younger, but who have gone from just talking and thinking about making their hopes reality to actually making it come true. These are the names we'll be seeing in the NCAA Championships in a few years, and probably in the Games in 2024 or 2028.

Pretty soon, the legacies will arrive, the next generation of women showing up to join. The daughters, nieces, even granddaughters of those who keep carrying their sport to stronger levels and greater numbers.

Where are we going with this analogy? Here's the significance.

Even gearing up for one of the biggest moments of their entire lives, not just their wrestling careers, everywhere the dozens of competitors looked, they saw familiarity. People they'd stood on the sidelines and watched. People they'd faced, defeated or lost to, or both. Even their own teammates.

And here's where the line between teammate and opponent truly gets broken. Many teams were represented in several different weight classes. Some teams had several members in the same class. Just days before, the same people who had helped one another sharpen their skills, had wished each other enough luck to fill the arena, might be the very last ones standing between a teammate and the Olympic Games.

As the trials finally kicked off that early April 2021 day at Fort Worth's Dickies Arena, one last set of obstacles would fall!

The Titan Mercury Wrestling Club sent 13 women to the trials, including 68-kilogram top seed Tamyra Mensah-Stock. Jacarra Winchester, the favorite at 53-kilograms, used to compete for the California squad, but she was representing the Army Wrestling Club at the Fort Worth contests. Sunkist Kids alumni Helen Maroulis (57-kilograms) and Kayla Miracle (62-kilograms) headed off their respective divisions and brought 10 of their teammates from Arizona. Sarah Hildebrandt (tops in 50-kilogram) and Adeline Gray (seed one in 76-kilogram) and two others from the New York Athletic Club were there to do battle.

"It points to having good partners in the room," says Joye Levendusky, vying for the 76-kilogram title with her McKendree University teammate Sydnee Kimber, "but you never want to compete against someone who's your friend." They, along with 57-kilogram contender Cameron Guerin, helped McKendree to its second consecutive National Collegiate Women's Wrestling Championship a few weeks before the trials.

Sarah Hildebrandt: "I feel like I've gone into world trials being a favorite, and I am really not trying to look at this any differently or put any extra pressure like it's some greater event that I've participated in before. At the end of the day, this is to make another 'world team,' and I've done that multiple times. I think just going in there and wrestling how I wrestle. I don't have to wrestle more or be better or bigger than I actually am."

It's sad that from a class that started so large, only six would be moving on.

But those women knew, before and after the tournament, that the ones who were truly part of the women's wrestling community would still be there a few days later. Even the dozens who didn't win would be behind them, eschewing bitterness to focus on doing right for their special sisterhood as a whole. They wouldn't be able to follow the squad to Japan—the Covid virus had halted those hopes—but they'd be crowded around TVs and computers and cell phones, watching the rest try to tear it up. And when the ladies returned, a heroine's welcome would be there. Sororities, which can number membership into the tens of thousands, are about pulling for people with at least something in common; this team would feel the same thing.

Everyone had their own story to tell, their own reasons to be on the team. "The underdog comes back to beat the opponents and the odds!" "I'm making my family proud, even if someone of them were stolen away recently!" "I'm out to prove that I'm for real, not a fluke or one-hit wonder!" And, of course, the old reliable, "I've worked too hard and sacrificed too much to go home empty-handed!" It doesn't matter from where the motivation came; all that counts is that it's here.

Hildebrandt and the rest of the top seeds might get to sit out the first few rounds. But they'd better take care not to rest on their laurels, mentally or physically. Just beneath and behind the first-round byers are dozens of competitors who'd just love to be the ones to reach up and disrupt the hell out of their concentration. Fourteen women line up alongside Hildebrandt for the 50-kilogram spot, and just as many are locked on Gray in 76-kilogram battle. There are 13 women, including Winchester, in the 53-kilogram roster, and Maroulis may have to bypass another 12 at 57-kilogram competition. Miracle leads a field of 12 in the 62-kilogram contest, with 10 looking to get Mensah-Stock lost in the 68-kilogram shuffle.

50-kilograms

Five years ago, one match ended up making the difference in history.

With a few steps between them and taking on the 53-kilogram world in Rio, Maroulis and Whitney Conder battled for the next spot on the Olympic squad as the trials wound down in Iowa.

And Maroulis took over from the start, overpowering Conder and running away with an 11–0 victory. This, as we've been over before and will touch on later, spurred Maroulis to the top of the world.

"That was a really tough day," Conder admitted. "I really contemplated retiring that day. It was a feeling I never wanted to have again."

Clearly, and very fortunately, that didn't occur.

"Wrestling always made me believe in myself and learn and grow," remembers Conder, who started wrestling in elementary school and became the first lady in Washington history to place in state high school tourney competition. "With wrestling, even if you've been wrestling your whole life, there's always something to learn and grow with, and you never know everything. Even though I've wrestled for about 25 years, I'm still wrestling and still growing in the sport of wrestling. You're never perfect in a wrestling match, but you can always achieve something great. Every wrestler is different, the way they respond to their coach. A technique may work for someone, but even if it does, it may not be exactly alike; there may be some small difference that wrestlers have to do to make that technique work for them."

In August 2019, she went to Peru for the Pan American Games in an event that would become a preview for the Olympics; while Conder took gold in the 50-kilogram event, Hildebrandt scored tops in 53-kilograms (she actually decided to slim down to 50-kilograms very soon before the trials), Miracle at 62-kilograms, and Mensah-Stock in the 68-kilogram tourney.

"That day, my coach asked me if I wanted to know who I was wrestling," says Conder, who'd previously won gold at the 2015 Pan Ams, "and I said I didn't care who it is, other than the lady from Colombia. My coach looked at me, and I knew I had my answer." She started out against Carolina Castillo, who'd wrestled at both the 2012 and 2016 Games, and-defeated Castillo. Then she slipped past Brazil's Kamila Barbosa and beat Yusneylys Guzmán of Cuba for the gold (Guzmán notched a spot on her country's 2021 Olympic team).

Later that year, in China, Conder scored a silver at the Military World Games, falling to China's Yuyan Li.

"When I first came into the military [in 2012], I stood out a lot," remembers Conder, a military police officer. "A lot of athletes do, because they're resilient. They're focused when they want to get that task done and do it correctly. A lot of people notice how focused we are. The schools I've gone through, I've done very well because of my wrestling. It's made me succeed in a lot of my courses." The Wuhan competition was her second foray into Military World competition, she continues.

"A lot of times when you go to the championships, the games are just as tough as the World Championships or Olympics, because those athletes are the same ones, competing there as well, serving for their countries, wanting to support their countries and show that they have a major love for their countries, just like we do. It's pretty amazing to see that competition, why it stood out for me a lot."

Along with that, she wants another shot at Hildebrandt, who convincingly defeated her at the Pan-American Olympic Qualifier Wrestle-Offs (the matches that laid the groundwork for America to qualify six weight classes for the Olympics) in February 2020 in Marietta, Georgia.

By this point, Victoria Anthony has won almost everywhere except the Olympics. A Junior World title in 2009, and another the next year. Later in 2010, she'd take her first Women's College Wrestling Association title for Simon Fraser University. Four years later, Anthony won her fourth such championship, the first person to ever do so—and just by a few matches; on January 25, 2014, she and fellow Fraser-ian Maroulis won their respective fourth titles a couple minutes apart. Later that day, King University won the overall team title, helped by Hildebrandt's first championship. The most recent four-timer? Miracle, who took four straight for Campbellsville and finished in 2018. This is clearly a who's who of wrestling.

Four years before, she came within a match of the 2016 Games, falling to Haley Augello for the 48-kilogram spot. Ironically, at the 2013 World Championships, she defeated Clarissa Chun, who would coach the 2021 Olympic team.

Anthony's also got as much momentum as any other athlete at the event; just a few weeks before, she won gold at an event in Italy. At the Pan Am Games the year before in Canada, she took tops in the 50-kilogram event, slipping past Castillo for the gold.

Then there's Emily Shilson, who's roaring into this event with both the strength of a rocket and absolutely nothing to lose.

First, there's the six state titles she took in high school in Minnesota, along with the Cadet World title and Youth Olympic Games gold she brought back to America in 2018 (the first-ever American to do so), all of which culminated in her winning 2019's national Tricia Saunders High School Excellence award, given to America's top high school woman of the mat. Then the 14–0 freshman year at Augsburg University, with two of those wins being national championships.

Add in the fact that she's just barely into her second decade (as in, well, young enough to be part of the 2024 or even 2028 teams), and she wouldn't walk out a loser if she never scored a point here.

"A big part of it is just planning and preparation," says Shilson, who lost to Hildebrandt at the U.S. Senior Nationals in October 2020 in Iowa, "knowing when everything is, having a set schedule of when I'm going to start peaking and tapering for the tournament so I'm not leaving anything to chance. It's about being very methodical in my preparation. I wrestle better when I'm not nervous. Sometimes I'm the top seed in tournaments, and now I'm the underdog. It took pressure off. No one was expecting me to win, except me. Those expectations helped me open up a lot more."

That works in her opening match, as she holds down Sage Mortimer, one of America's top recent high school graduates and one of just three grade-schoolers in the event, in just under three minutes.

"That was bittersweet," says Mortimer, whose skills won her a scholarship to King University. "It went by really fast, but now I know I can move on to bigger and better things, like being on a world team, winning world titles, winning an Olympic gold medal." Anthony tears things up in the round of 16 as well, teching Charlotte Fowler 10–0.

Them, in the very next round, Anthony uses her near-decade advantage in experience to make short work of Shilson, scoring a 10–0 technical fall.

"That's always hard," Shilson says of her uncommon loss. "I always go into tournaments thinking I'm going to win. I wanted to go into trials and come out an Olympian, but that didn't happen. But I can't let that get to me. I have to refocus and figure out what went wrong, and come back stronger. Recovery is really important, taking a break if my body needs a break. Focusing on recovery and nutrition is a big part of staying healthy." Mortimer beat Fowler and lost to Erin Golston in the consolation round, while Shilson teched Angelina Gomez; earlier that month, Shilson and Gomez each won their respective divisions at the National Collegiate Women's Wrestling Championships (NCWWC) at Ohio's Tiffin University, Shilson scoring tops at 109 pounds for Augsburg and Gomez the victor in 101-pound competition for Emmanuel, a win that cinched Gomez's qualification in the trials.

"I couldn't make the team, but I had to bounce back and come through the back side of the bracket," Shilson says. "I was there to wrestle, and I wasn't going to stop."

Anthony keeps going in the semis, holding off Alyssa Lampe, 7–6. Conder's trek ends before another shot at Hildebrandt, as she's pinned by Amy Fearnside.

Anthony gets right back on track in the finals, scoring an 11–0 defeat of Fearnside. Now it's time for a showdown with Hildebrandt, and a chance to avenge the defeat Hildebrandt handed her at Rome's Matteo Pellicone event in January 2020.

"I think it was advantageous sitting out," Hildebrandt claims. "I didn't care who came through. I honestly didn't watch. I'm super glad I earned that. I knew that the best person would come through that bracket, because it's a stacked bracket."

Now it's finals time and best of three. The first period of Round One is pretty close, one back and forth shot after another. One period in and through the first part of the second, it's anyone's match.

Then Hildebrandt goes gut-wrenching. Again and again and then some more. Her points start to pile up, and Anthony doesn't seem to be able to improvise out an answer with so little time. Suddenly the score reaches 12–2, and things end early. Anthony's quickly on the comeback trail.

Hildebrandt and Anthony appear to be having a tug-of-war with their mouths for the first moments of the sophomore battle, each head to the other's shoulder. Hildebrandt suddenly goes low, and Anthony nearly gets behind her, but they're head to head again soon.

Nearly two minutes in, Hildebrandt suddenly leaps in and gets her arms around Anthony's left leg. Anthony goes to her stomach, but Hildebrandt suddenly flips her over by her legs, racking up four points in seconds. She nearly gets another, but the whistle blows. Anthony nearly gets her leg as the period ends. This is looking a little different from the first match, and there's time for her to save the situation.

Anthony dives early, but Hildebrandt basically just guns her onto her stomach for a 6–0 lead. She goes back to Anthony's leg for another takedown. Anthony goes for some fancy footwork and another dive, but Hildebrandt gets around her and takes her down again for the tech-maker in a 10–0 win.

Then she collapses in tears.

"I don't even know how to talk about it," she says. "I'm just going to keep squealing. It's like a culmination of say many things, I feel like I was just speaking it into my wrestling. I know that sounds so cheesy, but that's how it feels, and I'm just grateful for the opportunity. For the most part, it's 'Be Sarah'! That's my mantra, and I say that all the time, and that's what I did. I brought a really good Sarah to the stage, and I think that's going to continue in Tokyo."

Sarah Hildebrandt: "A huge part of it is just not being afraid. Just stepping on the mat, and being like, 'Dude, I'm the best.' I think the pandemic offered some really crucial things that helped me to calm down and get things right [in my head]. Part of being a good athlete is finding ways through [trouble], and I did. I'm going to the Olympics! Holy shit!"

Shilson came roaring forward; one month after the Olympic trials, in events two days apart in Texas, she took the 50-kilogram gold at the USA Wrestling/United World Wrestling Women's Junior Nationals, then won a spot on the U23 Women's World Team, to commence in Serbia in November 2021 (she won gold there too!). The following March, she took an NCAA National title for Augsburg.

"It was crucial to keep from getting worn out," she says. "I never have a big break. Part of it is just loving the sport and having fun with it. I'm not where I want to be yet. I was still getting out-muscled, so I want to keep putting on muscle. I know what to accept for next time. I'll absolutely be at the 2024 trials."

53-kilograms

It had been bad when she was getting bullied back in her Oakland homeland, as too many with speech impediments still get forced through all the time. The knee injury

She didn't quite make the 2021 Olympic team, but Emily Shilson won two World titles later that year. Photograph provided by Augsburg University.

that had happened at exactly the wrong time to force her from the 2016 Olympic trials was awful. The iffy call that had cost her a shot at the gold in her World Championship debut in 2018 ... well, it totally sucked.

But she'd gotten past those in the mental sense, as much as anyone can, and her injuries had healed. Every wrestler has to bounce back once in a while, and some have to bounce back more often, and from a much greater distance, than others. Jacarra Winchester had been facing them since before her mat career had begun back at Missouri's Arroyo High, where she went from her first singlet to a state title in less than two years. Then all the way across the state to Missouri Valley College and a WCWA championship.

As common as torn ACLs and menisci are in wrestling, it doesn't make them any easier to suffer through, let alone return from. When they happen off the mat (in this case, a soccer game) and monkey wrench one of the biggest matches of one's career (in this case, the trials), it's like the ACL is looking up and laughing at us, like, "What did you expect, acting like that at that time?"

Winchester gutted it back, scoring a spot on the World team in Hungary. Up against Zalina Sidakova of Belarus in 55-kilogram competition, as the momentum swung back and forth, Winchester appeared to have scored it in the final seconds, notching a takedown that would launch her into the medal picture.

But looks were sadly deceiving. Sidakova's squad filed a challenge, and it turned out they were right—time had run out just as Winchester's move (and ultimately points) went through. While Sidakova got to the top match and lost to Japan's Mayu Mukaida, Winchester lost in the bronze round and ended up with nothing around her neck.

"Such a painful but necessary moment in my life," she told her social media fans. "My winning takedown was overturned in the semifinals of the World Championships last year and I lost the match. This is not a pity post. [I] just want you to know that every setback has a major comeback."

Damned right. Winchester found her niche, and it came at the U.S. Open. She won it in 2018, then again the next year. Also in 2019, that elusive World title finally arrived. Then came the 2020 Pan American Olympic Qualifier, which put her at the top of the trials.

But the worst was coming.

Even with everything Winchester got through, her Titan Mercury Wrestling Club teammate Katherine Shai has seen more, at least in time terms; twice before, the California native has gotten within two wins of Olympic-dom, notching third at the 2012 and 2016 trials (she also competed in the 2008 events, but didn't place).

"I had not prepared myself to be ready for that," she says of the 2008 event (that year, Shai won a world title at an event in Greece). "I had my head in the clouds before I really got down to it." She came back and won two consecutive WCWA titles for California's Menlo College, then saw her career upended by Tommy John surgery.

"It was very exciting to win, and then come back and win it again," she remembers. "It was very nerve-racking, the second year. It took a lot of mental work to prepare."

Diet changes and more trips to the gym got her back in shape and better than before. She started wrestling at 52-kilograms, then at 55. But she lost to future Olympian Kelsey Campbell at the 2012 trials, then, still on the mend from a broken foot, lost to Maroulis in 2016. Later that year, her shoulder went under the knife, and pregnancy came along.

"I kept finding a way to move forward," she says. "You take all the time to reflect and think about what you could have done differently. I wasn't sure if I had a situation that I could go back to, but like any wrestler, I couldn't stay away from the wrestling

A former world titlist, Katherine Shai (here warming up with coach Troy Nickerson) competed at four Olympic team trials. Photograph provided by Katherine Shai.

room. How could I approach wrestling in a different way? Could I do a better job, putting my training together without being relegated to the Olympic Training Center structure, but use the benefits that I had learned from that system? I went to find a training system in Denver, because I missed wrestling, the feel of training, the feel of wrestling. I was missing it, and I wanted to see how could I do it if I was on my own."

Then she started LuchaFit, an online support group and coaching program for female wrestlers.

"Part of it is to measure your own impact, and be a strong indicator for other athletes," she explains. "It depends on your training situation; it doesn't have to be traditional, and it doesn't have to be at the National Training Center. It gave people an opportunity to decide what they view their future as. Myself, I always envisioned making an Olympic team, winning gold, having a business career, and going out and starting a family. [LuchaFit] is all that smashed into one. It's allowed me to grow and expand in huge ways. I can do a lot more than I thought I could, and if I can't do everything at the same time, that's OK. Learning what to prioritize is big."

But there's someone else riding her own fire in this division. Winning a Cadet World title in 2015 had been nice, as had a national title the previous November. Now Ronna Heaton had a chance to not only realize the dream of every young wrestler, but settle a few scores as well.

One of many Sunkist Kids charges present, Heaton gets rolling with a hardcore 10–0 tech of Jasmine Hernandez, then shuts out Alexandra Hedrick, 4–0. Meanwhile, Shai defeats Heaton's teammate Alisha Howk, 10–0.

In the semis, Shai holds off Areana Villaescusa 2–1. Heaton holds down her teammate Dominique Parrish, the top contender behind Winchester, for her first pin.

Now it's youth against experience, and, for one of the few times of the event, youth comes out ahead, as Heaton pins Shai to move on to the finals.

Hernandez, Villaescusa, and Shai had something in common: all had beaten Heaton in the past. Now she's got a shot at Winchester, who defeated her at the Captain's Cup in Iowa the previous February.

"It was nice to get those matches back to show that I can be here and wrestle with these top girls," Heaton says. "Sometimes I get a little sloppy, so I just kept fighting every point. I progressed by working on the little techniques that you need to perfect."

Katherine Shai: "Athletes on an Olympic quest know and understand the extreme ups and downs of this journey. So when I returned to wrestling, so many asked me, 'Why? Why put yourself through this all again when we know it is such a hard path to walk?'

Despite this pain, despite the deep and intense feelings I am trudging through, I would do it *all over again*.

I would choose the pain, I would choose the joy, I would choose the moments of doubt about my training situation in Denver. I would choose the days when [my son] would cry and ask me to stay home instead of going to practice. I would choose the additional year where [my husband] and I got the opportunity to transform our lives into one completely devoted to wrestling. I would choose all the connections, partners, parents, and supporters who believed that my quest was one they wanted to join and help me see through. I have SO many people to thank."

Early in the final, it looks like Heaton might pull another upset, jumping out to a 1–0 lead. But Winchester takes over from then on, and scores a 7–4 victory.

The second match goes differently. Less than 10 seconds in, Winchester grabs a takedown. Moments later, she hooks Heaton's leg to go up 4–0 in the first minute. Ten seconds later, it's 6–0. Heaton stays on her feet for a while, but Winchester plants her to her stomach and nearly twists her into a C-shape to raise her advantage at the break.

Heaton suddenly explodes at the start of the second, hauling Winchester to her back, then over to her stomach. There's a break in the action, and Winchester returns the favor, shoving Heaton down and nearly out of bounds and holding her down for a near-in and the deciding points in a 12–2 tech.

"No surprise there," Winchester says. "I was happy. All your emotions hit you when you realize, 'I'm going to the Olympics.'" In late May, Heaton went to Guatemala City and brought home a gold in 53-kilogram competition at the Pan American Games.

But even so, there's still some bitterness in Winchester's sweet satisfaction.

"[I've felt] mixed emotions these last few days," she says. "The joy of making the Olympic team, but the sadness of knowing I wouldn't be able to make it back to California in time to say goodbye to my grandmother before she took her last breath. This life never seems to amaze me with the highs and lows it brings. Valuable lessons I've learned from life are to be kind, treat everyone with love, and forgive."

57-kilograms

Far from home, and twice as far from the spot where she'd shocked the sports world nearly two years before, Helen Maroulis nearly saw the end of her wrestling career.

Since taking America's first-ever lady wrestling gold the year before in Rio, she'd hardly slowed down, charging to Paris the next year for the 2017 World Championships and turning in an even more dominating performance than she had at the Games, shutting out every opponent for her second World gold in two years. Maroulis took a much-deserved break after that, but mat rust can be as much an enemy as any injury. Now it was a new year and time to get back to action.

In January 2018, she hopped on a plane to haul over to New Delhi, ready to captain the Haryana Hammers of India's Pro Wrestling League (PWL). Clearly with a different definition of "pro wrestling" than followed by much of the sports (entertainment!) world, it's an annual two-week event in which six teams compete against each other for point totals. Adeline Gray helped kick off the league's inaugural season in 2015, going 7–0 to help the Mumbai Garuda squad to the league title, and Erica Wiebe, who won a gold for Canada in the 2016 Games, competed in 2017.

Maroulis opened things against Marwa Amri of Tunisia. Even in her PWL debut, it was a rematch of sorts; the year before, the two had met in the finals of the 2017 Worlds. As had been her custom then and in the same event two years before, Maroulis pitched a shutout, charging through with an 11–0 victory to finish off an 87–0 performance from that event and the previous one.

Don't think Amri, who won an Olympic bronze herself, hadn't forgotten it.

Just as with the Olympics and a certain other type of pro wrestling, the competitors charged out to theme music; always the devout type, Maroulis used a Christian theme— tough to imagine the squared circle type of wrestling federation allowing that. Amri had a marching band–type tune.

Amri kept clawing at Maroulis's head and shoulders for the first minute. Then, almost in unison, the wrestlers pulled away from each other and lunged forward, Maroulis's face smashing into Amri's temple.

Amri appeared dazed, blinking at high speed. Maroulis grabbed at her face and nose. But the round wasn't even stopped, and both got back in action. As fans cheered and blew their own whistles (apparently easier than clapping), Maroulis built a 9–1 lead, then pinned Amri.

Behind her ever-present (except during matches) wide smile, Maroulis jogged off the mat and chatted with a reporter. But looks were deceiving.

Since long before the match, she'd been coughing, always lagging behind her breath. Dizziness and headaches started to kick in.

After not leaving her bed for the next two days, she fell behind 4–0 to a teenage competitor. She managed to come back to grab another pin, but then it was back to bed for four days. But it didn't help.

In her third match, for only the second time in three years, she lost. Clearly, this Maroulis wasn't the same as the one that dozens of opponents had fallen to over the past few years.

This was tougher than the torn ligament she'd powered through in the Paris event. It was even harder than the concussion that had knocked her out of action for a week back in 2015.

She was indeed diagnosed with another concussion, and loaded down with medications that, she claims, did little more than temporarily mask her suffering.

"I don't think that's what doctors in the U.S. would do," she says. "I've never had that experience before. Looking back, I'm not happy with that approach and the way that went." She couldn't stand up with her eyes closed. As soon as she quit exercising, her energy disappeared like it had been yanked out.

"What I learned," she says, "is every single concussion is different. It's not about how hard you get hit. You literally can barely get tapped and, for some reason, your symptoms are crazy. It's not like I had some traumatic blow to the head."

Back in the states, a doctor gave her special glasses to center her vision field and headphones designed to block certain sound waves. To an extent, things started to improve.

Yes—to an extent.

"Talking and making eye contact were two of the worst things that I could do," she says. "If I had more than three conversations a day, by the end of the night, I would get to this very weird place where I felt like my thoughts weren't really my own."

Halfway between shots at Olympic stardom, Maroulis was suddenly faced with sudden, involuntary retirement possibilities.

"I knew wrestling was always going to end at some point, but I don't want my life to be like this," she says. "I want to be normal. I want to be able to have conversations throughout the day, think the way I used to think, and process the way I used to process." She got on some new medications and changed her diet. Eventually, she started working out.

Then it all crashed down again. In August 2019, another concussion rang through Maroulis's brain. She vowed it would be the last.

"I just decided that I wanted to be done with wrestling," she remembers. Right around the 2019 holidays, she just *happened* to stop by Maryland's Capital Wrestling Club.

"Go visit, give back, maybe get a workout in. Didn't have any expectations," she says. "I knew that I still had symptoms, so I knew wrestling wouldn't be good for me. I just kind of thought a lot of the trauma happened in wrestling, and I think I just need to go back and be on the mat and figure it out. Could I retrain my brain to not freak out in any wrestling environment or situation?" One short workout later, she was in bed, praying off an anxiety attack.

It passed, and most of her pain went with it, although it returned every once in a while. But the more she worked out, the lighter her symptoms became.

Early that February, Maroulis stepped back onto the mat for the first time in over a year. And this was no warmup-level competition: it was the Pan American Olympic Qualifier Wrestle-Offs, the winner of which would get a bye at the trials.

Maroulis started off with a narrow win over Alli Ragan. Then she took on Jenna Burkert, the event's top seed.

Methodically, Maroulis built a 6–0 lead, then pinned Burkert just before the three-minute mark.

In the second of the best-of-three, Burkert scored her first point about two minutes in and kept her 1–0 lead for the rest of the period. Maroulis nearly took her down to start the second, but Burkert fought her way back up. Then Maroulis blasted in, grabbed Burkert's right leg, and took her down and over. About 15 seconds later, she'd scored the pin and first-round trial bye.

As one challenger after another qualified for the trials, Maroulis kept up her own training at Penn State. One day in mid–March, she hit the mat hard.

And screamed as pain blasted through one of her legs.

After taking a day off, hoping that it was just another typical bump, she decided it was time to check things out. She and her mom hopped in a car and drove three hours to a Maryland doctor.

Her MCL was torn. She'd be in a brace for six weeks.

That was unacceptable. Maroulis explained that she had less than three.

In the next few days, she barreled through therapy, trying to get range of motion back in the leg.

"They said it should heal as long as I didn't tweak it again," she says. With her injury taped up, she went into trial mode.

Right around the time Maroulis's Olympic career appeared done, Cameron Guerin saw her own road there clearing right up.

The Washington native had just returned from competing with her country's Junior World Team in Estonia. Next would be the Senior Nationals in Fort Worth right before Christmas, and a strong showing there would put her in the trials.

Then it all fell nearly apart.

That October, her father, Rich, one of the longtime driving forces behind her wrestling career, suddenly passed away.

"I took the whole month off," Guerin says. "I had been training for a tournament in Germany, and I decided not to go." Instead, she went back to her normal training grounds in Colorado Springs (she and Burkert had trained there together for seemingly forever), but couldn't find any motivation to exercise.

Eventually, her family helped change her mind and re-focus her goals.

"My mom and family told me how he would want me to keep competing," she says. Early in November, the Seniors coming back to mind, Guerin slowly went back to work.

"My mental state was crazy," she remembers. "When I was at practice, I wasn't sad, so that helped get me through it. When I'd go back to my room, I'd be sad and crying, but when I was working out, I was OK." She made her way to the Nationals and tore it up. Charging into the semis, she fell to eventual champ Abby Nette, but third place was good enough to get to the trials.

"When I went home, I regrouped with my family," Guerin says. "I was still young, I had some time, so I had that chance to get better. I didn't think about taking time off, just to train as best I could. I just wanted to find things I could get better at before trials."

Sadly, she wasn't the only one facing tragedy much more important than wrestling. About a month before the trials, Burkert's mother had undergone heart surgery.

"I didn't care about wrestling," she says. "I told my mom that I wasn't going to trials. She looked at me said, 'You have to go.'" It was one of the last conversations they'd ever have. In late March, about a week before the trials, her mother passed away.

Jenna Burkert: "I was a wreck after my mom's passing, in bed. I didn't even want to go for a walk. Everyone was like, 'You have to go. It's for your mom.' Wrestling's not like, 'I'm going out there and hitting a ball.' It's a lot harder than that. I felt cold, empty. [Wrestling is] not something you can show up to. You have to be physically and mentally sharp, ready to fight for what you want, and I didn't care. I was like the opposite. That was the most alarming part, because I always care. I was the number one seed [at trials] and I didn't care. I couldn't get myself pumped up. My big moment of hugging my mom in the stands was never going to happen. I didn't decide I was going to go until the Tuesday before. My mom's last gift to me was my freedom, to go out and wrestle at trials.

Wrestling wasn't the biggest thing, but my body knew how to do it, and I could do it very well. I could go out and feel free. There was no thinking involved. Usually it's 'If she does this, I have to do that,' or 'What if I lose?' There was none of that. Whoever is in front of me was in front of me, and I was there to do what I've been training for, opening up. It was so nice to go out there and just be free and have fun with it."

A few weeks before the trials, Guerin had closed out an undefeated season for McKendree University by defeating North Central's Amanda Martinez for the 130-pound title at the National Collegiate Women's Wrestling Championships (NCWWC) at Tiffin University, a win that helped McKendree to its third straight team title. The two went back to action to begin the trials, and the result was the same, as Guerin took an 11–0 victory. Now Guerin got a rematch against Nette.

"I really wanted to get that match back," she says. "My coach and I strategized against her. I was like, 'What was I doing wrong in 2019?' For next match, I knew what her offense was, and I was practicing my sprawling. I felt like I'd grown more patient." It worked: she slipped past Nette, 11–8.

Lauren Louive got things started with a 12–2 tech over Shauna Kemp.

"You have to carry that win," Louive says, "but at the same time, don't let it affect you so much that it keeps you from focusing on what you need to do for your next match." For the quarters, she was up against Ragan.

"I've been against her before," she says. "Alli's not my nemesis, but pretty close. This was the match that I wanted, and this was the place where I wanted it. I had been gearing up to beat her. I was probably a little but *too* ready for that one."

Rushing into things, she inadvertently stepped right into a throw and found herself down for a fall.

"I was disappointed," Louive says, "but at tournaments like that, you have to live in the moment. I would have deteriorated if I had stayed with that loss. It's not helpful to be in that place, so I had to move on. Yes, it's Olympic trials, but right now, it's not helpful for me to make that mean something more than that. Right now, it's any other tournament that I wrestle on the back side."

Burkert, who'd opened things by teching NCWWC 123-pound champ Cheyenne Sisenstein, had an identical result against Guerin in the semis.

"I don't know how she was able to compete just a week after her mom passed," Guerin says, "but I know God, and her mom gave her the strength to do it. I felt like I had more to show in that match. This past year, I've overcome a lot, and I've improved as a wrestler. At the time, it's hard to take those losses. You're wrestling, and you win, and your emotions are great. If you lose the next match, your emotions are all mixed, and it can be overwhelming."

Ragan had rolled to a 9–2 win over Xochitl Mota-Pettis, but Burkert held her down in just over two minutes in the semis. Time for Maroulis to get back into action.

Burkert got on the board first with a takedown, but Maroulis rattled off five consecutive points. Burkert escaped early in the third, but Maroulis held on for a 5–3 win.

"We're in the Olympic trials, and a lot of people think it's going to be a sweep for Helen," Burkert says, "and I was like, 'Who cares? What does it matter?' She's already won the first match, so there's no reason to be hesitant. Those are the matches we live for. We live for those close matches, shutting it down, scoring late. That's where it's exciting."

The second match went back and forth as well, with Maroulis ahead in the second.

Then Burkert leaped in and took her down for the deciding points in a 6–5 victory. For the first time, she'd come out atop Maroulis, and finally had some momentum.

Between matches, Burkert hurried to the back for a quick massage.

"I felt the fatigue a lot more, going into that one," she says. "I was feeling it, a lot of adrenalin. I was excited. I wanted to throw down. I have to win to be on the Olympic team. If I lose, I'll be the runner-up, and that sucks. We know how [Helen] wrestles, we know how I wrestle, and you have to keep moving forward."

If this is fate, you don't want to be in charge of it. As tough as it is to say, this probably *should* have been Burkert's moral victory. Here's where fate should have smiled on the tough underdog, felled by a horrible family tragedy, still gutsy enough to come right back, score the win over the heavy favorite (who herself had gone through some seriously rough stuff), and go on to glory, knowing that even her opponents are cheering for her and someone special's looking down from above and just as thrilled.

But it doesn't happen that way. Literally three seconds into the period, Maroulis reaches behind Burkert and yanks her to her back. Burkert attempts to bridge her off, and nearly does a few times, but at the 24-second mark, Maroulis records the fastest pin of the event.

Both competitors are in tears. Burkert cries, repeating, "I'm sorry, Mom." Maroulis embraces her former opponent.

"Grateful," she says of her feelings afterward. "I didn't know if this was ever going to happen. I didn't know if I was ever going to get to wrestle. I didn't know if I was ever going to get back on the stage. I knew adrenalin was going to help me get through it. After the second match, I wasn't wrestling well, and the coaches helped me get into the right mindset. It helps to be self-aware and constantly check in. I have mentors to keep me accountable. You have to be self-aware and realize what was working before, what I need to hold on to, and also realize that while this is a different go-round and what I need to change. I really believe I'm supposed to be on this team, supposed to go to Tokyo, supposed to win a gold medal."

Jenna Burkert: "The loss is one of those things that just happens in wrestling. It friggin' hurt. It's one thing to lose, but you don't want to lose that way. I wanted to go down fighting. It's a pouring of emotions, none of which were for the loss. It was crying out for my mother not being there. It's a lot to see yourself bawling on [TV]. It's intense to re-see it. I don't want to see it anymore; I experienced it. The good thing about it all is it's an unfortunate club to be in, the passing of a parent, but a lot of people go through it. That's been the intense, but beautiful thing, the amount of outreach I've had from people who have experienced it. It was a good moment to show strength, that you can always keep going."

Lauren Louive: "You gotta be happy for them, because they deserve it too. But a part of you burns, because you want to be experiencing it too. For me, goshdarnit, Adeline, Jacarra, Tamyra, these are my teammates who I train with every day. I wanted to be with them, and to not kind of hurts and sucks. But I'm not done. Do I care if I'm an Olympian in 2021, or 2024? I'm going to keep going after this next quad, going to keep chasing the dream. It's something that I want to use to inspire others."

Cameron Guerin: "This weekend was a combination of a bunch of mixed emotions. I had such a good time, not just competing but being around everybody. Right away, I felt like it was somewhere I needed to be. Being an Olympian was a dream that I'd had as long as I could remember. It felt like it lasted such a long time.

The next Olympics are three years away, and I'm going to go to as many competitions as I can. I can't wait to keep getting better every month, every year, because I know my time's coming. I know that I will get there one day. It's not a matter of if, but when it's going to happen."

62-kilograms

> "When I was four years old, I said that I wanted to win an Olympic gold medal. There wasn't even women wrestling in the Olympics at that time, so how could I know that was what I wanted, that that was possible? Each year, it kind of progressed. As I got older, I wanted to elevate my game. It's kind of like a tapestry; you look on the back, and all you see are tangled threads and tangled webs, but then you flip it over, and it's this masterpiece. It's beautiful. That's kind of like what the wrestling world is. I want to make a name for myself. I don't want to be in the shadows, in the backgrounds. I want to be at the forefront. I want to be the gold medalist. I want to be the first name that people think of when they think of great female wrestlers. The picture's so clear that how can it *not* lead to that? How can this path that I've been on for so long *not* lead me to that? That one super-blurry picture has led me to right here and right now."
>
> —Kayla Miracle

It's one of the most legendary calls in sports announcing history. Just put "miracle," "Olympics," and maybe, but probably not necessarily "hockey," and anyone with any business calling her/himself an American sports fan can hear the words.

"Do you believe in miracles? *Yes!*" Tossing out the impartiality that broadcasters so often pretend to adhere to, Al Michaels finished etching into history that glorious 1980 moment where our ragtag'ers beat the big boys, America knocking off the Soviets and getting to do so right in their homeland.

Well, many other people have believed in another Miracle. Like the Indiana wrestling community that saw her rise to a level that no other woman had when she was in high school. A mystique that spread through Kentucky and then the nation as she won four titles for Campbellsville University and many others around country while there.

Now, one small step for womankind at a time, it's moved across the globe, which watched Kayla Miracle grab one Pan American gold in 2019 in Peru and another the next year in Canada at the Olympic Wrestling Pan American Qualification Tournament, an event that grabbed her a first-round trial bye.

"I'm not peaking and going back down," Miracle asserts. "This has been my dream since I was four. I'm going to make it a reality."

It's not that a wrestling mat is tiny or anything, but there's room for at least *a few* people. You can walk into any team practice session and find a few (and sometimes a few *dozen*) people sharing one, rolling around, taking each other down, honing their moves one dive, one grab, one throw at a time.

And yet, in every tournament, things always come down to the old proverb: This town (in this case, a large mat with a couple of circles shrinking toward the middle) just ain't big enough for the both of us!

You just get into a mindset that winning isn't a possibility; it's a certainty. Losing? Not an option. Something that you're just not going to deal with because it just isn't going to happen. Maybe it's happened in the past, but we're not thinking, talking, feeling that right now. It doesn't even seem real, more like a dream you had or a book you read or maybe something you witnessed from the stands or the bench.

For some time, Miracle, Maya Nelson, and Macey Kilty had been helping each other find that mindset as their Sunkist Kids Club team rolled from its Arizona jumpoff point to and often over fellow clubs across the nation. Now things have changed, as Nelson and Kilty are the top two contenders to Miracle's bye place.

Macey Kilty: "When I started wrestling, I was all in, 100 percent. I knew I wanted to compete at the highest level, and I knew I had to devote everything to the sport. Family and friends are everything to me, but I knew I'd be committing everything to this sport. I've come way too far to give up on it now. I've done so much already, and I was surrounded by people who believe the same thing. Going in, I was as prepared and confident as I'd ever been. I was there to make the team, win the tournament, and then win my best-of-three series. I'd done my best conditioning. I was the strongest I'd ever felt."

Whoever wins this is going to have to take down someone, or someones, that have risen pretty high in the past; along with Kilty, Miracle, and Nelson's world titles, Emma Bruntil, Desiree Zavala, Waipuilani Estrella-Beauchamp, Zoe Nowicki, and Jennifer Page have all won national titles in the past two years.

"Trials are always one of the more fun tournaments," says Page, who took the U.S. Open national title the previous October. "We've got our little tunnel to come out of. It's been nice to get more competitions in, because we didn't have many in 2020, once everything was cancelled." She opens things with a resounding 11–0 win over Morgan Norris. Julia Salata goes one better in a 12–0 defeat of Nowicki, and Zavala routs Estrella-Beauchamp 12–2.

Nelson and Kilty catch fire in the quarters, Nelson roaring past Ana Luciana 10–4 and Kilty teching Zavala 12–2. Page stays alive with a 5–2 win over Emma Bruntil, and Mallory Velte takes a 7–3 win from Salata.

Now it's the semis, and Sunkist domination continues. Nelson takes Page out with a 6–1 win. Kilty has a tough time with Velte, but she holds on for a 4–2 victory.

"The hardest part of the competition is picking yourself up after not making the team, which is your whole reason for being there," says Page, who came back and did some more battle in the consolation rounds. "It was tough to get my mind right after that. I talked to our psychologist a little bit, and decided to go out and have fun anyway. Having fun should be the main reason we do this, so I just went back out and wrestled."

Now it was time for the battle to face Miracle. Two years before, Nelson whaled Kilty 11–2 in the World Team Trials. But this time, things go the other way, as Kilty takes control from the start and never gives it up with a 5–0 victory that's not as close as the score says.

Against Miracle, Kilty's out for redemption again, looking to come back from the defeat Miracle handed her at an event in France the previous January.

"I put a ton of pressure on my opponents," she says. "I get my attacks from my pressure, moving my hands and feet at the same time. I don't think anyone should be able to go six minutes with me, with my pace. You have to love what you're doing, just giving your full effort, doing everything you can do in your control, letting the other stuff take care of itself."

That doesn't work in the first of their best-of-three battle, as Miracle rushes off with an 8–4 win. But Kilty rebounds in the second, hanging on for a 4–3 victory and slight edge in momentum going into the final.

Miracle strides back and forth around the mat. Kilty's got a sudden case of tunnel vision, standing still, her hands on her knees, nothing else in her entire world except the next few minutes.

"Both knew what our tendencies were," Kilty says. "I was able to wear on her, and felt her breaking down. I felt that I needed to pick up my pace early in the second match, doing the little things I felt in the first that I was able to capitalize on the second. I was on a high, knew what was working. I knew I had a good feel on what she was going to do."

In her corner for one last pep talk, Miracle got a harsh reminder of what *hadn't* just happened, and what *wouldn't* occur unless something changed—*fast*.

"It's not going to be given to you," her coach dutifully explained. "We're going to have to take the hard road." Coming over her, Miracle felt that mindset that losing was no longer possible.

Miracle went downstairs, grabbing Kilty's left leg. As she went for Kilty's right, Kilty leaned forward over her back and grabbed her around her waist. Miracle slipped away and got behind Kilty for a takedown. As Kilty landed on her left side, something went wrong.

As her eyes and mouth shot open, the official quickly blew the whistle. She collapsed to the mat, medics quickly surrounding her. The competitor inside her flaring up, Kilty made her way back to the middle of the mat and knelt down. But as Miracle turned her over, Kilty cried out, and it was obvious that this one needed to end for reasons more important than any one match.

"I had never in my career quit in a match, but sometimes you just don't have a choice," Kilty says. "The trainers could tell something was hurt that couldn't be fixed right away. They took me back to the training room, people coming in and out, like a constant flow of people coming in. At that point, I was beside myself. It was literally the match to go to the Olympics, the match of my life on the line."

Eventually her diagnosis showed up as a torn labrum; basically, the meeting place between the shoulder's ligaments and ball-and-socket joint. She went under the knife later that month, then started six months of rehab.

In other words, a process hopefully finished well before the 2024 Olympics.

"This is just another setback," Kilty vows. "There's always setbacks. I don't think my goals should change because I have a setback."

One way or another, Miracle had been quite aware who would be standing at the end.

"Going into the third match, my mind was laser focused," she claims. "There was no way I was going to lose it. It's unfortunate she got injured, and I hope she heals up quick, but whether that match ended right there or it went the full six minutes, I was taking it. There was no other option. I didn't see anybody else taking that spot for Tokyo."

68-kilograms

> "[In 2016], I vowed, next time, I would be participating, because you have
> to be conscious of the words you say. If you say, 'Oh yeah, I'm going to the
> Olympics,' you'll go, but as a training partner. This time I'm participating
> so gosh, it's great, I love it."
>
> —Tamyra Mensah-Stock

Where had we seen this story before?

A young woman goes into one sport and does pretty well, only to give it up when the wrestling bug bites *hard*. She stays with it. She makes history. And now she's knocking on the brink of the dream of every wrestler.

That could have been Kennedy Blades's life story heading into the trials. After switching from judo to wrestling a few years before, the 17-year-old had rolled through mats far from her Illinois hometown. Her first flash to prominence had been as the first lady to win her respective division at the Illinois Kids Wrestling Federation state event when she was 12. In 2014, after she'd whaled every male competitor at an event in Tulsa, a special visitor stepped forward to congratulate her.

"This is what I like to see," he informed Blades, "a girl beating up all the guys." It was none other than the legendary Dan Hodge, the legendary college grappler whose name lives forever on the trophy award to the nation's top college matster since 1995 (as of 2023, a woman hadn't yet won).

Just two years ago, Blades was winning a national title in 16U competition, the same year she won the first of two Cadet titles.

Then she'd found a spot in the 68-kilogram competition, and started by teching New York's Rachel Watters, then shut out Alexandria Glaude, 5–0. Now she had to take on Forrest Molinari, the top seed below Mensah-Stock. She's won the last two Senior National titles and U.S. Open titles the last two years. She's also Blades's Sunkist Kids Wrestling Club teammate. No one could be more ready for Blades, and no one could be hungrier for a win.

It wasn't all *that* different from the division's leading seed. After placing among Texas's best in track and field, Mensah-Stock had wrestled on a whim. One day during track practice, her sister had learned of a new athletic opportunity.

"I said that I'd go to school at 6 a.m., but I wasn't going to practice. I ended up going, and my coaches said, 'Hey, you should put on some shoes and practice.' I was a germaphobe, so wrestling grossed me out; you're sweating on each other, extremely close to each other. I immediately loved it and hated it. I wanted to quit, but they convinced me to wait until our first dual meet."

She pinned her opponent, who herself had placed at state the year before. Maybe this would work.

Before her last name was hyphenated (she actually met her husband wrestling on the high school squad!), Mensah-Stock took two state titles for Morton Ranch High, the same number of national championships she'd eventually win for Wayland Baptist, and the same number of Final X golds she'd score, one of the qualifiers that placed her at the top of the 2021 trials. Her first Olympic "experience," if one can call it that, had been, well, something of a screwjob. But we'll get there.

"My coaches used to say, 'Stop smiling, Tamyra! Just pin the person!'" she remembers.

Right around her junior year at Morton, people started talking about her being in sight of the 2016 Olympics in Rio. But then things almost ended.

Her dad had just ventured down to Texas to see her take yet another tournament, ready to post a huge photo he'd just taken to the daycare he owned back in Los Angeles.

That night, the next morning, she called him. Then again and again. He didn't answer. This had never happened before.

Then her phone finally rang. It had to be him, up for their latest daily conversation.

It wasn't. It was someone with news that he'd been killed in a car accident the night before.

"I felt like all eyes were on me," she remembers. "What was I going to do next? Wrestling definitely gave me the support that I needed to survive, but at the same time I was blaming it. If I weren't a wrestler, my dad wouldn't have been there. I didn't want to study my Bible anymore or go to church anymore." She was out for a week, or it might have been two. Events like this tend to haze up one's memory.

"What kept me going was knowing how much my dad loved me being in wrestling," she says, "to see the enthusiasm that he brought to the gym. People always said, 'Tamyra, your dad's so loud!' He had this African accent, and he'd be yelling, 'Kill him! Beat him!' We'd say, 'Daddy, you're not supposed to say that!' Where I got the motivation, God only knows. I know I did not want to compete, at the same time, I know my dad wouldn't want me to quit."

Her eyes back on the Rio Games, Mensah-Stock became her own biggest critic.

"I was at the bottom of the food chain again," she says. "I All-American-ed every single year, but that wasn't good enough. When I got fourth at Nationals my freshman year, that's not good enough. I was way better than that. My goal was to be an Olympic champion. I wanted to go out and dominate everybody."

In early April 2016 in Iowa, her dreams appeared to be just about true, as she roared through three opponents (including Julia Salata, who's up for the 62-kilogram 2021 title) for top honors in 69-kilogram competition at the 2016 Olympic trials. Now she'd be home free for Rio, right?

Well, not quite. If her opponents couldn't hold her up, some red tape could.

Her country had not yet filled its quota for that particular weight class. In order to make Rio, she'd have to finish in the top two of a few more tournaments.

"I fell short three times," Mensah-Stock remembers. "I lost to [future Canadian Olympian] Dorothy Yeats in Texas, and my high school friends had come to watch. At another event, I was against a girl from Egypt, and all I had to do was take one more shot, but I was wrestling her way. She kept standing me up, and I kept letting her. My coach kept saying, 'Just *shoot!*' I could have taken her down and won. The next one, I was up 6–0 in a match, and I got complacent. I went for a sweep, she timed it, and she threw me to my back. I was not appreciative of where I was and I paid the price. I'm going to remember how this feels, and I'm going to use it."

Over the next few years, she took a U.S. Open title and the two Final X championships. A victory at the 2019 Worlds cinched her top trials spot—ironically, one of her wins there was a 10–1 defeat of Japan's Sara Dosho, who'd won the 69-kilogram Olympic gold that Mensah-Stock hadn't gotten a shot at!

So against whom would she utilize the redemptive pain of her past? Along with everyone else at the trials, she was about to find out.

And almost everyone is surprised. Not that the bout is one-sided, but in whose favor. Blades puts Molinari on the defensive almost from the start and never loses control, methodically working her way to an 11–1 tech win by the end of the second period.

Now it's the epitome of Blades's exuberance (and slight height advantage!) against her enthusiasm.

"I had the chills, butterflies," Mensah-Stock admits. "I was terrified because I knew how bad I wanted it."

The very day that North Dakota became the 30th state to sanction female wrestling, Mensah-Stock's home field advantage looks to pay off in the first match, as she walks away with a 12–4 win. But Blades scores a quick grab and near takedown to get ahead 1–0 about a minute into the second contest. It takes almost the full remainder, but Mensah-Stock leaps in and wraps her arms (undoubtedly two of the strongest at the event) around her waist for a takedown and 2–1 lead to end the period. Two more quick takedowns triple her score. Blades keeps trying to dive, but Mensah-Stock pushes her away. Then she telegraphs a dive, and Mensah-Stock gets around and behind her for another score. As it turns out, the last two are the final points she'll need.

The crowd gives her a hell of an ovation, and even Blades joins in. The applause continues for both competitors as they walk off the mat.

"I'm feeling excitement," Mensah-Stock says. "I'm feeling overwhelmed. I'm feeling like I could have worked harder.... It's a *lot* of hard work. No matter how naturally talented you are, there's so much work, satisfaction, and dedication in this."

76-kilograms

About Gray, good Lord, what else is there to possibly say? Is there any valid reason in the history of the universe to *not* cheer for her?

Is there another athlete, gender irrelevant, who has spent more time looking at one individual finish line without getting to cross it?

An unexpected loss that stopped her from the 2012 Games, and a shoulder injury that ended her 2016 jaunt, one that put her on the shelf for months.

A decision to give up parenthood for the time being to pursue her athletic dreams.

Having said that, there were 14 other women who wanted the Olympic spot as much as she did. Shortchanging them would be the epitome of unfairness and irresponsibility.

Ironically, had the Olympics proceeded as originally scheduled, Gray probably wouldn't have been able to compete. In mat battle in March 2020 at the Pan Am Games in Ottawa, Gray broke a few ribs. But the Games, and obviously the trials, were knocked back, and she had time to heal.

In January, however, as the trials grew near, Mensah-Stock bumped up a weight to battle Gray at an event in Texas.

Then she whipped Gray, 4–0. It was Gray's first loss to an American since 2012.

Just one more thing to come back from. Of course, more than a dozen contestants didn't exactly give her a stutter-step across the mats themselves.

At the end of the day, an opponent is just a person. Someone trying to score more points than you in one match, whether by takedown.

Of course, saying that, thinking it, writing it, and reading it is one thing. When you're out there, staring, or probably glaring, feeling like rays are about to blast right out of your eyes, right into those of your opponent, it might be hard to keep that in mind.

She might be the very person that inspired you to take up the sport a few years ago.

You might have modeled your moves and techniques after hers. She might have even been your coach at some point.

Now she's your opponent, and you're trying to defeat your own role model. Trying to overtake her hopes and dreams with your own. Trying to keep her from reaching a goal that she's been working for for longer than you have and take it yourself. Sometimes you can feel selfish for wanting to win.

Yeah, doing it is different from anything that comes before it. Very different.

"Growing up as a young wrestler," says Joye Levendusky, seeded sixth, "competing in tournaments like [trials] seems out of reach, so you have role models, but right now they were my competition." She's right below Yelena Makoyed, who beat her for the 170-pound NCWWC title in early March. Her McKendree teammate Sydnee Kimber, the eighth seed, owns a pair of NCWWC championships herself, along with becoming the first four-time state titlist in Alaska history.

Adeline Gray: "I want to share it. Please take some time for yourself to take just two percent of this dream and work a little harder in whatever you pick. Do a workout, be more consistent with eating veggies and less sugar, get an extra hour of sleep or start meditation. This is a nice dream: borrow it, have it motivate you by proxy."

Sports fans, even those training to become superstars themselves, sometimes forget that the very people they're cheering for, the ones they see as role models, were once fans themselves. There was a time, and usually not that long ago, that they had their own heroes, that there were people they wanted to be like, that they were once star-struck, and that, especially in the wrestling community, they may have had to battle their own role models.

Starting off, obviously with fewer role model options than those of today, Gray found herself take with female wrestling's trendsetters. Eventually, she'd have to face her own heroines. Per usual, she typically came out on top. As years passed and her name became household, others started to see her the same way.

"At nationals years ago, I teched a young woman in college," she remembers. "She ran up to me and said, 'You're my favorite! I can't wait to really compete against you!' These women are getting role models, something that women haven't always had. They're seeing that they can do things past high school, past college, past a world team, making a career for themselves, that women's sports are a real career. Being that role model and helping them reach new heights is important. It's about those young women competing against me to keep me on top, and one day, take me down. It's a worthy transition for sure." Such attempts would be arriving soon.

While many of her colleagues had shown up full of spunk and enthusiasm and time and everything else that youth carries along, Jackie Cataline had a different reason for not worrying about the future.

"It was my last chance," she flatly states. "If I won the whole trial, that was great, but if I lost one match, that was it. I'm 33 this year. I've been in wrestling for 21 years, and my last two tournaments, I was bouncing around my weight, and if I wasn't successful, maybe I was too old to be doing this."

The winner of a slew of national championships before she graduated from California's Millikan High, Cataline nearly permanently paused her career before she even reached drinking age.

Why? It becomes quite clear that her trademark bluntness on the mat extends far off it.

"Wrestling doesn't pay shit," she pontificates. "I can't pay my bills by being a wrestler. I had two kids and a lot of stuff outside of wrestling that's going to be there when wrestling isn't. But if you're gone for a certain amount of time, you miss it."

For her, that period lasted five years—plenty of time for wrestling to blast forward like it was just starting to at the beginning of her hiatus. Ironically, Cataline and Katherine Shai, two moms competing at the trials, were themselves born on consecutive days in May 1988!

"My skill is not ever going to go away," she claims. "I came back and won nationals [U.S. Open in 2014 and 2016]. I wanted to do it for my parents, because they'd put so much into this."

Still, there *might* be just a *bit* of personal redemption here, a shot at payback. In 2013, 2014, and 2015, Cataline made it to the finals of the World Team trials.

And each time, she lost the last match.

All … to Gray.

Cataline took third in the 2016 trials in 75-kilogram ranks (won, you guessed it, by Gray). Then she decided to take another sabbatical.

Then she cut it short.

"I became an electrician," she says (and we thought males had a majority in wrestling!). "It's a great career." But in early 2020, she felt the urge start to flare up one last time. If there was any shot of grabbing that elusive World or Olympic spot, she owed to it herself and her country to reach for it.

Resurfacing at the Senior Nationals Championships in October 2020 in Iowa, she notched fifth. Then, just days before the trials, she and the rest of the remaining hopefuls made it to Fort Worth for the (quite appropriately named) USA Wrestling Last Chance Olympic Trials Qualifier.

Four times she stepped onto the mat. And four times she walked off a winner. Minnesota's Marlynne Deede, whom Cataline defeated 10–0 during the event, also springboarded to the trials.

"I told myself, 'I'm not leaving here without first place,'" she says. "My skill is good enough to do that, but if my head and body aren't in sync, that's when you lose matches."

While her Titan Mercury teammate Kylie Welker techs Randi Beltz 12–2, Cataline starts the trials by holding off Levendusky, 3–0 (Kimber falls 8–3 to Life University's Jordan Nelson).

"You always want to win every tournament you enter, but I was really blessed to compete against some of the greatest in wrestling," Levendusky says. "Even walking off every match, I was taking it all in. Obviously, I wasn't really happy with the turnout of my wrestling, but it gave me a few things to work on. I'll definitely be working toward 2024."

Early in a match, Cataline explains, "You see how strong they are, and see if they're going to attack. I knew [Levendusky] wasn't going to take me down. It's very hard to take me down. I feel like my experience helped me in that match."

The five Titan wrestlers grab center stage in the next round, as Cataline, Welker, Dymond Guilford, and Victoria Francis win. Cataline's razor-thin 11–10 victory comes over Precious Bell, her own teammate.

"That was a tough match," Cataline claims. "I practice with her a lot. I didn't feel it was my time to lose yet. I went out and prevailed."

The all-Titan action continues. Welker, who'd actually started the meet at the bottom of the seedings, tears past Guilford, 8–0. Now it's Francis and Cataline.

The senior gal jumps ahead early. Things go back and forth for a while, but Francis grabs an edge and doesn't let go. When the last buzzer sounds, she's soundly ahead, 9–3.

Cataline is done. The losing bracket would be of no consolation.

She kneels down and takes off her shoes. The symbolic farewell of a wrestling great.

"If I won the whole trial thing, that was great," she says, "but if I lost one match, that was it. I could have wrestled another match, but there was no reason for me to wrestle for third. It was an awesome thing, to go to such a big tournament, then to retire with all these people there."

As it turns out, she doesn't stay still for long; the following June and July, she double-golds at two jiu-jitsu tournaments, in Las Vegas, then in her California homeland.

"I started training for jiu-jitsu in February 2020," she says. "All of the wrestling gyms were closed, and the jiu-jitsu gym was the only one open. I went there with the intention of practicing wrestling, and I picked up jiu-jitsu. Takedowns were the main thing; I used skills on people to take them down and hold them down, and I started realizing I could submit them."

In June, she grabbed two golds in Gi and No-Gi competition in Vegas, the main contrast between the two being the clothing: Gi competitors wear the arts' traditional kimono-like attire, whereas No-Gi eventers dress in rash guard shirts and shorts.

"The grips are the difference," Cataline explains. "If somebody grabs your Gi and holds you in a certain way, it stops you from shooting. It'll stop you from scoring."

The next month in Fullerton, she won No-Gi events against competitors from the 20–29 and 30+ age groups (competitors can battle younger opponents, but not older).

"I had five matches total," she says. "I won by points on one, and the rest were by submission. I used my armbar a lot. I hope to compete in the adult world championships."

Back at the Trials, the focus switches. Tied with Blades for the honor of event's youngest participant, Welker, a product of Wisconsin's Burlington High, won World Team events early in the year. Had the event not been knocked back a year, she'd have been too young to compete (participants must turn 18 before or during an Olympic year, not after).

With one match to go, Welker nearly pins Francis early on for a 4–0 lead. But Francis comes right back, making it to within 4–3 late in the final period.

A takedown for either wrestler will make the difference, and Francis goes for it. But Welker holds her back and gets behind her for the deciding points in her 6–3 win.

When Gray was trying to qualify for her first Olympic team back in 2012, Welker was in elementary school. Making her way up through the ranks, like a bronze in the 2019 Cadet games, Welker found herself someone to look up to.

"Adeline Gray was my idol at one point," she says, "and I worked until my idols became my competition." That's got to be one of the top sports quotes of the 2010s. Probably one of the strongest in wrestling history.

But her underdog Cinderella tale quest ends without much climax. Gray gut-wrenches and rolls her back and forth and all over the mat for a combined 21–0 two-match win that doesn't get anywhere near the distance.

Former national team member and multi-national champ Jackie Cataline says goodbye to the sport after her final match at the 2021 Olympic team trials. Photograph provided by Jackie Cataline.

At the end of the tourney, the six who started at the top ended up there. The ones who got to take the first round off got to save their energy for the big games.

"*Satisfied*'s a pretty good word," Gray says afterward. "Anytime you can score 20 points in less than three minutes, it's a good day."

CHAPTER 6

Women's Wrestling
on the Screens

Just as it's taken some serious time for female wrestling to expand across the sports landscape (as in, the speed of a one-legged fellow navigating quicksand), the entertainment world has been cautious about cinematic or even small-screen coverage of the mat battles. Remember, we're not talking about *pro* wrestling-based films; those are relatively easy to find, but are far less likely to succeed (*The Wrestler*) than to fail hard (*Ready to Rumble, No Holds Barred, Body Slam* ... hell, we could be here all chapter). In hindsight, it's kind of a sad surprise that we didn't see some sort of made-for-TV biopic of Helen Maroulis or Tamyra Mensah-Stock about three weeks after their Olympic golds.

Still, just as with the sport itself, amateur wrestling found (or is finding) a trek, one that's growing slowly, into the entertainment spotlight because women pushed it there themselves: first from before the cameras, then from behind them, as well as the word processors banging out one screenplay after another.

Nearly two decades before its actual state sanctioned women on the mat, girls' wrestling (more accurately, one girl's wrestling) hit the fictionalized small screen in 2001 as *Boston Public* arrived; Massachusetts native Danielle Coughlin, who'd become the fourth American woman to win a state title in 2013, wasn't quite into her own career of yet. About halfway through the show's rookie year in January 2001, the tales of Beantown's Winslow High School went where few had been—before or since.

A few months before, Lindsay Hollister had jumped cross-country from her Ohio homeland with a degree in theater and a sense of hope and enthusiasm that she hoped would lead to some performing resume entries. Unfortunately, Hollister could also see a pretty sizable obstacle (potentially) in her way, one that's overshadowed the talent of far too many looking to mark out in acting.

"At almost 400 pounds, I came to Hollywood knowing my weight would define me," recalls Hollister, who's significantly shrunk since way back when, "and I had already had auditions for all kinds of fat girls, but this was the first wrestler role. Back then, it was pretty original for the storyline to be about a bullied teenaged girl joining the wrestling team as an outlet and a way to be accepted by her peers."

Sadly per usual for plus-sized babes even today, Hollister's Christine Banks had long been looked down upon (not literally, for the near-six-footer), winning her terms of endearment like "The Blob," "Titanic," and other moving monikers. However, a new occurrence started ringing through Winslow High's halls: one loudmouth after another, *ironically* tormentors of Christine's, had suddenly turned up with a serious injury, with her just *happening* to be standing nearby at the perfect time!

One of the few with enough time and prowess to look beneath the surface for some dots to connect, Coach Riley (Tom McCarthy) sees a shot for Christine to get her own special revenge on all those on her case, and for his wrestling squad to rack up a few victories. She's resistant, her dad's not into it, and her future teammates can hardly comprehend it, but it happens. And for those who call it farfetched that a newcomer would be permitted to participate in a match the day after she joined the team, keep in mind that this was 2001; many felt that a *woman wrestling* in and of herself was still a pipe dream, as only Hawaii and Texas had sanctioned female wrestling, and the next state wouldn't follow until Washington pushed through in 2007.

"The show hired a stunt team and I had a man who worked with me on the wrestling moves," Hollister recalls. "We could make it look real enough without killing me. The worst part of it all was actually what I had to wear: a singlet. For an overweight woman, especially a young fat girl, wearing anything that's one solid piece is something nightmares are made of, *and* I had to do it on national television."

At typical TV show speed, Christine becomes a seemingly seasoned mat woman and the new school hit almost overnight. But this wouldn't have a happy ending.

"It was an emotional time learning the wrestling moves I would do for the scenes and do them in something that was less than flattering, which is an understatement," Hollister says. "Another factor was my body. I had back issues and have thrown my back out from time to time my entire life. The wrestling practices were more grueling than what was ever filmed. I did end up throwing my back out and was worried it wouldn't heal in time for filming. I knew I wanted to do as much of the wrestling as I could and I always give it my all. It's my job and my personality to be a huge overachiever. I think I did do some filming with a thrown-out back."

If only that were the worst Christine would face. As her final match winds down, her opponent's well ahead on points. But, gifted with some advantages in height and strength, she displays the shoulder throw that became her mat trademark, then crashes down on top for the pin.

Only she doesn't get up. Perhaps she hit her head and was knocked out. Or something worse.

Her dad, Riley, and everyone else looking on in shock, fear, and, most frustrating of all, helplessness, paramedics fire out the defibrillators, then start with CPR. Soon she's at the hospital, trying to come to terms with it all.

Everyone else will have more time than they could ever want. Christine has very little, soon dead of a blown aorta. Her friends, family, and viewers are left to pick up the pieces at her funeral, flashbacks of her show life playing as one of Riley's colleagues leads the group in a chorus of Blood, Sweat & Tears' "Hi-De-Ho."

It's almost certainly one of the lasting moments from the series' debut year, and probably from its entire four-year run. Her three-episode arc launched Hollister into consideration for an Emmy nod for Outstanding Guest Star, but she didn't score a nomination, the final award going to Cloris Leachman for a season-long appearance on *Malcolm in the Middle*.

"Since *Public* was never released on DVD [as of the summer of 2023, I can't even go back and watch the scenes for a reminder," Hollister mourns. "Maybe one day we will be able to enjoy the magic that was *Public*, but until then, the horrible singlet, the sweaty boys they hired as extras to wrestle with me, and the smell of the plastic from the wrestling mats will be what I remember."

Female wrestling flicks became quite the haven in 2016. By the time *Girl on the Mat* made it to short film festivals that year, lady mat action was a bit more accepted, though with still a ways to go. The tale told us about Hayden, a young lady facing parental opposition off the mat that made wrestling look easy. Her success in the mostly boys' sport had made Hayden something of a local heroine, but she couldn't feel it; outside the gym, she was alone. The same car accident that took her father's life nearly took her mother's as well, leaving mom an angry pit of self-pity, filled with booze and drugs, legal and otherwise.

Fresh off an award-winning portrayal of an abused daughter in the similar short *Broken* (2013), Julie Kline's new role put her up against not just the same sort of mother, but teammates that represent the sad reason that wrestling's still not sanctioned in the *Mat*'s Michigan shooting grounds (note: this changed after this chapter was drafted, as the Great Lake State did approve the game in May 2021).

"Hayden went through a lot of hardships, along with people giving her issues because she was a girl," explains Kline. "It was a huge struggle for her. [My trainers] shared a lot of that psychology with me." She spent several sessions training with some ladies who'd been through Hayden's journey, wrestling wise.

"I learned some moves that I would be doing in the film," she continues. "The guys who played coaches and wrestlers in the film were actual wrestlers."

She and the crew filmed all the match scenes in one day, the practices in another.

"I was wrestling for at least six hours that day," Kline says. "The coaches told me I'd have to take an ice bath that day. The next day, I was covered in bruises and so sore for the whole week. I was like a raging bull, like 'I want to do this!' I didn't consider my physicality."

No one, though, could ever consider or even fathom how Hayden's personal issues could affect her on the mat, even those who'd been there; everyone responds differently to these things. Some can put issues like abusive parents aside for the time it takes to go singlet to singlet, but others can't. Hayden did her best in a situation that no one could ever truly connect with.

"I sympathize with Hayden," says Kline, echoing the audience's mindset. "Sometimes, when you're put in a situation, even if it's not yours, you feel how people can feel, them being able to hone into empathy."

While *Mat* romped through short film festivals across the country, taking home several awards and even more praise from viewers, another flick was rocketing through box-office records across the globe.

During the early 2000s, whispers started to spread across India. Whispers grew into conversations, then into nationwide news. In a nation where women face controversy and suppression for so much as learning to read and write, cutting their hair, or showing anything beyond the knees and elbows in public, the concept of the country following other female teams onto Olympic mats was unheard of (to be fair, the country's male squad hasn't exactly been a bang-up show, with a grand total of five medals and no golds in history).

In the early 2000s, however, the nation was surprised to slowly see some changes. Inspired and trained by their father, Mahavir Singh, himself a former freestyle mat man, the Phogat sisters set their own trends in female sports, and charged all the way to medalhood in the 2010 Commonwealth Games, with Geeta scoring a gold and Babita a silver.

Two years later, Geeta became the first Indian lady to complete in the Olympics, falling just short of a medal. Later that year, she and Babita each took third in Canada's Women's Wrestling World Championships.

Julie Kline's Hayden faced opposition on and off the mat, in wrestling and in life in 2016's *The Girl on the Mat.* **Photograph provided by Julie Kline.**

Their accomplishments, along with the prominence they and other women brought to wrestling across the nation, convinced Nitesh Tiwari to put together the screenplay that would soon become *Dangal.* With him behind the camera, the cast starting coming together in the spring of 2015.

After a career that brought him international medalship, Kripa Shankar Bishnoi was brought in to get the charges in shape to portray the Phogats. Over the next six months, a few young actresses got a strong taste of what their role models had felt for years.

As if trying to make the jump from child to grownup star wasn't tough enough, Fatima Sana Shaikh now went out for one of the toughest roles any performer could grab. Actresses got sent through hormonal tests to see if they could "make weight," such an important part of real-life wrestling, and some were dropped then and there if they didn't pass. Dieticians kept them in shape before and during filming.

"I am ashamed to admit that I looked [Geeta Phogat] up on Google and found that she had won a [medal] for India," she remembers, "and I knew *nothing* about her. To my shock, she was a strong, tough girl and I was then thin and lanky, so I called up the agency and said, 'Listen! I do not think that I am the right choice!' But they asked me to try my luck, so I went for the audition more to show how I could act! Our workshops started and included six to seven levels, including how we run and work out, and there were scenes with Aamir Khan." Khan, who also produced the film, portrayed Mahavir.

For weeks, without any real assurance that the role would become theirs at all, she and the rest of the hopeful crew roared through wrestling boot camp.

Bishnoi, Shaikh recalls, "stated that [we did] not look like wrestlers. We had to train for that. For two weeks we trained, and my body would be so sore that I would hate getting up early and would cringe at climbing the three floors up to my house in the evening!" In early September 2015, she learned she'd passed the test: she'd become Geeta.

Now came the tough part—combining the physical training with actual acting. She and the rest of the crew (Zaira Wasim portrayed Geeta as a kid) stayed together at a separate house. Up at 6:30 a.m. for training, they'd go until lunchtime, then a quick siesta.

Schooling took place in early afternoon, then off to the gym. Often before 9 p.m., beds were the most welcome sight!

Often under the watchful eye of Geeta and Babita themselves, the *Dangal* crew told their tales. The sisters move from neighborhood to national heroes. Relations with their dad move up and down, with Geeta even forced to defeat him in one of the film's toughest scenes. As the Commonwealth Games move close, Geeta and her dad reunite, but she falls behind with just seconds remaining in the championship match. However— remember, this *is* a sports film!—she makes it through and wins anyway!

Just before Christmas 2016, a few months after Sakshi Malik's bronze at the Rio de Janeiro Games made her the first Indian lady wrestler to medal (Bishnoi was one of her coaches), the flick shot straight to history, winning awards all over the world (surprisingly, India didn't submit it to the Academy Awards' Best Foreign Language Film category) and becoming not just the highest-ever grossing Indian film ever, but the world's top sports moneymaker.

Earlier that year, *Restoration* took a slightly different tack. Some say it might have been the first film about female wrestling that wasn't necessarily about the wrestling.

"I have been interested in sports movies before," exclaims Victoria Anastasi, who calls the underrated Russell Crowe boxing flick *Cinderella Man* one of her favorite such films. "The role of Sam instantly caught my eye. Number one, I thought it was so awesome that she was a 16-year-old female wrestler, the only one in her school." The Sam in question is, like so many we've met and will see in reality, working her way up through physical mat war and suppressive sexism, trying to make it in a sport she's obviously been quite accustomed to for years.

And just as her coach decides to say goodbye, a new fellow at her grandpa's auto repair shop just happens to show up with a wrestling background, one that he'll eventually be almost hammerlocked into sharing with her. Once a man of higher-up regard in law enforcement, C. K. Erwin (Ken Stewart) lost everything in one tragic night. Many would have given away the rest and said goodbye, but maybe his background gave him a bit of strength even he didn't consider, or maybe he just didn't believe in being one's own executioner, but he's still here, and now Sam needs him.

He'll fill a role that Sam lost recently. Sadly, so had her portrayer. Remember the "Number one" reason Anastasi referred to? It has a sad sequel.

"Another huge selling feature of Sam was that her dad passed away," recalls the actress. "My dad passed away when I was younger, so I really felt a strong connection and bond to Sam because of that."

However, wrestling isn't really the film's focal point. It's more about the relationship between faith and humanity. C. K.'s losses have made him resistant to spirituality, and Sam and her family feel that things would get so much better if he'd just open up a little. Then he sees them ascribing everything that happens to a divine being that they trust, and it's easy to see such folk as too inclined to acceptance. The kind of acceptance that caused us to get disappointed and so much worse sooner than later.

"I auditioned one week," Anastasi remembers. "Then I drove back to North

Carolina, where I lived at that time, and as I was driving back, I got an email asking for me to do a screen test in Fayetteville. I changed my route and drove to Fayetteville, did the screen test that day, then found out I got the role maybe two weeks after that, and started filming the next week!" Typical small-studio filming, as any budding star or director will explain in all kinds of detail.

As the characters grow and change—C. K. realizing that one's got to go out and find new good once the first of it has been stolen, and Sam evolving as a wrestler and (not so willingly!) a lady, shoved into womanhood by … *dating!*—we see the main difference between *Restoration* and other lady wrestling-based films: that at the end of the day (or the flick), it's not really about the wrestling. More about finding strength elsewhere (or Elsewhere), and how much we should trust that strength, or its source. If we should trust it at all. Then things start to happen.

Unity. Hope. Hallmarks of religion like these start to ring through. The characters don't realize it, and maybe the audience doesn't either, at first, but soon things are showing.

All the time, Sam's working on the mat and in her grandfather's store, with C. K.'s help. To its credit, the film gets the requisite smartass sexist comment out of the way early, from Sam's first defeater, then just focuses on her as a wrestler, not a lady wrestler. Would be that this becomes reality for female competitors in the near future.

"I had been working out for months before all of this happened, so I was in pretty good shape!" Anastasi recalls. "I 'trained' consecutively about three days before the shoot and trained almost every day on set. This was a low-budget film, so we really worked with what we had. I learned a ton in that short amount of time. But it truly was physically demanding. Emotionally, I think I automatically connected with Sam. I felt like her soul, I already knew. So for that part of it, I kind of slid right into her. It was effortless to tap into it."

Some films, especially sports films, try to go too far with the happy ending (Disney movies, mainly). And see, that's OK if it's done right. But it's also the easy way out. It's the ones with the guts to try something a little different that we remember. When the individual final game is lost, but something bigger, more meaningful, more *lasting* happens. A game, you remember or you don't. Certain lessons, you carry with you forever, and you might find a little more success in doing so. Not just the film characters, but the audience as well. *Rocky* was probably the watershed of this, and 2011's *Soul Surfer*, similarly filled with religious tones, was the same way. *Restoration* followed.

Every athlete loses sometimes, and wrestlers tend to lose a hell of a lot more often than they win, at least early in their careers. No one unfamiliar with the sport can truly ever really comprehend this sort of thing. But the ones who we remember, the ones who end up making it to the big games—not only those who go there and win—are the ones whose names we remember. Bouncing back from a tough loss, seeing a shot at success become heartbreak, and, eventually, somehow making it back … these are lessons that every lasting wrestler carries.

And it's another reason that many have and always will turn to the holiness. Sam doesn't win her last match, but we can hope and believe that the faith that's carried her through so much will carry her on from here. It's C. K. who has the bigger moment: one that makes him see that, yes, there is something stronger than he is at work, and that that very thing is keeping certain people safe in ways they could never be in their previous lives.

"Sam and I connected instantly, so her lines were completely effortless," explains Anastasi. "I memorized them quickly. I hadn't looked at my lines since probably the table read the day before shooting. But I would be on set, and we film out of order, so I would just ask someone, 'Sooo ... what scene are we doing?' They would tell me, I would look at the script once, and then be like, "OK, I got it.' I didn't have to sit there and go over it; it was already in my body. Watching the film after it all came together was absurd. I had never really seen my face *that huge* on a screen before. At first, I felt almost like I couldn't watch. I feel like, for most actors, it's a bit difficult to see ourselves act. And that's definitely how I felt. It was a bit cringey, wishing I had done a few things differently. But after I settled in, it was just like watching any movie. I enjoyed it. And at the end, I was so incredibly proud of every single person on and off the set who made *Restoration* into a reality. It was one of the best experiences of my life." Looks like Sam and C. K. weren't the only ones to take something from the storyline forever.

Back in 2011, Olivia Newman had put together a short film about a young lady searching for a way to make it out of the rough streets of Brooklyn's Brownsville neighborhood and suddenly finding direction in wrestling.

"She was a young woman who was living in foster care that was on the boys' wrestling team, beautiful and very flirtatious," Newman says of her flick's protagonist, "but would get on the mat and wrestle with boys and be very aggressive. And I found that dichotomy really interesting. Then I happened to be at her wrestling practice the day she was hoping [her grandparents] would adopt her and they decided not to. It was then that I saw another side come out, where she was angry and would snap at people."

Over the next few years, Newman considered expanding her, or their storyline, not creation.

"I really wanted to tell a story about a young woman who was desperately craving family and that kind of family love," she explains. "Chasing after the family she thought were her real family and sort of inadvertently discovering a family on this boys' wrestling team, it kind of organically grew out of this experience I had making the short film."

As the script Newman had churned out for the first story expanded to a full-length piece, an up-and-comer in a different entertainment area saw it on the internet. Knocking out her own self-audition tape (note to hopeful performers: that's an initiative step that casting crews love), Elvire Emanuelle looked for her first lead.

"I got a call back and didn't hear anything for I almost three weeks," Emanuelle recalls, "and I thought to myself, 'Oh, they probably moved on.'"

Not even close.

"On first watch, I knew I'd found our Mo," Newman claims, "and then after her one-hour 'wrestling tryout,' our trainer took me aside and told me she was a natural wrestler. He'd never seen anything like it."

Now titled *First Match*, the story now told a longer tale of a girl named Mo in foster care, one parent dead and the other just out of jail. Looking hard to find some reason to get her dad to give a damn again, she'd followed in his footsteps to the local wrestling team, which ended up both connecting the two and driving them apart. But one thing hadn't changed; the film was still in the dark sides of Brownsville, the same same neck of the woods had birthed Emanuelle.

"It's crazy because I found out ... they were really looking for someone who lived in Brownsville, who was from Brownsville, and I was there when I was younger," says Emanuelle, who spent her first years in B-town before heading south to Philadelphia.

"But I just knew it as Brooklyn. I had no idea all that time that I had been in Brownsville. I called my dad and he said this is exactly where we used to live."

For about five weeks, she trained with a local wrestling coach, as well as the lady who'd carried the lead in Newman's short version years before.

Wrestling, she learned, "uses completely different muscles than I normally use. Even the stance—you have to have a certain balance and stance. What's crazy is that it's really hard in the beginning, but it's kind of cool that eventually your body learns it. It becomes more accustomed to it over time and things that were killing you before become easier."

When it finally arrived on Netflix in March 2018, audiences saw something both new and the same. The whole "scared underdog ends up as strong, confident leader" had been done for some time, as had "girl infiltrates boys' sport and becomes impromptu role model."

First Match was those, but a bit more. It's a sports movie, but the sports are more of a backdrop, just a supporting character to the plot itself. It's about a girl who knows that her father's a deadbeat, an unpredictable, selfish jerk, but she's convinced that he's her only or at least her best way out just because so few other people have ever given a damn for her. Family's family, whatever the hell that means to each individual.

Finally, there's its ending. As hard-hitting as wrestling is, and as much as sports films just *love* to pull the corny "winner takes all and keeps it forever" conclusion, *Match* didn't do that. The conclusion is more subtle because it's real; Mo's problems can't be solved as fast as a movie takes to finish, and there are clearly more ups and downs to follow for her, her dad, her team, and everyone else.

"She wanted love from her father, and to feel wanted by the person who created her," Emanuelle says. "I think we could all relate to that. Even if it's not our parents, we could all relate to wanting to be loved and having something that you fight for. I didn't have the exact life that Mo had, but I can relate to a lot of the feelings that she felt for different reasons. Imagining that her life could be my life was hurtful for me."

Our next cinematic exploit showed a different side of harm.

Alone Together was a drama. It didn't start out that way.

The short film began as a dream. It ended as a different sort of reality.

The roughest draft bore very little resemblance to the final result. That happens all the time in films.

What matters is that the finish line is worth crossing: to the creators, the performers, audiences, whomever.

"The idea hit me about two years ago," Katie Sponseller recalls of the 2020 release that she wrote, directed, and produced. "I had some weird dreams, like one that I was supposed to wrestle a lion. It went along with an idea I had, the other side of *Alone Together*, which was about sexual abuse and trauma."

Another recollection she used was from a more factual source.

"My brother wrestled in high school," Sponseller says. "He had to wrestle a girl, and he was flabbergasted. His coach said to just do it. I always thought it was interesting how much it intimidated him to fight a girl. He looked up in stands, like 'What am I supposed to do? Where can I grab her? Can I touch her? Should I give her an edge so I don't feel bad?' There were a lot of questions about what it means to interact with females in [wrestling]." A lady she'd seen try out another hardly female sport also inadvertently stepped into the preparation.

"[Alex] reminded me of a girl I knew that played on the school football team," she recalls. "I admired that girl, because I thought she must have a lot of strength inside her to do that sport, especially against a bunch of boys, so I started writing a script about a girl doing a similar thing. It started off as a bit more of a comedy, a story of girl using her wits to be antagonistic toward the boys. More and more, I connected it to surviving sexual abuse over time, and how we don't really talk about those things."

Also the sibling of a school mat man, Naomi Oliver brought her own athletic background to *Together*. After rolling to gold medal victories in figure skating, Oliver looked to balance acting with the perils of Harvard enrollment.

"Wrestling has always had a special place in my heart," she remembers. "When I first read the script, I was super excited that Alex was a wrestler. I immediately felt a connection with her on that level. I was also passionate about the themes surrounding Alex wrestling."

Intentionally given a gender-neutral name, Alex faced many of the same issues that too many female wrestlers battle today, mainly chauvinism and condescension from teammates and coaches still trapped decades in the past. But none of those were unexpected, or particularly difficult. Alex was facing something that far too many women still go through every day—and that hurts much worse and longer than B-words and other sexism.

"Her wrestling matches paralleled her internal struggles with bullying, isolation, and sexual abuse that she was facing off the wrestling mats," Oliver explains. "Wrestling physicalized her frustrations in this story and I thought that concept was enthralling."

Over the course of about a year, Sponseller brought *Together* to the page.

"One thing that pulled the story into a more dramatic direction was the truth in the story," she says. "What I felt when I saw that girl in high school, what her strengths meant to me, what I felt I couldn't obtain as a young girl, why I was inspired to be more like her, to tamper down my own fears to have a sense of self-awareness, inner strength, and value, I started seeing about what the character wanted. She was quiet and reserved in a lot of ways, relating to her difficulty being up front about fear. These things are very traumatic in terms of our own experiences, finding strength within ourselves. That's where the character started to take a more solid task."

Now it was out to find the woman who'd become the character and carry off the task. For weeks, Sponseller and the rest of the crew looked over hundreds of headshots and resumes and watched nearly as many live auditions at a small Los Angeles casting studio.

"It was really important that I understood her internal conflicts," Oliver says of getting ready for her tryout. "Part of what makes Alex so complex is that there is so much in what she is *not* saying. It was my job in preparing for this role to be able to effectively portray those very elements that she kept silent. I did this by immersing myself in her backstory, by developing a past and background that would create the Alex we're watching. I also worked on an internal dialogue, so that I could follow and portray all of the different emotions she was feeling at once." Adorned in a Kiss T-shirt and rocker jeans, she stepped into the audition and, she hoped, closer to Alex.

"There were several actresses that got it right," Sponseller says, "but [Oliver] was especially impressive. She had a very strong innocence, looking like somebody you didn't want to mess with, but was able to display this youthfulness and innocence."

For Oliver, things went past looks and demeanor, and now to physicality. After snaring the role, she spent the summer becoming Alex the matster.

"I worked with my castmates, as well as our wrestling choreography and stunt coordinator, to create and perfect realistic wrestling choreography. We had to learn basic wrestling maneuvers and technique so that they would read well on camera. Outside of wrestling practice, I also focused a lot on cardio. That way I'd have the stamina to do multiple takes of our wrestling scenes in a row without being winded or having too much muscle tone. We wanted Alex to be a normal, average, relatable girl, so it was important I maintained that balance between being athletic but not looking like it."

As with *First Match*, their piece had a greater focus than the sport aspect. Alex got grief on the mat, and struck back the best she had, hitting the mat with her opponents, often in the literal sense. But we also saw Alex's other reasons for the aggression that wrestlers use as an asset.

She'd been abused, and the person who'd done it hadn't gotten any just desserts (unfortunately, capital punishment still isn't an option for this sort of crime). As so many victims still do and always will, she had to carry around the burden that sex abuse victims shoulder while her victimizer walked around with nothing. She got bullied on and off the mat, and, again, per usual, those in charge just happened to have their heads buried in the sand at that exact moment. But when she finally struck back, shockingly, her tormenter suddenly morphed into a scared little victim with the backbone of a jellyfish. Administrators wussed out and took his side, sending her home.

But her dad, as any guy with a daughter worth his salt would, gave her a high-five and cheered her on. Sometimes breaking the rules is the best thing a lady can do.

After a year's writing and months of casting and other pre-production, filming took less than a week.

"We prepared so much in advance, by the time we started filming everyone was ready," Oliver says. "We had been training all summer for the wrestling scenes, and we had all worked on our character development beforehand. I had multiple meetings with Katie to map out the story arc, what each scene would look like and how we wanted it to feel, so once we were on set, we were already on the same page and were ready to shoot. I absolutely love Alex and all of the strong female wrestlers and resilient trauma survivors she represents."

And hey, if a biopic of Maroulis, or Adeline Gray, or Tricia Saunders, or any of the other ladies we'll touch on in this piece eventually does come around, Jaimie Alexander might have her next role—and unlike playing Thor's backup gal Sif in his lead debut in 2011, following him to *The Dark World* two years later, and making *Love and Thunder* roll in 2022, this would put her all the way at the top! Maybe with David Morse as Coach Terry Steiner, Halle Berry playing some sort of (dramatically created!) female mentor, and Michelle Rodriguez, Chloë Moretz, and Jessica Biel also on the acting bench!

After growing up in a home full of brothers, the Texas gal launched her own female wrestling team at Colleyville Heritage High School, where her brother Brady won a state title. Even a few years after her state became just the second to sanction female wrestling, Alexander (whose last name was then Tarbush) was forced to battle men in practice, waiting until competition times to face fellow females.

"I was so tall," says the five-foot-niner. "Compared to everybody else in my weight class, I stood out. I used the same moves over and over because everybody was so much shorter. I was able to sprawl and do the half—that was my pin move, because nobody could reach my legs." With the assistance of a few coaches from Iowa State University,

Alexander picked up the tools of the takedown trade pretty quickly, losing just twice in two years, mainly wrestling in the 120s.

"I've got [cauliflower ears]," she proudly proclaims. "They got smashed a little bit when I was wrestling. And I did have ringworm at one point."

Between spins as Sif, Alexander turned in the midst of Times Square in her tattoos and little else in the opening of *Blindspot*, which romped through a four-year run on NBC. As the gal originally known as Jane Doe looked for a past she couldn't always trust, as her body art became the blueprints for crimes that needed FBI solving.

"I get through all the intense physical training for *Blindspot* because of what I learned from wrestling," she asserts. "All the discipline and perseverance I have now comes from that sport."

One failed audition started Rachel Brosnahan's wrestling career. A successful one ended it.

"In my freshman year [at Highland Park High in Illinois]," she recalls, "I didn't get a part in the musical *Beauty and the Beast*. I was devastated, and wrestling was there for me. I loved it! I won some matches; I lost some. I remember wrestling someone who was 119 pounds (I was 112) and getting pummeled. But I enjoyed how difficult the training was and watching my body change because of the work I was putting in…. It taught me to find my unique skills and use them to my advantage. I was quick, and that meant I was often faster than my male opponents, even if they were stronger."

For two years, Brosnahan was the only female on the Highland mats, far from the 1960s Manhattan setting she'd inhibit a decade later as the title character of Amazon Prime's *The Marvelous Mrs. Maisel*, the dramedy of a domestic engineer who finds a knack for standup comedy in an age when it fell on the list of things that women just didn't do (hey, kind of like many people still feel about wrestling!).

"I loved the fact that, although it was primarily considered a boys' sport," Brosnahan remembers, "it was divided by weight class, so if you weighed the same, you might have different skill sets, but you're competing against one another, and gender has nothing to do with it. It was so hard and the workouts were insane, but I enjoyed that it was both a team sport and an individual sport at the same time. I wish I could have continued it, but I got a part in a musical!"

CHAPTER 7

Sports Entertainment—
and Other Wrestling(s)

"Let's get high school girls' wrestling sanctioned! When we support girls' sports at a young age, we do nothing but foster their growth in the future!"
—Stephanie McMahon Levesque, World Wrestling Entertainment chief brand officer, former WWE Women's champ, and mom of three daughters (Twitter post, May 21, 2021)

It hasn't happened yet, but it certainly could, and no one would be all that surprised.

To turn on the World Wrestling Entertainment or All Elite Wrestling programs sometime in 2023 or thereafter and see Adeline Gray, Tamyra Mensah-Stock, and Helen Maroulis in a six-woman tag team match against some of the most hated gals of sports entertainment (possibly wearing evening gowns and maybe even locked in a huge steel Hell in a Cell cage!), sounds like an absolutely plausible scenario ... and some serious fun to watch.

As more and more women walk out of school with the benefits of wrestling, it's more and more likely that numbers in the cagefighting and pro wrestling worlds will rise as well. Assuming, of course, that no one decides to coordinate a professional Women's Mat Wrestling Association. Could be a blockbuster, sports world! Here's where we'll meet some women who've experienced other types of grappling, often using their amateur backgrounds to do so.

Just as Mildred Burke and Mae Young set trends for other ladies both on the mat and between the ropes, more and more will, and they'll keep inspiring those looking to rise through the pro ranks.

For now, those armed with a dream can still find inspiration in those already in the business, male and female. New York has always been the cornerstone of World Wrestling Entertainment, and a grade-schooler from just over the Pennsylvania border sat in the stands at an early 1990s event and saw her future in the exploits of top stars like Ted Dibiase, Bret Hart, and Sgt. Slaughter. Years later, they'd be in the WWE Hall of Fame.

She'd eventually join them in the WWE. Then in the Hall too.

Looking over the winter sports signup sheet a few months into her career at New York's Notre Dame High, Elizabeth Kocianski knew what she wanted. She just wasn't sure if she could grab it. No woman in Notre Dame history ever had.

Kocianski took a deep breath, made her choice, and dropped off the paper. Soon after, she was called into the ominous lands of the principal's office.

The Notre Dame higher-up demanded to know just what the heck (it's a religious place, so mentioning hell would be, ahem, inappropriate) she was thinking. Maybe she'd blinked wrong and checked an inadvertent box, perhaps she was just looking for trouble, but girls didn't do that. Not before, not then, not ever.

Kocianski started out agreeing with tradition, and opted for track and field. But as her sophomore year rang in, the same box got checked, the same call came in, and a different decision was made.

She was gonna wrestle. And darn (not *damn!*) everybody and everything else!

Some liked it. Others, like her family, didn't, accusing her of just wanting attention.

But, "when I got past the noise," she remembers, "I was able to revel in the magic of wrestling, the camaraderie of my teammates, the respect they had for me when I just kept showing up." She'd become the first Lady Crusader (not Fighting Irish—remember, this is the New York high school, not the university!) in school history to take down a spot on the wrestling team. Before long, she was outlifting the rest of the team in the weight room, a tradition that would continue throughout her career.

After finishing life as a Crusader by reaching prom queen royalty, Kocianski went a few hours further northwest to Buffalo's Canisius College and became a first-ever matster for the second time in her career. Her first season culminated in a 75-kilogram victory at Brockport's Northeast Junior Wrestling Championships; the next year finished out the same way, with a title win and Most Outstanding Wrestler award at the same event. She also started working with USA Wrestling.

A few months later, women debuted at the Summer Olympics in Sydney. Kocianski's coaches informed her that some similar effort over the next few years might just win her a spot on the 2004 team.

By then, however, she was already looking forward a different sort of grappling.

"My heart was in pro wrestling," she recalls. "There were not a lot of girls built like me in my weight class. Most were very young. After a while, I saw it would not get me where I wanted to go, athletically."

That was north to Canada for training. The next May, she stepped into the ring for the first time. A few years in independent competition later, Kocianski scored a spot with Ohio Valley Wrestling, known as the WWE's minor leagues. Soon after, her name switched to Beth Phoenix.

Yes, this has been all about the gal eventually known as the Glamazon. Yes, the one who won the World Wrestling Entertainment women's title three times. The same lady who became the second of her gender to compete in the annual Royal Rumble (she didn't win). And, yes, the only female member of the 2017 WWE Hall of Fame class, and, as of 2023, the Hall's youngest-ever member.

However, it wasn't Phoenix's first Hall. That happened in 2015, when she became a member of the Dan Gable Museum. Four Mays later, she became the first female member of the George Tragos/Lou Thesz Professional Wrestling Hall of Fame, which honors pro wrestlers with an amateur background (Slaughter was honored at the same ceremony). If things keep up with women in wrestling, that list will probably have more new members soon.

Like the one we'll meet in a few paragraphs. We're not quite through with the Glamazon.

Since 2016, the Wrestle Like a Girl organization had been working like anything to spread awareness and opportunities for women of the mat. Early on, the group made it a goal to stretch sanctioning for female wrestling across every state in America.

Things went pretty slow in that regard. Alaska and Tennessee had added their names in 2014, but that brought the overall number to a grand total of four states, and no one had joined since.

Then things started hauling. Seven sports-supporting states superbly sanctioned the game in 2018. Early the next year, the group got a strong asset from the outside.

"I remember loving the sport of wrestling but having to join the boys' wrestling team because I had no other avenues," Phoenix tweeted through the organization, with which she's still involved. "Young women deserve equal opportunity in every aspect of their lives. It's time to sanction girls' wrestling in every state!" The amount of credit she should get doesn't need to be determined, but seven more states signed up that year, and more have since.

Right around Thanksgiving of 2019, a young woman from Lancaster, not far from Buffalo, was in the same position Phoenix herself had battled through. After a (admittedly short!) career of battling boys, Trista Blasz was ready to move to the Lancaster High junior varsity squad. Certain people with zero foresight and too much authority had tossed one roadblock after another in her way, but Trista and her family had battled back and won, and now she was strapping on the singlet.

Also like Phoenix had during her Kocianski days, Blasz had taken more than a few glances over the squared circle.

"I used to watch it," she says of pro wrestling. "I used to watch [Phoenix] on *YouTube* and stuff, because of how good of a wrestler she is, and how she went through the same thing [as I did]."

One day, she got a special message.

"I was so inspired by you and your passion for pursuing this sport," Phoenix told one of her many fans. "I wanted to reach out and see how you were doing and support your cause. There was just not a ton of support if I wanted to scrimmage or work with club sports. I had to wrestle the boys and there's a lot of tension and stress surrounding that."

Life is very simple for pro wrestling fans. You believe that the superheroes you see are real. You think that the heels, the villains who cheat and backstab (and back punch and back kick and back-hit-with-a-chair) them, are truly evil people. We don't really draw the distinction between wrestlers and reality that we do with movie actors and actresses. Even when we're young, we know that these people aren't *really* as cold in real life, nor are they as clean and wholesome as the good guy (and gal) in a film.

Wrestling is a bit different, up to a point. Before we get old enough to grasp the line between sports and reality, we still get angry at and scared of the heels. The bad guys. When we're young, we disregard these people as entertainers and talk about how evil and scary they are, regardless of how talented they are in the ring.

But see, that's OK. It's how wrestling tricks us. We're scared of these people, we want to see them get beaten down and pinned (*the* definitive way to beat someone, none of that count-out or disqualification shit), but we still put money in their pockets by buying tickets and add to their TV leverage by giving them ratings.

"I *hated* Ric Flair," recalls California native Erica Torres, referring to the guy who made more people spend time and money on a chance to boo him than perhaps any other heel in wrestling history. "I liked the Undertaker and Goldust."

The latter, himself a probable future Hall of Fame member, went back and forth between heel and face throughout his career, often with a lady at his side. One such woman was none other than Luna Vachon.

After winning state and national titles in high school, California's Erica Torres switched to a more entertainment-based type of wrestling. Photograph provided by Smitty Photographs.

Back then, it took serious guts to cheer for the bad guys ... and girls. Torres didn't care.

"I loved Luna," she remembers. "She wasn't a typical beautiful woman. She was mean, she was vicious, she had a look about her. She didn't care how she looked or what people thought of her; she was there to beat people up." While most ladies in wrestling from the 1980s on brought at least *some* sexuality to their characters at one point or another, Vachon went the other way: often walking around with at least part of her head shaved, tons of punk-rock facial makeup, a permanent fire-icing glare on her face, and an interview voice that sounded like Darth Vader's scarier twin sister.

As older siblings so often do, Torres found her own certain pleasure in tormenting the youths of her family.

"As the oldest sibling, I *couldn't* hit my brothers and sisters and be physical with them," she remembers, almost wistfully. "I'd do mental shit, like cheating at cards to get my sister's reaction. Once, we were playing Go Fish, and I cheated like crazy until she flew across the table, hitting and choking me. All I could do was laugh." These mannerisms would come in handy in her later ring career.

"I really wanted to get into pro wrestling," Torres remembers. "My dad said that if I wanted that, I'd have to do amateur wrestling." Her dad had done some independent squared circle work in California, which would come in handy later.

One day, as she and her friends worked out their academic aggression on a recess break, they noticed some team signup sheets all over the benches.

Torres saw one marked for soccer. She went past. Basketball also didn't grab her interest.

Then she glanced down and noticed one holding the mat sport label. The coach couldn't believe his eyes.

"He said it was the funniest thing," she remembers. The young girl scribbled down her name and roared off, adrenalin fueling her burst toward history.

"I ran as hard as I could right into a pole, and knocked myself out," Torres says. "In seconds, I was right back up and running around. The coach said, 'OK, she can do this.'"

Her parents, assuming wrestling would be a passing interest for her, secretly asked the coach to take it harder on Torres, hoping to force her out. Not happening; she hit the mat game as hard as anything. Every day after school, she blasted into the mat room. As often as not, her dad had to carry her out, having worked herself out a bit too much.

For years, every time Torres stepped onto a mat, a male stared back at her. It took all of a few seconds to get used to that; she took a second-place finish home from her first-ever tournament, then scored golds and bronzes for years.

"I think I was in the top four in every tournament," she remembers. "I was always seeded last, so I always had to face the returning champion. I beat two state champions."

Charging out for the second overtime period of her next title match, Torres glanced at her opponent. She had to fight off a smile.

He was laid out on the mat, with coaches and teammates fanning him with towels.

"His mom was saying, 'Don't you let that little girl beat you! You're a boy, you shouldn't let that girl beat you!'" she says. "I felt so sad, because they were putting all this pressure on that boy. My coach told me to let him go to give him a point, then take him down and get two." She did, and walked off with yet another hand raising.

Sadly, like so many lady wrestlers before and since, Torres was a victim of the unfair advantage men enjoy known as puberty, times of deeper voices, more hair, and larger muscles.

"It was strange," she says. "When I got to high school, it was a whole separate element. But people would still have to wrestle me, and say, 'Man, I lost to a girl!' Everybody would be like, 'Erica's not *just* a girl, so don't feel too bad.'"

As tough as her female opponents had been, physical strength didn't always transfer to the mental side of the game, she remembers.

"I beat a kid in my sophomore year in 30 seconds. When he went to shake my coach's hand, [the opponent] yelled 'Fuck this,' threw his headgear off, and never wrestled again."

When they did, it wasn't always so much better.

"One kid pretended he was sick to forfeit against me," she explains. "When I did wrestle him, I was beating him at the end of the first round. When we started the next round, he picked me up and did an illegal slam and *really* fucked up my shoulder. They disqualified him, and he just walked off the mat. But the guys on the team all knew me, and they beat him up in the wrestling room at his next practice." She overcame it, not losing a match throughout her senior year of high school and winning two state titles, alongside a 126-pound national championship in 2007. A college scholarship made her part of the first-ever female team at Oklahoma City University.

"With guys, if they have a problem, they'll duke it out and be done with it," she says, "but girls hold grudges. It's a whole different ballgame. In college, one girl stole another's shoe, so she couldn't work out. When she found out who stole it, she and her friends put fish in her bathtub."

That didn't push her away. A lack of gratitude became the final knockout.

"I was cutting 20 pounds a week to make weight," she remembers. "I was working out before, during, and after practice, losing five pounds a day, with no water. Then the coach told me I wasn't trying hard enough." Torres went straight home and downed a huge pizza.

The next morning, she stepped around campus, the theme from *The Last of the Mohicans* pumping some musical inspiration through her ears.

"I realized I didn't like it anymore," she says. "I was cutting 20 pounds for someone who didn't give a shit about me." She dropped by the coach's office to hand in her resignation.

"He was like, 'All right, see you later,'" she says. "I later found out that four girls quit after I did."

Back home, she was chilling and mulling the future. Her dad had been back to his old southern California wrestling grounds and had come back with a career resurgence, along with a message.

"He'd struck up a conversation with an indy wrestler, and decided to get back into it," Torres says. "He told me to come get into it too." Two weeks later, she was working on a new form of wrestling.

"They had me doing all kinds of bumps," she explains. "I like the physicality of it, the showmanship of it, the storytelling, being able to grab the emotions of the audience. I've always been a character, being loud at home. I loved jumping off of shit. Wrestling is a great outlet to get out energy and connect with people as well." She also took up MMA fighting shortly thereafter.

Back in Oklahoma, she started off as a new face, in every sense of the word, of Impact Zone Wrestling (IZW).

"I used my real name because I wanted people to Google me and see my credentials," she explains. "My amateur background would make me more legit." That was accomplished. But maybe, just *maybe*, people weren't quite showing her the respect she deserved. It's a common reason for babyfaces to jump to the other side of stardom.

Over the radio one day, Torres heard hardcore metal legend Rob Zombie, as only he ever could, tell the tragic tale of Salem's witch-hunts in "American Witch." It became her new musical anthem. Rather, it began Queen Erica's. By the end of her second year in the land, Torres was following in Vachon's footsteps, getting booed out of just about every arena.

"As a heel, you master the art of 'These people want to see me get my ass kicked! How can I give it to them?'" she recalls. Over the next few years, she took the IZW women's title seven times.

After IZW went under in 2017, she wrestled all over Texas, Kansas, and Tennessee. Then she, like thousands of other independent level wrestlers in America, saw their federations, and their careers, grind to a halt when the Covid pandemic kept everyone at home.

But she's still fighting, still working, still hoping to make a name. When the pandemic finally ends, she'll be ready to take another stab at the big leagues.

"When I looked back and see all the wrestlers who have amateur backgrounds, it's hit or miss," Torres explains. "They're great athletes, but they won't understand the psychology of [pro wrestling] and why [wrestlers] do the things we do. They're not lucky enough to have the trainers that I had. My amateur background helped me to do flips, rolls, and other maneuvers. I could take a whole new element and bring it to the table."

Note: In May 2023, Tamyra Mensah-Stock announced her intent to follow in the footsteps of fellow gold medalist and WWE Hall of Famer Kurt Angle, signing with the WWE.

"I just wanted to be in the WWE," says Mensah-Stock, who appeared at the organization's Summerslam pay-per-view event soon after winning her Olympic gold. "Something in the back of my head that's just been itching at me, a dream of mine for I don't know how long. I love watching the athletes just in the ring. I just see their personalities just shine through the television, and I see their strength. Just everything about them resembles me, and I've just wanted to be a part of that."

Beach Wrestling

"Life without martial arts...." Breanna Stikkelman's voice trails off. Clearly, it's a topic, a possibility that she's very glad never came true.

"I can't explain it," she finally admits. "I just can't be a regular person. I'd just be so bored. The thing about combat sports is that it's been such a big part of my life that I can't even think of a life without it. The family you build from it, the confidence, the self-defense is a huge thing."

Combat sports. That's a pretty interesting term. It makes you wonder if that's what knights called it while jousting to the death, or if the phrase was used to describe gladiators in the middle of an arena, slashing tigers and each other as bleachers full of people cheered (think people were doing chants back then? "Make him bleed! Make him bleed!"). Women like the ones we've profiled here in this piece would have been the prizes for said champs, and certainly competed for fiercely.

But this is now, and women are just as at home in battle as men are (and hey, wouldn't it be interesting if the next winnings of a ladies' MMA tourney included that lovely, elusive belt ... and a date with America's top male supermodel? Would that influence ladies to fight just a little harder?). Stikkelman's found herself in every form of "combat" from school mat brawls to cages over the past decade—but the one we're about to discuss, as of now, is one of the newest—not just for her, but for everyone.

"My dad was a wrestler," she remembers. "I grew up knowing a double-leg, a front headlock, stuff like that." One day, her dad came home and informed his kids of their new chance to follow in his athletic footsteps.

A general contractor, he'd just inked a deal to create the newest martial arts studio in central California. In exchange for his welding down the iron fabrication, Breanna and her bro could work out there.

"I did pretty well, but I had some really bad injuries," she admits. "I dislocated my shoulder 10 times until I had to have surgery. It'd pop out, and I'd put it back in and not train for a week or two. It got to the point where I couldn't even sleep without it being unstable." Most people would have stepped away from battles. She just went all the way over to jiu-jitsu, now the area's newest MMA hopeful.

"Martial arts makes me feel complete," Stikkelman asserts. "When I'm on a team, training all the time, I feel complete. Regular life is really unappealing to me. I like how primal [martial arts] is. You go through life, and there's a lot of bullshit. You have fake people, fake news, pandering, crazy politics. I feel like martial arts is one of those things where you can say you're good and act really confident, but when you're on the mat, that's it. It's a foolproof way to really prove yourself." Along with rolling to a purple JJ belt (the third of the sport's five levels of success), she also stepped into the submission style of grappling; in October 2017, she headed over to Azerbaijan (one country south of Russia), and scored a silver in 58-kilogram competition and a gold at 64 kilograms at the Grappling World Championships, the only American to take a gold at the annual event, and just the fifth American gal in history to take top honors. Less than a year later, she scored a bronze in international jiu-jitsu competition in Los Angeles. Stikkelman also competed in Belt Wrestling—a combination of both sumo wrestling and the "strap match" stipulation that's been done for decades in pro wrestling, competitors all but tied together with a belt as they battle for takedowns.

But it wasn't all easy, as if any of it ever had been. Injuries old and new kept Stikkelman from realizing her goal of becoming a firefighter, "limiting" her to the paramedic world.

"My doctor told me I couldn't be a firefighter," she says. "I couldn't fight, couldn't wrestle. He basically just told me to go to the gym." In March 2020, she stepped up to Canada for the Pan American Games, and didn't win in grappling. Then she tore an ACL working out. Then she got Covid.

"I couldn't walk or go up stairs for eight weeks," she says. "I gained 10 pounds. After I lost at Pan Ams, sometimes I couldn't get out of my head, wondering, why am I doing this?"

She needed a break, one by choice. In early May, a friend invited her to head down south, way down south, and across the country.

And yes, maybe a new "combat" foray might have been just a bit of an incentive.

Looking to make up for time lost to Covid and taking advantage of the relaxed social distancing that outdoor battles provide, hundreds showed up to get down and sandy at Jacksonville's U.S. Beach National Championships (held in North Carolina until moving south in 2021). Colorado, Idaho, Ohio, New York, and many other states (like, shockingly, Florida!) were represented. The competition welcomes any who have competed in club, school, or state competition, from elementary schoolers to college grads.

First, the obvious differences between this and one's typical wrestling meet. Like, say, lack of headguards and shoes, along with choice of attire (the singlets worn in school competition were an option, but many ditched them for the typical shorts and T-shirts). Competitors were still in the same circular area found on mats and in cages, but now it was filled with sand—along, of course, with pebbles, shells, dirt, and anything else one can encounter on a mini-desert.

Then, the scoring. Landing on one's knees costs wrestlers a point, so no shooting, no leg takedowns. Getting tossed from the ring also gifts one's opponent a mark. But a single takedown, one slamming to the back, gives the slammer three points—and that's all one needs to win. Officially, matches have the same three-minute period time limit as in school, but few needed anywhere close to that.

"I was having back and neck issues," Stikkelman says, "and you need a lot of upper body strength to get some Russian leg-sweeps, to get them to their knees to score points."

While she had come about as far as a competitor could for the event, and was using it as a bit of a bounce-back from a rough period, Kailey Rees had only ventured a few hours north from her Orlando homeland. And this would only be the start of a very busy weekend for the former freestyle Florida titlist.

"I saw a commercial about [the event] during the Super Bowl, and more people started posting about it," remembers the Cass High senior. "It looked like something fun to do, so about two months ago, I decided to do it."

Both had to adjust a bit. Used to battling at 122 pounds, Rees found herself bumped into the 127–132 class. Quite far out of practice, Stikkelman steeled herself against many much more used to the mats.

"All those girls were college wrestlers," she remarked. "I'm not on a college team, and I didn't have a Greco coach. I was just there to wing it and see how it went."

Her first opponent looked quickly for the offensive, pushing against her. Stikkelman faked her into thinking it was working, then hurled her to her back.

"I shocked myself," she admits. "I walked off shrugging my shoulders."

Her next match went about the same. Then she took on Amani Jones, who'd won her third consecutive Georgia high school state title the previous February.

Six seconds in, she grabbed Jones in a front headlock and took her to her knees. Normally, Jones would have stood right up and maybe powered her way out, but that's a quick score in beach battle.

Jones shoved her to the edge, leaving Stikkelman teetering one-legged on the side, almost all the way off balance. Just as Jones lunged forward to knock her all the way out, her right foot landed back down, and she surprised Jones with a takedown and a 2–0 lead.

As the two toppled back toward the edge, Stikkelman hit the ground mere milliseconds before her opponent, cutting her advantage in half. Then Jones tossed her to the ground, and had she not been right at the edge, Stikkelman might have gone all the way to her back for the loss. But the score was now tied, with nearly two minutes left.

And the climax didn't happen. After the two stared each other down for a few seconds, Stikkelman grabbed another front headlock and shoved Jones down. Her knees barely brushed the ground, but enough for the deciding point.

"I thought I was going to lose," Stikkelman admits. "We kept tying up, both trying to throw."

One win later, she was the champ, and hoped to use the title to springboard into professional MMA competition. Ally Graham, Zoe Wight, and Caitlin Cardenas, taking a few days off from King University's top-national female wrestling squad up in Tennessee, took their respective brackets as well. In male competition, Andy Hrovat, who represented his country in 84-kilogram competition in the 2008 Beijing Olympics, won a title.

If certain people have their way, beach wrestling might have as large an international audience as its amateur counterpart in a few years; the push is on to put sandy brawls in the Olympics as soon as 2028.

Rees did everything but walk up to her opponents ahead of time and say, "Hey, I'm going to dive at your waist, hook you behind your knees, and put you straight to the ground." It wouldn't have mattered; the identical technique helped her walk away undefeated in a grand total of about three minutes.

"It's crazy, because I've been wrestling for so long," says Rees, who started wrestling in first grade. "I never thought my first national title would be in beach wrestling."

She didn't have (or, fortunately, need) much time to recover; two days later, over at the nearby Prime Osborn Convention Center, she was rolling through a regional freestyle and club folkstyle event, and squaring off in a dual meet the following Sunday. In two days of mat wars, she stepped onto the mat 13 times—and won every time.

"I've been wrestling for so long," she explains, "that it's easy for me to bounce back, being able to throw and roll and shoot all the way through."

Kara Dover, Massachusetts: "I was in Florida wrestling in a beach tournament. You can get thrown in the sand, you can get sand in your eyes. My favorite part about the tournament was that between matches, I got to get my surfboard and just paddle out. Then I got to surf while I wrestled, two of my favorite things. I was trying to get some girls into wrestling, trying to coach some of them, recruit them on the national team like the older girls recruited me when I was young.

In my tournament, you had to get to three points: one for push-out, one for take-down, and three for hip-toss. The girl I was wrestling kept pushing into me so much, all I had to do was put my hips into her and throw. I pushed her out, and then I hip-tossed her to win."

She was already in town for a tournament, with a few hours to kill before the Summer Nationals. Too young to drop chips around a roulette table, Madison Healey decided to expand her wrestling repertoire.

"I was in Long Beach, near Atlantic City," she recalls of the July 2021 tourney. "I just thought it would be fun to wrestle somewhere not on a mat." Nearby was the Beach Bash event, a bit more difficult than Stikkelman's quest—competitors needed *five* takedowns to walk out winners.

"I was really cautious about keeping my feet moving, because your feet may get stuck in the sand," she says. "The sand kind of dragged me down. I did my normal thing with scoring points with takedowns, but I really had to be cautious."

Her first two matches passed as many of Healey's have: with her scoring quick victories. Then came one of the largest obstacles of her career.

"We were separated by age, but you could pick who you wanted to wrestle," she says. "I went against a 100-pounder, and I'm 60 pounds. He didn't have anyone in his bracket, so I decided to give him an exhibition so he could have a match."

If her opponent, and the onlookers, underestimated her because of her size, or lack thereof, Healey needed just a takedown to change their opinion.

"I didn't want to shoot on him, because all he'd have to do is fall his weight on me," she says, "so I was focusing on duck-unders and armdrags to get there." She took him down. Then she did it again. Then three more times for the win. That victory, along with five others (three of which were over guys), she walked out with a flawless record.

"It felt really good," she says, "because sometimes there's people in the back doubting you because of the size difference."

Sumo Wrestling

"My fiancée and I were looking for something fun to do, and we saw an ad for the 2019 U.S. Sumo Open, so we thought we'd go check it out just for fun. We ended up looking up classes, and we got to train with professional Japanese sumo wrestlers."

—Kellyann Ball, California

You know, it probably was like this at some point in amateur wrestling. Probably early on, when the wrestling population was very small, and the rules weren't quite hammered out.

No weight classes!

Consider a 112-pounder battling a 156'er! A (*gasp!*) 103-pound competitor up against a heavyweight? As common as things like that may be in *professional* wrestling, they fortunately don't happen at this level.

Well, sort of. Maybe not at the amateur level, the high school and college one.

In a different type of wrestling, however, the rules might change, and even fly right out the nearest window.

When one gets to the World Games of sumo wrestling, the weight classes are, shall we say, a bit more liberal. Anyone at or below 143 pounds can compete as a lightweight. Middleweight gals are between 144 and 180, and heavyweight is anyone 181 and above. We're already a hell of a lot less stringent than amateur wrestling levels.

And then there's the Open level, which is exactly what it says: wide open. Anyone with the guts can take on anyone else at any weight. The smallest of the lightweights taking on those far above heavyweight "requirements."

That's when things can get dangerous.

Kellyann Ball: "If you look at how the media portrays big women, you feel this pressure to look a certain way. In order to be pretty and presentable. Even going to job interviews, I feel that, as a larger woman, I'm already at a disadvantage because I don't fit the look.

After my first practice, I was hooked. It's the community, a lot of love, trying to take care of each other. Sumo's the only sport where I don't feel bad about my size. I've grown up being told I should be skinnier. But I never felt that way [at sumo], because traditional sumo wrestlers are bigger. There isn't a problem with me being larger. Traditionally, the women who do well are upwards of 300 or 400 pounds, so it wasn't awkward for me to be a larger woman."

"Rugby was my sport until I found sumo," remembers Mariah Holmes. "I was coaching a youth rugby team, and one of the coaches did sumo and looped me in. I went to practice and loved it. It was good that I was living out in California; Los Angeles has one of the largest clubs in the United States, and I had access to that. It gives you a lot of practice and variety, helping each other grow."

Literally on her first days of practice, Holmes found more support in her new sport than in her entire last wrestling jaunt a few years before back in Wyoming.

"I wrestled all the way from when I was five or six up through tenth grade," remembers Holmes, the state's top heavyweight competitor in her eighth-grade year. "It was a really small town, a small community, and girls didn't compete. What I was doing was really odd. I was the only girl in the state that I knew of that wrestled and played

After honing her athletic skills on rugby fields for years, Mariah Holmes (right, battling Poland's Magdalena Macios) won a national title in sumo wrestling. Photograph provided by Mariah Holmes.

football." She played varsity guard on both sides of the ball in her first two years of high school, and fired the discus farther than any other lady in Wyoming history had before.

"When I walked into [sumo] practice," she recalls, "being an athlete, I'm familiar with warmups and having really rigorous training. The training I was watching didn't look difficult at all, but as I started to participate and do all the techniques and the actual wrestling, even when the matches are 30 seconds, it was exhausting. And it was challenging. And there was this immediate connection. This is an insanely difficult sport."

The open arms of a sumo wrestler don't exactly call up a safe image, but Holmes kept finding a sense of welcome she'd never seen through much of her career.

"I went against males all the time," she says. "In high school wrestling practice, nobody really wanted to wrestle with me, and if they did, you could tell they were holding back. If you're trying to be competitive, you have to go 100 percent. To have the males in sumo that are taking you to the ground and go 100 percent with you, that speaks volumes. It's been a great sport to be a female in, because it has been so inclusive."

Ironically, she and the rest of America's (few but growing) female sumo wrestlers might be finding more, faster acceptance than those back at the sport's birthplace. As long as sumo wrestling as a sport has been a symbol of Japanese culture (Japanacana?) as a whole, even today's Japanese female competitors are facing as tough a battle as American women did when the first ones strapped on their singlets back in the 1970s. Though more and more arenas are slowly opening up to allow ladies across the Orient, women still can't compete in Tokyo's Ryōgoku Kokugikan, the Madison Square Garden of sumo wrestling. They also can't take part in ceremonies.

"First, there's the physicality," Holmes says. "It's a hard-hitting sport, physically exhausting. The bouts might only be a few seconds long, but it's like you played a whole rugby match. But at the same time, it's like a really elegant dance, so fluid and beautiful and graceful. It's not about brute force. It's about using your opponent's momentum against them. It's about feeling their movements and countering them. So in that aspect, it's a mental game. And that presents such a challenge that you don't get in other contact sports where you just go out and hit each other. Here, it's so tactical, so quick, your reactions have to be immediate. That is a huge draw for me. It's very spiritual almost. You're going in and centering yourself, really being in the moment and being present. With sumo, if you're not present and focused, you're going to miss your opponent's movement."

Kellyann Ball: "A lot of it has to do with balance. I always thought I had good balance, and I'm starting to see now that I don't. As a kid, I loved watching the World Wrestling Entertainment, and just wrestling in general, and this was a little bit of that without the extra gymnastics of the WWE. It's more about the physicality and the grappling of two bodies pushing against each other."

Just two weeks into her sumo career, Holmes was competing at a national competition. She won one division and took second in another, stamping her trip to the World Games.

For the next three months, she spent every other weekend at the Los Angeles club, tossing, throwing, pushing, shoving—all sorts of action. It's not about the amateur games, when one racks up points, or when a competitor within one false move of a technical loss can suddenly pull out a pin. In high school and college mat games, falling out of bounds earns a whistle and a restart; in the sumo wars, it's a loss then and there.

Scoring an amateur takedown earns a few points. One sumo takedown is all a competitor needs for a victory.

Remember those weight-related dangers we referred to back at the start? Here's when they got Holmes into trouble. As extensive as her pre–Worlds training had been, the 2018 Taiwan event put her against women who'd been honing their skills every day for *years*. Back in the Golden State, she'd been "rehearsing" on plastic mats. World competitors worked on a clay floor hardened to near cement.

"I always practiced by putting a hard step down and then shifting my weight," she explains. In Open competition, she was facing a lady who was pushing 400 pounds (think any school would have a gal of that size in amateur competition?). The usual technique didn't work.

"My leg went right out from under me," she says. "I tore my hamstring right off the bone." Just a few months into her career, she was in bed for months at a time, unable to even sit, let alone stand or walk.

Not until the next January did she get back on her feet. But Holmes was already looking to the next World Games.

"It just proved how much I loved sumo," she explains. "I hadn't been training, but I came back and qualified again for the world championships in Japan." That October, she was back in the world that makes sumo wrestlers into true giants of sports.

"The open weight class, it's a free-for-all," she says. "That's where I chose to fight. I saw some really, really big girls." But she became the first American woman in tourney history to make it to the semifinals.

"I would have gotten the silver if they hadn't called me on a technicality," she says. "The next round, I'm gonna get there."

Kellyann Ball: "It's wonderful. I go in and everyone there is my friend. In other situations, it might bother me, because it's a little weird to meet new people all the time, but in sumo, we're just a family. There's no pressure to look or be a certain way. It's just about working together and getting better. Now I go to the gym three or four times a week. It's given me a reason to get back in shape. I've been taking care of my body, taking care of what I'm putting into it."

Greco

This leads us into a brief discussion of a form of amateur wrestling that's well behind freestyle and even folkstyle when it comes to popularity amongst lady grapplers. Ever since female wrestling debuted at the Olympics, discussions have gone back and forth and up and down about introducing a Greco-Roman (GR) division for the ladies, but said conversations haven't gotten much past the hypothetical stages.

"I like it because it's something that most women don't do, and because it's more upper body, and that's my favorite," explains Cecilia Williams, who won a 16U Greco event in Fargo when she was all of 14. "I feel like I have more control over boys in Greco, because I've learned a lot more about it."

Before taking home a national title in freestyle action, Brittyn Corbishley scored three Greco championships in her Texas homeland.

"I tried it in my freshman year," she says. "I was scared to do it, but my coach was telling me that no one could overpower me. My coach was saying that all you do is not touch legs, and just do throws. I was always the person who did throws a lot. In Greco, I do lots of underhooks, two-on-ones, and body locks."

That upper body issue commonly gets the blame for giving the ladies hesitancy about giving it a shot. Unlike freestyle and folk, GR participants aren't allowed to grab each other below the waist or trip or shoot on each other. Without the natural leg strength and potential speed advantages they may enjoy, and often use, in other forms of wrestling, many ladies have a tough time making it with arm strength alone.

Maggie Smith, Wyoming: "Greco is my favorite. I like how intense it is. It's fun to throw people. It's harder, my kind of things. I like the difficult-ness of it. If you know how to move your hips, it doesn't really matter how strong you are."

"I'm also a gymnast, so I have a lot of upper body strength that boys also have," say-Kara Dover, who took second in a boys' Greco regional competition in Florida in 2020 and won a similar female tourney in May 2021. "When I go against girls, I feel like I have to take it easy on them. I don't want girls to quit, so I try not to be too aggressive with them. I try to become friends with them. It's tough when I wrestle boys, because multiple boys have told me to shut up when I'm congratulating them."

Years before she came within a few wins of making the 2021 Olympic freestyle team, Sage Mortimer also got rolling in the Greco game.

"I wrestled Greco since I started wrestling, when I was like nine," Mortimer says. "I like how there's big throws, and I understand pressures really well. It's a lot more fun, because you can just go out there and pull the trigger. As my coach says, you can go out there and 'shake 'n' bake.' Greco is a lot of upper body, but a lot of hips. As I started to get bigger, I couldn't compete with the guys as well, because their upper body strength was so overpowering. That's why I want girls' Greco: because I think it would be an equal playing field."

Cagefighting

> "Wrestling pushes you further than you knew you could go. It gets you into the best shape of your life. It is the best form of self-defense. If anybody were to ever attack you, you'd always have a fighting chance to defend yourself. I've had to do that a couple of times."
>
> —Shannon Williams

Over the next few years, or hopefully even sooner, the last names of Gray, Maroulis, Mensah-Stock, and so many others might become the sports world's newest household monikers, the role models for a sport a long way from its potential.

That's the same thing that opened up a new lifeline in cagefighting a few short decades ago. After men dominated the Ultimate Fighting Championships and the rest of mixed martial arts for years, women slowly and steadily emerged in the early 2000s, a new set of heroines for young female athletes to follow. Many female names from the sport became household, like Gina Carano, Cris Cyborg, Miesha Tate, and others.

Like, of course, Ronda Rousey, whose explosion into the UFC gets credit for shoving female cagefighting into the public eye with the speed and strength of a punch that carried her past and over so many opponents. It's interesting to consider how Rousey might have done had she started out on the wrestling mats (probably pretty well, considering not just her cagefighting success but her Olympic medal in judo).

Seven years after becoming the first American woman to win a wrestling Olympic medal with a silver in the 2004 Games and four years after her third World Championship medal, Sara McMann made her own MMA debut in May 2011. Two months later, she co-main-evented the Titan Fighting Championship 19 in Kansas City, defeating fellow former matster Tonya Evinger, whom we'll meet shortly.

Carrying an unblemished cage record into Las Vegas just after Valentine's Day 2014 for UFC 170, McMann was on the brink of sports history, main-eventing against none other than Rousey herself. But things ended in just over a minute, as Rousey blasted her with a pair of knees that stopped the match before she broke a sweat.

Long before Rousey was even considering a cage career, Evinger was tearing up wrestling mats back at Missouri's Odessa High.

"Guys would try to fight me on the mat, and coaches got crazy," she recalls. "I got a new coach in my sophomore year, and he tried to get me to quit. I never did, and I beat out other wrestlers to get the varsity spot. He would fight for me because I would get screwed out of matches I was winning. Refs just wouldn't give me the points." Such screwjobs would keep her from becoming the first woman in state history to make it to the state level, she continues.

"I lost the final match over a referee that didn't want me on the mat," she says. "The whole arena was booing. People were going crazy. I think I changed things for the good

After sharpening her grappling skills back home in Missouri, Tonya Evinger made her cage-fighting debut in 2006. Photograph provided by Tonya Evinger.

over there, because girls got to compete and not be biased against." In 2018, the Show-Me State sanctioned female school wrestling.

"I made the national team in my junior year," says Evinger, who also played football at Odessa. "I was the youngest person to ever make the national team at the time." Competing on said team, though, she got a stipend from USA Wrestling. She ended up paying a hell of a lot more than she'd been compensated.

As she arrived for her farewell wrestling year at Odessa, Evinger found that it wouldn't happen.

"They told me that since I'd gotten paid, I couldn't wrestle as a senior," she says. "That was ridiculous." Wrestling got her a near-full ride to Missouri Valley College, but bad luck would follow there.

"They only had women's wrestling because of Title IX," Evinger explains. "The coach didn't want girls wrestling. He had been a high school coach at our rival school, and I used to beat the shit out of his boys." Rather than take a crack at the 2004 Olympic trials, she decided to go into private training.

"I worked out in people's garages, churches, houses," she says. "It was my biggest struggle ever—it took me two years to get a fight. Nobody wanted to fight me, not just because I was a great wrestler, but because I didn't have a record. Get the hell out of here! If you could whoop my ass, you'd whoop my ass!"

That pretty much described Evinger's cage debut on May 13, 2006, pounding Brittany Pullen into a TKO in Oregon. But things went the other way on June 3, as Jennifer Tate (no relation to Miesha) choked her out in the second round at a California casino.

She got another shot at history the following February, as the Japanese American Cultural Center held California's first all-woman cagefighting event. This time, she came back through, cold-cocking Pullen in a mere 16 seconds.

She'd come out on top twice in the next two months, and debut for Elite XC that September. On the other side? Carano, who scored the first submission of her illustrious career by choking Evinger out in the first round.

After seeing her record bounce back and forth for the next few years, Evinger finally found her place, and her direction. The year before, Invicta had emerged as America's premier all-female organization; its first event came in April 2012 in Kansas City, with Olympic medalist Randi Miller (in her first and, as of summer 2023, last pro fight) appearing on the card with a win.

Six cards and 21 months later, Evinger debuted at Invicta 7 with a win over and defeated Sarah D'Alelio. The next year, she scored two submission victories, moving into position for the first title shot of her career.

Nine years and a month into her cagefighting career, Evinger (now nicknamed Triple Threat) battled Irene Aldana for the Invicta bantamweight title at Invicta 13 in Las Vegas.

Before the first round was over, the winner was all but blatant. Evinger got Aldana down and nearly elbowed her into submission. Then she caught Aldana in an armbar and nearly tore Aldana's arm right off before the savior bell sounded.

In the second round, she mounted Aldana and bashed her face and head with both hands. Finally, after maybe too long, the fight was stopped, and her title reign began.

"Invicta's not as big as the UFC with the money, but the title is well worth it," she says. "I always dreamed of being a world champion, and maybe the path wasn't exactly the way I pictured it, but I fought for one of the best promotions out there. Ultimately, I reached my goal."

In November 2016, she'd headline Invicta 20 in Kansas City, defending against Yana Kunitskaya (the card was titled "Evinger vs. Kunitskaya"). In the card's opening match, Miranda Maverick made her pro debut, submitting Samantha Diaz in the first round. This will matter in a few paragraphs.

Evinger got the Russian down early, but Kunitskaya grabbed her in an armbar.

What happened next was unclear. Evinger stepped on Kunitskaya's face to try to pry her arm free, which isn't illegal. However, the referee stepped in and forced Evinger to move her foot. Seconds later, she tapped out.

Two weeks later, Evinger filed a protest, and the Missouri Athletic Commission agreed, voiding the loss. The next March, she defeated Kunitskaya by submission, and headed off to the UFC.

One match in, she was already up for a title, battling Cyborg for the company's featherweight title in June 2017. Cyborg, who ironically had main-evented the card where Evinger won her championship, beat her in the third round. She'd finish her UFC career 0–3 before being released in March 2020.

"My shining moment was fighting for Invicta, a promotion that really gives a shit," she says. "Invicta finds [fighters] before UFC buys them up. Just being a part of that was my whole career."

As with so many young women yet to fully discover their interest in combat competition back during the Rousey Regime, Miranda Maverick (whose name just *sounds* like a perennial brawler!) saw some semblance of her future in UFC's first lady Hall of Famer.

"My dad said that I could do [what Rousey did]," Maverick recalls. "I said I didn't want to get punched in the face." Such fears wouldn't last, but jiu-jitsu became her athletic focus for a brief period.

But wrestling was soon to follow. And she'd gotten a bit of unintentional rehearsal in that sense. After moving from one Missouri town to another for her senior year of high school (she was in Buffalo, two hours south of Odessa), Maverick took a hesitant step into the wrestling room.

Eager to show the only lady there that she didn't belong (another joined soon after), her teammates did everything but literally try to push her out the door (and even attempted that a few times!). But years of working outside on Missouri farms had buffed this lady up, and the fellows learned the hard way that she wasn't going to go along with that nonsense.

"They thought I was weak, too girly to put up with their toughness," she laughingly recalls. "Even the boys on the team said I wasn't going to do well, and the coach was against girls wrestling. But when I won my first match with a pin in 13 seconds, he had to let me do what I wanted. He would have me train with the other female, then he started letting me pair up with guys."

It worked; she ended her debut and sole season at Buffalo High with a 21–2 record.

"It was amusing for my team to watch," says Maverick, who bounced up and down between 126 and 132 pounds at Buffalo. "I would act like I was weak for the first few seconds. We'd get into a collar tie-up and grab each other. When they would get my head down, I would go all the way and grab their leg and hip-toss them."

Without a wrestling team to look forward to at Drury University, Maverick's athletic finish line changed again.

"I had been an amateur MMA fighter for about a year," says Maverick, who went 7–1 in a single year before turning pro. "I couldn't find any more fights. I was posting crap on social media, saying no one would fight me because they were too scared." Soon after, Invicta came calling, and Maverick's debut came partway through her freshman year.

In her second year at Drury, the school began a wrestling team. One day, a gentleman who'd clearly put in his own gym time showed up to one of her classes.

"I hear you're a pretty good wrestler," he told her. "You could help the [Drury] team get some exposure. Join the wrestling team. You could work out with the boys." As a pro, and thereby paid, athlete, Maverick explained that she couldn't join a college team.

"I'm not wanting you to compete for me," he assured her. "I'm just wanting to help you and help our team, exposure wise, by having a female on the team. You'll be the only one with the freedom to show up or not show up there, three times a week." Along with buffing up her strength and conditioning, Maverick grabbed some MMA connections, as some teammates and local fighters asked that she show up at the gyms for some specific help. By June 2023, she'd racked up an 11-5 record and made it to the top fifteen in UFC's flyweight marks.

CHAPTER 8

Prayer's Role on the Mat

"It's by the grace of God I'm even able to move my feet. I just leave it His Hands and I pray that all the practice ... my coaches put me through pays off. Every single time, it does."

—Tamyra Mensah-Stock, after winning
Olympic gold, 2021

As with most sports, religion is a mixed bag in wrestling, as is the common man's response to it. Baseball players wear religious medallions, and football players bow and thank God for helping them score a touchdown or catch a pass. (Interestingly, you never see running backs pray after a fumble or a lineman who just missed a tackle genuflecting. Looks like they're not reaching for His hands when things go wrong.) It's not uncommon to see wrestlers bowing down just before a big match, hoping that Someone (He, She, It, Them, or whoever else) might give them the strength to make it through, even if overtime arrives.

Sometimes athletes don't have to ask. What they've already learned, and not necessarily in a school, is enough to know that guidelines from a certain Book are more important than the one extolling wrestling's rules.

For Helen Maroulis, it's all about the eternal message, the emotion that lifts us all. Not because we believe in or live a certain faith, or deity, or whatever else. Just about something that's hard to find, but always worth it.

Back in 2010, recalls America's first lady gold medalist, "I heard a sermon about love and it totally rocked my world." Since then, she's joined a church in Colorado Springs, and often discusses her faith in interviews.

In the Rio Olympics, not many gave Maroulis much of a shot, even as she worked her way up the 53-kilogram finals. For the last three Olympics, one wrestler after another had stepped into battle with Japan's Saori Yoshida and lost.

But Someone did give her a shot. Even in the biggest match of her life, Maroulis kept remembering a simple refrain.

"Christ is in me," she held in her mind. "I am enough." And she was, coming out on top.

For a time, it seemed to be more than enough. Over the next few years, injuries and other interests nearly ended her trek toward the Tokyo Games before it had much of a chance to start. But the same One kept calling her.

"I felt like He revealed to me that if wrestling is where your pain and trauma happened," she remembers, "and you run away from it for the rest of your life, you're not ever going to heal from it.... You know you're called to a journey and you definitely feel like God has led you, but until it actually happens, there's still that one percent of [doubt]."

99

As her battle with Jenna Burkert came down to the deciding third of a two-of-three bout in the finals of the Olympic trials, Maroulis looked to her faith to overcome the round she'd lost and the pain of a recently torn MCL.

"Who am I, Sovereign Lord," she asked, "and what is my family, that you have brought me this far?" King David inquired this of God in Samuel 7:18, and now she looked for her own answer.

It came in the form of a win. The next August, her newest answer arrived in a bronze medal.

"And Jesus said to him, 'Anything is possible to him who believes,'" she wrote on social media shortly afterward, quoting Mark 9:23. "Never lose faith, never give up."

Before she became the first-ever Nigerian to win an Olympic medal in 2021, Blessing Oborududu blasted across the sports social media world with her gold medal at the 2018 Commonwealth Games in Australia, her mat-kissing, rolling, coach-hugging celebration going viral.

"The joy," she says, "the joy of winning a gold medal, I didn't know how to express myself. That is why I rolled on the ground and said 'God, I give you the glory for making this possible for me.'"

Since women started wrestling, men (and boys, of course) have come up with all kinds of reasons for *not* wrestling them. We've already seen quite a few throughout this book, and we'll probably see and hear many more.

And mostly, those who say no are themselves made the villains. The Neanderthals still stuck in the past. The chauvinists who won't give women a chance because they're the weaker sex. The cowards afraid that a gal might actually defeat them.

These people are entitled to their opinions, as we all are. But we need to remember one thing, something that too many of us forget (intentionally or otherwise) in this "news everywhere" day and age: no matter who states it, no matter how many TV or internet channels they're on, no matter how many people read their words in print or on the net, an opinion is still an opinion, and saying it a million times to a billion people doesn't make it true. Or any more valid than any other time.

Very rarely do we try to see from their side. The possibility, the slightest chance, that just maybe these guys might have a legitimate reason to step away, or aside, for a loss that's worth it.

How about because it's the way that many of us were raised? When you've been taught for decades that any sort of physical action against women—*any sort*—is wrong, that's hard to overcome.

That however a woman may be challenging us, even if it's for reasons of sport, sometimes we can't just push that aside. Even as tough as women are, and always have been, the image of getting physical with her, and the idea of her getting hurt because of us, would be all but impossible for us to overcome. Facing that is a reality that many men can't stomach even facing.

And those who say we should, or badmouth us for doing so, just like to climb up on their pedestal and look down, laughing. Giving away a win is worth it to avoid some possibilities that we've been turned away from for far too long. As tough is morality is to locate in sports sometimes, these guys hold true to their values.

"We're taught all throughout our lives as men," explains Kelly Benton of Wrestlers for Christ, "don't put your hands on a girl, don't fight a girl. Guys get yelled out to go out and rip her head off. I have sons, and I wouldn't allow them to wrestle girls. I didn't want people to think I was against girls wrestling, but think sanctioning it is the greatest thing [he formerly coached high school wrestling in Kansas, which sanctioned the sport in 2020]. Being sanctioned gives girls a way to grow and flourish, and it takes that pressure away from boys."

Back in February 2011, Iowa's Joel Northrup got raked over the coals for saying no. No to wrestling a girl. No to taking a chance on hurting her. No to getting into combat with a lady.

And far too few were willing to hear why.

Just one more thing that so few knew, or would ever take the time to figure out.

Northrup had actually been there before.

"Back in sixth grade, I was in a youth tournament, set to wrestle a girl," he recalls. "I didn't feel it was right at the time, so I didn't. I thought that if I ever had to do this again, I'm not going to wrestle a girl."

After home-schooling all the way to high school ("I weighed 100 pounds soaking wet in eighth grade!" he recalls), Northrup snared the lightest spot on Marion's Linn-Mar High School's squad. Two years in, he finished near the top of 112's Linn-Mar Community School Districts—and now on to state.

Then he found something out.

About 20 minutes north of Marion, Cassandra Herkelman was making history at Cedar Falls High School. In her rookie year, she'd also made it to state, taking second in the Cedar Falls District at 112 pounds.

This marked about her seventh year in the sport. "At a family Christmas, I was wrestling with my siblings, and my grandma said I should wrestle like my dad and uncle did," she says. "I asked my dad, and he thought I was joking. I kept bugging him about it, and he signed me up. Wrestling was something that I loved. You can't blame anybody but yourself. At some point we all want to blame somebody else, like a referee, but this is such an individual sport. My huge motivation was to keep going and see how far I could take it. I was going to two tournaments a weekend, every weekend for three months a year. I'd see the same people on the bracket at these tournaments. Sometimes I'd beat them, and sometimes they'd beat me. As soon as I saw them, I was like, 'OK, how's it going to go to today?'" After 84 years without a female in Iowa state competition, the 2011 event would have two: Ottumwa sophomore Megan Black joined Herkelman at the games.

"When Megan Black and I qualified for the state tournament, I think that had a huge impact on women's wrestling in Iowa," she says. "Back then, going to state tournaments had 80 to 100 girls, and now our high schools have over 400 girls participating."

After knocking out a 35–4 record during the season—impressive for anyone, especially a sophomore—Northrup could have made it to the top of Iowa (he'd ended at third as a freshman). And defeating Herkelman would have been his first step.

Would he have? Odds were, yes. Despite her district title, Herkelman had "only" compiled a 20–13 record that season, and Northrup was two years older than she was, gifted with both experience and puberty's natural gifts. Nothing's ever certain in wrestling, but betting probably would have gone his way were it legal.

Without a pro team in the state to cheer for, Iowa sports fans don't always have much to get excited about. That's why, every February, the state high school wrestling tourney becomes one of the biggest events of the year. 2011's event nearly jammed the Wells Fargo Arena, some perhaps there just to see how the ladies would do.

Herkelman and Northrup stepped to the scoring table to check in. Then Herkelman yanked off her jacket and motored to the center of the mat, ready for battle.

"The week going into state tournament, my parents had taken my phone. I was off social media, and I didn't watch TV leading up to it," says Herkelman, whose team had scrimmaged against Northrup's school before, though she'd never worked with him directly. "That day, I was ready to go. Then I walked out to the mat, and everybody was like, 'I guess they are going to wrestle.'"

But Northrup didn't follow. He strode off the mat, and the official raised Herkelman's hand in victory. She'd made history, but not in the way she'd especially wanted.

"It had nothing to do with sexism," asserts Northrup, raised deeply evangelical. "It was grounded in my Biblical beliefs that God made males and females different. Males are better at some things, and females are better at some things. I don't believe it's right to physically hurt a female, whether it's on the mat or on the street."

Not surprisingly, the two immediately became more famous than anyone else who found much more success at the event. Magazines, newspapers, news programs, and websites from around the world jumped all over the gesture. And, also not a shock, much of it was against Northrup.

At least, out in the open.

"Does any wrong-headed decision suddenly become right when defended with religious conviction?" asked longtime *Sports Illustrated* columnist Rick Reilly. "In this age, don't we know better? … Body slams and takedowns and gouges in the eye and elbows in the ribs are exactly how to respect Cassy Herkelman…. If the Northrups really wanted to 'respect' women, they should've encouraged their son to face her."

However, it wasn't the most stressful moment for Northrup's family at the time; his mom was about to deliver his seventh sibling.

"For the kid's sake," Reilly childishly and self-righteously chided, "I hope it's a boy."

With microphones and cameras suddenly jammed in his face, Northrup won the first consolation round match, then fell in the second. Herkelman and Black each lost their next two matches.

"It was crazy for a few weeks," Northrup remembers. "I expected it to be a little thing, but it blew up. Everybody was trying to

Cassandra Herkelman, celebrating a big win with her dad, Bill, was one of the first women to reach Iowa state competition. Photograph provided by Cassandra Herkelman.

interview me." He, Herkelman, and Black stayed friends after the event (the teams shared a hotel, tossing everyone together) and cheered one another on for years afterward.

Herkelman eventually took a cadet national title and some other nationals, and made All-American ranks at McKendree University until a torn ACL ended her shot at the 2016 Olympics, eventually coming home (almost!) to coach the new girls' team at Denver High, about 20 minutes north of Cedar Ridge, along with following her father and grandfather's footsteps into law enforcement.

"I was surprised," she says of Northrup's decision. "He was number three in the tournament. Not to be negative about myself, but I expected to go 0–2 for the tournament. I probably shouldn't have thought this way, but I should not have won. I can't complain about being the first female to win a state match, but I can't change it. A lot of people tried to put down Joel Northrup, but he made the decision, and he's still very religious. I don't have much to say on that."

The next year, Black transferred to Eddyville-Blakesburg, headed back to state, and scored a 10–0 defeat of Don Bosco's Jacob Schmit to become the first gal to take a forfeit victory, ending eighth in the event. She then went on to compete at both King and McKendree Universities, scoring All-American honors, and became a member of the 2021 class of Iowa's Glen Brand Wrestling Hall of Fame.

Publicly, our egotistical nature being what it is in America, many couldn't wait to get on their columns and websites and shows and talk down to Northrup and all like him (whether they'd have had the guts to say it to his face is a question many were lucky enough not to answer). On the quiet side, the results were a bit different.

"I got tremendous support from people all over the world," Northrup says. "I got a thousand letters in the mail from people who support what I did." He'd finish fourth in the state the next year, then finish with a third-place win in his senior season. He'd eventually wrestle at and snare a degree in science from the University of Iowa.

"I still stand by the decision I made," he says. "Wrestling a very physical sport. If I were to wrestle her, I might accidentally give her a black eye. I don't think it's right to do that physically, especially to a woman."

Since 2008, Benton's organization has been spreading the Word at matches and practices from the kids to the collegians.

"I go out and do the opening prayer before and throughout tournaments," he explains. "I serve as the tournament chaplain. I'm on the floor with coaches and athletes, and sometimes they want me to tag along on a long trip. I come out and talk to the team, giving them the motivation to drive and not quit. At tournaments, they're all faced with stress and pressure. When we're there, it gives them an outlet to reach out and get some spiritual strength. I've seen a lot of girls over the tournaments basking in the glory."

It took time, but girls' wrestling grew in Iowa. In 2019, the state held its first-ever all-female state tournament, and more than 500 women came out the next year. The spurt was halted because of Covid, but the state sanctioned female wrestling in February 2023.

"I'm totally supportive of it," Northrup says of all-gal mat battles. "It's only right for women to have their own league, so they don't have to wrestle in a men's league."

> "And Jesus came and said to them, "All authority in heaven and on earth has been given to me. Go therefore and make disciples of all nations, baptizing them in the name of the Father and of the Son and of the Holy

Spirit, and teaching them to obey everything that I have commanded you."

—Matthew 28:18–20

Right after Georgia became the seventh state to sanction girls' wrestling for the 2018–9 season, Lisa Hankins got an email.

For about eight years, she'd been working with the Fellowship of Christian Athletes (FCA), bridging the gap between God and the sports community. Since 1954, the FCA had been inviting competitors and their coaches into a new relationship; wrestling had become a group focal point in 2008.

Hankins had been working with local clubs for years, and one up north in Georgia's Gainesville area wanted her to spend more time with its lady matsters.

"God was saying that we had all this stuff for boys," she explains, "and now girls were starting to grow in the sport, and we needed something for them."

She called the area director, ready to ask about faith expansion. As it turned out, they'd already contacted him.

"I poured my heart out to him," Hankins says. "It was amazing that God could use me. It's as if He just pushed me and said 'This is what I want you to do.' He connects all these dots in our lives. I can look back and understand that some of the most painful things I have been through are some of the most relatable to these girls. My favorite saying is 'You can't be a tour guide to a place you've never been.' God uses it all if we let Him. My hope is that they never feel alone, knowing Jesus is with them and for them."

Just as Christians believe Jesus shared with His disciples and with others, and just as, biblically speaking, His former enemy and converted apostle Paul wrote a letter to a teenager he'd met named Timothy, encouraging him to accept the same Spirit that Paul had, Hankins and the FCA were handing out the same motivation.

"When going in for first time, you make a strong introduction," she says. "You can't trust somebody you don't know. We don't talk at them, but to them. I share who I am, about building relationships and trust, the vulnerability of being real, being genuine and honest. I let them know that I don't have all the answers, and that I'm not somebody they need to impress."

Just as acting out of sudden impulse and emotion can pull a loss out of nowhere out on the mat, a quick decision of fun and pleasure can hurt someone down the road, and today's enjoyment can be tonight's detriment.

"Jesus doesn't want to take the fun out," Hankins explains. "He wants us to live an obedient life. We engage, we equip, we empower. We get to know them, build their situation, and build their trust. It's about being someone who understands enough about their situation to gain their trust. Our overall goal is to empower them to give what they have learned to someone else, like a domino effect."

Yes, refusing a match in the midst of a season is one thing. Doing it in the biggest event of the season is quite another.

Doing it *twice*? Unheard of. Unthinkable. But not when Brendan Johnston is involved.

A wrestler's success is defined not by the coach, the school, or the team, but by the person. Most, particularly the guys, will scream at you that that means standing atop the platform! Hoisting the trophy! All or nothing at all.

Wrong. Being the best in wrestling means being the best for yourself.

Johnston *could* have made a strong statement during his junior year at the 2018

Colorado state games. He'd lost his first match, but the Classical Academy junior had a chance to rebound in consolation competition, ending a tough year on a strong note and raising his outlook toward his farewell tour.

Nope. Encountering (alliteration alert!) Conifer's Cayden Condit's name on his bracket, Johnston stepped aside and let her win. Then he headed home with his head high.

"I'm OK with the decisions I made," he says. "I'm peaceful. I'm fine. I'm calm. [My coach] always says, 'Wrestling is what we do, it's not who we are.' So I know who I am. And my identity lies elsewhere. I'm fine with that."

The next year, Johnston came right back in 106-pound warfare, churning out a 37–4 record before stepping into the Pepsi Center in February 2019 for the final state games of his career.

And almost right away, he knew he wasn't heading home with a medal. Because Jaslynn Gallegos of Skyview was his first opponent. It would be the easiest win she'd had all year.

In consolation rounds again, Johnston could still end his career on a winning note. But what does a medal or a victory mean if every time you look at it or think about it, you have to remember when you became someone you didn't like much at all?

Seeing his next opponent, he considered it. For about two seconds.

The name was Angel Rios. It was the fourth time he'd face her this season.

And just as he had the first three times, Johnston lost without competing.

"I feel good," Johnston says. "I'm not really comfortable with a couple of things with wrestling a girl. The physical contact, there's a lot of it in wrestling. And I guess the physical aggression, too. I don't want to treat a young lady like that on the mat. Or off the mat. And not to disrespect the heart or the effort that she's put in. That's not what I want to do, either. And there are more important things to me than my wrestling. And I'm willing to have those priorities." Rios and Gallegos ended up fourth and fifth at the event, the first time that one woman, let alone two, had placed at state. Johnston soon headed to Wheaton College in Illinois.

Jenna Gerhardt was a little luckier; by the time her senior season rolled forth at Devils Lake High in North Dakota, the state had already sanctioned female wrestling, eliminating the need for gender-caused inner conflicts (yes, her school is Devils Lake, as in plural rather than possessive, and absolutely, it'll seem *really* ironic in just a few paragraphs!).

Still, she'd been calling on a special Fan since long before her mat career had started in the eighth grade.

"Wrestling's brought me closer with God," recalls Gerhardt, baptized Catholic before she could crawl. "I pray before matches with my coaches and teammates." Through three years at Devils Lake, she'd won a pair of unsanctioned state titles and (quite) a few other all-gal events.

"I've had a mindset of 'I'm gonna win. I've worked really hard, and I deserve it,'" she says. "Sometimes when I lose, when I'm down, I pray to God for strength, and it takes my fear and anxiety away. I remind myself that I'm a hard worker. I can do this, God made me strong to fight my way out of my struggles. I like to thank God after matches."

Every female wrestler dreams of hitting the mats of Fargo, the sport's national cornerstone. Living in its state gave Gerhardt and her North Dakota colleagues a bit of a head start, their state tournaments held at the Fargodome since the inception.

As the state's first sanctioned event became Gerhardt's farewell tour in February 2022, she got a little extra inspiration. Just before the matches got rolling, the FCA, which itself had recently started a chapter at Devils Lake, held an impromptu event. Wrestlers chatted about how the biggest wins fade away and the toughest losses drop off (albeit always seemingly taking so much longer!), but how Someone special is never too far away, one way or another.

Gerhardt listened. She kept praying before and after every match. And then she went right out and charged past three opponents, culminating in a 44-second pin of Central Cass's Anna White to become Dakota's first-ever sanctioned 105-pound champ.

"God makes you a better person," she says. "I want to become a nurse or counselor as a way to help others. A lot of my teammates and kids at school come to me with their problems because they want to have somebody to talk to. A bunch of people at the tournament came up to me like, 'Wow, you're like my idol. I want to wrestle you!'"

CHAPTER 9

Warming Up for the Olympics

"I think we have a very strong team, a veteran team, an experienced team. Many of them have been here before, and they're more motivated. They know what their capabilities are. Sometimes you have people on the team who are just happy to be there, and we don't have that with this group. They want to come home with a medal."
—Terry Steiner, U.S. women's wrestling Olympic coach

Time out! Let's get a quick update on those few short months, weeks, and ultimately days between the Olympic trials and the Games themselves.

They had just fought some of the toughest battles of their careers. They'd gone against the best their country had to offer—and, one way or another, they'd come out on top.

Now would come the harder parts.

America's women's wrestling team would be facing the *world's* greatest. Women's wrestling would be showcased in a way that it never had been before in any Olympic competition.

And not only that, but this would be far from home. Right in the middle of the country that had long set the standard for the sport. They were heading to the heart of a nation that has won 17 medals in three Olympics (gold in every lightweight, middleweight, and light heavyweight competition that's been held), along with 23 of 28 World Championships. They'd be in a country looking to put on a show for a homeland that hadn't hosted the Summer Olympics since 1964.

Just reading all that sounds like enough to intimidate the hell out of most people, even those who have been through what the American women faced and faced down. But these aren't the kind of women who get scared all that easily. And in the decades over which they have competed, dozens of tournaments and hundreds of matches, at *no* time, no time at all, had they ever gone anywhere to lose. For anyone who makes it to this level, motivation's never an issue, no matter from where it's found, and few things are more inspiring than a shot at a place in history.

So now it was time to get started. And there were some tools to draw the starting line and run across it.

To a point, the preparation started in early April, in the days just after the Olympic trials. Some sharpening came along the way, like the next May, when future Olympians Kayla Miracle, Tamyra Mensah-Stock, Adeline Gray, and, for the sixth time in her career, Sarah Hildebrandt, had won gold at the Pan American Championships in Guatemala.

Along with enough enthusiasm to rise to the top of the nation, there was the familiarity. Gray and Helen Maroulis had been to the Olympic Games before. Virtually all of the women had teamed together before. They'd worked together. And they'd all worked with coach Terry Steiner, many several times. Nothing to adjust to in those departments.

Of course, the Covid virus was still going to be a problem. But they'd gotten around that enough to not worry too much.

The first thing was to create the atmosphere. Get used to more than just on-mat expectations. This was different than most camps, tournaments, and other events, where overwhelmingly most, if not all, of the warmups take place in the wrestling room or mats beforehand. It's not like *just* sharpening up one's mat skills and then going into battle. Most wrestling events are almost all about the physicality; here, it's a part (maybe the largest, most significant part, but still a part) of a much larger expedition.

Throughout June, the women warmed up in Georgia, then worked out in Colorado for some time. For the final round of homeland training in late June, the team (most of it, which will be elaborated upon) arrived in South Bend, Indiana. About three miles from Notre Dame University (the two schools share a student exchange program), the group set up at Saint Mary's College. Away from the public, away from the media, away from everything but their teammates and some there to assist, Steiner and his staff created a makeshift Olympic Village.

The on-mat skills were already there, and had ample time to improve. Now it was time to turn these women into true Olympic athletes. No surprises on or off the mat.

Along with a few dozen others there to assist, the women were turned into everything but athletic cyborgs.

The coaches laid out the exact times of day that each specific lady was to compete in Tokyo (they were scheduled to hit the mats on August 2–3). Just as if they were at the Games, the women were placed in a makeshift warmup area, staged similar to one in Tokyo. People were there to lead them out on the mat, just as in August. Surrounded by their coaches, the women worked out in their official singlets. Real-life Olympic officials officiated their warmup matches. Theme songs played as the women emerged. Even an audience was brought in to cheer for them.

"They got a feel for those days," Steiner explains. "It's a very different time than we are used to [Japan is 13 hours ahead of America], and we had to get a feel for how that day will play out, what our protocol will be on those days. It definitely brought out the emotion that competition does. We could sense everything coming up in Tokyo."

Makeshift matches were staged on mats around the Olympians, getting them used to whistles, cheers, coaches' shouts, and everything else that can reach out and disrupt a wrestler's concentration. After working out, athletes were paraded out of the arena, through a constructed press row to get ready to debate with the media—again, just as they would after the Olympics. The same hydration and nutrition schedules for the Olympics were followed. Personal coaches and workout partners gave the women the same assistance—literally word for word and move for move—they expected to in August.

"They had two rounds in the morning, and then a long break before semifinal matches in the afternoon," says Steiner, echoing the Tokyo schedule. "During then, how will they handle that time? When are they going to come back and warm up? They got used to the schedule. The next morning, on day two, finals aren't until 9:20 p.m., so they weigh in in the morning. How are we going to spend that day? We let them sleep in, enjoy the morning, get the body feeling good, maybe get them a massage, then come back in for their hard warmup to get that intensity high, ready for their matches." Back at the Olympic trials in April, the six qualifiers (a) only had to win one match to take it all, albeit a two-of-three battle, as all started as top seeds and, therefore, (b) were walking into said match fresh, while their opponents had been through three or four mat wars, and (c) were squaring off with people whom they probably at least knew of and usually had had it out with before, so were as easy as wrestling can offer in terms of preparation. In the Olympics, they won't have these advantages.

Sarah Hildebrandt: "I feel like I don't have the words to just be out there. You worked so hard for this. Everyone has put so much into this. I feel it with Team USA on my singlet. Everybody is in that."

Over a decade before the Olympics, about 20 minutes from St. Mary's, a young woman from Penn High started her wrestling career. In her varsity debut, Sarah Hildebrandt won five consecutive matches and a tournament title.

Now, in 2021, she hoped to have similar results in 50-kilogram competition in Tokyo. In one of the last simulated events in South Bend, Hildebrandt burned through a pair of matches by a combined 20–0.

"It's unreal to have started my wrestling career here," said Hildebrandt, who trained in South Bend with Gray, Jacarra Washington, and Tamyra Mensah-Stock (because of Covid issues, Maroulis and Kayla Miracle trained in Arizona), "and then to have my last Olympic preparation here it's like—to just to come full circle like that—is so cool." Her team was scheduled to have one last round of warmups in Nakatsugawa, a few hours west of Tokyo, in the last days before the Olympics.

Just after the South Bend training ended, Olympic organizers announced that Covid concerns would render the Games audience-free.

"We thought that was coming," Steiner says. "We knew our friends and family weren't going to be there, and we didn't care if Japanese fans were there or not. I think the team is fine with it. The honor is the same, and that medal around your neck is going to feel the same as it would be anywhere else."

Terry Steiner: "They're laser-focused. They know what's at stake. For a lot of them, their legacies are on the line right here, and at stake, and they're here to do a job."

And right around that same time, the women got a new shot of motivation when United World Wrestling (UWW) released its seeds for the Games. Lining up competitors by the number of UWW events in which they'd participated in recent times, the UWW played out its Olympic favorites.

Gray was at the top of the 76-kilogram class. Mensah-Stock was first in 68-kilogram.

That, however, was all. Miracle wasn't among the top seeds at 62-kilograms. Winchester was left out of the top of the 53-kilogram list, as was Hildebrandt at 50-kilograms. And Maroulis, the defending champ herself, hadn't racked up enough points to even be counted in the top four of 57-kilogram competition.

Even the ones who made the game ranks didn't think that four of the top six American ladies had it in them.

Just one more group to prove so, so wrong.

Adeline Gray: "We are trying to chase the Japanese team and show we can compete with that greatness. We want to knock on that door and I'm sure they will want to answer!"

CHAPTER 10

From the Gridiron to the Mat,
and Sometimes Back

"I was blown away by how much harder [wrestling] was than football. Other football players can't do wrestling. They won't last a match; they're stronger, but they lack basic technique, coordination, and conditioning for a continuous six minutes. Football is like, a few seconds, stop; a few seconds, stop. You always have time to reload. In wrestling, you don't. You have to listen, you have to think, you have to move very fast, you have to outdo your opponent. You have to think four moves ahead. The conditioning for one match is beyond anything I experienced in football, and [out there] I ran a lot, in extreme heat, wearing very heavy equipment. But to condition for football, I would do wrestling conditioning because it was so much more difficult. You have to simulate reality, even if it is a controlled environment. It's different in football, when you're running plays you're going to run in the game. In wrestling, you could have moves down to perfection, but if you can't anticipate what your opponent is going to do, all the moves you thought you were going to do just got thrown down the drain, and now you're in a pin.

Wrestling was immediately something I could be aggressive with, and it was immediately embraced that I was an aggressive person. I'm very dedicated and very articulate, and I love to condition. It may sound weird, like a disorder or something, but I loved being able to throw up, run back to wherever I was at, and show everyone, that no matter how dehydrated and exhausted I may be, that I'm going to outperform you. I want you to try to beat me, because I know you probably can't."

—Angel Celaya, California

Even with women's numbers going all over the place in wrestling—and, as we've seen, in other hardcore contact sports as well!—there's still at least one sport in which ladies still struggle to make their mark.

The one involving helmets, pads, tackles, touchdowns, and everything else that brings thousands into stadiums every Sunday (for the pros; those cheering for younger players start earlier in the week!) and have turned Super Bowl Sunday into a symbol of Americana, nearly as big a holiday as Christmas.

Look, it's not that ladies haven't tried to break into football; the U.S. Women's Football League, Independent Women's Football League, Women's Football Alliance, Women's National Football Conference, and so many others have taken a shot at getting women out of the stands and off the sidelines and onto the field. And they're still trying; in 2022, the number of females playing high school ball lifted past 3,000 for the first time, a number that had increased for seven consecutive years and probably

Angel Celaya both wrestled and played football at California's Golden West High, one of many women to wear both a helmet and singlet. Photographs provided by Susie Youngs

would have gone higher had the Covid pandemic not monkey-wrenched American sports.

Well, if certain health issues finally get straightened out, certain authors might get a new female sports history book to write very soon. But for now, let's meet some ladies who broke some athletic mold in not just one, but a pair of formerly male games!

It's rarely an asset to have to step onto a mat packing less than five feet of weaponry to throw at one's opponent, no matter the weight class. However, as tough as wrestling matches can be, at least a matster has but one opponent to face. No double-, triple-, or quadruple-teaming in this game.

Now imagine entering a different situation in a very different sport, but built about the same. Sure, you've got pads and helmets—but there could be up to 11 monsters out there looking to smash you straight into the grass! And, this being middle and high school (as in, the puberty years), they're probably going to outclass you in the size and strength departments!

Attempts at sarcastic humor aside, however, this story doesn't have a happy beginning. Homeschooled since early on, Angel Celaya stepped into California's Visalia Technical Early College (hereafter, V-Tech) as a freshman at 13, high placement tests bumping her a grade ahead of the normal public school pack, her eyes and mind already on college. Too soon, however, she would see and feel a hell of a lot more of the wrong things.

Not long before starting on a wrestling career that took her to a 2002 national title at Oregon's Pacific University and a spot on the first-ever Olympic team two years later, Tela O'Donnell dipped her cleated toes into the Homer High junior varsity gridiron squad of her Alaska homeland.

"Safety, cornerback, a little guard," remembers O'Donnell, never one to boast, "but I wasn't very good."

Before she won a Cadet World title and Junior National Title within a few weeks in the summer of 2018, and came within a trials match of making the 2021 Olympic team, Macey Kilty battled her way through gridiron defenses in Wisconsin youth league ball.

"I played fullback for my first few years," Kilty remembers. "Then I got to middle school, and the guys were getting a little bigger. My teammates wanted to protect me, so I played quarterback. It was cool, calling the shots. I enjoyed being the quarterback more than the running back, because I didn't get hit as much. Football was like wrestling: combat, a very physical sport. I played until my freshman year in high school, when I gave it up because my opponents were getting too big."

As these women learned as they moved from shoulder pads to singlets, from helmets to head guards, football and wrestling have some pretty strong commonalities. First is the gender issue; just as with wrestling, a lady football player gets accustomed pretty quickly to being the odd woman out in the gender sense. But there's also a skills crossover here: at least for those who played defense, the objective is to get that ball-carrier to the ground as quickly as possible. A play ends as soon as his knees hit the ground, which is obviously a different end goal than the necessary shoulder-shoving three-count, but the opening is the same.

"Wrestling and football are very similar in their setups," explains Celaya. "The stance in football is similar to the stance in wrestling; you have to get low, take out your opponents at their knees, just like in football. In wrestling, a lot of the conditioning is in body weight and being able to move somebody else's body weight, shoving someone out of the way. In football, it's a lot of strength training, with added weight, because you train with all the pads. Together, I did them both, and it's phenomenal endurance that you're able to get. The moves I would learn in wrestling, the perseverance, wrestling in extreme heat, with tons of layers on, and being completely exhausted. When I was going through Hell Week in football, everyone else was dying of the heat, but to me, it was just another day, preparing myself for the next. Football and wrestling complement each other very well because they are both very demanding. Both require you to be good at your technique."

"With football, you tackle, so single- and double-leg takedowns came pretty easy," explains Paige Gershmel, who got started playing linebacker in middle school and moved up to the freshman squad at Montana's Billings Senior High. "I like defense better than offense. As middle linebacker, you get to call the plays defensively and run the field, and I enjoy that. In football, it's always keep going, keep going. Wrestling's the same way. There's always something to do; you keep going and you keep learning."

Her first season on the Billings wrestling squad didn't get off to as great a start, Gershmel continues.

"I lost five of my first six matches," she sadly recalls. "I wasn't afraid of losing, but I was about to break after losing so much. Then I had one more match."

With one period left to go, her opponent held both a three-point lead and Gershmel down on the mat. Then she escaped.

Her coach, also on the football staff, had a brain surge.

"Paige," he shouted to the new gal in the game, "just tackle her!"

She did, and two points came her way. Not going for a pin just yet, Gershmel let her opponent up. Then she went right back and took the lady down again, escaping with a 9–8 lead, and a win that Gershmel carried on the way to finishing third in Montana at 132 pounds in her state's first all-female state competition in February 2021.

A quick clarification on Celaya's tale: V-Tech would do a hell of a job getting her on the way to a high GPA and a trek towards a physical therapy career. Unfortunately, the place didn't have much in the way of a physical education program. Actually, it had nothing. For a brief period each school week, students headed elsewhere to keep their bodies as sharp as their minds.

This didn't appear to be an issue at first; Celaya could walk to the nearest public school. That would prove to be about its only convenience.

Knee-high socks. A skirt. A blouse. Doesn't seem too risqué (or even unusual) for a student's attire, when you read it. No one had mentioned much before.

"My mom had dressed that way in high school, and she let me pick out my outfit," Celaya recalls. "If my parents had no problem, why should anyone else? A lot of adults saw me as a respectable individual. Until I went into the school system, I didn't realize there was anything odd about me until I was there."

Maybe it was because she was the new girl in town. Maybe students didn't like someone whose voice and heart outsized her pint-heighted (again, below five feet!) body. Maybe, in all their jeans-wearing tradition, they decided to take someone so sacrilegiously dressed and do everything but burn her at the stake. It's not as if teenagers are especially rational, or need an excuse to get aggressive with someone even within walking distance of their clique.

"I was sexually harassed," Celaya says, her voice getting slow and deeper for the first time. "I was kicked down a flight of stairs by a group of girls in my driver's ed class. Apparently, I overdressed a lot, and it was said that I dressed like a porn star."

She went back, just like she always had. Martial arts became her athletic pastime. Then, one day, a classmate approached, as condescending as her "girlfriends."

"You're so tough!" he schmoozed. "Why don't you go try football, like me?"

OK, now it was time to take that aggression and move it out of the passive area. Every teenager is loaded down with defiance, but that's helpful if it's directed at the right areas. Like, say, an idiot classmate.

"I don't do well when people undermine me, especially for generic reasons like the way I dress," Celaya asserts. It took her mere nanoseconds to take him up on the proposition. Sports related, it sounded like a great idea.

Just one problem.

What the *hell* was football?

Sydnee Kimber, Alaska: "I played defensive end and linebacker. I was trying to be one of the boys, and most of the boys were also on the football team. I was trying to distinguish myself as a girl playing a male sport. I had to prove that I was good enough. I had proved it in the wrestling room at that point, but proving that girls could do other sports was great too."

Kaden Campbell, Colorado: "I started playing football when I was seven, playing running back and wide receiver. I was really fast. I scored quite often. I started wrestling when I was eight, and played football for two or three more years. I was always really tough, and all the boys were like, 'You should come wrestle with us.' I wanted to, but I didn't want to wear what they had to wear. I was raised to be very modest, but I decided I wanted to do it."

Lexi Janiak, Illinois: "I played football from third to seventh grade, because I was getting too small. In Pop Warner, I was a linebacker, and also played fullback. I was the second-string quarterback. I scored a lot. I was a lot more accepted in football than in wrestling. I don't think I had a single person tell me that I shouldn't be out there playing."

Living hundreds of miles from any of the Golden State's football hometowns, Celaya might not have recognized a football if someone gave her a handoff. Barely able to figure out the gist of a helmet—the mask goes *in the front*!—she stepped toward a group about as accepting as her classmates had been.

"I knew nothing, and the coaches were no help," she says. "I explained how little I knew, and I can understand them not having the patience when they had other people who knew far more. I knew that it would take time to show them that when I start something, I finish it. I ended up going online, reading about every position, reading books, watching old games. Studying like crazy, from its origins to now, how to get faster, how to get stronger—the shortest NFL player to ever play, and how did he get to his position?"

Note: There's actually an interesting story there. In the infancy of the NFL, Jack "Soupy" Shapiro stepped onto the field twice for the 1929 Staten Island Stapletons; at 5'1", two inches taller than Celaya herself, he became the answer to her question, and probably in every other edition of Trivial Pursuit. However, she and every other vertically challenged hopeful gridiron-er can look to Barry Sanders, who maneuvered his minuscule (well, per NFL normalcy!) 5'8" frame to the Heisman Trophy, the Hall of Fame, and what many will always consider the finest running career in NFL history. Tommy McDonald, an inch below Sanders, who made six Pro Bowls in the '50s and '60s, is the tiniest resident of Canton.

Two weeks after making her gridiron debut, Celaya was on the field—taking the very position of the guy who'd needled her there to begin with. But things didn't improve around the school or the squad. "I still got a lot of sexual harassment and verbal abuse from the rest of the team and even a few of the coaches," she says. "Not all the guys, just a few morons."

After practice one day, a teammate took roughness well past the unnecessary level.

"I was abused enough to get my toenail removed," she says. "I played it off like I had a difficult practice. I practiced for three days until blood was coming out of my cleat, and my dad was like, 'What happened?'" She broke down, insisting that she could still make it there.

"You're not quitting," he responded. "You're just starting something new." Shortly thereafter, she was continuing her career at slightly farther away Golden West High—and there would open the door to her newest athletic expedition.

Tonya Evinger, Missouri: "I'm into physical sports, so I played during my freshman year in high school. I played tight end, strong safety, on the kickoff team. I only played one year because I was like, 'Goddamn, these boys are so big.' Most of the other teams tried to kill me when they found out I was a girl."

Maggie Smith, Wyoming: "I started playing offensive and defensive line in third grade. I live in a small town, so lots of people know who I am. It's not uncomfortable for me, but the older I get, the farther into high school, the harder it is, because there's such a size and strength difference compared to junior high and little league. The past couple of years, I haven't gotten as much playing time as I usually do, and the coaches tell me it's just because of my size. When you're on the line weighing about 170, you can't go against people weighing 300 pounds. It's frustrating, because at practices, the coaches will be like, 'Everybody watch Maggie! Maggie has the right form!' and then I don't get to play. But I knew this would happen when I got to high school. This past season, I got to play in my first varsity game. It comes naturally for me to tackle in football because the motion of a tackle is the same as a [takedown]. Staying in my stance and staying low and all the techniques as a lineman, I get from being a wrestler. The only difficulty is managing my weight. In football, you like to bulk up and be bigger, and in wrestling you sometimes have to slim down."

Before starting off at Golden West, Celaya "warmed up" with some city league ball.

"Being 13, 4'11", and then 134 pounds, I wasn't too much trouble for the guys," she says. "They were in eighth grade, so I was at their playing skills. The coaches were willing to work with me; I learned about the three-hole, the four-hole, even the Hail Mary. I was working out three times a day: before school, during school, then going to practice. I could out-condition the guys." Elsewhere in the school athletic community, someone else started to take notice.

"Most of the time, my opponents didn't know I was a girl," she says. "I'd tuck my hair in, and my uniform was so big, I looked like a short, stocky guy. The only thing was, sometimes I would paint my nails the brightest pink I could find. After a tackle, you'd look through my facemask and be like, 'Wow, I just got hit by a girl!'" On the other side of the ball, she became the first lady in district history to carry the ball into pay dirt.

About halfway through her first season, she received another visitor, this one a *bit* more diplomatic.

"A girl came up to me and said, 'You do football? I do wrestling. You should go out for the team,'" Celaya says. "It seemed like that's what other girls who thought and acted like me would do."

For the first few seasons of her new career, Celaya battled men and women. Mostly guys, though, for some specific reasons.

"A lot of the girls were complaining that I was too rough," she says. "I didn't want to be too rough, but I knew that if I practiced in a less aggressive form, I'd begin to play that way, and I don't like that. I feel like I need to execute a move like I'd execute it on the mat. I could do that with guys." Though never quite making it to state-level competition was her biggest disappointment ("I was always one match short!"), Celaya cherishes the memory of suffering a broken nose early in a tournament, then coming back and finishing in the top five of a field of 30.

Yes, the verbal abuse continued. The slurs, the threats, sort of the same stuff that had happened at her old school. And maybe it was just as bad as before and maybe it wasn't, but she had new ways, new *whys* to ignore it. Maybe not to ignore, but to overcome. Her teammates and coaches were a new source of help there, along with a ton more from within.

"Wrestling is an escape for some people, and for me, that was my escape," she says. "One time where kids were a lot more decent to me, where I knew what I could do. I could prove to myself that, in spite of my height, my weight, my background, whatever people said was wrong with me, I was obviously right in something, because I was doing better than those who said I couldn't. Coaches from colleges started messaging me, telling me they wanted me on their team. It was amazing, because I didn't think I was that good."

Remember, for a long time, many couldn't conceive of even a handful of women on the wrestling mat, let alone enough to have an all-female team, and forget about an all-female tournament! But once these things started happening, the small snowball rolled down into a boulder, and it's getting bigger with every new signup and state sanctioning. And someday, if certain people come together and work as hard as the people we've met throughout this book, the same could happen for gals on the gridiron.

CHAPTER 11

The 2000s

"I wasn't that worried, but I didn't think it would be that easy."
—Sissy Lyle, after winning her second consecutive Pennsylvania girls
high school wrestling title, February 6, 2000. A senior at Ambridge
Area High, Lyle won three matches in a total of 79 seconds.

"I like to pin them fast so I can have more strength for the next match."
—Eastwood (Texas) High's Tressa Yocum, who finished the
season at 30–0, all pins, and took the 165-pound title in
2003-4 University Interscholastic League competition

Kent Bailo, founder, United States Girls Wrestling Association: "The gender issue is the idiot issue. When people say that the girls are being touched in inappropriate places, I would counter by saying that the boys are the ones being touched inappropriately. The idea is to gain control and maintain a pin. Nobody shakes hands on the mat to get a date for the prom."

As the new millennium arrived, numbers kept going up for lady matsters. By the start of the 2000-1 season, more than 3,000 women were competing on high school teams across the country, albeit many of them still in the few sanctioned states.

But when the Olympic ruling went mainstream, the news that they might get to wrestle in the global spotlight in just a few short years gave women a whole new incentive to try this "new" sport. Numbers started to explode. More and more women started making history. More and more whispers grew into public speech about not just women gearing up to face guys, but just maybe getting enough to spread co-ed competition past the exhibition ranks.

Keristen LaBelle, Michigan: "When you're out there and the referee raises your hand and the other guy's head is hanging down, that's the best feeling."

Enough stories to fill three or four of these books have been told of women in wrestling who took every chance to *not* boast of themselves or their accomplishments.

That's OK. Those are the ones who tend to last. Those who get into the sport to be seen as great (or even pretty good) *wrestlers*, not *women*, tend to stay longer.

And it's OK for them to downplay their importance. That's where authors like the one behind this piece—and the media, which I used to be a part of—come around.

"I think people are making way too big a deal over this," admits Keristen LaBelle. "It's good in a way because other girls will see this and say, 'Hey, I can do that.' But I'm not that special."

Yeah, others might disagree.

Like those she defeated in 50 wins in less than two years on Davison High, an accomplishment that won her recognition in *Sports Illustrated*, on CNN, and in an HBO documentary on the sport.

Or those whom she made history against in February 2000, when she pinned her way to victory in the school conference championships—the first girl in Michigan history to do so.

"Everybody was saying, 'Good job!'" she recalls. "That's when I thought, I just won the Big Nine." She'd qualify for the state meet the next month, but not place in the tournament. This wouldn't occur until 2009, when C. C. Weber notched fourth in the event. Weber, who never lost against females in state competition during her years at Goodrich High, went on to win national titles at Fargo and medal at the 2008 Junior Pan American Games.

Interestingly enough, 2000 ended up being a pretty lucky year for women who had to take an evening off from their mat career to trade their headgear for a Homecoming Queen crown. Holly Haritan, who went 29–0 her last two years and won a state title for Florida's Lyman High, snared the royalty honor, as did Shoni Plagmann of Oregon.

A few years before, Plagmann had been competing as a 13-year-old in the Oregon Wrestling Classic at Oregon State. She held down a woman seven years older to take the 104.5-pound title. At the same event, her mother, Vicky, won the open for ages 19 and above.

Breaking onto the Lebanon High squad in 1997, Plagmann grappled with a guy.

"Why don't you go home and make cookies?" he sneered in mid-lockup. In a just world or a Disney movie, she'd have hurled him to the mat and pinned him before he knew what the hell was happening.

That didn't happen; he still came out on top. But Plagmann got the last laugh. Accompanied by her teammates, she walked up to him afterward. Then she held up a cookie. Embarrassed, her opponent stormed away.

It wouldn't be until the next year that she'd win a varsity match, but she'd become the first area female to qualify for the Class 4A district tournament in February 2001. Two months later, she'd win a USGWA national title. Currently known as Shoni "Silent Fury" Esquiro, she went 2–2 in pro mixed martial arts competition in 2009–10.

> "Wrestling: Something Women Do During Girls' Volleyball Season"
> —Brandy Rosenbrock, Michigan, state titlist in 1999,
> won three national titles by the summer of 2001.
> Also national referee by age 16.

Jessi Shirley started the millennium the same way she'd finished the previous one: by winning.

Before she'd finished middle school, she'd won middle school tournaments and state events all over Ohio, racking up a 19–1 record and national ranking in eighth grade. Things kept going for her in high school, as she debuted with a pinfall win in her freshman year at Northmor High on the way to a 14–6 record, albeit with about half the wins coming by forfeit. This came along with two state titles in all-female competition at the Keystone Open in October 1999.

A shoulder injury kept her out for her sophomore year, but she came back strong in 2000, her second-place finish in junior level competition at the World Team Trials in Michigan winning her a spot on the Pan American team for the Games that summer.

Sadly, they'd never take place, as political unrest ravaged across South America, including the Games' host country of Peru. The next year, she'd finish up her high school career by becoming Ohio's first female winner of a district tourney match.

During her time at Northmor, Doug Blubaugh came by in the midst of working with another squad. Noticing Shirley doing her thing, he remarked that he wished his lineup had her drive and work ethic. Blubaugh happened to have won a gold medal at the 1960 Olympics.

Shirley scored a place on University of the Cumberlands's wrestling team alongside future Olympian Toccara Montgomery and overcame an early ACL tear to go to school mat warfare for years. Eventually, she'd come back to the Northmor area to coach her own daughters in the mat game.

Her sister was one of the first wrestlers in the family's Hawaii homeland history, winning state and national champs.

Her brother plays in the NFL.

But some might still call Lalelei Mata'afa the top athlete in her family, partly because she managed to pull off both games.

"I used to beat him on the beach wrestling," Lalelei remembers of her big bro.

Hercules was drafted to Minnesota in 2018 before switching to Washington in 2021. But the first NFL game he ever attended was as a kid in Indianapolis; that halftime, his sister took the 8–9 girls division of the league's Punt, Pass, & Kick nationals.

"I was fifth in the nation the year before," says Lalelei. "I trained better and won the

Lalelei Mata'afa celebrates one of her four Hawaii state titles. Not a single high school match even went the distance during Mata'afa's career. Provided by Lalelei Mata'afa.

whole thing. My strong point was passing. At eight, I threw about 30 yards. Later, I could hit 60 yards."

By then, like her big sister Lia, Lalelei had already hit the mat game. Unlike Lia, she was working with a state that had long since sanctioned wrestling.

"My whole family wrestled, and I started when I was four," says Lalelei, one of six siblings. "Polynesians and Samoans look older than their age, so I was able to be passed off as five years old. I made boys cry, and they don't like losing to girls, but there was no one disrespectful to the talent I had."

Long before she arrived at Lahainaluna High, Lalelei was already racking up AAU mat titles. Then she really made some serious history.

"I like the attack style of wrestling," she explains. "I like to make [my opponents] adjust to me. I'm not going to let them attack me and try to counter it. I like to throw them off, to go after it. I'd practice against the boys, doing attack style and making them adjust to me. I never got put into a situation that I couldn't get out of against girls. If a boy got me into a situation, I'd find a way to work out of it. I also had defensive weapons. If somebody took a shot at me, I was good with my hips and throwing them."

Her freshman year? State title.

Her sophomore year? Another.

People kept doing what they could to prepare. Trying to find some weaknesses to exploit. Somewhere.

Didn't happen.

"There was this one girl in my junior year, who'd been a judo state champion," she says. "She ended up being my finals opponent. My teammates were saying that this other girl was going to beat me, but I wasn't nervous. Just having the thought in the back of my mind that other people thought I was going to lose put fire under my butt, to show them that I was capable of still being there and retaining my crowd." Her third state crown took all of 28 seconds.

The next year, she became the school's first-ever student, gender irrelevant, to take four Hawaii titles. Not one female opponent even took her the distance.

"I'd wrestle boys and usually pin them too," she says, "but they gave me a harder match."

College took her to the University of Hawaii and away from wrestling. Off the mat, she was now in the water polo pool, a sport she'd also played at Lahainaluna.

"It was empowering to get into something and work towards something," she says. "My goal was always to do my best and put all the practice to work and get results. Wrestling is a great transition sport for the position that I play now in college: center at water polo. If you wrestle, it can translate to other sports. At my position, there's a lot of wrestling, trying to gain position. Through years of wrestling, and grappling, it's a little easier for me to hold on to someone and use it to get position."

Leigh Jaynes, New Jersey: "Women's wrestling has been recognized to a point where the Adeline Grays, the Victoria Anthonys, the Alli Ragans and myself, boys are wearing us on the back of their shirt, and that's something that hasn't happened in the past."

If wrestling didn't out and out save Leigh Jaynes's life, it sure as hell grabbed her existence by the lapels and hurled it in a straighter direction than it had ever been, and maybe ever would have been. If she'd said no to a person whose profession revolves around encouragement and instruction—and we know teenagers just *love* authority—no telling where or how things would have ended up for the Jersey gal.

From middle to high school, Jaynes was living in a Jersey group home. One of the leaders took the residential crowd on a rock-climbing trip, and noticed that she went at those mountains like they'd done everything wrong to her.

The sort of energy and emotion all too often becomes a hair trigger to trouble, but he just might have known a way to not remove, but utilize it.

He mentioned to Jaynes that he also coached the high school wrestling squad—and that she might want to come out and try it.

Unless, of course, she was scared.

Reverse psychology like that is an unsafe bet, but it worked here. Not that centering all that energy was especially *easy* off the bat.

"At first, I was running on adrenalin, just scared," recalls Jaynes, who knocked out an opponent's tooth in her first warmup. "I was wrestling boys, and I did not win a lot of matches my first year. At the end of the season, my coaches decided that I needed some more opportunities to wrestle women."

Then again, little had come easy for her.

"I was never the kind of kid that would be engaged in drugs or alcohol," Jaynes vows, "but a lot of people would come to my home, mainly guys. Me being young and naïve, I would entertain myself by talking to these people." One day, in the midst of a, shall we say, gathering, she started feeling ill.

Rushed to the hospital, her system turned up a shock—for anyone, let alone an 11-year-old.

"I'm back positive for barbiturates," she says. "I didn't even know what barbiturates were. I'd never even taken a puff of a cigarette." But they didn't believe her, albeit with a bit of reason. Her dad hadn't come back alone, on the inside, from Vietnam, and certain people just figured his issues were bleeding over. She became one of the youngest drug rehab program residents in American history.

"The first step was admitting that I had a problem," she says. "I'm brutally honest, so I don't have that gene that sugarcoats things. My only problem was that I was in a drug rehab program and I didn't do drugs." Figuring that the denial stage was just sticking around, counselors held her there for as long as they could. But when she kept insisting she was OK, Jaynes got sent to a different facility, certain people desperate to find a problem to solve.

"I was transferred to the psychiatric security ward," she says. "I cried the entire time I was there. I couldn't believe I was in this situation. Because of the constant tears, I was diagnosed with manic depression. To this day, I stand my ground. I'm not going to allow them to bully me into believing something."

Certain people deciding she'd be better in a group home than her own, Jaynes was left with some others in the unwanted world. If wrestling hadn't come around, it's tough to guess what might have happened, if much at all.

"Wrestling is a sport where you're always getting knocked out and you have to get right back up," she says. "I really think you take those losses and you go back to the drawing board and you figure it out, and I do believe that wrestling and training took my mind off the challenging circumstances in my life. It also helped me find ways to dust myself off, get back up again, and get my hand raised. I felt like wrestling was symbolically like my life at the time. I became addicted to the wrestling culture of the wrestling family and how hard it was to get my hand raised at the end of the day."

But many would have quit after the sort of first year she made it (or suffered) through.

Not a single win.

She was sent halfway across the country to compete in the national championships in Michigan—and if her losing season record hadn't ruined her confidence, that experience about obliterated it. At first.

Two matches in, Jaynes thought she was already done. She'd gotten whomped in both.

"I couldn't believe it," she remembers. "I was sitting in the hallway crying."

Then came a message—she'd been put into the wrong weight bracket. Back in action, she rolled to the top six in the country.

"Getting called back to the table was like my second lease on life," Jaynes recalls. "If I wasn't successful, there wasn't going to be a bailout plan. I had no one to come help me pay for cars or school or anything. I had to push harder because I knew that my life was at stake if I didn't."

The next summer, someone desperately wanted to take a chance on her. With little more than one bad year and one good tournament to show for it, Missouri Valley College hurled a scholarship straight into Jaynes's lap. To be fair, it was one of, quite literally, a handful of women wrestling-offering groups at the time, so pickings may not have been all that plentiful.

And her college wrestling career's start wasn't much stronger than that "way" back when. But in her sophomore year, another outside force strengthened her singlet focus.

Jaynes decided to try out Army basic training. The next year, she was enlisted.

"I made it all the way to captain," she proudly asserts. "Being the only female, or one of the only females, on a wrestling team helped me to understand guy culture. I was very well respected in the military because of my athleticism and my commitment to helping people to achieve their goals here. Nobody gets mad at the person on the team that can max out their PT test."

Right around the time the announcement finally came that women would get their shot at Olympic competition for the 2004 Games, Jaynes snared a spot at the U.S. Olympic Training Center.

One morning in May 2004, the first-ever women's trials kicked off. In the first such match in American history, Jaynes went to 136-pound battle with fellow Missouri Valley gal Tina Arns—and came out on top.

"But things didn't work out," she remembers. "I think I ended up going 3–2 and fifth place." Sadly, this would become a pattern for her.

One small technical error at the 2008 tryouts cost her a fourth-place loss to Jennifer Page. Then came the 2012 Games, which really makes you think that fate was working her over as hard as any mat opponent.

Arriving as the top seed at 121 pounds, Jaynes was ready to take it home. But her trek would end before the first match even started.

She missed weight—by all of *0.1 pounds.*

It might have been enough for Jaynes (who, to her credit, defeated Helen Maroulis twice and was ranked in the planet's top three in 2012). By the next year, she was a married mom. But as her little Evelyn started to grow up, Jaynes felt that wrestling allure start to call (at least) once again.

And her answers didn't seem to ring true.

"I lost all of my matches in 2014," she says. "Psychologically, I was having trouble believing that a 30-something-year-old mother could be capable of doing better than I had in my athletic drive. I wasn't sure I deserved it enough." At one of 2015's first tournaments, a coach stepped in to straighten her out.

"I had a coach say to me, 'Why not you? Why not now? Take out the fact that we don't know if you deserve this or not. Just say that the person who puts forth the best effort in the matches deserves to win.'" She ended up scoring a win against fellow Olympic trial competitor Sally Roberts.

Jaynes's fire was re-lit. Later that year in Las Vegas, she won a bronze medal.

Her fourth Olympic tryout ended short of the team, but Jaynes didn't lose all the way out there, either—she helped train Brazil's Joice Silva, who made her second Games appearance.

"Most girls from the U.S. Olympic team didn't want anything to do with me because I was really good," Jaynes says. "Nobody wants a training partner that if you get hurt they're going to go in and take your place. I was blacklisted from being a training partner to the U.S., but other countries found me useful. I felt that if I was going to go to the Olympics, going there to help the host country would be an amazing experience, and it was."

As any wrestler will tell you, some more openly than others, no one in their profession can have one without the other.

No victory without defeats along the way. No exultation without serious frustration. And no triumph without pain. Serious pain. Pain that doesn't go away, sometimes ever. Pain that undoubtedly makes some in the sport consider whether it was really all worth it.

The answer? Well, sometimes that depends on the day. Mostly, it's a strong yes. Usually. After a while, the injuries don't heal any further, and when something brings them back a few years after competition, things don't always seem so.

If we consider how Mary Kelly's on-mat career finished, the tale might not appear to have a happy ending. Checking it over as a whole, or examining what has happened since, that might be another matter.

"I grew up in an old-school kind of family mentality where if something hurt, you pushed through it," remembers Kelly, the next generation in a family full of wrestlers. "My dad still tells stories about how he won nationals with broken ribs. There can be a price to pay for those things, and you don't really know what that price is until later. You can't re-calculate how you would have done had you taken a break and let something recover and then come back. Would I have been more successful? Maybe I wouldn't have." Her uncle and father both won Illinois and national wrestling titles.

Her first bout with take-home suffering was about par for the course in early wrestling. Kelly's dad had *happened* to hear of wrestling pioneer Tricia Saunders putting on a clinic against future Olympic medalist Zeke Jones, and if Saunders could do it, why not his elementary-school-aged little lady?

Well, maybe a few reasons.

"My first day, showing up for practice," Kelly remembers, "I was feeling so awkward and out of place. I was looking at my mom, and she said, 'Get out there!' My first year of wrestling, I came home with at least five black eyes."

Eventually, as is typically the case in high school sports, the team changed (we didn't say evolved!) into the typical near-dysfunctional lot that most families, particularly those with several small siblings, become. As in, we'll torment you to our black hearts' content, but anyone else messes with you, and we're *all* coming down on them!

With the (*usually* eager) backing of her teammates and family, Kelly turned into one of the top area grapplers, going 67–2—by far the team's top record—in her seventh- and eighth-grade years.

Both losses came in state tournament competition.

"A real bummer!" she sadly recalls. However, in eighth grade, she did make a bit of state history after making it to the semifinals.

"I couldn't cry, but I also couldn't celebrate, because that would hurt the boys' ego more," she remembers. One win from the title match, though, she fell short, and the audience couldn't wait to rub it in deeper than third-degree mat burns.

"The crowd gave a standing ovation when the boy beat me," Kelly says. "I think they wanted to see me lose. When I came off the mat, my dad whispered in my ear that if I had to cry, to go to the back, to not give them the satisfaction. I was fine after he told me that, and I knew I had to refocus, because I still had another match." She took the advice, and then the third-place match, becoming the first female medalist in Illinois Elementary School Association competition.

Soon after that, her competition changed—and her audience expanded. *Greatly.*

It took over 20 years, but the Cadet World Championships finally found a place for women in 1998. Kelly took home a silver in 38-kilogram competition. The next year, buffed up to 43-kilogram battle by a weight-training program she'd snared from a local college football coach, she scored a gold.

"The first year I made the team, we had to pay a few thousand to go," she says. "My family was not well-to-do, but my parents spent all their extra money on getting me to tournaments and other training. My first year, we organized a Cowshit Bingo event, where we painted a hundred squares on the ground and let a cow walk around until it 'marked' a square. Every other year, USA Wrestling funded me."

Then it was back to Mahomet-Seymour High and co-ed competition. Four years, four varsity letters, one regional individual title, one team state title, and an overall 75–36 record.

Kelly headed far from home to continue her career, but Kansas's Neosho College dropped wrestling at the end of her freshman year. If only that would be anywhere near the biggest inconvenience she'd face.

Just before returning home to learn under her dad's tutelage at MacMurray College, she attempted to shake off a urinary tract infection on the way to Turkey for a tournament.

"I was having bad back pain, and I was really tired," Kelly remembers. "I thought it was because of increased practices and the time change. I was having cramps from my period, and my stomach started hurting real bad. I thought it was from brushing my teeth with the water. I took a ton of Pepto Bismol, so much that I thought I'd OD'ed."

She still managed to score bronze at the event, and made it back to the states. A few days later, future Olympic medalist Randi Miller walked into their dorm room.

Kelly was collapsed on the floor.

"I had drool coming out of my mouth," Kelly remembers. "All I could say was, 'Daddy, I'm dying.'" Rushed to the hospital, that infection she'd been fighting had battled back and nearly won. Her kidneys had been victimized, and were on the edge of failure. Another day out and about, and Kelly may not have made it.

As she was laid up for days on antibiotics, Kelly's weight dropped back into double digits. Her first (and, as it turned out, only, as she'd switch over to Northern Michigan for junior and senior seasons) year at MacMurray became an impromptu rehab, although it did culminate with a fourth-place finish in the 2004 Olympic trials.

After medaling at the World Team trials the next two years, Kelly could feel herself winding down, at least for the time being. Her unsuccessful foray at the 2008 Olympic trials had required neck cortisone shots, never a great indicator for athletes.

"I decided to give my body a break," she remembers. "I took a year off and coached, to see how I felt and if I missed wrestling." It took less than a year to realize that she absolutely did.

Her ailments seeming on at least a temporary fix, she rolled roared into the 2009 World Team Trials with little more than experience under her singlet—no training had been done. She notched fourth, kicking off a new round of practice and enthusiasm that spurred her right back to Worlds the next year.

And it seemed to be working, as she made it to the final match. As her opponent went for a takedown, Kelly felt a tweaking in her shoulder. A crash landing kicked the pain up about a *million* notches.

"I was screaming," she says. "I don't think the referee blew his whistle for a while. I remember wanting to desperately stop, but I didn't." She managed to get back to her feet, but her shoulder kept popping out, and she was forced into every wrestler's dirty distinction of an injury default.

"It took me about a month before I got an MRI," Kelly says. "I had two labrum tears, a torn tendon, and a torn ligament by my bicep." If losing a match for injury is tough on a wrestler, having a few weeks or months of time stolen away by one is almost insufferable.

"I went to rehab, but you feel like you're missing a lot," Kelly says. "You feel like everybody's getting better, faster. You want to get back on the mat." Over half a year later, she slowly made her way back to the mat, ready to make at least one more run back to the top, maybe even the 2012 Olympics.

And then came her painful coup de grâce.

In one of her first reentries into practice, Kelly was still worried about her shoulder. Even as she was being taken down, keeping it safe was on her mind.

Moments later, her mind wasn't focused on much; she'd been dropped almost straight onto her head.

"It was a couple of days before I said anything," she remembers. Her head ached like hell. She was dizzy half the time and bushed the other half.

Weeks later, the symptoms were still around. Then came months. Even longer.

"I had post-concussion syndrome for two years," she sadly estimates. "For those two years, if I tried to read too much or even have a conversation with someone, I'd feel exhausted. A five-minute conversation was like if I was taking the SAT. Sometimes my headaches would be mild, but if I was stressed or if I tried to exercise, it would get worse. It was getting to the point where I thought this might never end. I'd never have some sort of regular life."

But she did, albeit away from the mats for the final time.

"Eventually, I started to feel like I was coming out of it," she says. "One of the things that helped in that transition was just getting to take care of myself again. I didn't even think about the fact that I couldn't wrestle anymore." Eventually, she'd move to Hawaii and go into personal training. In 2019, she was inducted into the Illinois Wrestling Coaches and Officials Association Hall of Fame.

So, the bug that nearly killed her? The back and neck issues that still bother her once in a while? The two long years of fear, pain, and uncertainty? The price she paid for her time on the mat?

Was it too much, too high? If she had known that wrestling would follow her for so long, would she have changed her path?

No way. No way under the hot Hawaiian sun.

"Wrestling shaped and molded my whole life and gave me my greatest experiences," Kelly insists. "It helped support me in getting a great education. No way could my parents have afforded for me to go to college. I went to 15 different countries. I got to go to the Louvre and see historical landmarks, several multiple times. I got to see so much of the United States and what it has to offer. If I hadn't wrestled, I probably would have stayed home and been comfortable with that. Instead, I got to go to China and France and England. I got to live in Colorado and South Carolina and Kansas and northern Michigan, all these areas and different subcultures. I met the best people in the world, people that know struggles, know commitment, know integrity, and got to call them my friends."

Pella Wisniowski, Arkansas: "Wrestling was my body; when I lost it, I lost myself. Wrestlers are a whole different breed from any other sport. You hurt your knee, you dislocate your shoulder, you tape it up or pop it right back, and you go back in. You deal with the pain. I've had several different concussions, dislocated my shoulders, and still wrestled. My memory's not great."

As rough as Kelly's physical obstacles turned out, and are still turning, at least they didn't come around to much of a degree until after she'd solidified her spot in wrestling. Pella Wisniowski wasn't so lucky.

"I was around 152 or 160 in my freshman year of high school," recalls the Arkansas native. "I was against a guy who was 182. He snapped my leg forward and tore one of my muscles. I was out for a month or two." And even when she made it back to Conway High, Wisniowski, one of the few people on her squad with the guts to jump up a weight class once in a while, didn't fare very well by the halfway point of her high school career.

It was then or never, and, up to a point, she'd be making it on her own. Her teammates had their own careers, and coaches their other commitments. If she was going to move up in the sport, she'd have to take the first few (and more than a few) steps by herself.

"I wanted to take it to the next level," Wisniowski recalls. "I was doing two or three practices a day, running extra on the side, going to the weight room after practice. That's when I started to really get better. Going out on that mat, being calm and collected, being able to decipher my emotions, just to have something to control in my life, something that was mine for once, made me fall in love with it. I didn't have to rely on anyone else. It's a team sport when you look into it, but when you're on that mat, no one else matters but you and that opponent."

As her state hadn't yet sanctioned the sport, Wisniowski battled boys during the regular season, then squared off with women when school time ended.

"I dealt with a lot of slander from guys, guys telling me I shouldn't be on the mat," she says. "As soon as I stepped on the mat, as soon as I started winning, people started respecting me more, but I still had guys telling me they only let me win because I'm a girl. Their coaches would come up to me and tell me otherwise. When I would win my matches in general, it was a great feeling."

The summer before her senior year, Wisniowski, already a signee at Kansas's Central Christian College, became the first Arkansas lady to place at Fargo's Junior Nationals.

"I had to get out of my own head and stop thinking I wasn't good enough," she says. "I had some confidence issues, but I just said screw it—I win, I win. I lose, I lose. When I did that, the results showed. I know the only reason I placed in Fargo was all the work I put in."

Doug McGuire, Arkansas, state wrestling coach: "Pella wasn't extremely talented, but her work ethic was incredible, which is something you don't see a lot in wrestling. My boys didn't want to work with her, because she just worked that hard. She kept them busy and got on them for being lazy. [At Fargo], she'd already signed to wrestle in college, so she didn't have to do it. The first morning, she tells me, 'Coach, I'm placing here.' First match, she loses. If she loses another, she's done. Then she comes back and wins four in a row. That'll always be one of my favorite memories from coaching."

In March of 2018, she carried off the Arkansas female state title.

"Wrestling taught me not to give up," she says. "I was told to give up by other guys, that I'd never be a good wrestler. It was about pushing past what everyone thought [about] me and learning not to care. It was empowering to see that there were other girls wrestling guys."

At Central, though, those injuries she'd managed to hold off finally caught back up.

"I was weightlifting, squatting, and the bar slipped and hit my back," she says. "I dropped 215 pounds on my lower back, and my coach wouldn't let me take time off to go to the doctor. I found out that I had two bulging discs and arthritis in my spine. I decided that it wasn't best for me to be there."

Physicality wouldn't be her only lasting opponent, even after she finished on the mats.

"I've had several different concussions and still wrestled," Wisniowski says. "My memory's not great. I regret not taking care of my body, and not finding other things that I was interested in. Wrestling was my body, and when I lost it, I lost myself. Wrestlers are a whole different breed from any other sport. You hurt your knee, you dislocate your shoulder, you tape it up or pop it right back, and you go back in. You deal with the pain."

Someday, and hopefully someday soon, she'll be helping others with similar issues; Wisniowski hopes to become an ER physician.

And maybe for her, as for Kelly, all that suffering was worth it as well. Concussions, back injuries, these things tend to stick around for far too long, to a point, but Wisniowski feels it's better to remind herself of this, rather than running away. She's adorned with a tattoo of Dan Gable, a fellow who overcame it all for one of wrestling's most successful careers, but paid his own price, heading under the surgical knife multiple times since he called a competitive quitting.

"Wrestling was and is a part of me," she says, "and [the tattoo] helps me remember on the days when I can't do anything, that I've had worse times in my life."

Silvia Cortez, California: "If a girl is 112 pounds and a boy is 112 pounds, there should be no difference, and let the best wrestler win. I'd feel extremely ashamed if I couldn't beat someone my own weight. If some of them are jerks, I'll rub it in and tell them, 'Hey, you lost to a girl.' If they're upset, but nice about it, I'll try to talk to them about it and let them know it wasn't a fluke. I've worked hard to be able to beat some of the guys."

Over in California, Silvia Cortez had been perfecting the art of not losing.

Things had gone back and forth for the Hanford High student. After starting her mat career on the junior varsity squad, Cortez blasted off by winning a male tournament and rolled all the way to Most Valuable Wrestler at 112 pounds, then notching fourth at the 2001 nationals in Ohio.

Cortez didn't take long to impact the varsity, knocking off three male classmates to represent her team at 112. But not until her senior year did she, well, go insane.

Charging through the season, she took match after match after match, and the country started to take notice. Maybe there was someone who could beat this gal—but they weren't going to find her in the Golden State.

That became finalized at the state events on February 1, where Cortez finished an unbeaten season by slipping past Yesenia De La Mora, 3–0, her second victory over De La Mora in a few weeks. She competed in the first-ever all-female match at the California Interscholastic Foundation event in early March.

Now it was back to taking on America's finest at the United States Girls Wrestling Association High School championships the next month in Michigan.

That began with a pinfall of homeland heroine Heidi Haughn, then a 15–0 tech fall over Ohio's BreAnna Oswalt. Candice Pellerin of Florida gave her a closer fight, but Cortez took out a 3–0 victory.

Then Pennsylvania's Rachel Groft managed to do what no one else had accomplished since the season before. In the semis, she defeated Cortez, 3–1.

After winning so much, many might have been heavily affected by a loss, especially one so close to a national title during her senior year. Not Cortez; she came back with a 7–2 defeat of Leilani Akiyama of Washington.

For the bronze, her opponent was looking to make the third time a charm for third place. It was De La Mora (Groft fell to Hawaii's Caylene Valdez in the final).

The two fought through regulation 1–1. The first overtime ended the same way. But Cortez scored the tiebreaker in the second to cinch the win, and the medal.

> "[Wrestling] looked interesting and challenging, but the coach said, 'Girls shouldn't do it. They should play with dolls.' I took it as a challenge to prove him wrong. I don't play with dolls. It's the hardest sport, physically and mentally. You have to lift, run, watch what you eat, and work on your technique."
> —Sarah Peasley, Wisconsin, two-time USGWA champion, 2004-5

> "Last year, this kid cried when I beat him. It was my first match and my first pin. I didn't expect him to cry, but he did. It was a great feeling!"
> —Jenny Ryder, matster of Northeastern High (Ohio), December 2005

> "No, I don't want to be like her."
> —Lisa Maslowsky, February 2005, first female in Nebraska history to win a state meet match, after a reporter asked if she felt like Britney Spears

"I go to the [national] tournament every year. A bunch of girls there are in high school and some have wrestling varsity. I don't get to talk to them as much, but it's really cool to see that there are other girls out there doing this."

—Sarah Dorsay, who won the 2006 New Jersey state high school title as an eighth-grader, one of three state titles, and seven-time USGWA national titlist

"I never suspected freshman year that I'd come this far. Oh my God, I came to practice, and I was so nervous that first day."

—Ana Hernandez, two-time New Jersey USGWA state champion, 2004-5

"I figured if I would lift his head a little more, [the official] would call a pin. It feels good. I hope it encourages younger girls to go out and try their best."

—Sammie Gonzalez, February 2008, first female in Kansas history to win a state meet match

"This was a dream come true for me. I hope this inspires other girls to do the same thing. I like what I'm doing. I want to keep going and try to get better. I just wish I could have gotten a couple of takedowns when I had the chance. I missed a few chances early, and that pretty much changed the whole match for me."

—Elissa Reinsma, March 2009, first Minnesota female to compete in a state tourney match

The year before Texas gave its official OK for women across the state to go to battle, Scott Tankersley was asked to expand his coaching arsenal.

"We had to have a full team or not have it happen at all," recalls Tankersley, already leading Caprock High's basketball and baseball squads. "We called a meeting in the gym the next Thursday. We were looking for troublemakers, tough girls if you will." Expecting a few, he was floored by the 20-plus turnout.

Were they there to go to war? Maybe. But even if so, these looked like the type of ladies who were used to roaring into battle without much regard for rules. Long baggy pants, opened-button shirts ... if the dictionary wanted a photographic representation of the term *chola* (officially a young woman belonging to a Mexican American subculture close with street gangs), this could be a group shot.

"Looking at this group, this unique group of girls," Tankersley remembers, "I could teach them." Things started as smoothly as such a situation could hope for.

Then the principal called. Some students had heard about the program, and wanted to join. Problem was, past fisticuff action had kept them from campus.

The coach immediately agreed. One of the women in question would take a state title that year.

"I caught a lot of flak in the school because they didn't like that I had started the program," Tankersley recalls. "Other coaches, parents, people in community were giving me dirty looks. At a regional tournament, people got up and left the gym while the girls were wrestling. Another coach's wife approached me and said, 'You're an embarrassment to yourself.' I got comments like that all the time. But I didn't care; people just couldn't see beyond their noses."

With the help of Toni Adams, who'd nearly win a spot on the 2004 and 2008 Olympic squads, Caprock won the 2000 state title, just a year into "sanction-ship."

Four years later, the Lady Longhorns would kick off a streak of *nine* consecutive such championships.

"We went 104–2 over seven years," Tankersley says. "We went to eight tournaments every year for six years and won them all."

Maci Alvarado, state champ: "I first got into wrestling when I was approached by the greatest coach ever, Scott Tankersley. He approached me at track practice and told me I should give wrestling a shot. I was in eighth grade at the time, invested in basketball, but gave it a shot and the rest is history.

I stayed with wrestling for so long because I loved it. I loved the discipline, the structure, and most of all, the energy. The most memorable moments were the tournaments. We from Caprock would walk in and the other teams knew they didn't stand a chance. Our camaraderie was great, and I loved my coaches. At the time, I hated the conditioning, but it was definitely worth it. I honestly don't have many bad memories.

Away from the mat, it pushed me to do better. I graduated because of it. I've made a lot of mistakes in life, but I've learned never to give up. The structure and discipline was something I was looking for. To keep wrestling, I had to be on time. I had to focus. I had to gain the stamina to last. It was real work.

Wrestling is both a team sport and one-man team. You can advance alone and with a team. Overall, you want everyone to do good. We're a family in practice. We struggle together, we learn together, and we overcome together.

It was the duel that gave me so much energy, knowing that I had what it took to win because our coaches instilled in us tenacity and the drive to succeed. They taught us the tools and techniques we needed to win. Some of my top accomplishments were the wins, of course, but also the capacity to know I gave my all.

My mistake was trying to take the easy way out. Instead of following all the hard work and goals I worked toward, I fell into a crowd. I ended up selling drugs. I caught two [charges for] organized crime, three manufacturing, and two possessions with intent to deliver. I did six years flat on 20 and made parole.

I was on my way to my parole class and got pulled over for speeding. My best friend's gun was locked in the console. I got four years. So I'm [incarcerated] on parole violation. When I get out, I'll renew my license for massage therapy so I can work. I will work hard and dedicate my time and effort to my boys. The traits I learned in wrestling are perseverance and dedication. Basic structure keeps you in check mentally and emotionally, so I can stay strong and accomplish the goals I set for me and my family."

Before the Caprock roll began, Casey Brittain helped Palo Duro High to the 2001 championship.

"I was always tomboyish and scrappy," she recalls. "I had two older sisters, and I was always being picked on. I wanted to go slam girls where it would be OK. I was always kind of mean, and I thought it would be fun."

After hearing about certain people *trying* to get the sport sanctioned since before she'd even started at Palo Duro, it finally came true for her, and Brittain didn't waste time, making it to the state tourneys her junior year.

"Then I got a knee injury," she says. "I remember bawling and crying, and my dad saying that I had to get it. I got fourth."

The next year, she didn't lose. Not during the regular season, which included a team win over Caprock. And not during the state event, which her team won. With a win over future Olympic medalist Randi Miller, Brittain took the 165-pound championship.

"It was a while before we left the gym," she says. "We got to strut around school like we were tough stuff. I could have gone to the Olympics, but I didn't want to leave my family. I was more intimidated, didn't want to leave my boyfriend, shoulda, coulda, woulda."

Far too much of Amberlee Ebert's early wrestling career was "not quite."

Getting to Wisconsin Interscholastic Athletic Association's Division III sectionals for Wisconsin's Reedsville High in 2003–4, but not quite winning much there.

Scoring third in 152-pound competition in the 2005 USGWA

Amarillo's Palo Duro High set a state point record in 2001, winning both the Texas and national title. Photograph provided by Steve Nelson.

Nationals in March 2005, but not quite enough to reach the title match, and not as high as fellow stateswoman Sarah Peasley, who took the 126-pound title.

Not winning the Senior Nationals in Vegas. Making it to the 148-pound title match in the Asics USA Wrestling Nationals the following August, then falling to Ohio's Vanessa Oswalt to score the silver. Some losses, however, end up mattering in a different way.

About eight months later, things finally turned around for Ebert—all the way. Back in USGWA tourney competition in Michigan, Ebert scored a comeback win over Texas's Lindsey Brooks, then an even closer victory from Ashley Westman of New York.

The next day, her first pin of the event came before the end of the second period, holding down Ohio's Sara English. But the performance that not only convinced the USGWA crowd that she deserved not just the tourney crown, but the top national ranking she'd already earned came in the final, when she roared over California's Teri Milkoff 12–1.

Then things moved up. While Ebert hadn't won in the two Nationals events, her performances there scored her a spot on the 2007 Junior Pan American team. In July 2007, she'd make her international debut in Venezuela.

She rolled out pretty smoothly in 67-kilogram battle, pinning Dominican Yoheidi Solano and roaring past Anibel Diaz of Venezuela 6–0, 5–0. Against Canada's Erica Wiebe, however, she almost hit a fatal stoppage.

Early in a career that would take her to a 2016 Olympic gold, Wiebe won the first round 1–1 on riding time.

"I was so nervous that first match," Ebert remembers. "After the first period, I thought, 'I really want this.' That's when I stepped it up." She tied things up in the second, and slipped away for a 3–0 shutout to take the gold. The win helped her squad take first overall in the event.

"I don't think I'm ready for [international competition] now," she says. "Usually, I think about my coach and my team, but there it felt like so much more. It felt like I was supporting my country."

In April 2008 in Oklahoma City, an early mistake nearly kept Ebert, now studying at Missouri Valley College, from the Olympic tryouts. As she battled Oklahoma City's Ashley Sword in the Women's College Wrestling Association Freestyle National Championships, Sword suddenly gunned Ebert straight onto Ebert's back. Sword, who had split with Ebert in their previous four career meetings, went for a pin, but Ebert managed to maneuver outside the ring for a restart.

"She threw me right in front of my coach and teammates," Ebert recalls. "I'm on the mat looking at them on my back going, 'Oh my gosh, I'm going to lose.' I saw that my friends were yelling at me, 'Scoot out!' Once I was in that second round, I knew I got it." Not right away; it took a takedown with 15 seconds left for her to escape with the 147.5-pound title and the berth in the Olympic tryouts the following June.

"I would love to be in the Olympics someday," says Ebert, who ultimately did not make the team, "but I just want to see how far I can get. It's not like I *have* to go to the Olympics. I love the sport, but it's not my first priority in my life."

"She's got it in her heart," one of Tia Forrester's opponents said of the Georgia mat woman. A legitimate compliment of course, especially from someone who'd become one of the few to defeat her, but also inadvertently prophetic.

Moving arguably farther than any other lady in the Peach State (and most of the males), winning more than 150 matches during four years at Buford High and four appearances at the state tournament weren't Forrester's toughest accomplishments. Fortunately, they were the ones she was old enough to remember.

As "un-tough" as Forrester may have seemed (pre-match, of course), at just over five feet tall and 103 pounds, that was 100 heavier than she'd been at birth. Showing up three months early tends to have that effect.

She'd survived a serious intestinal blockage and two major surgeries that kept her in the hospital more than out over her first year. And, yes, a serious heart murmur. So many different things that could have taken her before she was even old enough to walk, let alone go for a takedown.

Even if she'd never know about it all, wrestling with both boys and sexism—still too alive in Georgia, a state that boasted fewer than 200 female wrestlers during Forrester's high school years—was one hell of a lot simpler.

Just before a 2007 mat battle, Forrester's opponent slunk up to her. Maybe to wish her good luck. Maybe to psych her out.

Or maybe to almost beg her—his daddy had offered him a c-note if he won.

Not good enough. She took him down and pinned him. And the dough stayed in pappy's pocket. Then there was the guy who lost to her in a tournament and never wrestled again. And then there was a whole team that battled her off—or tried.

"One school would not allow their kid to wrestle me for two or three years, they said for religious reasons," she remembers. "Then it was the finals of a big tournament, and they suddenly decided he could wrestle me. I beat him; I was not about to lose after all that." Forrester became the first Georgia gal to make it to state competition all four years of high school.

"I was actually thinking about playing football," she says. "They said, 'No, you're too good of a wrestler. We don't want you to get hurt!'"

Sadly enough, she even experienced the other side of sexism, or saw others suffer because of it.

"A girl will come up to me and say, 'I want to wrestle like you,'" she says. "But then her parents will be like, 'No, you don't want to do that.' I say to let them do what they want to do. Parents and girls are too scared of what other people will say about them."

"There's certain people that think just because I wrestle, I want to be a guy," says Forrester, who'd eventually move to wrestle at Cumberlands. "That's not how it is. I can be as much of a girl outside of wrestling as any other girl out there. But when I'm on the mat, that's all I'm thinking about."

> "I'm at a high level for my age, but I don't like to think that I'm better than everybody. I want girls wrestling to blow up, and me being here encourages young girls to keep wrestling."
>
> —Tatiana Padilla, 2008 California
> girls state wrestling champion

As liberal as California has always been, it's kind of a surprise that it took the state so long to sanction female wrestling. Granted, the Golden State was just the fourth to do so, but it still took until 2011—over a decade after Hawaii and Texas broke the ground—to establish itself as a new cornerstone for female wrestling.

For certain people, however, sanctioning was just a word. When a wrestler's on the mat, terminology like official and unofficial don't matter too much. If a wrestler's mindset is, "I'm not going to try my best, because this event isn't of formal enough levels!" she's not going to do much.

Even before California did the sanctioning, it had already established the nation's top individual tournament, as hundreds of local ladies descended on the Hanford West High Event Center for the third annual California Girls Invitational in early February 2008.

Almost two weeks before, Gaby Corona-Zamarripa had warmed up for States by pinning four opponents at the Southern California Regional.

"It's not just about going out there and winning," said the Hanford West High senior, who'd only grabbed up wrestling during her freshman year, "but about achieving your goals…. I feel like I have seniority over other girls, more mat time."

Recovering from a badly broken leg in her sophomore year and a rough outing in a junior year in which she didn't place at states, Corona-Zamarripa made it to the 146-pound final against Brittany David, coming off her own regional title.

The wrestlers fought through a scoreless first period, but Corona-Zamarripa nearly ended things early in the second, planting David for a near-pin and 3–0 lead. But David grabbed the momentum and almost the match in the third, pulling out two takedowns for a 4–3 lead.

If David had been a little less aggressive with her crossface, she might have finished on top. But the officials ruled she'd struck too hard, handing Corona-Zamarripa a penalty point.

Overtime started the same way the match had, with the two squaring off all over the mat. Corona-Zamarripa appeared to finish on top, but the referees did not automatically give a point, and David rolled her over.

Corona-Zamarripa's side launched a protest, and officials conferred. Then they ruled that she had scored the deciding points and declared her the winner.

"Everything paid off for me," said an emotional Corona-Zamarripa. "This is what I've been waiting for. It just came down to who wanted it more."

If her career had only convinced *most* Californians to sanction female wrestling in the state, Amanda Hendey's did the rest at high volume. After nearly taking the state title as a Beaumont High sophomore in 2009, she did so the next two years, along with helping her state to a dual teams title at the 2010 USAW's Junior Folkstyle Nationals in Oklahoma. The next March, she gave Oklahoma City University a preview of (they expected) coming attractions, winning a national folkstyle title, pinning both opponents without allowing a point.

Just before her Beaumont career ended, Hendey scored a silver medal at the 2011 Pan American Games in Colombia. After starting off at OCU, she switched to King University, helping the school to several national titles and scoring the 2015 U.S. Open title.

Injuries and hypothyroidism derailed her shots at the 2012 and 2016 Olympic squads. But she might not be done.

"I tore my left ACL twice and my right ACL once," says Hendey, who became an assistant coach at Colorado Mesa University in August 2021. "Because they postponed the Games, I could have tried out, but the issue I ran into was a stable training place. They kicked everyone out of the Colorado training center because of Covid. In California, they were shutting everything down, I was working out in random people's garages to work on my strength and conditioning. It proved to be too hard to make anything happen. There have been numerous times when I had a plan, and I was disappointed and heartbroken. Right now, I'm not trying to tell myself that I'm training for the 2024 Olympics, even though in my mind that's the track. I know that if I show up healthy, that I have a chance to make it, but I'm trying not to think about that, and focusing on the next steps: getting into competition shape, competing again, maintaining the integrity of my knees."

The sonofabitch never could have seen it coming.

Before he'd hardly moved, she'd caught him in a chicken wing, his hands behind his back like a jailer's manacles. She'd braved football gridirons earlier in high school, and this wasn't all that different. Maybe even easier.

Now he was caught, and he wasn't getting away.

But this guy could only *wish* that an official was there to slap the mat or break it up. He wouldn't be lucky enough to stride off the mat, *only* seeing her hand raised. Then there would be rules.

But there were no rules here. He'd already broken some, and tried to break some more, and this was far from a wrestling mat. Even if his opponent's tactics were similar.

"I was driving, with my Nana in the passenger seat," remembers Brittany Delgado of the August 2011 incident. Her sister Brieana sat behind them.

The Delgados had cheered each other on throughout wrestling careers that had started in elementary school. Well, for them; their dad and brothers had been on the mats before that. Both had rooted their way through middle school, high school, and, starting the next season for Brieana, college. This day, however, would be a bit different. As in, even more wild than any of the hundreds of matches the two had sloughed though.

As Brittany made her way through northbound traffic in Oklahoma City, a driver made an illegal left turn right in front of her. Brittany's front met his side, and her car went careening off into a stop sign.

She and her sister weren't hurt, just shaken up a bit. And their grandmother seemed OK, but our elders need a little extra consideration in times like this.

As the Delgados tended to her, the other driver stood nearby, looking like he might actually do the right thing.

Then he took off running. Doubtful he'd get away with his wrecked car there for identification, but panic can take over at times like this.

Fortunately, so can instinct. And the sisters had those to the hardest core.

After just a few quick steps, Brieana had the guy on the ground. Many opponents had given her a tougher time than this impromptu bout.

As she planted his hands behind him, Brittany "helped" them both up, then maneuvered them back to the scene. Officers arrived quickly, fighting off smiles and snickers at this guy's misfortune. Then residents poured out of a nearby apartment complex, detailing what had just occurred. Not long after, the incident had gone viral.

The driver went to the hospital, then to jail. And all three Delgados were just fine.

They didn't know it at this point, but the next year, the sisters would have their only season together on the Oklahoma City University squad that would take its fourth straight Women's Collegiate Wrestling Association (WCWA) title.

"I have always been a rambunctious, physical person," Brittany admits. "That was never *not* the case. I was a three-year-old, watching my four-year-old brother out there rolling around having a good time, and I was just supposed to sit there? I was going stir crazy just sitting there."

Heading a state north from their South Carolina homeland for a tournament, Brittany finally saw another lady in a singlet.

"I went to my mom and said, 'See, Mom! Girls *do* wrestle.' She said, 'OK, you can wrestle, but once you start, you can't quit until the end of the season.'" That commitment would last for decades. Not long after, Brieana would begin her own.

"I got good and met some really cool people," Brittany says. "I was winning, getting shiny trophies." In one tourney, she stepped onto the mat with none other than Reid Fliehr, whom pro wrestling fans will recognize as the son of squared circle legend Ric. Delgado won.

Not until she was about to roll into middle school did Brittany actually get to battle someone of her own gender. Two of her opponents were none other than Nicole Woody and Helen Maroulis.

"I was a hundred-something pounds," Brittany says. "They were 75- or 80-something. But they just put us all together and had us wrestle each other."

That rambunctious physicality she mentioned earlier started to grow. It began to focus. And once in a while, it got out of control.

"I was in middle school before I leveled out and focused into the type of wrestler I wanted to be," Delgado says. "I was pure fire and explosion, and that included my temper." At a tournament, one win stood between her and an All-American honor in wrestling.

Then came the sort of subtle discrimination that she'd seen before. Something that almost every female wrestler has felt and seen at some point.

"The official didn't think that girls should be wrestling boys," she says. "I had two back-to-back three-point throws, and the official gave the points to my opponent, and he tech-falled me. He told my coach, who he didn't realize was my dad, that girls don't belong on the mat." When she happened to run into the ref the next day, diplomacy flew out the window.

"I might have lost my temper and said some choice things," Delgado says, *might* being a questionable way to put it. "I cursed out the official." A guy named Archie Randall informed her that she wouldn't be wrestling there again. But the two would eventually even up.

At Simpsonville's Hillcrest High, both sisters would win national freestyling titles and roll to All-American honors. Brittany took a Junior National Duals title and some events in Fargo, her two-years-younger sister a Pan Am championship.

And someone was watching. Someone who knew what to look for. Someone who remembered a certain showing of extreme emotion, and recognized that it might just become Brittany's asset if he, and eventually they, could reach out and adjust its focus just a bit.

"I saw you at nationals," said the voice on the other end of the phone. "You were a whole different wrestler. I saw how much you've grown as a wrestler."

Two years before, Randall had kicked off the male wrestling program at Oklahoma City University and finished things in the national rankings. The very next year, the OCU women's squad debuted at second place in America, losing the WCWA title to the University of the Cumberlands by a single point.

Sounded like the perfect landing spot for the recent Simpsonville grad. Once there, however, Delgado found there to be quite a difference between battling women once in a while at a tournament and being part of an all-lady squad.

Brittany Delgado: "I didn't know how to function, because it was so dynamically different than being on a guys' team. On a dudes' team, you get mad, you wrestle it out, you go about your day and all is solved. But with girls' teams, I was introduced to grudges. It was a whole new dynamic. I was not ready for that at all. The wrestling was the easy part. It was the social dynamic that was hard for me, to be a part of a team that was nothing but celebrities. A year before that, the USWA had put out all-star posters. A lot of girls on the posters were in the same room as me. You go from being a powerhouse to being just another person when you're in a room like that. Being on a guys' team, I was one of the guys, and now I wasn't. The girls valued me as an athlete, but not necessarily as a teammate. It was difficult to adjust to doing stuff with the team and being accepted. If I demolished my wrestling partner in the wrestling room, that partner would hold it against you to get back at you, which I had never experienced on a guys' team."

She adjusted, charging to a 24–5 record and third in the nation. With Michaela Hutchison, who'd just made history by becoming the first lady in American history to win a high school state title back in Alaska, helming the squad, the Lady Stars took the 2009 WCWA title, roaring past Cumberlands by 31 points in the final.

"My freshman year, I suffered a wrist injury," Delgado says. "They thought about red-shirting me. My teammates called me Hellboy, because I had separated the tendon from my wrist. I couldn't turn a doorknob. I ended up having surgery on it. They had me in a cast, and the coach would wrap it in bubble wrap. It made my arm look like a club, so disproportionate."

Soon, the team would grow into a juggernaut. And the addition of a certain someone became icing on the cake for both Delgado and her team.

After nine World Championship medals, nine U.S. Open championships, and enough other accomplishments to fill a book longer than this one, Kristie Davis showed up in Oklahoma City (to be fair, she was from Mustang, just 20 minutes southeast).

"My biggest thing was having Kristie Davis as wrestling partner, both as a mentor and a friend," Delgado says. "She really pushed me to be a better athlete."

Early in the 2009–10 season, Delgado sent a message to the rest of the WCWA by holding down Lindenwood's Evanie Paulett in all of eight seconds. Less-than-a-minute matches would become a trademark for her college career.

The next spring, she, Hutchison, Amberle Montgomery, and Stephanie Waters took national titles, OCU's 124 score well above Cumberlands' 76. And Davis debuted alongside her in title-hood in 2011. One year before qualifying for the 2012 Olympic trials, Nicole Woody rocked her own championship, as did Ashley Hudson while the Lady Stars made the third title a charm, the first three-peating college women's squad to do so.

A few months after the Delgados performed their infamously impromptu law enforcement act, it was back to OCU action, together for the first time. The results wouldn't change.

"We were wrestling at Missouri Valley," Delgado recalls. "Everyone was like 'Beat OCU!' and 'Beat Brittany!' because I hadn't lost in two seasons." But the unthinkable appeared near.

"I get tossed out of bounds, and the whole stadium goes crazy," she remembers. "Everyone was like, 'Ooh, Brittany's gonna lose!' *Right.* I get up laughing. Archie looks like me, like 'Dammit, Delgado!' I was like, 'Don't worry, Coach. I got this.' Two seconds later, I tossed the girl and pinned her." Her 100th win and third national title (along with OCU's fourth) arrived that year, with Brieana notching fourth at 130 pounds. Brittany would finish her entire college career without ever getting pinned.

Kiaya Van Scoyoc, Washington: "I've never met a woman who wrestled for more than a season or two and said she hated it and would never do it again. Every person I've wrestled, even those who weren't athletes, said that wrestling was the best thing. It challenged them and made them grow in a way that other sports couldn't push you towards. It gave them a sense of accomplishment that they'd never felt before."

A few years later, one of the Delgados' colleagues happened to be in the right place at the right time for people who needed it.

Some gifts that wrestling gives never go away, not in totality. Like the guts to do the right thing just because it's right, and to never shy away from the hardest works. Even, as we've already seen, those without rules or referees. Even years after she was bringing national wrestling titles home to Washington state, Kiaya Van Scoyoc still carried these things on.

And on September 5, 2021, they may have, to a point, meant the difference to someone's health and life.

On the way to a friend's house with her fiancé, Van Scoyoc glanced down the road and saw a group of cars swerving all over the lanes, like something large and dangerous had fallen in the midst of the street.

A man emerged, bolting down the middle of the lanes, seemingly trying to get to the side. OK, maybe he was just trying to keep from meeting a car head on.

Then Van Scoyoc saw something else, and the evening atmosphere darkened. Fast.

On the very side the man was looking for, a young woman was running herself—and it appeared not in fear of the vehicles.

"It was like watching a scary movie," Van Scoyoc remembers. "Someone is running and keeps looking back fearfully. Is he following me? It was obvious that she wasn't OK." She managed to pull up next to the lady.

No time for banter here. The young girl blurted that the man was after her. He'd already come after her and her friends. He'd touched her. He'd told her what he wanted to do to her. He'd done shit that many people feel should warrant castration as punishment.

"I instinctively told her to get into my car," Van Scoyoc says. "By the time she did, the guy was on the other side." But the girl wasn't alone; two of her friends were on the other side of the street, and the guy was after them as well.

After one of the most impromptu U-turns in driving history, Van Scoyoc and her man had grabbed all three women. But the man wasn't giving up.

"He came up to the side my fiancé was in," Van Scoyoc says. "We told him to get away."

"Just give me one of them!" pleaded the dirtbag. "I just want one!"

That did it. That pushed things up a notch. Running away wasn't going to get rid of this guy.

Van Scoyoc's fiancé stepped out of the car. The jerk may have managed to avoid the cars, but an oncoming fist moved too quickly for him.

With him safely toppled into a nearby ditch, the group finally took off, soon on the line with the cops. About 15 minutes later, the guy was in cuffs and off to booking.

"Thankfully, I'm the most aggressive driver, so [my fiancé] wouldn't have been able to do that," Van Scoyoc claims. "But he's the more aggressive puncher, so it all worked out."

The local contact sport scene had been getting a taste of Van Scoyoc's aggression since long before she'd put on the headgear.

"I had a black belt in judo, which is a sport I'd still be doing if I weren't so busy," she remembers. "It's really brutal and hard."

She tried something new in her farewell middle school tour, becoming the only lady in the league. But when she got to Lakes High and went 30–0 on the mats in her freshman year, it was clear that this was no fluke occurrence.

"Wrestling is such a unique sport in a way that you are in control," she explains. "It's such an intense sport that when you're out there in a circle, it's a fight, a battle. Women, in my opinion, excel under pressure. Some of their best moments are under pressure. I remember certain matches, like the nationals, when I'm in the spotlight, with people all around. That was an immense amount of pressure. In the sport of wrestling, women are strong, malleable, flexible. We learn quick."

Some, however, weren't all that anxious to learn, as Van Scoyoc herself found during her undefeated sophomore season.

"I went around to all my friends and got a handful of people to come out," she remembers. "The biggest question I'd be asked was, 'Are there other girls?' My dad was asking the same question, because I was a 160-pound girl, not nearly as strong as a boy at that age. Boys are filling out with all their muscles, and we're filling out in different areas—not muscles! It was a big concern for our friends and parents. I was able to say, 'You won't be up against boys.' As more women joined the sport, it attracted more women."

After sweeping her way through Lakes and the rest of Washington in 2011–2, Van Scoyoc finally lost a match—in the finals of national competition.

"I won the state championship, but it wasn't my proudest moment," she remembers. "I was totally not as good as I should have been. I was just throwing people. I was sneaking up on people, throwing, and winning. Everybody found out that I was a thrower, so for the next two years, I wasn't able to sneak up on people. [My state accomplishments] were practice, because I wasn't ready to bring my best to the table."

So she adapted and improved. In 2013, Van Scoyoc finally won a national title at 172 pounds. The next year, she bumped up to 198 and grabbed another.

"I was supposed to be at 172, but I waited too long to cut weight," she remembers. "I was so dehydrated. That's where judo prepared me: a lot of fitness, and size doesn't matter. The way that throws are designed, you're supposed to throw somebody, no matter their weight. You change your technique and your position. Wrestling bigger girls, I didn't notice the difference, except that I was shorter. These girls weren't fat, but they were tall."

She roared out of Lakes and, scholarship in hand, towards Oregon's Warner Pacific University. But around then, another issue arose, one that's become the wrong type of tradition for too many matsters (probably more for women, but some for men).

"I had bulimia really bad, and no one knew," Van Scoyoc admits. "I had struggled with it in high school. I didn't *know* I was struggling; I thought I was just doing what I had to do. When I got to college, I was around other young women, and I saw them doing what I was doing. It made me not like what I was doing to my body, and I didn't want to live a life like that. I had to figure out a way out, because that's such a bad way to live. I wrestled my first year and almost all of my second year, but I had an awakening in my second year, and I had to step away. I didn't get to finish my college experience, but I think it was for the better."

> "Sometimes they throw their headgear down. And sometimes they don't shake hands."
>
> —Savannah Fitzgerald (Virginia), 2009–10 Southern Valley District champion, on males' reaction to her

Sometimes, being prepared isn't enough. Even if you know exactly what your opponent is about to try, you can't always be prepared for it. She might just be too strong to stop, too fast, too intent, too anything. Maybe she's just worked too hard to turn back, or be turned back now. It's just her story now.

After four years of helping set the work ethic standard at Virginia's Fort Defiance High, Savannah Fitzgerald kept losing at or near the top of the Southern Valley District. In 2008-9, she'd been content with becoming one of the first ladies in Old Dominion history to get to regional competition in her junior year.

Rolling into the last weeks of her wrestling career, Fitzgerald banged out an 11–6 record, by far her most successful season. On January 16, 2010, she quickly added three wins to the higher column, only one of which went to the second period.

For the finals of the 21st annual News Leader Wrestling Tournament at Fort Defiance High, she battled it out with Waynesboro's Connor Jarvis. After nearly two full periods, things had gone back and forth. Then, literally in the last seconds, she managed to strap a half nelson across his neck and shoulders and rolled him backward. With a single second to go, the ref slapped the mat in her favor.

"I've been in [the tournament] for four years," she said afterward. "I'm just happy to be the champion." But there was one more thing.

And it came a few weeks later in front of her home school.

Right back in the 112-pound finals, on the brink of state and personal history, she took on Rockbridge County's Jake Ailstock, responsible for two of her previous losses. Starting off the second period, both competitors looked for an advantage. Locking up, Fitzgerald reached down to grab his leg, then pushed forward into an ankle pick. As Ailstock fell backward, just as she had all season, Fitzgerald snared another half nelson. Less than 30 seconds in, she was the champ.

"I was just trying to do my best," she said.

For years back in Texas, Anthony Carter waited and waited for women to come out to wrestle.

Of course, this didn't mean that the Hanks High coach would know exactly what to do about it if they did.

"We'd have girls who wanted to come out for wrestling," he remembers. "It was boys versus boys, and I would welcome them, but they needed to bring a training partner. They wouldn't last. Some looked to do it just to get noticed." When Texas's sanctioning came through and gals' numbers across the state started to skyrocket, however, things changed.

"I told them to bring practice partners," Carter says. "They did! I had eight girls show up. I went to the principal, saying, 'I don't know I how I feel about this.' She said, 'Either you welcome the girls or get rid of the boys!' I said, 'Welcome, girls.'"

Shania Villalba, Texas: "I hated wrestling, hated fighting, hated confrontation, I'm 5'2", so how could I play basketball and get a scholarship? My stepdad, uncle, and father wrestled. I joined wrestling because I knew I had it in my blood. There were some wrestlers that worked out twice as hard as me, put in all their effort, but they would pray before wrestling me on the mat. I was dominating. I knew what to do. I could have put in all the effort, but I didn't feel like I had to, because I was so good at it. It just came natural to me.

I thought about quitting after freshman year. I weighed 99, then down to 95. I didn't want to lose weight and work out any more. I did not go to state. I didn't get anywhere my freshman year. I quit for two weeks, and I felt so bored. There I go, running back to Coach Carter to allow me back. He said, 'You can come back, but you will not have your varsity spot. You'll have a wrestle-off for it at the next event we have.' But he didn't keep his word; I was on the varsity squad as soon as I came back. But it definitely was a wakeup call.

I was runner-up in state my sophomore year in 2015. My junior year, I was ready to go through everything. I think I lost twice during the year.

In my junior year, my final wrestling match was crazy. [My opponent] goes in and takes me down, and somehow my headgear gets on top of my eyes. Coach Carter taught us to bring in a sock, a bandana, a headband, something to cover our eyes. We wrestled blindfolded the whole week to know the feeling of the moves. Not to see it, but the action, the push, the pull, what's going to happen if I do *this*. I love that he did that for us. My opponent was running me in a circle, but I was in a really firm base, and I just kept telling myself, hold still, be stable, get your arms and legs out. Still blindfolded, I knew she was going to try to pull me down, then I switched and I got on top of her. I did a grapevine to get her arms and legs up and pinned her.

A lot of people would boo Hanks's wrestling team because we were so good. We'd walk into a tournament and just see death stares. Hanks was a very hated wrestling team because we were baddasses and always won, but they would call us divas. I would wear makeup all the time. I would go to wrestle with a full face of makeup, eye shadow, eyelashes, foundation, mascara, with my hair curled. I wanted my hair to be short enough that I didn't have a wear a hairnet. If your hair was curled, you didn't have to wear a ponytail. Every match that I won, I'd take off my headgear and shake out my hair. It became my trademark.

At one point, it was Hanks against Caprock at a tournament. The whole crowd was cheering that we lost. One person was running around yelling, 'Hanks lost!' We were hated, even though we put in that much effort to be that good! We would practice all night, from morning to night, and sometimes we would work out during lunch. You want parents to support their kids, but in wrestling, they would hate us.

In my senior year, I wore makeup at districts, and in my first match, the female co-coach [of the other team] told the ref that I needed to take my makeup off. I'd been wrestling like that my whole season! I took all my foundation off. I always did my eyes the color of the school we were going to.

The ref was like, 'You have to take that off too.' I was so mad, I was crying. They were telling me, the foundation was oily, it makes a problem, it gives me an advantage. I was furious. I took it out on the girl I was wrestling. I put her in a guillotine. She's screaming, 'Aaah, ahh!' The refs are looking at each other, like, 'We have to stop this.' I was telling her, 'Your coach did this! You think my makeup has anything to do with this?'

After Hanks won at state, I put gold glitter on every single girl on my team before the end of the tournament, when we were about to get our trophy. Seven of 10 of our girls won first."

Hanks took six state titles from 2014 to 2019.

"Here I am, who didn't want to do this," Carter reflects, "and look at all the accolades! God has a sense of humor. It goes back to the eight girls that started the program."

Even at a historic beginning for female wrestlers in Michigan, Johanna Palshan could only see how far she'd come. The year 2019 marked a new beginning for her and the increasing number of ladies of the mat, but it was just one more step in her trek.

It wasn't too long since the days back in elementary school where opponents and their coaches would rather sacrifice points than their precious male egos. The times when so few ever figured that the state would have enough women serious enough about wrestling to have a tournament, let alone the sanctioning that so many of their geographical colleagues had braved.

Those seeming cliches that so many athletes, in and out of wrestling, toss back and forth until they seem so overplayed now seemed so true. The ones about never giving up. The ones that assure us we could do anything we wanted if we set our minds to it and worked hard enough.

They were coming true. Many of them already had.

"I was seven in my very first tournament," she remembers. "It was two out of three. I lost the first match, but beat the guy the second and third time. It showed me the things could always change."

And they did. But it took far too long. And she was around to see them take their difficult time. Not long after her debut, one of her most memorable matches didn't happen.

Out for a match, she and the referee waited for her opponent. And waited. And waited.

He stayed away.

"I was confused when he didn't come out," she says. "I thought he was hurt or something. Then he wrestled his next match. I was confused because I worked just as hard. It annoys me to this day. I'd been doing the same thing that they had been doing, working as hard as they had, if not harder, and they didn't have the respect to at least even wrestle me."

It kept happening all the way through the rest of elementary and middle school, and even when she started out at Southgate Anderson High—but less and less.

If her winning records didn't convince them to worry about the wrestler first and the gender second (she won three all-female national titles by the start of middle school), a certain decision she made before ninth grade showed everyone how much this sport meant to her—and changed both her life and Southgate forever.

She didn't live in Southgate, but in nearby Taylor. Not too long a distance, but there were quite a few schools she could have been zoned for right there in town.

Just one problem; none of them had wrestling teams. Fortunately, Michigan has a "school of choice" program that allows students to attend schools a distance away as long as they're in the same district. Palshan had nothing to argue about.

For two years, she had to be satisfied with co-ed competition. But for her junior year, the Michigan High School Athletic Association finally sponsored an all-girls event. On February 3, still a little weary from a meet at Anderson the day before, as well as trying to adjust from jumping back and forth between 103 and 112 pounds during the season, Palshan showed up at Adrian College for the tourney.

She started off with a first-period pin, then roared away in the semis for 16–1 victory. Now it was her and Saline's Alexis Poupore for the title. And Palshan broke things open early, roaring away to a 13–3 win. In a single tournament, she'd won more state titles than all the Anderson mat men from history combined.

"It was mind-blowing to me," she admits. "I was on cloud nine for days."

Over the next season, the competition grew in Michigan, as did the numbers. More opponents, all with the added incentive to knock the champ, herself on a farewell tour, off her pedestal. Palshan attempted to fend off the attacks she was all too aware would be hitting soon and hitting hard.

"I was less worried going into my senior year," she claims, "because I knew all the best girls in Michigan. I had traveled with them and I knew they were going to be in my bracket."

Need proof of how much women's wrestling had grown in those years? While 142 *competitors* had showed up for the 2019 tournament, 149 *teams* were at the 2020 games, back at Adrian in February 2020.

Now in the 117-pound class, Palshan says, "I had a point to prove: that last year wasn't a fluke, that I was the best in Michigan at that weight." First-period pins in her first three matches drove that home pretty well.

"I just got into a mindset where I didn't talk to anyone," remembers Palshan. "I came here to do a job. I didn't get distracted, going off by myself and listening to music. I was pumped and ready. I had no idea who my final opponent was." It happened to be Alana Nuorala of Westwood, who'd come within a win of a state title at 119 pounds the year before.

It's frustrating to lose to someone despite knowing almost exactly what she's going to do ahead of time, but Palshan's opponents had been feeling that way for years. Nuorala managed to keep her back off the mat, but couldn't score a point, and Palshan stormed to a 6–0 victory.

"I have proved again that I was one of the best in Michigan," Palshan says. "All the lessons that it taught me. It's a mental tool more than a physical tool, knowing you might not be strong enough to wrestle people who weigh as much as you, but you hope your technique is good enough. You can't really say wrestling is for boys if I win."

Olivia Rondeau, Maryland: "I started taekwondo when I was four or five, and got my black belt when I was 10. At Poolesville High in Maryland, they didn't have many girls. I was the only one on the wrestling team.

It was pretty nerve-racking my first year, as a girl and a freshman. I got pushed into varsity if someone didn't make weight. The coaches were pretty cool. They treated me like one of the team. The nerve-racking part was going to another school and seeing the other team realize a girl was on the team. They were like, 'Oh, I don't want to wrestle a girl!' If they lost, they'd refuse to shake my hand and run out of the room.

The most major thing was a referee in one of my first matches, like my third match ever. It was a three-school match, and I was the only female. He told me, 'This is a boy's sport, and you can't cry if you lose.' A lot of people are still backward, like it's still the 1950s, where women couldn't play sports.

I loved how confident the sports made me. I broke out of my shell when I won a match and my hand was raised. I never got super-competitive in taekwondo when I was kid, because I didn't grasp the competition. When you win, it's all because of you. You didn't have to credit someone else for your winning. It gave me a voice and confidence in my opinion. I'm a journalist, and when I write, I feel more confident about putting myself out there and commenting on things that may seem controversial. It increased my leadership abilities, like when I coach small kids in wrestling. If I hadn't gotten through certain losses and criticisms in wrestling, I wouldn't get to own it and become unapologetic about certain things in my life.

I won folkstyle, freestyle, and Greco state championships in high school. Then a few months prior to the AAU Junior Olympics in 2017, the first one that girls were allowed to participate, I tore my ACL, so I couldn't practice.

I was supposed to be at 172 pounds, but that meant I'd have to lose 20 pounds in three or four days. Officially, I didn't do this, but I was running and spitting in a trash bag, using creatine and Pedialyte. After I got down to 172 in weigh-ins, I went to IHOP and had *lots* of pancakes.

It was hard, but the motivation to get there made it OK. I was rejuvenated. I pinned both my opponents in the first round. Technically, I was the first female a win a medal at the Olympics.

[Note: After becoming the first Poolesville wrestler (not just female) to make All-American honors, Rondeau transferred to Wyoming Seminary (actually in Kingston, Pennsylvania) to train for the Olympics.]

I won the Super 32 championships in October 2017 in Greensboro, the first girls' competition and one of the biggest on the East Coast. I was on the Olympic development team, full of tough girls that didn't like me. We were on a bus for 11 hours with teammates that didn't like me. They didn't like black people. I'm not the type to call people racists, but they told me straight up that they didn't like me because I was black. I heard the N-word. There was one other girl who liked me, and she also won. I was confident because I knew that they didn't want to see me succeed."

Driving home from an impromptu mat battle in South Carolina in 2017, Bella Hoffman watched herself on the web.

Earlier that night, she'd been asked to exhibit a quick wrestling match at a mixed martial arts event, and the announcers hadn't exactly been in her corner of the octagon. At first, that might not have been too unreasonable; the eighth-grader was facing a high school senior, clearly overmatched in experience.

But as things moved forward with the match, the commentary and the rest of the audience quickly switched over. Not so much a case of hopping on the Hoffman band-wagon, just an acceptance of reality.

The rules were that the first to five takedowns would be the champ. Hoffman had come out on top—five zip. For the rest of the night, event winners kept calling her up on the stage to give her their gloves.

"As we're wrestling, [the announcers] talked about how [my opponent] came from a really good school," Hoffman recalls. "Afterward, they totally flipped gears and started to really love me, I was the 'Next Big Thing,' a reminder of Brieana Delgado." A graduate of Hillcrest High, about an hour west of Hoffman's Fort Mill High, Delgado lettered in high school before making All-American honors at Oklahoma City University, where she later coached.

It wasn't the last time that people would have a pessimistic first impression of Hoffman.

"Before a match, I'll be warming up, and I'll wear a hoodie for the surprise that I'm a girl," she says.

"For most guys, when they see a girl in her first year, she doesn't even know how to tie her wrestling shoes or keep her head guard on. Then they see a girl that knows what she's doing and they're kind of dumbfounded."

Pacing back and forth before one of her first-ever matches, Hoffman heard a noise from the bleachers behind her.

"I have this girl Bella to wrestle," the guy said. "She's nothing."

Bad idea. Extremely bad idea.

"That made me mad," she says, "and I wrestle better when I'm mad."

Quickly, *very* quickly, she got him down, nearly mashing his head into the mat. Then she hooked an arm and leg around both of his legs and turned him over, leaving him helplessly spread-eagled for a few embarrassing seconds before the ref smacked the mat, ending things in a mere 12 seconds.

It's called a spladle. It's a legitimate wrestling move, but to be put in it, to be held under someone else's authority in it for a time, let alone to be pinned with it, is not a wrestler's proudest moment.

"A spladle doesn't happen that often," she says, "so when it happens, it's usually a really, really bad guy getting pinned by a really, really good guy. It wasn't that I was so much better than him; it was that he put himself in a bad position and I capitalized on it."

By the end of her freshman year, guys were going out of their way to compliment her on her moves. College coaches showed up to scout some of her male teammates and opponents, only to end up studying her.

Hoffman ended up working so hard against the guys that the concept of all-female competition became an afterthought. Hardly likely, so why worry about it?

"I prefer wrestling guys because I'm used to it," she says. "When I go into a national event against girls, it's totally different. You have to think more. With the guys it's all about muscles and 'I'm gonna do what I can to win.' I don't get to go against girls very often so when I do I want the mat time against them. I've wrestled at the national level, so coming to wrestle at the high school level is not as big of a sport in South Carolina as it is in California where they have over 200 girls. Here in South Carolina, we have about 150 who are all relatively new."

But by early 2011, there were enough; the Carolina Invitational, a showcase for both junior varsity and varsity matsters across the state, added a female division. In January 2020, a certain Fort Mill junior stepped into Lexington High for the latest event.

And she didn't take long. Three matches, three pins, and the title was hers.

As was the event's Most Outstanding Wrestler honor.

"It's a big deal," she says of the MOW award, "because it's the coaches from all the teams in the entire tournament voting, so that meant that not only did my coaches like what I did, but other coaches that didn't even have girls on their teams noticed how well I was doing."

The actual victories, however, didn't seem as special, and not because they arrived so quickly and simply.

"I've always been so caught up in winning against boys that I've never really thought about winning girls' states in the way that others think of it," Hoffman admits. "Winning at first, it was just another tournament. Later on, I realized that it was a very big deal. I just won a state championship!"

Meanwhile, in the ladies' junior varsity division, Morgan Grimsley was pinning her way to the top as well.

"I was doing jiu-jitsu in seventh grade," recalls the then-eighth-grader. "One day, my coach came into the cafeteria and asked if anyone wanted to try out for wrestling. Lots of girls signed up, but no one stuck around."

Except her. By the start of her last year at Dawkins Middle, the team's only female was voted captain, not to mention being ranked in the top five in South Carolina.

"I worked on my snapdowns and power half nelsons all year," Grimsley recalls. "I learned something from every match and tried to fix it." Much like Hoffman, she preferred coed competition to all-gal.

"I never got pinned during the regular season," she says. "Well, I got pinned once, but I don't think I got pinned. The referee overreacted."

For the Carolina tourney, she eliminated such a possibility.

"My first match, I got a pin in the first round," Grimsley says. "My second, I pinned her in the second round."

In her finals battle, though, things didn't go so fast. As time wound down into double, then single digits, Grimsley clung to a small lead, and to her opponent, holding her down.

"I pinned her with five seconds left," she says. "Everybody on my side was jumping around. The people I'm around keep me motivated. They're always there, like a family. It was a great experience."

Lilly Gough, Oklahoma: "I was watching my brother and the one girl on the team before me. She begged me to start doing it. I saw my brother doing it, and I got so much adrenalin watching his matches. I picked it up a lot easier than most kids do. I'm a very aggressive person, very hands-on and fast-paced. This sport goes along with everything I'm used to doing. I grew up working with my dad in construction, so I was naturally strong. When I got into it, I was stronger than most girls."

Before she'd had much of a chance to become a real part of Oklahoma high school wrestling history, Lilly Gough was about finished.

Before her state had even given her and the increasing number of mat women their own tournament, she was close to done.

"I was wrestling boys at 145 as a sophomore," remembers the Jay High junior. "They didn't want to lose to a girl, because their whole team would shame them. So they'd go twice as hard with me as with a guy." Early in the season, she'd been battling an aching ankle that she'd convinced herself was just a sprain, fighting it off with ice, tape, prayers, braces, everything.

But that wouldn't be the worst thing. One evening in the middle of a match, her opponent got on top of her, and went for a half nelson. Gough looked to bridge her way out, and her opponent flipped her.

He was half-successful; everything below her waist stayed on the mat, but the top twisted to the mat. Then one of her ribs popped out.

A couple of cortisone shots helped her finish up the year. Then, for the umpteenth time it a very short while, she took her bum foot back to the doctor. He informed her than the sprain wasn't a sprain.

She needed surgery, or the bone could die completely. Nothing was worth that.

By the start of her next season, she felt ready. Gough had been working out all summer, albeit modifying the leg strength and speed that had been two of her biggest assets in her debut year. And now she had a new incentive.

For the first time, the Oklahoma Secondary School Activities Association (OSSAA) was offering a girls wrestling championship. Now her name could stand forever in state history.

But every other lady in the state was thinking the same thing. One dual match into her junior year, Gough found out her finish line might have been farther away than she'd predicted.

"I was winning 9–0," she says, "but when the second period came along, I gave [my opponent] things, little mistakes. It was 9–9 in the second, and no one scored in the third. In overtime, she got an escape, got on top of me, and won the match. I wasn't in the right mindset, but opened my eyes for the rest of the season."

In March 2020, she and the rest of the few hundred female wrestlers in the state gathered in Oklahoma City for their state's first-ever all-female tourney.

As she walked into the gym, her coach glanced at her.

"You're going to be my first state champion," he said. Encouragement, hope, or simply the truth, it was enough.

"I was looking forward to it, make his words come true," Gough recalls. "I got out on the mat, and I could not let my coach or my team down." Then, though, came the same sort of reminder she'd gotten at the start of the year. Norman's Trinity Crump hadn't come anywhere to lose.

"I had worked with her coach, so she knew all of my moves," says Gough. "He gave her everything I did. She came in educated." It was a war—but as she clung to a small lead late in the second period, she managed to plant Crump's shoulders to the mat for the win.

Stillwater's Aubrianna Smith was just as aggressive, but not quite as effective.

"She kept hip-tossing me and slamming me on my head," Gough says. "I kept getting away and got saved by the clock. She was getting upset that hip-tosses weren't working. We fell over, and she shoved my head into the mat. I look over at my coach with this disgusted face. He was like, 'Get to the line and don't touch her.'" Gough got away, 18–12.

Now it was down to her and Alison Conway of Putnam City High. Gough's season-opening loss had been her only defeat of the season, but Conway was walking in with a 22–2 mark herself.

"I made sure that my mind was set," Gough says. "If you don't have fun wrestling, it messes up your head. If I think about it too much, I mess up really bad. If I'm having fun, I do really well."

The two battled through a close first period. Early in the second, they locked up again. Gough grabbed Conway around the neck, then spun her around and to her back. It's called the twister, and it can take an opponent from the feet to the mat, from stability to "What the hell happened?" in about two seconds.

It worked; less than a minute into the period, her shoulders were down, and Gough had it done.

"I was so overjoyed," she says. "I started crying for a minute. I just kept thinking, 'I actually won!'"

One month after the event, the OSSAA Board of Directors voted to sanction female wrestling in the state. But right around that time, Gough's old enemy came back, and she couldn't out-point this one.

Her repaired ankle had held up well enough over the regular season, but the pain was increasing. This time, with no upcoming matches (but possibly her career!) to lose, she headed back under the knife.

"The first surgery didn't take, and it had become bone loss and arthritis," Gough says. "They filled it in with bone marrow, and put a plate and seven screws on top of it." Laid up for a while, she came back just as rough the next season.

And finished with not just her team's Most Outstanding Wrestler honor, but her second state title—and then a scholarship to Central Methodist University.

If Olivia Shore had made the wave in Ohio wrestling, Grace Jones jumped on and rode it the very next year—as did a few (hundred) others.

"It's been crazy," says the London High graduate, about an hour east of Shore's Buckeye State homeland. "What started it all was Olivia Shore making it to boys' state and winning a match [in March 2021]. It's just been growing. More girls are staying, more opportunities for wrestling. Now we have tournaments for girls to wrestle girls."

After needing everything but a court order for her to be given a spot on the London Wrestling Club's youngest teams when she was in kindergarten, Jones found all kinds of gifts across the mat.

"It was mainly against guys in wrestling," she says. "I liked the physicality and hard work. It made me more disciplined. I got into weight lifting. I was working out a lot. Wrestling boys gave me a sense of self-respect. It gave me confidence."

She found them elsewhere for the next few years. But in her second year at London High, Jones just *happened* to venture into the wrestling room.

"I took stats for the wrestling team," she says. "Being around that environment made me miss it, so I came back. I was on an all-boys team. It was very nerve-racking, being in a room with all dudes. It was definitely a challenge to be around them. But wrestling them was like riding a bike." But even the best riders bump and fall once in a while; Jones managed a 15–22 record in her return to the mat, still good enough to qualify as an alternate for the male district contest.

Over the 2019 summer, she went full force into making up for lost time. "I wrestled on a girls' national team," Jones says, "working with a bunch of different programs, mainly boys. I started getting stronger to be at a higher level. Trying to push it all together, training all the time, wrestling against boys put me at a higher advantage."

As she was getting back into the mat game, hundreds of others were arriving as well; Ohio women wrestling numbers more than doubled from 2018 to 2019, soaring past 500. The Ohio High School Wrestling Coaches Association considered it enough to finally hold an inaugural girls' state championship.

On February 22, 2020, history was made at Hilliard Davidson High. Jones was the 116-pound favorite.

"But I felt like the underdog the entire time," she says. "I always feel like the underdog. It gives me a humbling sense. I knew that no matter who I was wrestling, it would be a good match."

After bye-ing her way through the first round, Jones held down Tinora's Jordyn Hoffman in less than a minute, then pinned Jada Schafer of Minerva in about three minutes.

"It felt good," she says of the first day of competition. "I was feeling more of my adrenalin." Massillon's Shi'anna Bamba had grabbed Ohio's attention in her freshman year, tearing all the way to the state semis. But experience overcame enthusiasm, as Jones built a solid lead over Bamba before pinning her in the third period.

"I needed her to put me in a good match to get ready for the finals," Jones says.

She and the rest of the finalists had about three hours to prep for their title matches, and they made the most of it in all kinds of ways.

"I rested for a good amount of time," Jones says. "Some of the boys from my team were there [she'd missed a team tourney for the state games], and a group of us got together to help me warm up. My coach showed me everything that I'd messed up on in the matches before. I felt a lot more confident."

Now it was her and second-seeded Eliana Paterra of Indian Creek. It was a war.

Jones managed to jump out to a 4–0 lead, but Paterra tied things up, and got atop Jones with less than a minute to go.

"I was on the bottom, one of my weakest positions in wrestling," Jones remembers. "I told myself to get it together. She was running a move, and her leg got a little loose. I felt it fall to the side of me, and I was able to pick it up and force myself on top of her. It was the longest time of my life."

Obviously, she hadn't had much time to gaze over at the scoreboard.

"I did not realize that I had won the match until I looked over and saw my coaches cheering," she says. "It was amazing. It felt like everything that I worked for, wrestling all the boys, the disappointment I felt when I lost to them, was worth it."

But the best, or at least the just as great, would come just a few short hours later. As Jones and her mom got back to London, a line of cop cars appeared.

Had she done something? Had someone threatened to do something to her? Of course not.

The cops and some fire trucks escorted them all the way through town, and to her school. Clearly, news travels fast in this neck of the Buckeye State.

Surrounded by sign-wavers, chanters, and a few of her teammates, she put the next notch in a school tradition.

"We have this bell at our school, and the teams ring it every time London has a big victory," Jones says. For the first time in school history, a lady wrestler would knock out the notes.

Jones grabbed the instrument, and a very special sound rang through that cold night.

"It was awesome," she says. "That whole day didn't even feel real. I sit here and it still doesn't feel real."

Gillette Stadium might have had a morose aura that day in April 2018.

Its New England Patriots, led by a certain quarterback named Brady, had won eight games there the season before, including a pair in the playoffs, but had fallen to Philadelphia in the Super Bowl. The Foxborough spot would have another title to celebrate less than a year later, but that wasn't in mind just yet.

So someone else gave it a reason to cheer. One that had never before been experienced in the entire state.

In a time when previous experience was hardly even available, let alone necessary, Jim Peckham had roared to the top of the wrestling world. Without a day of high school or college experience, Peckham had made it all the way to the 1956 Olympics in Greco Roman competition, then on to coaching Olympic and World tournament teams, and eventually the National Wrestling Hall of Fame.

Shortly after Peckham's 2011 passing, his friends and family put together the Jim Peckham Memorial Scholarship, there to help out upcoming area matsters.

Diana Peckham (left) presents the Jim Peckham Memorial Scholarship award, named in honor of her dad, to Massachusetts's Bella Ricchiazzi, the first woman to win the award. Photograph provided by Bella Ricchiazzi.

Every year, hundreds from across the state applied for Peckham's help. The 2018 ceremony marked the first time the winner would be a lady.

"My brother wrestled, and I was always at the meets, the 12 hours it takes for a wrestling tournament," remembers Bella Ricchiazzi. "Then they put out an ad for all-girls wrestling camp, and I was the only girl that showed up! But I got to go one-on-one with the women's coach, and fell in love with the sport."

What made her scholarship victory even more impressive is that Ricchiazzi didn't have the attention of high school wrestling; competing for longtime powerhouse Framingham High in a state when female wrestling wasn't sanctioned (that happened for the 2018–19 season, after she'd graduated), most of her matches were (a) on the junior varsity level (although, "On JV, I beat them almost all the time!") and/or (b) against boys, coming up on the wrong side ("Varsity, I was a little less than .500!").

Off campus, however, it was a whole separate story. That's where she showed why she deserved the award.

Ricchiazzi took three state titles and two New England championships. In her junior year, she finished fifth at the National Folkstyle Championships.

"My coach said, 'You're going to be on the podium next year,'" she remembers. "In the off-season, I had 54 matches in 10 states. I set a goal high, but it was attainable."

That could refer to both her mat goals and scholarship. Applying, she says, "was a cool thing, to put this into my own words and share it. I wrote about my experience wrestling, what I'd had to go through, my whole experience."

Right around the time she learned of her Peckham victory, which she'd use to attend Cumberlands, Ricchiazzi charged into her farewell showing at the National Folkstyles in Oklahoma City. She'd roar all the way to the title match at 138 pounds, where she lost to California's Destiny Lyng.

"My goal was to place higher," Ricchiazzi says, "and getting to the semis, you place higher. Win and you get into the top two. I won in the semis and started crying with joy. All my hard work paid off for the national finals." Ricchiazzi, who also played lacrosse at Cumberlands, finished in the top eight nationally in her freshman year.

If nothing else, Ashley Iliff should definitely have won the crown for surrealism alone.

Consider this—you're at a beauty pageant, and it's time for the talent segment, which probably emphasizes individualism more than any other aspect of these events. You expect to witness some great singing, dancing, instrument playing, bird or hog calls, whatever.

Five minutes ago, someone was firing off the latest rendition of "Somewhere Over the Rainbow," and now we're seeing demonstrations of throws, takedowns, and Granby rolls. And if she'd had to do all those things in the prototypical pageant dress and heels? Yeah, guts like that would have automatically solidified her as a cavalcade legend.

And you know what? As Iliff looked to qualify for the 2018 Miss New Jersey pageant, she might have done exactly that. Unfortunately, pageant rules prohibit contestants from having any, ahem, *assistance* while competing.

"The opening interviews had gone well," she remembers, "but walking in heels was a struggle. But the talent was hard. I decided to do motivational speaking, talking about empowering women to do anything they want." With music playing and a Powerpoint telling and showing the story of a young lady who brought state and national titles home to the Garden State, Iliff discussed her real-life Cinderella story…

She told them about a young girl who'd been thinking of wrestling since early in middle school, but didn't or couldn't. She was too skinny, and girls were too weak to wrestle anyway.

The pageant, and the list of those she'd already won, were about following in the steps of a mother who'd had her own beauty pageant past. Wrestling would be more about being like her two-time state champ father.

"He brought me to a practice, and I was supposed to be the practice dummy," she says. "Then I started wrestling back, and my dad was frustrated. He'd try to teach a move, and I'd be taking the kid down. He was against women's wrestling, but what was he going to say to me? He didn't have a good reason to stop me."

Walking onto the mat for her first tournament, she was struck. Fortunately, not literally.

"The other wrestler was so cute!" she remembers. "I got twisted up, but the mentality of getting beat up and going back, I fell in love with. I did not win one match that first year, but the next year, I won my first tournament. That's when everything started igniting for me. I got into it, and so did my dad. It was kind of like the game-changer for me: the determination of knowing I can get knocked down and get up and come back. I was taught never to give up, that if you work hard, you earn what you work hard for, and wrestling embodies that."

And as wrestling embodied it, it empowered her as well. Enough to be the first women in co-ed competition to make it to New Jersey state levels, and winning four state titles and a national title on her own. And then helping King University to three national titles.

> "I have suffered broken bones, stitches, a torn labrum, and my meniscus was removed from my right knee. I still refused to quit, and I refused to give up. My losses, they became wins; my wins, they became championships. By my senior year in college, I was ranked number one in the nation and became a four-time All American. In 2016, I competed in the U.S. Olympic team trials. I suddenly realize the magnitude of my accomplishments. [Duchess] Megan Markle once said that women need a seat at the table, and if that invitation is not given, then women need to create one. It is said that girls with dreams become women with vision. May we empower each other to carry out such vision, because it isn't enough to simply talk about equality. One must believe in it, and one must work at it. Let us work on it together, starting now!"
>
> —from Ashley Iliff's pageant speech (sadly, she didn't win)

"I always saw wrestling as the sport I went to after school," Iliff says. "After my earrings and makeup came off, my game face went on. I once had a ref come up to me and say, 'I remember you in the finals of a varsity tournament, right after you came out in a dress and heels!'"

Unfortunately, some of these stories come to the saddest of ends…

> "She was part of our developmental program. I met her in Colorado Springs. She was a hard-working kid. What stood out the most was her wanting to learn, her thirst for knowledge, her ability to push herself.
>
> We know that losing a wrestling match is hard, but life's harder than that sometimes. But the constant struggle to fall and get back up is done on a daily basis in wrestling, and I reminded her, 'You've learned how to deal with this. You're further ahead than 90 percent of society at your

age, because you've known struggle and you fight through things and get yourself back up. Failure is a part of learning. She was very responsive.

I was in Omaha for a volleyball tournament for my daughter when I found out. I knew Allycin was struggling. I went to the funeral. It was important for me to be there because there were a lot of young kids there, and I wanted them to hear that it should never come to this. We should be celebrating people's victories, their birthdays, their marriages, their first kids. I don't want to come to a funeral.

You can handle life. Nothing is this bad. I thought it was important for them to hear that. Winning medals and championships is one thing, but that's a small thing. Through the sport of wrestling and its trial and tribulations, we prepare them for life. Obviously, something got too tough that she didn't handle the right way."

—Olympic coach Terry Steiner on multiple All-American Allicyn Schuster of Nebraska, who took her own life on April 25, 2021

She'd be very proud of it all. Many are of her.

It took certain people far too long to admit it, at least to her face, but there were people all over the Wyoming wrestling community on both sides of the gender equation who saw a young woman who planted her feet, raised her hand, and, even speaking alone, said that enough was enough.

The Wyoming High School Activities Association (WHSAA) had done everything but carve in stone a rule that would define a boys' sport as a boys' sport and a girls' as a girls', and that the twain wouldn't meet. Not then in 1998, not in 2011 or 2028 or 3098 or any other time.

In the middle of the state in the town of Casper, which would be the place's biggest city if Cheyenne were to break in half, Sarah Tolin said no. And yes.

No, in that she wasn't going to stand around and watch guys have all the fun. Yes, a girl should get a chance to try, for one minute, one match, one season, or whatever.

She just walked in and challenged the WHSAA. It became something of an athletic Cold War; no explosive drama, riots, fiery rallies, media blowups, none of that. The WHSAA didn't welcome the change, but they didn't really fight back against Tolin either. Just took a few years to make their mind all the way up.

Tolin wasn't too concerned with that. She didn't have time. The state's first-ever high school female matster had to contend with a Kelly Walsh High squad that took much longer to welcome her.

Like the WHSAA, the team didn't shove a blockade in her face. Having the school find a place in not just Wyoming, but national high school wrestling history wasn't enough of an incentive. They just didn't react right away. At practice after practice, guys would avoid her when partners were picked. Opponents and officials just gaped at her like she had five arms when she showed up to wrestle.

"I kind of expected [the publicity]," she remembers. "Nobody really knows about women's wrestling, and it was something new. I would rather have people acknowledge that it's a real sport."

She pushed it aside as much as any teenager can. Enough that she won two straight state girls' freestyle titles and two more Rocky Mountain Regionals at the University of Wyoming, and notched a spot in the top five at a national tournament in Louisiana. More tournament titles after her wrestling career continued at Kansas's Neosho County Community College.

And there's more. There always will be.

After Tolin opened the door and rushed through it, and dozens, then hundreds of others followed her. Hundreds of them compete every year at tournaments carrying her name. Hundreds more will continue to do so; in June 2020, the WIAA, the same WIAA that had nearly needed to be spladled into allowing women to compete at all, voted to sanction the sport in its state.

Tolin proved that even a person a few inches above five feet can stand above anyone and lead them to success.

She should have made it to the top of the nation and beyond. She should have walked out of her eventual alma mater of the University of Oklahoma with a double major in sociology and history.

She deserved all of it and more. As much as she accomplished, she had much more to collect.

But because of that heartbreaking day in early March 2005, Sarah Tolin never will.

And certain people will never be convinced of why not.

What few facts have ever made public come from Tolin'sthen-boyfriend.

Himself a former Neosho wrestler, Joe Blackwolf told police that the two had fought (not necessarily physically) in Tolin's apartment until she had decided to go to bed. But when Blackwolf went in to check on her, he found something unthinkable.

Tolin was hanging from a bedroom doorknob, a computer cord wrapped around her neck.

Blackwolf claimed he tried to resuscitate her. About 12:20 a.m. on March 7, paramedics arrived on the scene to take her to the hospital. She was dead on arrival.

A few issues immediately sprang up. An emergency room doctor noticed bruises and other discolorations across her body. It not being wrestling season, he suspected she'd been in a different sort of combat, one with no rules or referees.

Adding to that, her body had already stiffened before even leaving the apartment. As this usually takes at least an hour or two to take effect, it calls into question the timeline of Blackwolf's claim of fighting and Tolin hanging herself soon after.

Still, mere hours after her death, Tolin's passing was ruled a suicide; the pathology report claimed the examination showed she'd tried suicide before, such as diagonal scars on her wrists, as though she'd tried to slit them.

University police, however, continued to investigate, and her friends and family held out hope that a mistake had been made, somewhere. But the following November, the cops closed their investigation in agreement with the earlier verdict.

The beginnings to their respective wrestling careers could hardly have been more different.

Less than a year after strapping on her first singlet, Emily Callender was rocking through the finest in her Texas homeland, scoring a state title victory.

"When Emily was 12, she wanted to play football in seventh grade," remembers her mom, Rosie. "We told her that wasn't going to happen. We made a compromise that she could do wrestling, and she fell in love with it."

Over in Kansas, however, Hayleigh Wempe's debut was significantly less successful.

"It was hard those first few tournaments," her dad, Carl, remembers. "She was getting destroyed by tough kids and I thought she would quit. But she was so tough she just bit down on her mouth guard and went right back out there."

As things kept coming together for Emily, her family could feel itself almost breathing a collective sigh of relief. And of hope. Before she'd done much even in grade school, Emily had begun showing sorts of moods and behavior that looked to go much deeper than is typical for a seven-year-old.

But not in a good way. Maturity as a word has a positive connotation attached to it, but growing up fast—by force or otherwise—can be rough. Emotions change like the wind for every elementary school student, and Emily had always been mostly your typical happy young girl, but when the dark side hit, it hit hard and stuck around. Doctors told her family that Emily was a textbook for the reliable misbehaving young adult standby attention-deficit/hyperactivity disorder, but also saw concern for her waist-deep anxiety and depression.

"How do you deal with a seven-year-old suffering from that?" Rosie still wonders. "As a parent, you don't understand that." The ethics and accuracy of even trying to diagnose and treat a seven-year-old for mental illness (especially with medication) are still hot debate topics across America, and they didn't work here. Emily was medicated, which just turned her into a hardcore insomniac and made her emotions spin even farther out of control at times.

Still, sports had always been something of a temporary immunization for Emily's issues. The idea for her football career had come from her middle school gridiron coach, impressed by how Emily made that checkered sphere *hers* on the soccer field. Those who even dared to take it away paid dearly, and sometimes a foul call can be a soccer player's friend: mess with me, and I'll toss the rules aside for redemption. Is it worth it? That sort of intimidation carried over into her mat career.

Hayleigh had always been on the wrong end of tenacity—per usual for full-figured women surrounded by hormone-crazed immature nitwits known as middle school boys—but after her first tournament win in a 12U event in January 2018, those who'd been going out of their way to make her days a little darker just *happened* to start staying away.

"She always talked about how girls wrestling in Baldwin City started with her showing up and the other girls saw how tough and strong it made her," Carl says. "They also saw how she wasn't getting picked on by the boys anymore because they were afraid she would slam them."

But like Emily, Hayleigh could be her own toughest opponent, as Lord knows she'd been mistreated enough to do so. It didn't always take much to reach right out and yank away that confidence she got from a trophy here and a medal there.

Sometimes she had reason. One of her first-ever tournaments had Hayleigh up against a lady who was walking in with last year's state title. Talk about a shot at an early Cinderella story for the newcomer!

A mere 12 seconds after it started, the match was done. Hayleigh was on the wrong side.

She had another shot, as the bout was best of three, but she was about ready to forfeit. Why get embarrassed again?

Well, because some way, there was something to learn, to be proud of and take away. Her coach and family gave her a goal: this time, last a little longer. Just one second longer will mean improvement.

It's not baby steps here, more like ant steps. But she did. It took her opponent 21 seconds to put her away, and few would be too proud of that, but she was. It's about finding something to carry out of the toughest outing.

And she kept carrying, and adding to her load all the while. Hayleigh started 2019 with five straight tournament titles. St. Patrick's Day brought her a shot at her first state folkstyle title, the Kansas USA Wrestling event in Topeka.

Olivia Stean handed Hayleigh a tough opener in the championship, holding her down in less than four minutes. But Hayleigh looked back to the loss she'd rebounded from before, and knew she could do it again; this event was the glorious sort of double-elimination that gives the bad starters one last shot.

She held on to beat Olivia 5–2 in the second go-round. Time to grab all that momentum and become the winner that would take all.

Hayleigh scored a quick takedown about a minute into the first period, but couldn't turn her over before the break. Olivia began the second period on top, but Hayleigh fought her way upward.

And then the end came almost by accident. With the two nearly face to face, Olivia attempted to pull Hayleigh down, but tripped and brought her opponent down on top of her. She quickly rolled to her stomach, but Hayleigh ran her over to her back. With less than 10 seconds to go, she'd scored the pin.

Before the ref could raise her hand (remember, this was pre–Covid, so physical contact wasn't quite taboo!), Hayleigh hugged her opponent. One of her trademarks was in swing.

"She won her first and now only state championship," Carl remembers. "The moment she pinned her opponent, she stood up and looked at me and we both cried so ugly it was unreal. It was on the big screen at the arena and it was a moment I will never forget."

As Hayleigh readied to tear through another set of opponents soon after at a co-ed event, he could hear her future opponents sitting nearby.

"One boy behind me told his group that he had that state champ girl," Carl claims, "and he knew he was gonna get destroyed in front of his friends and family."

Well, he was right, and it took her less than a round. But after having so many of her flaws gleefully pointed out at high volume, Hayleigh wasn't going to put him through it.

"She hugged him and told him he'd done a good job," Carl says. "She was so good about letting other kids know it was OK to lose, that there were always going to be more matches and days."

Not long after closing out 2017 with a title of her own down in El Paso, Emily managed to "convince" her little sister Sarah to start accompanying her to practice.

Maybe for the physical and emotional benefits. Or maybe Emily just needed an extra practice model to toss around. It's just what older siblings do.

But Sarah stuck around.

"I didn't like it at first," she admits, "but after one or two hard practices, I fell in love with it. Having to rely on myself made me a lot more independent and disciplined, because it's all on me."

In the classroom, Emily was hurling herself at the books just as hard as her opponents. Gifted classes were all but simple to her. She'd come home from school, spend hours poring over her homework, then head to practice. Sometimes one or both of those activities would get a little extra attention as the day, evening, and night took their respective turns. Most middle school—hell, most *college* students!—don't have as much of a work ethic. For a parent, though, sometimes it's too easy to ascribe this sort of thing to pure luck, rather than our child's almost *need* to make her workload heavier. To feel like she's never doing enough until she crosses the line to too much.

"She was off-the-charts smart," Rosie recalls. "She was the kind of smart where she could just listen to someone and absorb all the information. She liked psychology and murder mysteries. She was fascinated by serial killers—why did they do what they do? What makes them evil?"

Early in her high school career, Hayleigh rolled into 2020 action with a win over state titlist Jolie Ziegler, herself coming off an undefeated season.

"Thirty minutes out, we would find a quiet space and talk," Carl says. "We talked about mental toughness and how great she was. We walked through her first moves. We would get forehead to forehead and I would tell her how much I loved her and how proud I was of the person she is. And right before she stepped on the mat, I got a huge hug and an, 'I love you, Dad.' Then it was all business." Ziegler injured her shoulder late in the loss, and Hayleigh wouldn't celebrate until she was helped from the mat.

"Then she leapt into my arms and got to celebrate her victory," says her dad. "That look on her face was so amazing, like she just conquered the world. What a great night."

While Ziegler bounced back to win the state title in early 2021, however, things didn't go Hayleigh's way at the event, as she lost in the first round and ended up taking fifth.

Since before that, however, signs of depression had started to creep through Hayleigh's existence. She'd talked things over with a therapist. Aside from wrestling (both on her school squad and several club teams), she was also playing volleyball and softball, hoping to make it to Iowa University, then to the Olympics, with forensic anthropology calling her name in the (non-athletic) career field.

A lot to worry about. Maybe a little much.

Hayleigh had harmed herself in the past. She'd talked about doing worse, though never really flat-out, never in much detail. And when she pulled herself out of the post-state loss funk and won a national title in Missouri in late March, things seemed to be turning around.

Spurred on by her new practice partner, Emily walked into the Texas Open in early March 2018 and came out with a state title, inspiring Sarah that one day she could get there as well. Then she went to Iowa for another match, and a big step toward her future, meeting coaches who all but fought over who'd get her on their next dual meet squads.

"She came back with a renewed sense," Rosie says. "She was saying how she loved wrestling, how she was made for wrestling."

On April 29, 2018, Emily Callender, just months into her teenage years, took her own life. Three years to the month later,

Opposite page and above: **In honor of the memory of her sister, Emily Callender (opposite), herself a former state champ in Texas, Sarah Callender (center, above) won her own state wrestling titles in 2019 and 2020. She is pictured at the 2019 Texas USAW/UWW State Free-style Women's Championships with second-place finisher Aylan Pagan, and Lillian Jukes in the 3rd place spot. Photos provided by Rosie Callender.**

just a week after her Missouri victory, so did Hayleigh Wempe. This time, certain pressures had gotten too strong.

There are no instructions for this. No teaching. No coaching. No practice. Not even remotely possible to ever be the same again. Not anyone. Not these women's teammates, coaches, opponents, especially families. All that's left is to focus on the journey they took, the ones so many were accompanied upon—yes, the trip itself, not only its ending.

And those who lose their loved ones take on a certain responsibility as well. Just to remember. Just to keep the memory alive, and not just for the time being.

Hayleigh's high school and her club teams keep her name alive, all three naming their respective Most Valuable Player awards after her.

"I always gave her 24 hours to celebrate a great win and lament a hard loss," Carl says, "and then it was back to work. Be coachable. Always show good sportsmanship and be a great teammate by lifting others to greatness because it will lift you as well. That's how I would want her to be remembered: as an outstanding teammate. She cheered and coached other girls, hugging them after a match, win or lose, and always had their back every day. That's her legacy—a great daughter and big sister and the best teammate anyone could ever ask for."

Hayleigh Wempe always got a few late words of encouragement from her dad Carl before she headed out for battle in Kansas, where she became a state champion. Photograph provided by Carl Springer.

In her sister's honor, Sarah continues to wrestle.

"I'd only been wrestling a month or two when Emily died," she says. "It was really difficult, but I know that's what she would have wanted. I stuck with it because it's the closest thing I would have had to her."

Just before the 2019 state games in Texas, the wrestling community held its own collective tribute to Emily.

A priest gave an invocation, and a tribute to Emily and others who'd lost their lives to suicide. Then Sarah and Emily's coaches walked across the El Paso County Coliseum and placed Emily's shoes in the center of the wrestling mat.

Olivia Stean pays a final tribute to her late friend and common opponent Hayleigh Wempe after winning her second-straight Kansas state title in February 2022. Photograph provided by Mike Garza of Furious Fotografy.

That November, Sarah scored the first gold of her career at a tournament in Colorado. A few weeks later, she won two national events back home in Texas, a feat she'd repeat in 2020. In October 2021 alone, now living in Alaska, she won three tournaments.

"Winning a match against people who are ranked higher than me, and going out and giving it my all and winning is wonderful," she says. "I love having a close match, and at the very end, I pull out a move and win. It's crazy, but if I keep working hard, I can make it. I don't know if I would be as competitive if Emily was still here, but she would be higher than me if she'd stuck with it. She'd be proud of me. We'd be pushing each other to be better."

On April 4, Olivia Stean had chatted with her friend Hayleigh.

"She was my best friend," remembers Stean. "I had met her in 2018, the year I started wrestling. She was one of the funniest people I've ever met. She cared about people with everything she had. She just lit up the room." At meets, the two tended to go from one extreme to the other; on the mat, they went at it with as much ferocity as two opponents ever would (the past January, Stean had jumped up a weight class to take on Hayleigh at a Kansas meet, and won). But when one was against someone else, the other was in the stands, firing up the crowd behind her colleague. Such a thing is pretty commonplace in female wrestling.

And almost every day, by phone or FaceTime, the two caught up and down on the major happenings of the past few hours. In her typical upbeat mood, Hayleigh let Stean know that the next time the two met on the mat, she'd be ready.

But that would never happen. As opponents or best friends, the two would never meet again. Stean's family woke her up the next day with the worst news of her life.

"We never thought that she would have done this," Stean recalls, "but we never would have thought that she would have done this. We're so upset about it, and we still are."

It took her a few weeks to get back on the mat, but she managed to finish out her freshman season with a state title. And as her sophomore year at Bonner Springs High came closer, Stean knew it would never be even close to the same without her friend there—and now she had both legacies to carry on. She'd taken third in a national tournament in Fargo over the summer, and thought about Hayleigh the entire time.

"It's still upsetting, because I know that she should be at these meets," Stean says.

An October 2019 car accident nearly ended Jas Alexander's life—but it didn't even end her wrestling career. Photograph provided by Grand View University.

"Fargo was especially tough, because she should have been there with me." Even tougher was an early season match at Hayleigh's home mat at Baldwin High.

"I've competed in seven tournaments in two weekends," she says. "My coach asked me if I wanted to wrestle on Thursday in a boys' tournament, Friday in an all-girls' tournament. I got home at 3 a.m. on Friday, and had to be back at school at 6:30 a.m. on Saturday to wrestle girls in a tournament and wrestle a guy in an exhibition match." But it kept paying off—dozens of times she stepped onto the mat, and came off a winner (and usually a pinner) every time, sometimes against opponents upwards of 200 pounds. Along the way, she'd also fought off a bout with Covid and a tough respiratory infection, both of which her asthma exacerbated like crazy.

"I started taking shots, instead of trying to go all upper body," she says. "It paid off tremendously." On February 23, 2022, equipped with a 42–0 season record, she stepped into Park City's Hartman Arena, looking for a second-straight 170-pound title.

"It was nerve-racking," she remembers. "I didn't want to let my team down, I didn't want to let Hayleigh down, and I didn't want to let myself down." It took her a quick arm spin and pin—all of 15 seconds—to take care of Spring Hill's Lexi Suter. She took down Gianna Redcorn of Wichita-Kapaun Mount Carmel, then turned her over for a 30-second win. Olathe-Northwest's Val Galligan nearly got behind her, but Stean grabbed her for another quick pin and takedown. In less than a single period's time, she'd racked up three wins.

"I just went back to the hotel," she remembers. "I wanted to make sure I was good on everything for the next day. I was out before 8 p.m."

For the third time this season, she'd be up against Basehor-Linwood's Mandy Wilson. Stean had scored a quick pin of Wilson in their first outing, but Wilson took her to the third period in the second.

Just before she made it to the center circle, Stean glanced aside. No one heard her, and one needed lip-reading to tell this, but she knew that someone special was there ... somewhere, hearing her.

"Come on, Hayleigh," she mouthed.

And maybe she heard Hayleigh's voice. Maybe if she glanced around quickly, she might have seen her for just a brief second.

She and Wilson grabbed each other, then pushed apart. They did it again. Face to face, they clasped hands.

Then that shooting technique she'd been utilizing all season came roaring back out. Stean went down and grabbed Wilson's right leg. Wilson got to her feet, but Stean powered her back down. In a bit over 40 seconds, the pin, the match, and the title were hers.

Stean fell to her knees, and clasped her hands together like she was praying. Then, just as she had all tournament, she pointed skyward. If Hayleigh was looking down—and everyone knew she was—she had something special to see.

A few weeks later, Stean took a state folkstyle title in Topeka. Someday, Fargo and other national— even international—events might come along.

"I'm trying to make Hayleigh proud, because she can't for herself," Stean says. "I hope she's proud of me."

Just a sport?

Only a game?

Wrestling is not these things. Not just them. Not to everyone. Means more. Means *much* more.

Some might call this saga too tough to buy. Maybe it's a piece of fiction that slipped into a historical fact piece by accident, the layout for a novel on its way to publication.

No way. It's all real. Read it, feel it, react to it. It might cause inspiration. Disbelief. Undoubtedly someone on the extreme spectrum. The right people will be on the good side of it. The others won't be able to comprehend it. Or even worse, won't even try.

That's OK. There's quite a bit about wrestling that's tough to fathom for some. Plenty of reasons not to get into it. But those who don't (or can't or won't) understand Jas Alexander's story, and her reasons for staying in the game for so long, even today, simply don't have to.

"I wanted to be a Special Victims Unit detective," the Hemet, California, native says, almost sadly. "I wanted to work with women and children who had been raped. But with my injuries, any line of work that can be too vigorous or dangerous to my face, I cannot do."

Tough story with a rough ending, although not entirely uncommon for a wrestler, right? Well, you'd expect to hear a statement like that *after* a career. You wouldn't believe how far from right you'd be.

If she'd been like very many of the past, Alexander might have quit the mat game her first year at Waldorf University. Early in her wrestling career back at San Jacinto High, a disc in her back had maneuvered its way out of place, along with a small crack in her spine. The feeling in her lower body danced in and out of coherence, then started to disappear. Even getting out of bed was a challenge.

Of course, no one else was going to see that. It's amazing what the mind can do when it's focused enough, including blotting pain out for as long as it takes to finish a match. But wrestlers are still just human, albeit of the extraordinary type, and before her freshman year was done, Alexander was forced under the knives and needles.

"Wrestling was one of the most important things," Alexander asserts, perhaps an intentional understatement, or maybe not. "It was all I had that I was successful at, and that no one by myself could take away."

Her walker got the boot, and before long, so did some more opponents, as Alexander took the Waldorf Open early in 2017. But that November at the Missouri Valley Open, her head hit the mat and her career a wall.

"I'm not sure what happened," she admits. "I've looked back at the film multiple times. I continued to wrestle despite my head hurting as bad as it did." Not long (fortunately!) afterward, her coach pulled her aside. A training partner had noticed Alexander's voice slurring, her face displaying all sorts of random, strange expressions. It was time to get looked at.

Doctors noticed that her eyes weren't focusing. Not surprisingly, a concussion was the culprit.

But maybe she'd been hurt before then, or perhaps aggravated it by continuing her career. Concussions are still way in the dark of the medical field in terms of diagnosis, prediction, treatment, everything. Everyone thought and hoped that her issues would recede and vanish.

They didn't. Not over the next few days, or the next week, or even a month later. The circuitry in her brain wasn't reconnecting, preventing her eyes from staying still or focused.

Months went by. Doctors flatly informed her that her career needed ending. No telling if this would worsen, let alone improve. Concussions prevent their victims from doing most any physical activity, and Alexander felt her strength and skill slipping away.

Then, the next spring, right around the ending of the school year, things finally started to clear up. Her eyesight healed. Her balance was back. Her speech and facial expressions calmed down.

Still, her brain and her spine, two of the most important areas in the body, were tentative at best. Many would have said the hell with it after just one. But all she could think about was getting back to where things make the most sense. She switched to Grand View University. She made a slow and steady return back to wrestling.

But now came the worst yet. Here was the moment in which much more than her wrestling career almost disappeared. Then came the tragedy that pushes this story from the tough to the incomprehensible.

That quote from earlier about head injuries affecting her career? She wasn't talking about the concussion, or at least not only about that.

In the dark morning hours of October 19, 2019, Alexander and a friend sped off from Grand View for a tourney about two hours away in Waterloo, near Des Moines, there to do some table work.

"I remember when we left that it was dark, and that it started raining on the way," she says. "I remember waking up to ask him if he was OK." It might be better if she *couldn't* remember the next part.

As her friend apparently dozed off himself, the car went off the road, then flipped over. Metal and glass smashed together in a terrifying tune. Her head and body whipped around, hitting everything.

"I believe I was in shock," Alexander remembers. "I was still in the car, screaming in pain. Something was hurting, but I didn't know what." It soon became easier to distinguish where she *wasn't* suffering.

Her face was almost literally bashed to pieces, fractures everywhere. Her teeth were chipped. Both eye sockets crushed, tearing apart her tear ducts.

A hole through the top of her nose bore so deep that paramedics could see her brain. They flew her to a hospital, not sure if she'd be there when they landed. A police officer called her wrestling coach at Grand View and advised that he might want to come say goodbye. Her mother was in California; even if she left right then, she might not get to Alexander in time.

But her mother did arrive, as did her boyfriend. Her teammates from Grand View showed up, and some even came in from Waldorf. Eventually, the View male squad came around.

Alexander hoped it was all a nightmare she'd wake up from, maybe just as she and her friend arrived at the tournament. As stitch after stitch rolled through her body, plate after plate inserted throughout her face, every day she struggled to accept that this wasn't the case. That for all she'd been through before in such a short while, now there was far too much more.

"I couldn't open my left eye, and had broken both eye sockets," she says, "the left one so severely that my eyeball had basically fallen into my skull, and the swelling was so severe I remember several doctors coming in several times a day to try to open my eyes. The most painful part was that my eyes were not ventilated, so they wanted to know if I still had a functioning eye."

Seeing again would have been great. Being able to move without feeling like spikes were poking through her skull, yeah, she'd be fine with that. But forget about that.

One of the most annoying coaches' interview mantras is, "We're taking this season one game at a time, and not overlooking anybody." That quote, or some variation of it, tends to work its way into just about every press conference.

The hell with that. Alexander was staring *far* past tomorrow already. There were some hurdles dwarfing Mount Everest between now and there, but all she could see was the finish line.

"From the moment I woke up in the hospital, I knew I wanted to come back," she remembers. "You'd think I'd be worried about my recovery, but all I thought about was coming back to wrestling."

The doctors looked at her like she needed a team of their psychiatric colleagues. She'd gone through something like that, and now all she could consider was maybe going back onto the mat? Just how powerful a pull does this sport have?

Well, one hell of a strong one, and not just on her. Alexander's teammates became regulars at the hospital. Her wrestling colleagues from around the nation, and even some from across the globe, reached out to her. Even the Wrestling Hall of Fame, itself located in Waterloo, held an auction for her. It's how the sport's community helps each other out.

"I started discussing returning to the sport in February or March," Alexander says. "The doctors said that wouldn't be a possibility. One good strike to the face could ruin the structures they had built." That, and more surgeries were already on her docket.

She wouldn't be back to the mats until June—as in, an eternity for her, but a million times sooner than the *never* label she'd been given by almost everyone else!

"With the head injury and headaches, I still could not finish a full practice," she admits. Wearing a huge mask with eyeholes cut out wasn't the most convenient way to focus on an attacking opponent either—and people complain about having to cover their faces and noses for Covid protection!

"I was nervous about it," Alexander says. "If someone gets into a crazy position, I might not be able to see them because the holes might be covered."

Against training partners still iffy about getting aggressive with her, before coaches, teammates, and fans slowly getting back in line to cheer and believe, Alexander made her way to Indiana Tech for the Warrior Women's Open, a few weeks before Christmas 2020.

"It was almost like I wasn't ready," she says, "the fact that it had been two whole seasons since I had last competed, it was more difficult than I thought it would be. No training and practice can fully prepare you for when that whistle blows." Then in did, and she lunged straight at Tech's Riley Horvath.

Horvath juked back, and Alexander's head appeared to smack into the mat, chin first.

Everyone watching stopped breathing. Would everything be undone? Would the first good blow knock her back out? It's not often we get to see a moment of truth, live and up close, but this could qualify.

But the pause off the mat didn't extend to the midst. For everything she'd been through, Alexander had slipped back into wrestling autopilot mode where one doesn't feel, let alone stop. She was back up and all over Horvath, using her height and reach advantages to maneuver her around the mat. Before the second period was through, she'd finished off a 12–1 tech fall victory.

"That was nice," Alexander remembers. "It was a great redemption to everything I'd gone through. I was tired. I had been throwing up all weekend, and I went to throw up afterward. I couldn't focus on how happy I was." But reality quickly ruined her come-back tale, at least for the day; Alexander lost her next two matches, then pulled out of her last one after her head began to bother her.

She didn't compete much the rest of the season, but still took second in a tourna-ment the following February in Missouri.

"I don't give up on things," she asserts. "Once I decide to do something, I don't like anybody or anything else determining that I can't do it. Wrestling got me through it 100 percent. It's very scary to know that any time I hit my head, it could be over, but I think it's worth it for how much I love the sport. I have enough protection on my head and face that nothing major will happen. It makes me feel strong as an individual, makes me feel important to people around me. They support everything I do."

For many, that's what wrestling's about. A sense of belongingness, even when one's alone. There's a strong control issue involved, and defending that, beating back others who even think about stealing it, that's an urge tough to find anywhere else. This is *my* mat. *My mat, motherfucker, and you don't have any damned right to be here! It pisses me off that you even stepped out here to face me, and you'll pay in inflated dividends for your nerve!* Saying that, even silently, makes you feel like the rulemaker. Backing it up pays things off even stronger.

For Alexander, and others who have and will battle through pain and laughed in its grimacing face, there's just nothing else to do.

> "I didn't start wrestling until my freshman year. I think I only wrestled one girl my whole high school career, and I won. Other than that, it was all boys. By the end of my career, I had 106 wins. I was the first girl in Iowa to get 100 wins. In my freshman year, I saw some of my teammates get 100 wins, and I wanted to be a part of that. In my high school wrestling room, they had banners with state qualifiers, conference champs, and people who got 100 wins, so naturally I wanted to be on as many banners as I could. I was a three-time conference champ, so I got to be on that ban-ner, and of course I got to be on the 100-win banner. I think the thing that made me do so well was that I *hated* losing. I've always been very com-petitive, ever since I started doing gymnastics at a young age. It carried through me. The hate of losing drove me to get to where I am now, and where I was in high school."
>
> —Felicity Taylor, Iowa, now at McKendree University

> "My school has a plaque on the board with the names of all the people who have 100 wins, and I really wanted my name up there. At the start of my senior year, I just focused that I had to get 15 more wins to get to 100, but I also focused on winning my next match and hopefully making it there. I didn't think it would be possible, because I didn't have a nor-mal high school season because of Covid. My school had one match, and then some people got Covid, and my high school season got cancelled, so I had to do it on my own, with club teams. [Maryland allowed its state wrestlers to include victories in club tournaments so as not to hamper their chances for college scholarships and other benefits.] [In late Feb-ruary 2021], I passed it at the state championships. I did not know that I was a couple of wins away, and I'm glad I didn't know, because that would have really stressed me out."
>
> —Julianne Moccia, first woman in Maryland history
> to reach 100 wins, finishing her high school
> career at 120–41, with 79 pins

CHAPTER 12

Women on the Go

The streets are like a maze. Not *that* different from any other, but still new. Down that street, around that corner, you don't know what's there. Not yet. These unfamiliar buildings, fields, houses, whatever else. They can be intimidating. May even scare you a bit.

Hey, why shouldn't they? Probably happens to everyone, for a while. You may have never seen them before. You may be a long way from home. Maybe farther away than ever before. It's OK to feel a little off.

Then you finally get there. You walk into a building, an enormous building in the middle of a place you've never been before, where few know you, even if they're aware of why you're there.

And suddenly arrives a wave of relief. Comfort. Five feet outside the door, you wouldn't have been less balanced if you were ice-skating backward and blindfolded. But you can walk into any wrestling tournament in the world—and you have, to a degree—and know exactly what's going on, where you're supposed to be, what you're supposed to do. Win, of course, but there's more to it than this.

In a huge, strange room full of fans blaring for 10 different matches at once, loud-speakers calling for the next competitor and giving play-by-play on the matches, and brackets that just switched one team from this mat to one halfway around the building and an hour earlier than originally scheduled, a wrestler feels right at home.

That's life for the lucky wrestlers. That whole "season" that they go through back home in school is barely on the side of relevant. It typically starts just after Halloween and finishes up near to March (globe-crippling pandemics notwithstanding, of course). But before, after, and oftentimes during that period, the phone might ring or a message appear in one's inbox, informing—sometimes begging and pleading!—for just *one more member* on *this* team at *this* event! We need you! Be a part of it!

Yes, it might be miles, cities, states away. Yes, it might involve teaming up and squaring off with people whose name we were unaware of until shortly before. It's about going to places that we might not have been able to pick off of a map, and showing up to give our all. But it's part of going the extra mile for a wrestler, sometimes in many senses of the word.

See, once her match started, she wasn't thinking about the few days that she'd spent traveling all the way across the country for a few days of mat action. That jet lag mess, those time zone changes, forget about all that. About as far from her California home-town as she could get without leaving the country or continent.

And damned if she wasn't going to make it count. This wasn't just *any* tournament, not that any event is unimportant. See, this was the April 2021 National High School

Coaches Association High School Nationals event. She'd motored all the way from the Golden State to Virginia's Old Dominion, and anyone who'd gone through that much time and distance and trouble hadn't shown up to lose and go right back home.

Just a few weeks before, Janida Garcia had ventured about *half* as far—there *are* degrees of everything in life—to the USA Wrestling Girls Folkstyle Nationals in Iowa, and zipped through four wins before a shutout in the finals knocked her to second.

Hardly a cause for shame, but that's not what she's about. One good thing about a year-round season is the quick chance it offers for redemption; a wrestler loses a tough one, but doesn't have time to sulk about it—because shortly thereafter, somewhere, she can charge right back on the mat to make up for the last loss time. The state and national titles she'd already won before the end of her sophomore year were nice, but her opponents in Iowa, here at Virginia Beach, and elsewhere may have had just as many or more, so a long résumé wasn't going to intimidate anybody.

Hey, maybe that's a downside of having so many takedown obligations. They sure don't give the mat women much time to rest on their laurels, do they? You won a national title last week? Great—but imagine how nice it would be for *this* lady to say she smoked you just a few days later!

As hundreds of her colleagues warred across the Virginia Beach Sports Center, Garcia blocked it all out and focused. Now she was home. Now the queen had a castle to defend.

After appendicitis almost creamed her high school farewell tour before it started, Montana DeLawder had roared right back to score her fourth state title, an accomplishment that, along with a 2019 national title and a list of other history-making wins, won her a scholarship to King University. Earlier in April, the sole female on an all-Pennsylvania squad had scored the only pinfall as her team beat an all-star squad from across the nation in the Pittsburgh Wrestling Classic, a few hours east of DeLawder's Gettysburg residence.

The Beach, however, had always been one of DeLawder's few downers. She'd been hitting city mats since her middle school years, but still hadn't taken home a top spot. She'd be graduating from Gettysburg High in a few short months, so this might be her last chance to go out a winner, at least right here.

And nothing was getting left to chance; in 120-pound competition, DeLawder ended her first four matches in the first period, then finished things with a 10–0 rout of New York's Ally Fitzgerald, herself a national and state titlist.

"I started traveling when I was 11, so I've been doing it probably the last seven years," said DeLawder, who won a national title in Oklahoma early in her career. "During the school season, I'm wrestling boys [her 80-plus victories there are the most by a gal in Pennsylvania history], so I already have a different mindset at all-female tournaments." One week after the Beach event, she headed down to Texas and came back with All-American honors in two separate divisions.

"You're traveling, but you're not going on vacation," she asserts of the travel schedule. "You're going there to get a job done. You're getting into game mode while you're traveling. Now that I'm older I try to give it my all. I want to make sure I don't waste my parents' money, traveling so far. It's cool that you get to do a lot of stuff that not a lot of kids get to do."

In one of her own finales before furthering her academic and athletic careers at Presbyterian College, Catherine Grace Bertrand took the 112 title, giving up just one point in five matches.

"I'm kind of nervous, but I'm just excited to wrestle my last tournament," says Bertrand, who helped Mount Pisgah High to a state title the February before, becoming the first lady in Georgia history to finish in the top four in the state competition in consecutive years. "It's pretty nerve-racking; you're traveling to a big tournament so you want to do well, but it's also exciting, because you get to prove yourself and see how you can do against the other good girls in the country."

She'd get to do that. She'd at least get to try. But as soon as she'd stepped through the sports center doors, Loralei Smith had felt her confidence drop out of her like her body was a trapdoor. Without DeLawder's or Bertrand's poise (at least, not *yet!* she's still a sophomore!), the whole non-local tournament world was still new to the West Virginian.

"Since I'm a sophomore, I wanted to get some experience in my first *big* tournament," she says. "I was planning to be in the winners' bracket the whole time. I was nervous that I wasn't going to make weight at a big, big tournament, but I got back into it. All my confidence left as soon as I saw the people warming up, but when I got out on the mat, it all came back. I wrestled girls from Alabama and Georgia. I'm not used to wrestling people from so far away." Her battle with Tennessee state champ Jailynn Tindall would decide the 144-pound championship.

As the last buzzer sounded, the scoreboard read 8–6.

"I got my colors confused, and I thought I'd lost," Smith said. "I was worked up and started crying. My coach looked at me, and said, 'What are you doing? You won!' I looked down at my ankle band, and I was so excited. It was a whole rush of emotions."

Want to talk about the importance of experience? Last season, the Ohio wrestling community found out how deceiving looks could be. In just her first year on the Whitmer High squad, Savannah Isaac brought home a district title. Then a state one. Now against the nation's best, she was the only freshman in 185-pound combat.

And why change what works? Isaac pinned two opponents and held off another for the title.

"When I won districts and state, I thought it was time to take it to the next level, so I came here," Isaac explained. "I just came with the right mindset: just going out there thinking I'm going to win every match, doing what I've learned from my coaches. It feels good, everyone telling me congratulations."

Having shed a few pounds since her Iowa event, Garcia held down her first three opponents at 128, but Colorado's Alicen Dillard took her to the limit, Garcia just managing to escape with a 2–1 win.

Her trip a few states north from South Carolina hadn't been a cakewalk for Aniyah Kelly, but nowhere near the trek that Garcia had been shoved through. And the incentive (heck, the obligation!) of not wasting such a long trip, along with a new urge to prove herself after nearly falling to Dillard, handed Garcia more than enough adrenalin to step to a 5–0 lead early in the last period.

It appeared to be more of the same; Garcia planted Kelly to her stomach and held her down, her arms clamped around Kelly's shoulders.

Kelly attempted to power out. And a strange look came across Garcia's face.

Not the strain of holding her down. Not even intensity, zeroing in on holding on for those last few minutes. More like shock. Utter astonishment. Like, *huh*? What was this woman doing? Did she actually think she was going to score, let alone win? Did she not *know*, had she not realized, at least by now, just whose event this was?

The audacity of some people, right?

In any case, it didn't work; Garcia kept her down until the time finished out.

"Traveling's hard, but it's worth it," Garcia said. "I want the better wrestlers. I want the challenge. I like the solo sports, because there's no one you can blame but yourself. There's always going to be someone better than me, and knowing that there's someone out there better than me keeps me going. I've been sacrificing a lot of my free time to wrestle, and it's nice to know that my work has an output."

Just weeks after wrestlers from across the nation roared through Virginia Beach for the Nationals event, hundreds more came right back for the National High School Coaches Association's National Duals. Without a female-only division this time around, the event's few lady competitors, especially from non-sanctioned states, were left to take on the guys.

"I've been wrestling for five years, and traveling is better competition because you're not wrestling the same people," says 10-year-old Cordy Zalota, of Pennsylvania. "I get to go to really fun places. I've been to Indiana, Ohio, Florida, Delaware, New Jersey, and I want to win at the Olympics for the U.S.A."

Just as they have for years, the upcoming mat women across the country continue to battle anyone they can find, even if they have to go elsewhere to find them. Even if it's an opponent they've never heard of in a place they've never been. Just another aspect that sets wrestling apart from so much of the sports world.

Because every woman at such an event has a dream of one day that gets closer all the time, taking one trip that may carry them farther than any other, but will show them to dream of every gal who straps on a singlet every weekend, even if the school season's out.

Like, say, a journey to Paris for the 2024 Olympic Games. And for those who can afford to wait even longer, one across the country (although not for Garcia and her neighbors!) in 2028 when the Olympics come back to Los Angeles for the first time in nearly half a century.

And maybe, perhaps hopefully, events like this, especially in unsanctioned states—like, say, Iowa and Virginia!—might convince certain people across the country to step up, raise their hands, cast their votes, sign some papers, do whatever the hell simple tasks were still left undone to add to the 30-plus states that had sanctioned lady wrestling by the fall of 2021.

Oklahoma. Iowa. Wisconsin. Utah. Nevada. Texas. Hungary. Elsewhere in their Arizona homeland.

No matter where the Pastoriza sisters wrestled in 2021, they came back at the top.

"I like the traveling part of wrestling," says Lisa, an upcoming high school freshman. "A lot of the places we go, it's because of wrestling, so we go to a lot of new places."

It all started down in Tulsa for the aptly named Kickoff Classic, where Sierra Linda High junior Erica strolled away with the title. Her triumphant return arrived soon at the Tulsa Nationals, bringing another championship.

Something else happened in the interim, but we'll come back to that. The next event helped both make a certain form of history.

Its title may be a bit misleading, but the April 2021 Reno Worlds event (actually just a battle of America's finest!) ended in titles for Lisa and Erica. It also made Erica the first Lady Arizonan to score the World of Wrestling's Trinity Award, handed to those with a strong enough combo of skills, luck, and endurance to walk off with three national club events in a short while.

Before that, however, Erica had torn through the USA Wrestling Girls Folkstyle

Nationals the March before in Utah, rocking through at 16U 94-pound competition. And the month after Reno, she'd roared straight to the top of the 2021 Women's Nationals in Cadet competition in Texas, ironically defeating Minnesota's Gigi Bragg in the finals of both events. That victory got her a spot on Team USA's Cadet World Championship squad, heading to Worlds in mid–July in Hungary.

"We've both won a lot of tournaments," says Lisa, who'd finished first in 2019, "but I think that was the most exciting."

Erica could have kept conquering America, but the globe presented a larger challenge. While her colleagues battled it out at a national tourney in Fargo in early July, she and the rest of the Cadet World Championship squad hopped on a plane and jumped over to Budapest for the World Games later that month.

Her first round didn't last long, as she racked up a 10–0 advantage on Kazakhstan's Aizhan Muratbay for a tech fall less than a minute in.

Up against Anastasiia Polska of Ukraine in the semis, Erica scored two quick pushout points, then got behind Polska for a 4–0 lead at the break.

Erica headlocked her opponent for much of the second period. Polska held her in front for the period, but couldn't escape or get an advantage, as Erica maintained the physical status quo for the victory.

Now it was Erica against Romania's Alexandra Voiculescu for the World title. Erica grabbed her in her own headlock early on, and Voiculescu shot in for a leg. Pastoriza reached over to grab Voiculescu's leg, then rolled her over and ended up behind her for a 2–0 lead.

Then Voiculescu managed to escape and get behind her. For the first time all tourney, Erica had been scored on. But one stoppage later, she came back for one more quick takedown and a 4–1 lead. Rolling Voiculescu onto her back got her two more points, and, less than 90 seconds into the match, she scored a World title-winning pin.

Time for a breather, right? Kick back, lie around, enjoy the rest of her summer? That's not a wrestler's way.

Back in Las Vegas in late August, Erica went 3–0 for the Supreme Women of Wrestling Club, helping her squad to second place in the Supreme Summer Girls High School Duals (Supreme took second to California's Empire Wrestling Club). Then came as big a challenge as any American wrestler her age had ever seen.

For nine years, FloWrestling had been holding the aptly monikered Who's Number One event, pitting the top two matsters from across America against each other to truly find out who *is* number one in the country. When her first opponent pulled out, Erica got a chance to compete against Florida's Valarie Solorio, who'd won the Fargo event that Erica had missed for the World Games.

"It challenges me," Erica explains. "It gets my name out there. Who wouldn't want to be the best in the nation, in your weight class?"

She'd never faced or met Solorio, but the two had several mutual opponents.

"I had seen her in videos," she recalls. "She had wrestled a bunch of girls I had wrestled, and done pretty well against them." Solorio walked in with a slight weight and height advantage, but that was commonplace for 4'10" Erica, who'd been wrestling for a year longer than her opponent.

Solorio used her reach and leg length for a quick underhook, then planted Erica to her stomach. She went for a headlock and looked to turn Erica over before the refs called a stoppage.

Erica went for a quick headlock, and then dove at Solorio's legs. She attempted to power Solorio to her back, and Solorio tried shoving her off. But she rolled to her stomach, handing Erica a few takedown points.

"I got confident after that takedown," Erica says. "I knew I was better than her, but I had to prove it."

Solorio looked to get behind Erica, who grabbed her around the right leg. Solorio pushed free for a reversal point, but Erica took her down again, and, just as she had against Voiculescu, motored Solorio down for a pin with three seconds left.

"I wanted to make a statement," Erica says. "People were saying to watch out for my ankle pick, but she couldn't stop it. They gave her too much credit. You can be a champion once, but to be it multiple times is pretty good. A champion has to defend her title."

As the high school season started, Erica and Lisa went back to their original agreement: if they end up facing each other in the finals of a tournament, the match doesn't happen. It's double forfeits all the way; the only intra-family competition takes place at practice.

"We're great partners," Lisa says. "We help each other because she's faster than me, and I'm heavier and stronger. I feel like my weight and strength help her when she goes up in weight. Her speed helps me control the tempo. I know what she's going to do, so it makes her work harder for the move."

Cailin Campbell, Indiana: "I started [traveling] when I was in seventh grade, so it's been about five years. The first place I ever went wasn't that far; it was in Illinois. But it was still new to me, and I enjoyed it. The farthest I've traveled was to Texas for nationals. I've been to Oklahoma City, West Virginia, North Dakota, Colorado, Iowa. Most of the time, I find out about it a couple of months early, but some of the smaller tournaments, sometimes they just randomly ask me a couple of weeks in advance. It's fun, because I get to see a bunch of places in advance. I love traveling, so it gives me more experience, since I don't get to travel that often. I don't get to go on vacation that much because of wrestling, so wrestling is kind of my vacation.

The long drives get really tiring, because you're sitting in a car for several hours. The bus we took to North Dakota, it was 17 hours on a bus filled with teenage guys and girls, so it wasn't terribly fun, but getting to travel gives me a bunch of knowledge about other people and places.

Whenever you don't eat for a day or two so you can make weight, and you have to sit in a packed car, it messes with your mental state and drives you crazy. You're cutting weight, and you're sitting in a car where parents and people who aren't cutting weight are sitting right beside you.

There are instances in a national tournament where I didn't do as well as I wanted to, and it bums me out because my parents paid a lot of money for me to go there and I let them down. Once, we went to West Virginia, and I was wrestling, and I had gotten food poisoning the night before, so I couldn't wrestle the rest of the day. It bothered me that they had paid for me to wrestle and I couldn't."

Vada Burton, Missouri: "There's early mornings, not very much sleep, and long days. Usually when I don't get to wrestle much, I get upset, but at least I get to wrestle. If I don't do well, I learn from my mistakes, like maybe the others were better than me. I've traveled for about three years, since I've been on the Missouri women's national team.

I've wrestled all over Missouri and Kansas, and in Fargo. Sometimes I have to travel, and end up wrestling my own teammates, which is awkward."

Audrey Jimenez, Arizona: "Going to the bigger tournaments, it takes about 16 hours. It's difficult. On the way up, I would be cutting weight, and it was a draining drive, but it was worth it. I'd lean out and spit, or we'd stop, and I'd get a little workout in. I went to Panama in 2019 when I was on the Pan Am team, and I've been to Georgia, Wisconsin, Nebraska, everywhere. It gives me more exposure to different types of wrestlers, and getting more titles and matches. I've met a lot of different people and styles of wrestling. The weather can mess with the way you wrestle. If I'm cutting a lot of weight, and I were to go to Colorado, being high up on inclines, it can mess with you. You try a little harder, so the whole trip wasn't a waste."

Bryanna Luihn, North Carolina: "The people that go to [travel events] are typically a whole lot better than the people you wrestle in season, so they help you get better. Most of the time, in lower weight classes, you're going to find a harder competition when it's national tournaments than when it's in season. If you're doing mediocre at these, you're going to be more successful in the season. I like to challenge myself. It's not that I want to beat the other person; I just like to do better than I did before."

Lyric Hetzer, Ohio: "The farthest one I've gone to has been in Texas. I've gone to about 15 other states so far. I started about two years ago, after my family knew that I was going to be good. I knew it wasn't going to be easy. But when you stay in one state, you wrestle the same people over and over again. [Traveling] helps you meet new competition. You meet new people and see what they do. It helps more people know me and look up to girls' wrestling. They see that a little girl [like me] is making the biggest statement."

Maggie Smith, Wyoming: "For state wrestling or other tournaments, we travel as a club. I bond with my coaches, hearing how they feel about me as a person, not just as a wrestler. That always is heartwarming to hear. At states, like the Wyoming wrestling tournaments, young girls come up to me and say, 'Are you Maggie Smith?' It feels awesome to be a role model for girls all over the state and especially in my town. I've helped coach young boys on the team. The coaches always want me to come and show youths. They can depend on me to help the younger kids."

CHAPTER 13

Up Against Covid

"I lost my maternal grandparents to Covid. It was tough with the family loss—faith and family are above everything in our culture. That became everything for the time being, but we took the time to get the cardio in, to get the weight training. It was probably the biggest mental challenge that I've had.

Getting ready, it was mentally hard to stay in a good, positive place. We managed to figure out some training, considering our situation. I knew, looking forward, that I had the responsibility to stay ready. During the corona times, everybody's training schedule was different, so I had to do whatever I could on my end to progress.

It was tough when it first happened in March, and we had so little information. We had to get creative, running outdoors and finding hills to sprint up. We had home equipment. I had some bands, some dumbbells, and a little slab of mat. I was reaching out to my dad or my coaches to figure out a game plan to stay on top of it."

—Tiare Ikei, Hawaii, state champ

This book almost didn't get finished.

When it started in early 2020, not many had heard much of the Covid virus. A few people had gotten sick here and there, but most figured it would just flare up and disappear fast. More and more people got sick, but you didn't hear too much about deaths. People became ill, but they just lay around for a while, maybe got on some meds, then came back. No worse that the flu or a cold, right? After all, our (elected!) leaders had all but guaranteed that there wasn't much to worry about here, so it had to be true, right?

This book was going to finish up right after the Olympics, and that would certainly be a happy ending, right? Our gals were destined to do well, to let the world know that America could wrestle in front of the world.

Well, that didn't happen. And that's why this book didn't finish in late 2020. Now let's look at how the wrestling community handled an opponent no one of then had seen before.

With masks, social distancing, and limits on public meetings, sports that require physical contact got hit hard. What were competitors supposed to do, mime out their takedowns or play charades and paper-rock-scissors for points?

Catherine Grace Bertrand, Georgia: "A lot of the training centers were closed down. Then they started taking your temperature. My dad had [Covid], and I lost my sense of smell at the same time for three or four days, so I'm pretty sure I had it. I'm not too concerned about getting it again, because I think the chances are pretty small of getting it again."

Wrestling got as big a beating from Covid as its most savage competitors have ever given each other. In September 2020, it came out that matsters would miss out on the prestigious Beast of the East, Ironman, Bethlehem's Holiday Wrestling Classic and Tony Iasiello Memorial Christmas City Classic, and Trojan Wars. These, along with so many other grade school and college district, regional, and state events. Hundreds of teams and thousands of fans missed out on some of America's top tournaments.

One year after she became the first woman in Virginia history to coach a male high school team, Warry Bonney had become the first female to have her peers vote her the district's top leader. As February rolled forth, she and the rest of the Falls Church High squad were ready to make her the first gal from the Old Dominion to help her squad to a regional title. Maybe even the state.

Then, ironically on the very day Bonney notched her coaching honor, the virus reached right out and stopped everything short (saying "stopped everything dead" would clearly be inappropriate here!).

Someone on her team took a test and failed, and an F-grade would have been a million times better of an outcome here. The Falls Church squad was shut down for a two-week period, knocking everyone out of the regional event that would fall within the dark "window."

"It was devastating," says Bonney, who, in news that drags this tale down even more, had recently announced that family transportation matters would make 2020–21 her farewell tour at Falls Church. "It was probably the hardest two weeks of my life. We had worked so hard during the year, and we didn't get to go to regionals, which obviously meant we wouldn't get to go to state. But there were many teams in the area that didn't get to have a season at all, so we were fortunate to get to have a season. I'm glad that we even had that chance."

Far too many seniors never got to enjoy their farewell tour. Coaches couldn't stroll around looking for the newest class of recruits. The NCAA offered its wrestlers an extra year as an option to make up for time lost, but many didn't have the means to take it, and this certainly wasn't an option for those in grade school!

And, yes, the Olympics were postponed to July 2021. Fortunately, a certain group of editors were willing to wait for them to be included here.

"It's been a mess," Sylvia Pierce, a Michigan competitor, remarked in February 2021. "So far, we've only been running and conditioning, but no practices or matches. I wrestle on a travel team, so I can wrestle in different states, but I can't wrestle for my school team at all."

And for those who weren't allowed to ply and improve their trade, legality wasn't going to protect them for Covid's wildfire-speed blitzkrieg. Those allowed to practice and compete sometimes hesitated to do so—people wouldn't be able to test positive for the virus and then say, "Hey, I was permitted to practice, so Covid isn't permitted to infect me!"

Many found this out in the saddest ways. In September 2020, the University of Wyoming saw outbreaks on both its cheering and wrestling teams. Two months later, more than 50 high school student-athletes tested positive after a tournament in central Florida, and dozens more were infected at another event in Louisiana in early 2021. That's hardly even scratching the surface of the effects this epidemic has had, and will carry on for a period of time that's impossible to predict at all.

"We were actually at the [National Association of Intercollegiate Athletics] Nationals

Left without physical or even face-to-face contact during the pandemic, wrestlers like Alyssa Randles of Idaho were left to improvise on their own, at home and elsewhere. Photograph provided by Alyssa Randles.

in North Dakota when they announced that quarantine was happening," remembers Virginia's Jessie Erice. "It was March 15, and we had just finished the last weight-cut practice for weigh-ins when the director of the tournament came up to us and said, 'Sorry, we're cancelling the tournament.' I hadn't heard much about Covid. They were warning us about not shaking hands, which was weird, since we'd been touching each other. [At home,] we were in school for about two days, then the school said we had to go home for the rest of the semester."

Over the coming weeks and months, wrestlers around the country, and presumably the planet, looked for *some* way to find *some* way to stay in wrestling shape until that glorious day of new throws and slams.

"It was usually me she was wrestling with," says Chantel Vitale, whose daughter Madison became an elementary school stalwart in Pennsylvania over the past few years. "The coaches would do instructions over Zoom, and the kids with a wrestling mat in their home would follow suit. They'd do outdoor activities five or six days a week."

Back home, Erice and many others forced into physicality solitude just did the best they could.

"I ran every day," she says. "I did a virtual 5K, then a 10-miler. My parents got a small 10-by-10 mat, and I did some drilling by myself, trying to keep the feeling of wrestling. Something was better than nothing. Conditioning is about finding your emotions: if you stop doing it for even a couple of days, you feel rusty."

Katrina Worthington-Dover, Georgia: "[My daughter] got some private lessons. The coaches keep it in very small groups. If anybody got caught with groups more than six, they could have gotten into some trouble. A lot of us parents hired out coaches for private lessons. She did a lot of swimming. Gymnastics made her so much stronger than all the boys. She grew about nine inches and gained 15 pounds in nine months.

It's frustrating; the lives we live are in sync, with a strict schedule, a strict routine. Covid blew that out of the water. Before, she didn't even question practices, and now she's like, 'Do I have to?' The shutdown caused kids to say, 'Do I really want to go back to the grind?' When you go to a tournament, the refs aren't shaking hands, and everybody's got facemasks on. You can't even shake the coach's hands. The kids don't shake hands after matches."

Ella Beam, North Carolina: "The virus doesn't scare me so much. I know there's a lot of unknown and everything. If I get to have a season, that's great. Wrestling's like you're making out with somebody without actually kissing them. You're all over them. If you have it, they're going to get it. I'm doing weight training. Wrestling taught me respect and how to be more determined in everything. When I started, I wasn't as determined as I am now. If you want it, you have to go the full mile. If I take any shortcuts, the whole thing will start over again."

Chloe Dearwester, Ohio: "I've been quarantined three times, twice from exposure to classmates and once because of strep throat. It was very weird, because we couldn't wrestle for two weeks. If you know how to wrestle, you know how to wrestle for the rest of your life. You just get rusty. I practiced on my little sisters.

[Starting back], I had two matches on my first day and three on my second. I was kind of confident, but very nervous. After my semifinal match, dehydration hit, and I felt like I was spinning. I focused on the opportunity right in front of me. You only get so many of these opportunities in real life. At any point, you could get injured or paralyzed, so you never know if this will be your last match. I won the final, but I was still feeling under the weather."

Aesabelle Castanares, California: "I didn't work out because I was so discouraged by Covid. It was really hard. I tried to work out at home to stay in a little bit of shape. I was going from having a full day's worth of wrestling and not coming home until 9 p.m. to staying home all day and not doing anything. I always had fast metabolism, so I watched what I ate and drank lots of water. I gained weight, but it was muscle weight. My coach had a mat I could go on, and my parents woke up at 5:30 a.m. to take me to the gym and came home at 5:30 to take me to practice. Seeing how excited my parents were, what my coaches are doing for me, it's encouraging. I worked for that, and if I were to give up now, it would kind of suck."

Alyssa Randles, Idaho: "When the quarantine started, I was having trouble not wrestling. I struggled a lot, because wrestling has been my 'friend group.' It's the thing to look forward to. My dad ordered me a mat so I could wrestle. I've been working out a lot more. I've been wrestling with my brother, doing motions."

Maggie Smith, Wyoming: "I worked on my mat, with my dummy at home. In the summer, I tried to work on it every day. This year, the coaches worked with me. I did weights, I ran, anything to make me a better athlete in general."

Evelyn Holmes-Smith, Alabama: "I ran a lot, and we have weights here at home. Coaches do Zoom meetings a lot, so I would get on there and train with him that way. We eventually could go to our own gym and train there."

Esther Levendusky, New York: "It was a roller coaster of emotions. Thinking that I wasn't going to have a season was very disappointing for me. Now realizing that I do have a season was exciting, but very different. [Note: New York's wrestling season didn't start until mid–February.] Our coach had us practicing at a greenhouse. We were able to stretch some mats out there and work out. We have a small mat in our garage where I could practice with my brother once or twice a week, so that helped keep me in decent shape."

She and her twin sister Catie had been tearing up the mats of Indiana's North Montgomery High School for years. Before that, Cailin Campbell—herself the younger twin by a single minute—and Catie rocked out down in San Antonio.

"I wouldn't say that one of us got into [wrestling] first," Cailin recalls. "We both always loved it. We always tried to get our dad to let us wrestle." Even before moving back to their Indiana homeland, the two had been each other's top training partners, in and out of the official mat room.

"It got frustrating during practice," Cailin says. "One of us would win, and then we'd switch. I knew that, since she could beat me, she'd make me better, and I'm sure she felt the same way about me." Then the two went out and showed it to some serious non-believers.

"Since our state hasn't sanctioned girls' wrestling, we mainly wrestled on boys' teams," Catie explains. "In high school, I would beat the guys that people think I wouldn't beat." Even without official "sport-hood," the state High School Wrestling Coaches Association puts together the Indiana High School Girls Wrestling State Finals every January, giving Indy ladies (more than 100 state schools have female wrestlers) a chance to compete.

In their first two years at Montgomery, the Campbells had finished at the top, but never together. Freshman year, Catie won her weight class, with Cailin second in hers. For their sophomore seasons, the places were reversed.

Then, in mid–January 2021, things finally came together: Cailin took the 120-pound title, Catie the 126-pound championship.

And just as quickly, things came crashing down. Prepping for a visit to the legendary female wrestling school of Life University, Catie had to take a Covid test.

Positive. After spending much of the past year coming all the way back from a serious back injury, now she had this to worry about.

"We self-quarantined the week before states, but I still got it," she remembers, "probably from someone I wrestled. I wasn't really scared, because I didn't think it would affect me, but it was still a bummer, having to work out at home and not really getting to go anywhere."

After qualifying for regional competition against the boys that year, Cailin found herself in involuntary seclusion. After her sister and a practice partner both tested positive, she got quarantined out of the rest of her junior year, despite coming up negative herself.

"It was sad," she says. "I wish I was out there, but I tried to be supportive of my teammates."

In January 2022, both made it all the way back, as the Campbells each finished their junior years by taking Indiana state titles, Cailin at 120 and Catie at 126.

Like virtually every other state, Missouri found itself handicapped by Covid as its season rolled near in November 2020. After coming *this close* to state competition in her debut the year before, Polo High sophomore Vada Burton was ready to prove that no one on the mats could stop her from getting there.

Maybe she was right. Maybe no *one* could. But something else, something a hell of a lot more dangerous than a shocking throw, just might.

Early in November, she had been coughing quite a bit, breathing coming and going. As these symptoms can have, oh, about a *million* causes, she didn't worry very much. But on November 13, just before the season started, she became the next in a list of millions of Americans to get the scariest health news.

"It was a surprise," Burton says of her Covid diagnosis. "I was upset, because it would take time off from me wrestling." As Covid could hardly be treated, let alone cured, she was left to sit around for a few weeks and hope (as, to be fair, is usually the case with the virus) that it would die out on its own.

Maybe because of her conditioning ahead of time or the best of luck, it worked.

"I had to get a physical and an EKG, and the doctor had to check my breathing," she said. "The first week, I could only practice for 30 minutes at a time, and I was exhausted. It was driving me crazy, watching [my teammates] work out. I started jogging three miles a day." On December 11, she stepped back into dual competition, and won. In January, she started going to the gym every day after practice. Slowly, she started weight training again.

For one of her California colleagues, things went in the other direction.

Like anyone else who'd seen the virus reach in and yank away her game, Kyrra Young was frustrated, kept off the mat by an opponent she couldn't even see, let alone gun down for a pin.

Someone was going to pay. She couldn't hunt down the virus and personally beat it down and out of existence (Lord knows the wrestling community would have gone *insane* at such an opportunity!), so she'd take it out on someone, somewhere else that couldn't feel the pain and didn't mind being worked over.

Young went back to where she'd only been sparingly in the past.

"I wasn't serious about weightlifting before," recalls Young, who started wrestling as a Valley Center High freshman. "I would only do it when I was in gym class."

With no one to practice against, no matches to battle, she needed something. Something that might require a mask—never comfy during a workout—but would be there when she needed it.

Up and down went the lifts, the jerks (clean and otherwise!), the curls, and everything else for her.

"I stayed consistent with it," she remembers. "I've been eating a lot more, gaining some weight. I'd started at 180 and gone down to 133 in my freshman year, and now I was back up to 143."

Before long, it showed. Then it showed even more. Wrestling singlets don't hide the arms and legs, and hers started to show why her nickname had become (in a playful sort of way) "The Beast."

"Once I noticed I was getting stronger," she recalls, "I really enjoyed the feeling. It was really helping me improve with wrestling."

When Covid tainted her California season, and put her on the individual shelf early, Kyrra Young tore through the weight rooms and a multitude of opponents in her senior year. Photograph provided by Mike Young.

She started off by sweeping through the Goddess of Olympia event just before Christmas, then she tore through the Queen of the Hill event.

But when the 2021-2 holiday season rolled around, the most unwelcome of gifts came visiting.

"I had Covid for a couple of weeks, so I wasn't able to wrestle or even go to school," Young remembers. "I missed a few tournaments, but the tournaments I did go to, I didn't lose." She restarted by charging through divisional and Masters competition in early February.

State, however, would be tougher.

At Bakersfield High, Young needed just over 30 seconds to pin Golden Valley's Elyse Flores. Jocelyn Yepez of Paramount made it to the last round, but Young held her down as well. In the quarterfinals, however, Jo Forman of Montclair managed to do what no one else had during the season, holding off Young for a 7–6 win. While Forman went on to take the title, Young rebounded by pinning Valley View's Alexis Jimenez for seventh place, finishing the event 4–2.

"I actually didn't expect myself to do as well as I did in state," she asserts. "I didn't have as much confidence in myself. I'm happy with how I did."

Just a few weeks after becoming the first Bedford High lady to win a state title, Sylvia Pierce found herself out of a sport. So she switched all the way over to another.

"I had been introduced to powerlifting at a very young age, but I never got into it until my junior year of high school," says the Michigan woman. "I liked the physicality of it. It gives me a little more diversity, so I can lift and wrestle without getting bored in one of them. I wrestle freestyle, so there's a lot of throwing. Deadlifting comes in handy when you're picking people up off the ground, and getting people off of you. It helps in the physical aspect and the stamina." Around the end of 2020, she learned of a national tournament, just a few hours south in Toledo, Ohio. Seven weeks is a short time for any powerlifter to train for a tournament, let alone make her debut in one so large, but she went for it.

On February 6, she stepped into the event. With just two lifts, she changed the world.

Knowing that the American female bench press record in the Junior Age 18/19 ranks was 170 pounds, Pierce lay across a bench and whaled it on her first try, hoisting 176 pounds into the air. Nice, but not enough.

One press later, she became the national champ with 187 pounds. Then came some news.

That lift hadn't just put her in the lead in her homeland. It set a new *world* record (well, unofficially—as it wasn't an official world tournament, it couldn't be counted)!

"I happen to bench really heavy," she remarks. "I had not known previously what the record was. It was pretty exciting."

That same weekend, Burton was a few states west, at a sectional tourney in Missouri. The first day, she won a match and got a bye victory. Then she went 1–1 the next day, and stamped her ticket to the Missouri games.

"At one point, I was wrestling a girl that had beaten me twice, and I was at the point I was about to give up," she admits. "But I took a second, and I said, 'How bad to you really want this?' I kept going and beat the girl. I was back in the groove."

CHAPTER 14

The Games Finally Arrive!

"I know once I get to Tokyo, it's gonna elevate every emotion even more. I'm ready for it. Shit, I'm excited. I am so excited to do this. By this, I mean wrestle, to be out there and just to give it my all.

Today I met with one of my sports psychologists and he said to commit to the way I want the experience to be. I want it to be fun. I want to be proud of the effort I give. I want to showcase my skills and ability. I want it to bring me closer to the people I am with, who support me. When I look back at this competition in ten years, (or) one year, shit, just a week later, I know there are the things I want the experience to represent. I know I want to win, but I don't want winning to be defined by one obvious destination. I want winning to morph into something that isn't only possible from analytical definition for it to become something extremely unique to me.

I want winning to be a process, to be emotions, effort, gratitude, family, and teammates. I want to be the best version of myself honoring everyone and everything who have added light to my own. When I take the mat on Friday, I will be glowing with light of so many individuals, and we are gonna *shine!* I'm committed to my experience. I'm committed to myself. I cannot miss."

—Sarah Hildebrandt, journal entry, July 28, 2021

So much to do, so much to worry about, so much to focus on, so much to be forced to miss.

One after another, and sometimes almost two at a time, the American women's Olympic wrestling team was heading into battle. And even in one of the most individual sports in history, they were almost all alone.

Look, it wasn't that their teammates didn't *want* to be there to cheer each other on. Far from it. It was just that, with more than 80 matches scheduled to rage all over Makuhari Messe Hall on the first day of competition alone (men and women included), the competition would flow like Niagara Falls that August 1. One ended and another started. Adeline Gray and the rest of the 76-kilogram class would be the only women to compete on the first day, but after that, things would split up, one or more weights having it out, leaving the team little time to cheer for each other or even think too much about who or what a teammate might be facing.

Many didn't or couldn't even attend; all it would take was one bad Covid test to knock someone out of the Games and straight home; in the past weeks, fellow Americans Coco Gauff (tennis), Kara Eaker (gymnastics), Katie Lou Samuelson (three-on-three basketball), and Sam Kendricks (pole vault) had seen their Olympic dreams dashed by the virus.

Tamyra Mensah-Stock (left, with Elena Pirozhkova) became the second American woman to win an Olympic gold medal in 2021. Photograph provided by A. J. Grieves.

It was just safer to stay away from the crowds, as minuscule as Olympic officials had made them. Back when the virus had first hit, many amateur matsters from across the country had seen entire tournaments suddenly halted because someone, somewhere had tested positive. It wasn't beyond the realm of possibility that some official could suddenly barrel in at any moment and yell, "Sorry, everyone, but this virus is getting too strong for comfort! Games over!" Anything could happen.

Nothing to do now but try to focus on the opponent across the mat. That was about the only thing that the women could control—and if they could keep doing so, they might walk out with a couple of heavy necklaces.

The wrestlers hadn't marched in the opening ceremonies when things got rolling. They weren't staying at the Olympic Village, instead warming up at the U.S. wrestling training center in Nakatsugawa, about 150 miles west of Tokyo.

Arriving there, however, the ladies and their coaches got one hell of a heroine's welcome from thousands of Nakatsugawans.

"The streets were lined with people, from little kids to the elderly, and everyone was just waving as we drove through," Hildebrandt says. "Some people had American flags and wrote signs in English so that we could understand. It was really amazing, and it reminded us of what the Olympic movement is all about." As their Olympic counterparts went into action in the Games' first week, the wrestlers worked out elsewhere, not showing up in Tokyo until July 31, the day before their battles began.

Meanwhile, between takedowns and stretches, they go to XBox and Nintendo Switch war, and out-sing each other on a karaoke machine, rapping and rocking and even singing the Word's praises once in a while.

"I didn't want to sit in my room and just let the time go by slowly, dreading the fact that I'm going to the Olympics," Tamyra Mensah-Stock explains. "So I'm like, enjoy yourself."

> "The female wrestlers today get a chance to live at the Olympic Training Center and get a full-time coach and other high-level teammates to train with. Back when we first started wrestling at the national level, we got to stay at the Olympic Training Center for a week to get ready for our bigger international tournaments. Most of our time was spent in a local high school training with high school boys."
> —Shannon Williams, four-time World medalist

It's enthusiasm versus experience to get things rolling; in the very first female match of the Games, Gray opens 76-kilogram competition against Tunisia's Zaineb Sghaier, who was trying to break through in the 2018 Summer Youth Olympics just three years ago. Now not even a year into American voting age and the youngest wrestler out here, she took gold at the 2020 African Wrestling Championships, then, literally on the same days that Gray and her teammates were securing their Olympic spots, qualified with a silver at the 2021 African & Oceania Wrestling Olympic Qualification Tournament (Egypt's Samar Amer, who finished first at the event, lost her Olympic opener to Russia's Natalia Vorobieva).

Gray walks out, Steiner and the rest of the minimized crew behind her. It's not entirely unlike a gravy train you'd see as the boxers stroll out for the main event of a title fight. There's some music playing that sounds like a cross between "Radio Ga Ga" and "Eye of the Tiger."

Herself a titlist from the 2011 Dave Schultz Memorial International in Colorado, Norway's Kristina Ness is overseeing the action. Three years older than the ref, Gray powers Sghaier down twice about a minute in for a 4–0 lead, then grabs her and twists her nearly in half a few moments later. Sghaier manages to her stomach, but Gray (an announcer calls her "Madeline," which shows some lack of homework here) twists her back again for the pin just over two minutes in. Covid fears still raging, Ness can't hold her hand and raise it, only indicating the winner with her own lifted arm (even sadder, but necessary, is officials not being able to place medals around the winners' necks, just holding out a plate with the medals on it and having winners grab them and decorate themselves).

Just as she's been doing for some time now, Gray tosses her own powerful limbs skyward and stretches a stunning grin across her face.

Hardly sweating, Gray rolls back to the locker room. Before her next opponent is determined, a few surprises happen.

First, she won't get another shot at Vasilisa Marzaliuk, who ended her Olympics drive back in 2016, as the Belarus battler falls to Aline Focken of Germany. And defending champ Erica Wiebe will not repeat, as she's unable to return from an early 5–0 deficit against Estonia's Epp Mäe, who defeated Gray in 2018.

But she can't worry about that right now. Some spilled milk will never be cleaned up, and now it's time to move forward—and straight into Yasemin Adar, whom Gray denied a bronze medal in the 2013 World Championships. Six years later, Adar got a gold at the European Worlds, while Focken scored a bronze. Whoever wins here, the German lass will have a score to settle—assuming she can get through her own opposition.

Gray wraps Adar up in a bearhug early on, and scores a quick takedown. She goes for the same twist that worked on Sghaier, but Adar keeps crawling forward until the ref calls a break. Gray goes for an armbar, but Adar powers out.

Then Gray suddenly goes for a shot at her left leg, and Adar topples backward. Her shoulders hit the mat, but she rolls over. Gray nearly brings her back with a cradle before she rolls back again and another break is called, and no one leaves her feet for the remainder of the period.

After some more arm-wrangling, Adar goes for her first takedown, grabbing Gray's left leg. Gray stiffens up and grabs Adar around her stomach until a break is called with about two minutes left.

At the 100-second mark, Gray scores a takedown, and Adar's nearly back on her back before she manages to roll over. Gray looks to snare her left ankle before things go out of bounds with 86 ticks left.

With both sides' coaches shouting through their protective masks, Adar goes for Gray's waist, and now Gray turns her own back into a steel bar and grabs her. Her arms turning red from effort, Adar hangs on to her waist as Gray attempts to reach over and grab her leg. As she climbs over Adar's back, Adar snares her left leg and tries to tackle her, holding on to her leg as Gray attempts to get back atop her. They're out of bounds again with a minute left, and, down 6–0, Adar is starting to realize that only a pinfall will get her elevated.

She goes for Gray's waist again, and this time it works, flipping Gray over her back. Gray on her backside, she resists Adar for a moment before conceding the takedown and points, moving to her stomach. Then Adar grabs her around the legs and rolls both of them over, grabbing two more points with 11 seconds left.

Then she rolls Gray over again. But they're too far out of bounds, and a break is called. Adar shoots for her leg again, but Gray straightens her legs and anchors her down. She gets behind Adar, but just lets things expire for the win.

For the semi match the next day, she'll be up against a sort of Cinderella story itself.

Walking into the Games unseeded, Kyrgyzstan's Aiperi Medet Kyzy got things started by walking it, 8–1, to 2016 bronze champ Elmira Syzdykova of Kazakhstan, then followed things up with a 12–0 walloping of two-time medalist Natalia Vorobieva, the event's Russian representative. Now she's the underdog looking to knock off the legend.

Through nearly five minutes of action, Gray can manage just a pair of escape points. Then, with about 1:20 left, Gray leans on Kyzy, who pushes right back and maneuvers Gray onto her side. Both women go for armbars, but Kyzy lets go and grabs Gray around her side, trying to crawl onto her back. Gray grabs for her left leg and snares it, but Kyzy's leg slips over the line, and the ref calls a break.

Kyzy's coaches are ticked. One slams his hand down on the challenge buzzer, demanding another look at the action. But the call's upheld, and with it comes a point and 3–0 lead for Gray. That point's going to end up making one hell of a difference.

With less than a minute left, Kyzy goes back at Gray's leg and lifts it into the air. Gray falls onto her side to cut her lead to 3–2, and tries to pull away. With 20 seconds left, she's on her hands and knees as Kyzy grabs at her feet, looking for a roll-over that could put her ahead. But another break is called, and Gray underhooks Kyzy into bay for the remaining seconds. Had the challenge worked, or if that roll had been pulled, there's no telling what could have happened here.

Forget just stretching and smiling: Gray's roaring, "Yes!" and embracing Steiner as a small group of fans nearby chant, "USA! USA!"

Now it's going to be Gray and second-seeded Focken, who slipped past Japan's Hiroe Minagawa Suzuki (who herself had earlier defeated Mäe) 3–1. They have history as both opponents (they've wrestled each other tons of times for over a decade, and Gray beat Focken in the semis of the 2019 World Championships) and friends (Focken was on the guest list for Gray's 2017 wedding), and now they'll make more. Gray will be the third American lady to win a medal (a number that could increase within mere hours), and Focken will be the first female ever to win a medal for Germany.

As the men rush through their second weight class's worth of Greco-Roman battles (no one's really had a serious discussion about incorporating that type of combat for women of yet), Gray heads back to her teammates and a break. Over in America, most of her fans aren't even awake—it might be about 6 a.m. on the eastern side of Old Glory—but she's heading down for the evening. She's been here before, and then she hasn't; the Olympics are the only competition there's left to conquer.

Adeline Gray: "My cadence got off and I wasn't firing as many shots as I'd like to, but definitely felt like those matches were in my control for most of the match. Something that I've always had is that I can take people down and turn them in these matches, but I've gotten multiple takedowns these last few matches and scored in a multitude of ways. I get nervous every time I wrestle. I had similar nerves at the nationals when I was beating people up, versus here when I was beating people up. Wrestling hard makes you want to puke; it's hard to eat, hard to do anything after your adrenaline is pumping that much, but I went out there and wrestled.

[Focken is] tough and she's a gamer and I'm looking forward to wrestling her. She definitely has a few very straightforward attacks and I'm just looking forward to going out there and battling. It's going to be an awesome final."

Tornadoes. Hurricanes. One tsunami after another.

Two matches into the Olympics, Tamyra Mensah-Stock is becoming a human impression of these wraths of nature.

Her 10–1 defeat of 2016 medalist Sara Dosho of Japan in the 2019 Worlds might have seemed decisive. In the first round of the Olympics, however, Mensah-Stock kicks things up even farther.

Just over a minute into their 68-kilogram August 2 rematch, she takes Dosho down twice. About 40 seconds later, she does it again. Shortly into the second period, another takedown ends things early.

Hours later, she's back in action. And there's an incentive here too.

In January 2020, up against China's Zhou Feng in the finals of the Matteo Pellicone tournament in Italy, Mensah-Stock was one move from the title. Up 8–0, a tech fall was moments away.

Then it happened. Feng battled back. Mensah-Stock's edge fell away. In the brightest moment of one athlete's career and the saddest of another's, Feng came all the way back to victory.

Not this time. Four minutes into the quarterfinals, Mensah-Stock's back up, 8–0. Chances are, she's been thinking quite a bit about the last time she was here.

With 90 seconds left, Mensah-Stock forces Feng to a sitting position. Knowing that turning over will give away a match-ending takedown, Feng goes for an underhook to power her way out. But Mensah-Stock crawls up her body and turns her over for the tech fall.

And things keep happening. Mensah-Stock heads home for a quick rest. Very quick. That very evening, she's in action again. "Five minutes and I'm right back at it," she quips, a legitimate exaggeration.

Three years ago, Alla Cherkasova scored a World gold for Ukraine, while Mensah-Stock was left with a bronze. Now the women are one match away from the finals here.

On a two-match winning streak against Mensah-Stock, Cherkasova puts the American behind for the first time of the event, taking her down for a 4–2 lead early in the second period.

Then Mensah-Stock, well, goes insane. As friendly, even laid-back and fun-loving as she can be off the mat, when she's out there, there's one thing, one person standing between her and victory. Today, said obstacle is named Cherkasova. And that's not going to work.

Tamyra Mensah-Stock: "You've got to beat the best to know that you're the best. And that's what I keep telling myself. It doesn't matter the draw. You go out there and you beat whoever is in front of you because that's how you tell somebody that you were the best. I'm the bad draw."

Easy? Hardly. She only makes it look so.

An escape later, the score is tied. A takedown later, she's up 8–4. Before Cherkasova can react, let alone get back on the game, the lead is 10–4, and it stays that way.

"I actually appreciated [that win]," Mensah-Stock says, "because I didn't want to come out, like, unscathed. It would have been cool, but to be able and be in the finals, that would mean more than getting techs and pins. Be like, 'Nah, I fought for that.' That was freaking awesome, so I appreciate that…. I like to showcase what God's given me, so going out there and inflicting my will, it's fun because it makes me surprised what I'm capable of. And when I go out there and I do it, it's awesome. So I love getting that moment."

A few hours later, it's finally Gray's shot at a moment she's been awaiting for over a decade. Through all the victories, all the injuries, all the dedication, all the tough choices she's been making for so long, it's here. This is a moment that every wrestler dreams of. Now it's reality.

Focken scores a quick point, and things go back and forth for much of the first period. Then, near the end, Gray goes for a shoot. Perhaps ready for this from their past battles, Focken overcomes her momentum and plants her down, nearly pinning her for a 3–0 lead and all the momentum at the break.

Thirty seconds into the second, Gray goes for another shoot, but Focken grabs her in a headlock and flips her onto her back. Gray immediately rolls to her side, but Focken's upped her lead to 7–0. With just over a minute left, Gray nearly scores a takedown, but can only get Focken out of bounds to score just one point.

Back in action, she finally scores a takedown, but Focken manages to stay on her stomach, and just enough in motion to avoid a stalling penalty.

With just seconds left, Gray goes for a headlock, but Focken pulls away as the final seconds tick off. Focken collapses in tears, and Gray hugs her in congrats. As she trudges off, Focken grabs the German flag and roars around the mat.

It didn't happen. That gold medal that so many predicted for Gray for today, as they had four years before, didn't arrive. Sometimes even the highest expectations, the surest things, don't come true. Reality often overcomes hope at the worst times.

Adeline Gray: "I didn't come out with a win, and you don't come to lose. But I came out here to fight and I gave it my all. I took some shots and I went in there and battled, and she threw me off my game and unfortunately, I didn't come out on top. I'm still coming home with a silver medal. It's going to take a little while to soak in, but that loss is here.

There was so much mental fortitude, even making the decision to come back, honestly. The year off was so wonderful. I was like, 'Do I want to do this?' I can win matches and still be dominant and still be powerful and still learn on this journey, and that's what I did over the past five years. I've made a better me, and I know it doesn't show it by the color of my medal, but I'm still coming home with hardware and I'm just happy that this journey has been what it's been and I've really proved to myself that I'm a powerful force. That's going to take me a long way in this life."

At times like this, there are a few things to remember.

If an athlete isn't enough for herself without a gold medal, she won't be enough with one. And one's legacy, especially one of the longest in her sports history, isn't defined or remembered by one loss. It's a pretty strong bet that, if this is Gray's mat farewell, or if such an event occurs soon, there's more than enough for many to remember for more than just a few months or years.

As hard as Focken worked, she deserves to be a heroine in her own right—and becoming the first German gal in history to win a medal of any kind solidifies her own legacy. Before and after her medal win, Focken asserted that 2021 would be her Olympic farewell tour.

> "Adeline Gray is my favorite. I absolutely love her work ethic. She is an absolutely phenomenal wrestler. She's accomplished a lot. She's definitely a dominant wrestler; like that, I think of myself as not liking to take backward steps, because that gives your opponent some momentum."
> —Oklahoma's Olivia Brown, 2021 Tricia Saunders award winner

The third day of competition gets off to a sad start, as China's Long Jia comes back for a 3–2 victory to end Kayla Miracle's quest for a 62-kilogram medal in one match. Soon, it's Mensah-Stock's turn.

She might not be exactly in tip-top shape, even for the biggest match of her life. Three matches in one day, even wins, some aches and pains are bound to carry over.

As she tried to drift off to sleep the night before, some neighbors upstairs were making serious racket—never mind what sort, even if it was in a hotel! Stirring awake, she weighed in, then returned to the hotel, trying to focus with a few episodes of *Walking Dead*.

Finally, longtime colleague Maya Nelson, there to help the Olympians stay in shape, showed up and helped woo Mensah-Stock back to the welcome slumberland for a few precious hours.

The history keeps coming. Now Mensah-Stock's the target.

Since 2009, Blessing Oborududu has won 10 medals in African competition in three different weight classes.

Blessing Oborududu: "When I was growing, my parents used to tell me wrestling is for boys and not for girls. But when I saw female wrestlers shining in the sport and traveling outside the country, I said, 'I want to be traveling like them, I want to [wrestle].' A lot of people would see me and [say], 'You are not a wrestler; you don't look like one.'

I kept doing it for me and my coaches. They believed. Whenever I went to the Worlds, Olympics they always encouraged me that, 'Blessing, the best is yet to come. You just need to focus, because you are strong, you are young, you can make it.' This is what has kept me going for the past 10, 12 years."

In 2018 and again last year, Mensah-Stock and Oborududu went to battle on the mat. Both times, Oborududu fell. Now, in her third Olympic appearance, she can get revenge in front of one of the biggest audiences in wrestling history.

Oh, and she's about to become the first Nigerian ever to win a wrestling medal. That's a pretty strong incentive to put one's moniker in the history annals, right?

Mensah-Stock goes for a few shots early, and Oborududu nearly flips her to her back. Nearly. Not quite.

Mensah-Stock escapes a headlock and gets behind Oborududu for a 2–0 lead about a minute in. Mensah-Stock tries to flip her over, but she throws a little too hard, nearly tossing herself onto her shoulders as Oborududu almost holds her down. The escape allows her to cut Mensah-Stock's advantage in half as the action breaks.

Oborududu grabs Mensah-Stock's knee, the one that once sent her under the surgical knife. Mensah-Stock shakes it free. This is a specific drill she's worked on in practice a few (hundred) times since the medical work. Moments later, Mensah-Stock's fireman's carry works for two more points at halftime.

The two women armlock and headlock their way through the next period. Mensah-Stock goes for some more shooting, but Oborududu is able to withstand. Like the rest of the people Mensah-Stock has battled over the past few months, though, she's also unable to find a way past the American's defense.

With about three seconds left, one last armlock breaks apart, and Oborududu rushes forward. Mensah-Stock backs away, and steps right into sports history. The second American woman to win a gold, and the first African American to do so.

But rather than raising her arms above in celebration, she makes her hands into a heart. She's been doing this all event, as have her teammates. The gesture means a few things.

It can be saying thanks to the fans. It can be a sign of connection to those watching back at home. And it's a way of remembering those who couldn't be here.

If her dad were around, he'd be out-shouting everyone in the building. He'd be running around the room, letting everyone know that, yeah, this was his little girl, and he was damn proud to brag about it. There are some friends and teammates who couldn't be here either, but it's easy to believe that they, like him, are all watching from somewhere.

"I love representing the U.S.," says Mensah-Stock. "I love living there. I freaking love it, and I'm so happy I get to represent U.S.A.! I felt that I could be an Olympic champ, so I kept going." In this case, going right back to the hotel for (at least) one last karaoke rendition of Carrie Underwood's "Champion."

"I'll be the last one standing," Underwood vows in the song. "Two hands in the air, I'm a champion."

Here's hoping the video accompanies Mensah-Stock's tune: it shows everything from civil rights action to the MeToo movement to athletes like UFC champ Amanda Nunes and New York marathon victor Shalane Flanagan. Her heart-hand gesture also took off, becoming a common sight in both men's and women's events across the globe.

"I am invincible, unbreakable, unstoppable, unshakeable," the song's chorus promises. "They knock me down. I get up again. I am the champion, you're gon' know my name. You can't hurt me now. I can't feel the pain. I was made for this, yeah, I was born to win. I am the champion." Sounds like it could be the mantra of almost every athlete with the guts to make a dream happen.

Tamyra Mensah-Stock: "Like I always say, my biggest enemy is me, and even I can't stop me."

Here's an interesting tale: each country chooses its own rewards for the medalists, and some, like New Zealand and Britain, give nothing but thanks (that must have been tough for the homelanders back at the London Games, knowing that people were coming to their place and walking out with more dough than they were!). Others don't give cash, but barter with everything from houses to lifetime beer supplies.

The biggest rewarder? None other than Singapore, who pays out $740,000 (in American bucks) to its golders. America's not nearly so generous, dishing a paltry $15,000 for the bronzes, $22,500 for a silver, and $37,500 for the toppers.

Right around the time she got larceny-ed out of a medal shot at the 2016 Games, Mensah-Stock promised her mom, Shonda, that she'd buy her a food truck if she did score that medal. Doing so now would cost Mensah-Stock nearly her entire paycheck.

But before she could, one of the millions of countrymen and women whom she touched came through for her and did her one better. Cruising Kitchens, a Texas truck manufacturing company (the globe's largest of its kind), announced it was handing Shonda a truck worth $250,000—for free.

Cruising Kitchens, said operator Cameron Davies, "fell in love with the person [Mensah-Stock] was."

And as it turned out, she and her fellow winners, whom we'll be meeting soon, wouldn't have to be content with a single source of compensation. She'd get $250,000 from the Living the Dream Medal Fund, while Gray's silver notched her an extra $50,000. Should any not-yet-competitors score a bronze, they'll score $25,000.

And not only that, but just after the Games, back in Mensah-Stock's Katy hometown in Texas, the waterpark Typhoon Texas announced an extra tribute to its special sports daughter, decorating a huge waterslide with red, white, and blue lights.

One Olympics ago, few expected Helen Maroulis to walk out with any medal, let alone a gold one. But she did.

With a high accomplishment such as that, however, comes a burden. There are few larger cap feathers than to knock off a world champion—and Maroulis's record had had its share of blemishes in the past few years—along with one she'll be remembering shortly. That, along with the personal issues that had been as troublesome to her as the mat opponents, had ruined any aura of invincibility she may have had after Rio.

But past reputation can make a strong impression in the minds of outsiders, both the audience and the opposition, so many might have chosen, even expected Maroulis to win simply because she already had.

Helen Maroulis: "I know people know who I am and what I've accomplished. But at the same time, I've been injured, I've been out of the loop. It took me a long time to really work to get my wrestling back to where it is. And so I think some people might think, 'Oh, she was good,' or maybe they don't think that anymore. Either way, it doesn't bother me."

She'd packed on a few kilos for the new games, storming into 57-kilogram competition against Rong Ningning, who'd been winning gold medals all over Asia since 2018. Disregarding the head trauma that had caused her so many problems over the years, Maroulis, quite literally, went head to head with Ningning for the first minutes, no one able to gain an advantage.

Then, with about a minute left in the first period, Ningning gets a point. After a break, she grabs a single leg takedown and almost gets Maroulis all the way over. The American gets to her hands and knees, but falls back 3–0 with less than 20 seconds to go.

But Ningning gets impulsive; rather than riding out her lead, she tries to turn Maroulis over. And Helen's ready, reversing at just the right second to smack down Ningning's shoulders to the mat. Ningning escapes just before the buzzer, but Maroulis has chopped her lead to 4–2 at the half.

Thirty seconds into the second, Maroulis goes hardcore offensive, flipping and rolling Ningning to her back to tie the score. She looks to leg-lace Ningning over, but the two roll out of bounds.

Undaunted, she gets behind Ningning for another takedown and her first lead. Another score with just under a minute left puts her up, 8–4. The two go back to head contact, but no one's able to score again.

Neither she nor her next opponent get much of a break; just before Maroulis's win, Tetyana Kit scores a tight 2–0 defeat of Siwar Bousetta (Tunisia). After a breather of just five matches between them, Maroulis and Kit square off.

That last win by Kit, a last-minute injury replacement for the Ukraine squad, was a wakeup call for those who didn't see her as serious. But if the majority of Tokyo's crowd wasn't familiar with her, Maroulis sure as Hades was; Kit beat her 8–2 at the Poland Open in June.

This isn't going to be another upset, as Maroulis lunges forward with a shoot and takedown in the first 30 seconds, then another a minute later. She repeats herself in the second period for an 8–0 win that was her all the way.

Four years ago, while Maroulis was winning her gold at 53-kilograms, Japan's Risako Kawai notched tops in 62-kilogram competition. While Maroulis added to her poundage for Tokyo, Kawai shed from her own. Now they'll meet for the right to score a second-straight gold at 57-kilograms.

Kawai scores a quick technical point in the first 10 seconds, and it stays 1–0 until the half. Another such point doubles her lead, but Maroulis gets a point of her own with 20 seconds left.

Kawai grabs her in an armlock. Reversing it into a takedown would put Maroulis ahead. Shoving Kawai off her would tie the score.

The action breaks with 16 seconds on the clock, and Maroulis goes low. Kawai grabs her around the head, and Maroulis goes for an underhook as the clock gets to single digits. Maroulis goes down for another shoot, but Kawai doubles back and catches her as the final buzzer sounds for the win.

Helen Maroulis: "Day in and day out, I studied [Kawai]. I worked on my game plan, all these moves, everything, and I wasn't prepared for her game plan to change so drastically. I never in a million years expected her game plan to change so drastically. I never thought that she would not shoot. I thought my defense was great, hers was great. I could have made more adjustments. I transformed my mind, my heart, my body. I did everything in my power to be worthy on this stage."

The next day, Kawai's younger sister Yukako wins gold in the 62-kilogram division. And the day after that, Kawai takes her own 57-kilogram title. Safe bet as to who will become Japan's newest sports heroines!

But Maroulis is still in the game. She may not become her nation's first double-golder, but becoming America's first two-time medalist is one hell of a bragging right. Her work against Kawai was hardly a bad performance, but it's nice for that shot at redemption to still be within reach.

She's got the next morning off. Meanwhile, Jacarra Winchester sneaks by Russia's Olga Khoroshavtseva 7–4 to start off the 53-kilogram rounds, but falls to China's Pang Qianyu in the quarters.

But she gets a special gift, a second shot, in the form of a repêchage.

Literally, repêchage means something along the lines of a second chance. But there's very little that literal about it after that, mainly because different Olympic sports define who gets another kick at the can (or medal) and who doesn't.

In the supposed simple version of wrestling's rendition, athletes who lose early on are placed into their own bracket. If the ones to whom they lost lose their own matches, those in the defeated bracket are eliminated; basically, wrestlers have to cheer for the very women to whom they lost!

For if their defeaters keep winning, they get the repêchage: another shot at maybe a bronze medal!

When Long lost her quarterfinal match back in the 62-kilogram event, Miracle was eliminated. But when Pang defeats Belarus's Vanesa Kaladzinskaya, there's suddenly a new hope for Winchester.

But first, it's Maroulis's last chance; if not of her career, then for this medal. Now it's Maroulis and Mongolia's Khongorzul Boldsaikhan.

Maroulis kneels down for one last prayer, shaking her head, perhaps in one last hope for Someone's burst of assistance.

Boldsaikhan grabs her left arm, and Maroulis attempts to jerk it away. It takes about a minute, but she does so for a takedown, and grabs Boldsaikhan around the head.

Boldsaikhan fights to her feet and grabs Maroulis again, but the process repeats for a 4–0 lead as the action pauses. Maroulis gets a quick escape point, then another takedown to go up 7–0, then, shortly after, 9–0. With less than 10 seconds left, one last takedown ends the match just a little early.

"If this *is* my last event," Maroulis says (it wouldn't be), "I wanted to go out there and enjoy it, just be able to tap into my old mentality and wrestle great. Being on the mat was such an amazing feeling…. This bronze medal is so special. I wouldn't change it for the world. A reporter asked if I was bitter than I didn't win the gold, and I was like, 'No, absolutely not.'"

After what she'd come back from, just getting to the trials, winning them, just making it back to the top stage in sports history, all of that meant success. Outsiders might only respect greatness when it's confirmed by authority (Jane won a title and Julie didn't, so Julie's a failure!), but wrestling is about living up to one's own expectations, and just one's own. A wrestler defines for herself when she's a success, when she's *made it*, and when she hasn't. A wrestler may win an event and not feel satisfied with her work, while another may finish near the bottom and be more than pleased.

That can be the biggest regret of all: *not* doing your best.

"If you go out there and you lose," Maroulis explains, "and you feel like you were a little bit timid or held back, that's the worst feeling. Because you can't ever go back and re-do that moment. Wrestling's also about doing your best. Win or lose, it's about leaving everything you arrived with out on that mat."

Helen Maroulis: "I have such a peace about [bronze]. And I'm like 'Man, why am I not more sad?' I spent four years trying to get back, my wrestling, just to not have fear. That is the biggest gift. If you told me in 2016 what I would have had to go through, I probably would've retired right then. This was harder. This was harder for sure. There were really deep, dark, dark moments. But this is way more rewarding."

Winchester hauls right back into battle as competition roars on August 6, thrashing Cuba's Laura Herin Avila 5–0 to snare a shot at a gold medal. Not long after, Sarah Hildebrandt follows her up in her 50-kilogram debut, walking an 11–0 defeat to Turkey's Evin Demirhan. She does about as well in the quarters, needing less than two minutes to foil Miglena Selishka (Bulgaria), 12–2.

On to the semis, Hildebrandt grabs control again early, charging to a 7–0 lead over China's Sun Yanan. Sun scores a point late in the period, but Hildebrandt is within a few takedowns of her third straight technical victory.

In the second, though, the pendulum swings back. Sun didn't win the 48-kilogram bronze in Rio by accident, and she's not quitting now. Two takedowns cut Hildebrandt's lead to 7–5, and Sun gets another point as the two fall out of bounds, a break in the action coming with less than 10 seconds to go.

Sun attacks, and Hildebrandt goes for an underhook as the clock reaches seven. But Sun gets her hands near Hildebrandt's waist and flips her to her back with five to go. She finishes the throw and gets its four-point reward for a 10–7 victory as the buzzer sounds.

As shocked as her coaches, fans, and viewers, Hildebrandt stares at the mat, shaking her head, wishing someone could or would just *do* something.

Sarah Hildebrandt: "I don't think I'll ever understand it. It didn't feel real, it still doesn't, but I had to forgive myself. There was a time in my career where the worst place for me was being up, 8–0. I would find a way to lose the match, get pinned. There were multiple times in a row when that happened. I had worked hard to get past that. Sure enough, we went to the break, and I thought I had to hold onto the lead, and she shut me down."

For third place in 62-kilogram action, it's Winchester and fellow former World champ Kaladzinskaya, looking to avenge not only her earlier loss to Pang, but her quarterfinal defeat to Canada's Carol Huynh back in the 2012 London Olympics.

A minute in, there's no score, with Winchester narrowly missing on some shots and Kaladzinskaya not quite able to reverse. But at the 90-second mark, Kaladzinskaya catches her off guard with a headlock and plants her to the ground.

Winchester holds her off for a few seconds, then attempts to roll and bridge her way out. Already up 4–0, Kaladzinskaya locks her into a headlock, then rolls her over just far enough for the win in 2:09.

Now Hildebrandt was the only one left.

After her tough loss, she admits, "They had to peel me off the floor. I didn't want to do it. I didn't want to cut weight. I told them I was done, that I wasn't going to weigh in. I didn't sleep at all." At around 4 a.m., she decided to go for a run.

As the sun started to rise, an idea made its way through her tired, troubled mind.

"I thought, 'The sun is up, so you have to say good morning to everyone you see!'" She started doing so, then watched a video on her cell phone. That's when she knew that her last chance was worth taking.

"I said, 'We're going to win the bronze. That's it.' The semis were in the back of my mind, and it was whether I was going to let that impact me negatively or positively. I could *not* let that hold me back. I wanted to know, even if I lost [the final], that I had left it all on the mat, and that I had done it Sarah-style."

Before heading to the hall for their final match, a coach got in Hildebrandt's face.

"Second sucks!" he declared. "Bronze rocks!"

That's a pretty profound statement. Wrestling's not like a track or swim meet, when there's several people competing at the same time, and three people emerge from the pack. In wrestling, as in any one-on-one sport, a silver medalist ends things with a loss; whoever gets the bronze can say her finale was a victory.

From the Ukraine, Oksana Livach charges up to the mat, jumping up and down, ready to rock and roll. Her pursuit of gold had also been ended by Sun, but repêchage action allowed her to charge by Cuba's Yusneylis Guzman Lopez earlier this day. Her face darkened by both a bruise and an icy stare, she's here for that medal herself. Hildebrandt strides out quickly, looking ready to go—typical athletic attitude after a tough match— yet not entirely comfortable. Sleep deprivation and heartbreak can have that effect.

Coming off a break after a minute and a half, Hildebrandt still looks a bit sleepy. Livach pushes her away and avoids her grip, then scores a quick point. But with less than 10 seconds left, Hildebrandt grabs her left leg and tries to maneuver behind her. Livach holds to her right arm, but Hildebrandt pulls it free and puts Livach on her stomach at the buzzer for the lead.

The second period starts the same. With a minute left, the score hasn't changed.

But then Hildebrandt grabs another takedown and locks on one of the leg laces that's become an impromptu trademark of hers. Another takedown gets her up 6–1.

Rather than a pin, she pulls out the familiar weaponry. With 22 seconds left, she flips Livach with a lace for two more points. Eight seconds later, she's twisted Livach over two more times for one last technical win, and the bronze.

"When I get on top, it's almost animalistic, like 'I will break your ankles,'" she says. "It was a very Sarah match. Sweep singles, leg laces, that's something you think of when you think of my wrestling. To end with my medal with something that was very much me was very cool."

Hildebrandt's win ends up making a bit more history. It pushes the women's team total to four, their highest-ever point total. It ups the overall American count to nine, the most of any team of the Games, one above Russia (Japan, in third place with seven, has the most golds, with five). That's the most by any American team since the 1984 Olympics, in which a boycott meant that they didn't have those pesky Soviets to worry about.

That Living the Dream fund we mentioned? Run by a group of intentionally name-less donors, along with USA Wrestling and the U.S. Olympic & Paralympic Commit-tee, it will pay a record $950,000 (the fund also hands out bonuses for the Senior World Championships). Since beginning in 2009, it's handed out $3.7 million to America's top wrestlers.

And, while many more medals will come America's way for the rest of the Games, without Mensah-Stock's title, Old Glory would be tied with China for most golds. We won there, 39–38. And overall, America's 113 medals were quite a bit ahead of Japan; try 25.

Should we pile on more? Hell, why not? These women deserve it!

Consider this: once again, America's overall medal count was 113, a full 25 above second-place China. The Russian Olympic Committee was third with 71, followed by Great Britain with 65.

Impressive, right? Now look at this: our women out-won our men 66–41 in Ameri-ca's medal count. Therefore, of the 186 countries that won a medal at the Olympics, our women *by themselves* won more than 184 of them!

Are our gals amazing, or what?

Note: This next part was one of the last additions of the piece, written months after the previous few paragraphs.

Mere days after finishing up at the Olympics, Gray announced she'd be right back to her old World Championship stomping grounds, heading down to Norway for the 2021 Games the following October, along with several of her classmates. And once again, she proved just why she'll always be considered a role model for upcoming ath-letes, regardless of sport or gender.

She started off 76-kilogram competition by pinning Ayşegül Özbege of Turkey, then followed suit against India's Kiran. Gray then had her way with Egypt's Samar Hamza, roaring to an 11–1 lead before yet another pin.

Now it was Gray and Mäe, the latter also looking to rebound from Olympic disap-pointment and repeat her win over Gray from three years prior.

It looked like it was to be. Mäe closed out the first period with a surprise takedown for a 4–0 lead at the midpoint, and held Gray off for the first minute of the second.

Then, at the 100-second mark, Mäe went for a takedown. But Gray was there to meet her and pushed right back, muscling Mäe onto her back for two points. The pair landed out of bounds, and Gray went back to work, getting behind Mäe to tie the score with 40 seconds to go. Then she rolled Mäe over for her first lead.

What to do next? Would she hold Mäe down and out for the remaining time, or get aggressive again, risking a potential escape and maybe reversal for a shot at a pin? There were less than 20 seconds to go, so maybe the best thing to do would be as little as possible.

Nah. Not her act. Gray kept rolling, and Mäe inadvertently helped her out, kicking her legs and landing on her shoulders. With two seconds left, Gray secured her fourth pin of the tourney (a World first for her) and sixth title of her career (a record for her country).

Adeline Gray: "How many times do you get four pins all the way through the World Championships? That's dynamic wrestling, not letting people score on you. That's groundbreaking for me. I usually tech people, but the pinning thing went very well for me. You can tell, when people get on their backs, they don't know which way to move and where to adjust.

[After the Olympics,] it was a struggle every single day. My coaches were talking me into this every step. It's too short of a time period to cope with everything, good and bad. In the Olympics, you end up with some memories and experiences than can only happen with something as special as the Olympics. It takes time for those to process and become part of you, and there hasn't been enough time. I just feel like this buzzing high has stayed through since the Olympics, because 14 days later, we had to decide whether to do this World Championship. It's still a blur; I'm still on Japanese time. The pressure there never let up. [Worlds] aren't that different from the Olympics in that you have your high and low days. It's just the focus seems a little more clear."

CHAPTER 15

Mat Women of the Future

As we near the end of our journey together, let's look toward the years to come.

Puberty typically breaks the deal when it comes to coed wrestling. Once boys suddenly get those extra layers of muscle and inches of height, along with all that testosterone-fueled aggression, it's tough for women to keep up, at least in the middle to upper weight classes.

In other areas, though, women are already ahead. And unlike with the physicality, they typically hold this advantage early on and keep it throughout.

We're talking about mental maturity. In that regard, women rise ahead sometime around early middle school … and that's a lead that men don't (and probably can't) ever cut into.

Intellectually, it may not be so much that women are smarter, per se, but they usually think *more*. Much deeper. Analyzing, critiquing, considering, reviewing, searching out all the gray areas, looking a few levels under the surface. Men are more superficial about this; they see, they act, they react, they move on, they forget.

Even in the warp-speed world of wrestling when decisions must be made and plans go from A to Q in nanoseconds, the analytical female mind often finds the needle in the haystack and threads it to victory.

"We're smarter than [boys]," asserts New York's Ally Fitzgerald, "and you have to think about all the scenarios, the technical aspects. Boys get hotheaded easily, and you focus on technique and not them just coming at you. They try to pull my singlet down, pull my headgear down, pull my hair out. I've gotten punched in the face a few times. You can't let them get to you if they're immature."

Surprisingly, her Big Apple land, typically ranked among the most liberal states in the union, still hadn't sanctioned female wrestling by thespring of 2023. So, in 2018, after a recent Lynbrook Middle grad finished up a loss-less career there (along with setting an all-school, not just all-female, record of 110 consecutive pushups), Lynbrook High had a new weapon to unleash on the fellows.

More was the pity. Right off the bat, Fitzgerald roared past everyone (as in, a full male opposition) to a Nassau County tourney win.

"I was wrestling at 99 pounds, and I beat a senior boy in the final match," she recalls. "That was crazy. I started using technique and flexibility as an advantage over their strength and muscle."

Hardcore debuts had long been a habit for Fitzgerald; her very first tournament, at age eight, resulted in pinfall losses for all her opponents. Three years later, she'd rolled through her opening female tournament, finishing up with a 15-point-plus slaughter victory.

Winning titles all over New York helped Ally Fitzgerald make a mark in one of the remaining non-sanctioned states—and, she hopes, start a trek all the way to the 2024 Olympics. Photograph provided by the *Lynbrook/East Rockaway Herald.* Copyright © 2017 Richner Communications, Inc.

"I destroyed everyone," she proudly asserts. "I get obsessed with winning. It's something I could always count on. It brings happiness to my day. I love proving people wrong, showing people that a girl can do anything a boy can do. When people told me I couldn't do something, it made me want to do it more." Along with winning national female championships during both her sophomore and junior years at Lynbrook, Fitzgerald made it to 63–17 against guys along the way (she switched to Long Beach High for her senior year).

"A lot of dads and their boys were intimidated," she says. "Dads were scared their sons would lose to a girl. Coaches took me lightly, but they changed when they saw what I was about. I quickly gained respect all over Long Island and all of New York. Not many people disrespect me around here anymore."

She keeps moving forward, and taking past and future with her. In January 2020, for the first time in over four decades of its existence, the Eastern States Tournament added a female bracket. A certain someone was at the head of the 113-pound class, one of 70 ladies at the event.

But she was almost gone before getting anywhere. With Fitzgerald ahead in her first match, her opponent twisted her hand and broke her ring and pinky fingers. The woman was given a warning.

Undaunted, Fitzgerald stayed ahead. Then, with about 20 seconds left, her opponent grabbed her hands again. Trying to pull free, Fitzgerald's elbow smacked the woman's face.

"I was just trying to get my hands out, and it wasn't even that hard," she claimed. "Her mom and her coaches were going crazy. Her mom's friend started cursing my mom out. Two other moms were screaming at my mom."

She was disqualified. Seventeen seconds from an almost-sure win, it looked like she was heading home.

Then her coach and the tournament director stepped in and overrode the decision. Both were allowed to stay in the tournament. Fitzgerald took out her next two opponents in a combined three minutes. Now her opponent was Riley Dalrymple of Copenhagen High. Fitzgerald had been in this same battle in national competition over the years, and come out ahead all but once in seven battles. But no one in the state had beaten Dalrymple this season (she'd pinned the woman who'd beaten Fitzgerald earlier in the event).

Until now. Fitzgerald tossed her across the mat to jump out to a 5–0 lead and dominated all the way to an 11–2 victory. Not long after, she became the first lady in the Nassau County sectionals, finishing third.

"I wasn't ranked," she says. "They didn't even want to rank me, because the top people didn't want a girl taking their spot. Some of the teams and coaches are supportive, but others are not."

Events like this and wrestlers like her just might someday convince enough people that the rest of the gender deserves its own New York sanctioning. By then, Fitzgerald looked to make waves in some even higher competition.

Like as a member of Sacred Heart University's team, which started in September 2020. And by 2024, maybe somewhere else.

If her high school accomplishments weren't enough, competing on USA Wrestling's Cadet Women's National Team helped her glimpse the globe's best in her sport.

Maybe a World Team appearance. Or a shot at the Olympics.

"Having to prove myself to so many people, I think I'm a pioneer," Fitzgerald says, "and having to prove myself through most of my life, the advantage of training and competing against boys, where a lot of the girls in the Midwest and West only go against girls, make me a stronger competitor."

Just because a wrestler is enjoying herself doesn't mean she's not out there giving her all.

And just because she's having fun doesn't mean she's not taking it seriously.

For the last two seasons of her high school wrestling career, Taryn Martin learned to straddle the line between the two.

And it took her farther than most other mat women in the nation.

Per usual for incoming freshman lady wrestlers, despite their success beforehand, Martin felt intimidation sneak up on, and maybe even ahead of, her enthusiasm in the early days of her career at Grove City High. The 30–10 record she'd pulled in at Jackson Middle, even the state titles she'd brought home from Pennsylvania and her Ohio homeland, didn't feel like they'd be enough incentive to even strap on a Grove singlet.

"I didn't want to wrestle in high school," Martin admits. "The boys were bigger and stronger." Back in 2017, no one was talking too seriously about sanctioning female wrestling in her state, so it was coed or nothing for her. Maybe the track, softball, or soccer careers that were already going pretty well for her at that point would be a better switch.

Then, just as she was ready to remove the headguard forever, one of her old coaches from Jackson rang. She had a chance to trek to the Mecca of American female wrestling.

The Cadet freestyle nationals were happening soon.

Why not? Even if this was her farewell, why not end against America's finest? She'd gone to Oklahoma City the previous March for the U.S. Marine Corps Girls Folkstyle Nationals, and had a pretty good time of it, coming back with a silver medal. What bad could emerge from one last kick at a similar can?

It might overshoot to say the Fargo event changed her life, but it sure as hell focused it. Once again, Martin made it back to Buckeye Land with a second place and a stronger direction.

"It proved to me that if I could compete with the best in the country," she says, "a couple of boys here and there weren't going to stop me from what I wanted to do." At this point, she was wrestling in the 94-pound class, which will matter soon.

The next year, Martin became the first of her gender to win a match in the Central Ohio area. She won a place on a national Pan Am squad. But then came a few more snags back home.

First was a relocation; she switched over to Olentangy Orange High for her sophomore season.

"I was going through a lot of life stuff that year," Martin adds. "Wrestling wasn't my focus. I wasn't sure if I wanted to go to college."

And here came a major change in her career, as well as her life.

Gaining a few extra pounds is always hard on the nerves of a young teenage female, especially one in a sport where weight maintenance, or lack thereof, can mean the difference between even getting into a match, let along winning one. In her first year on the Orange mats, Martin had bounced from 120 to 106 and back and all over the place. It's a tough burden for someone who, as all high school sophomores do, already had more than enough to hoist up and carry around.

Coming back for her junior season, she was in the 137-pound class. And no one, not even Martin herself, could have ever guessed how well this would work.

"My weight change made me work harder," she says. "Everything flowed well. My coaches were always supporting me in everything I did." Now with female wrestling spreading all over the state, she and the rest of her growing "family" had an extra incentive at its finish line, as the Ohio High School Wrestling Coaches Association would be handing them Ohio's first all-female tournament in February 2020.

By then, Martin had about made up for her time off the year before; when she stepped into Hilliard Davidson High for the state event, Martin had defeated *every single one* of her 14 female opponents, pinning all but one.

She started the state tourney with two quick pins, then got a little experimental against Piqua High's Beth Herndon, rolling to a 17–2 win for Martin's only technical fall of the season. Western Brown High's Lacie Reese got her to the second period, but Martin ended a perfect 19–0 season by holding down Big Walnut High's Aliya Martin in one of her quickest victories of the season.

Over the next few months, the local community started to see a bit more of Martin. She was still practicing or at the gym all the time; that hadn't changed since her career had started.

"I put in a lot of extra time," she says. "There were a lot of new girls eager to learn. I was coming in early, staying late, working with coaches, tweaking little things like hand placement. Tiny details like that will help you win a match."

We're talking an increase on the literal level.

"I used to be 5'5", wrestling at 100 pounds," she remembers. "Now I'm 5'8", still pretty tall compared to everyone else. Every time I'd be done with the season, I'd just put on more weight, because I wasn't fighting it anymore. I was eating instead of cutting weight, and it felt amazing. I was still eating healthy. I didn't cut at all in my senior year, because I wanted to be a role model for my teammates to show them that they didn't have to. The number on the scale doesn't determine your ability." By the time the season kicked off, she was in the 170-pound class.

But don't think we're talking about fat here, as looks were deceiving; much more of Martin's bulk was in, shall we say, a wrestler's weaponry areas, not her belt size. She would undoubtedly shock the emcee in a "Guess Your Weight" contest.

And bigger may not have been better, but it was just as good: Martin rolled to a 19–0 record during the regular season. No decisions, no tech falls, none of that. Two of her opponents never stepped onto the mat; the other 17 were pinned.

"I'd wrestled for six years, and I'd never just had fun," recalls Martin, who scored a scholarship to continue at Tiffin University during the season. "Not having to cut weight was fun, and being excited to go to practice was a huger part of it. People know my name, and I have a target on my back. Wrestling was just who I am and doing what I do. Win or lose, I'm going to go out there and wrestle like I wrestle. I look at who I wrestle, and I like to watch and learn. A name doesn't scare me. I like to know what's coming, and deal with the moves they hit, knowing that if I lose, it's not the end of the world. People aren't going to remember one loss in 10, 15 years."

That might not be accurate, considering how her high school career concluded. Marching into Hilliard Davidson High on February 21, 2021, Martin was riding a 39–0 mark over the past two seasons. Ending that streak and maybe getting a state title in the bargain would certainly be something to brag about.

"It was very nerve-racking," she says. "It was worse than my first year, because I knew this was the last one. My goal going into state was the state title, but I wanted the least amount of mat time in the whole tournament." Racking up her first two pins in a minute (combined) was a hell of a start to that one, and Abi Miller of Mount Orab's Western Brown only lasted 80 seconds in the semis.

"I was nervous going into my final match," Martin remembers. "I hadn't wrestled her before. She was second in the state."

Equipped with a slight height advantage, Kaylee Griffith of Casstown's Miami East attempted to lock Martin up for the first few moments. But Martin suddenly dropped to her knees, flipped Griffith over in the fireman's carry that had become one of her trademarks, and rolled on top of her for a pin.

The time? *Thirty-three seconds.* Martin's total mat time for the entire event? *2:53.*

In less than a full period's worth of time, she'd held down four of the best the Buckeye State had to offer. Yeah, her goal was reached with plenty of room to spare.

But Martin wasn't totally invulnerable.

Up in Fargo the next July, she got off to a familiar start at the U.S. Marine Corps Junior tournament, whaling her first three opponents.

Then came a lady from even deeper south.

Much like Martin, Brittyn Corbishley had given dozens of opponents some very short and very disappointing outings over the past few years, racking up a 66–0 record and two Texas titles in her last years at College Park High. But not long after finishing up, Corbishley got a reminder of her own vulnerability, falling to perennial champ Jaycee Foeller of Missouri at a national competition, pinned in the first period.

"In my head, I'd been hyping [Foeller] up," Corbishley admits. "I thought I wrestled good for 20 seconds, then I stopped wrestling good and let her do what she wanted, and that's why I lost."

Clearly new, or at least unfamiliar, territory for someone who didn't even debut on the mats until her first year at College Park.

Like so many others, she'd been used as a practice prop by her older brother.

"He'd cradle me and beat me in a lot of stuff," she remembers. "That made me so competitive. I used to have a goal in beating a specific person, or getting a certain amount of pins, or getting the fastest pin on the team. Little goals that I've made for myself have done wonders for my career. They just made me that aggressive. I used to take things slow, but as soon as I realized that I'm really good at wrestling, I started to pick up the pace with these goals. I wanted the fastest pin, so I'd go out and take a shot and pin them as fast as I could, or take a certain amount of shots in a match. They all came together, and it made me one of the best wrestlers in the nation." All four years, she took tops in local district and regional competition.

Just after her sophomore season, Corbishley headed to the nationals in Fargo and came back with a silver. It would be her last loss for quite some time.

After rolling through the 2019–20 state tournament with four consecutive pins, finishing with a win over Nicole Blinn of Katy's Tompkins High for the 185-pound championship, Covid kept Corbishley from Fargo redemption. Then she went right back to work in Texas, knocking out a 20–0 record on the way back to state competition.

And there was more of the same. Three matches, three pins, a first-period pin of Blinn, and another state championship.

Just one thing left to try. Much like the Olympics that would be starting the very next week, the new Fargo meet had been tentative until a short while before, with Covid still around and much stronger than anyone had hoped. But it happened.

"I felt really pressured," Corbishley says. "Every year I'd been getting better. This year I had to win it, or I'd have been really sad. At Fargo, my goal was to make it to the finals again. This year I wasn't going to choke. I loved the feeling of that."

Kansas rep Grace Johns was her first opponent, although *victim* might be a blunter, more accurate term. It took Corbishley a mere 36 seconds to rack up 10 points and a pin. Sierra Chavez didn't have much more success, Corbishley jumping to an 8–0 lead before pinning her in less than two minutes.

Now it was time to reach back and remember the success she'd had with the technique of focusing on just beating a single person. She'd been thinking, on and off, of her next opponent for two years, and, college competition notwithstanding, she wouldn't get another chance.

"My coach had told me not to look at the brackets," she says, "so I really didn't know I had her. Which was good, because usually I'll look at the bracket, and it'll make me think, 'Oh, they'll beat me, or they'll give me a good run for my money.' But it felt great going into facing Jaycee. I was getting what I wanted." Foeller had overtaken her first two opponents even faster than Corbishley had, and she wasn't looking to fall either.

Corbishley muscled Foeller over for a quick takedown, then managed to get behind her for a 4–0 lead about 30 seconds in. Foeller got Corbishley to her knees a few times, but Corbishley managed to hold her off, using her left arm to keep Foeller from getting behind her. Wrenching Foeller's leg, she made it behind her again for another takedown. Foeller appeared to get Corbishley down, but Corbishley hip-tossed her off and jumped behind her.

Then Foeller nearly stole everything. Corbishley attempted to roll her over, but Foeller managed to twist over, grab her in a headlock, and nearly plant Corbishley to her back. Corbishley managed to push her way out and notched another takedown, raising her lead to the deciding tech fall total of 10–0, all in one period.

"Everything I did clicked," Corbishley says. "It gave me a lot of confidence."

Now one of the two-time state champs would get a rare loss. Would it be her, or fellow finalist Martin?

Corbishley sent a message at high speed, slamming Martin down for a 4–0 lead in less than 10 seconds on the way to a quick victory. It would take longer than with Foeller, but she finished things with another convincing first-period 10–0 win.

"I didn't realize it for a second," Corbishley says. "I ran over and hugged my coaches. It was amazing. Two years before, I had been so nervous, I couldn't have done anything like that. I felt loose this year. I'd earned that title."

Right around the end of her high school career, she'd announced she'd be continuing her wrestling career at Texas Wesleyan University.

Wrestling, Corbishley explains, "gave me a purpose throughout high school. I went in my freshman year thinking I didn't know what I was going to do. I had no idea what to do when I grew up. Since I wrestled, it's given me a good purpose. Now I have a college and a career path, and I'm really glad about that. Right now, I'd like to go into business. Hopefully, when I start learning business management next year, I'll have some good ideas."

Not much can rank higher on a wrestler's accomplishment list than taking home a tournament. Coming out atop everyone else, standing above them on that pedestal of ledges … what's better?

How about doing it twice in one weekend? Maybe even on the same day?

She's done that. Before she was finished with middle school, Alyssa Randles got accustomed to it. Taking home a championship in freestyle one day and in Greco the next. Beating one group of adversaries in the morning, taking a quick lunch break, then taking down another one by sunset—which does happen quite early in Idaho winter and spring!

Well, maybe there is something better than that. Or at least just as good.

Vowing you're going to do something, spending years busting your hump and hips for it, and finally making it real.

Randles has pulled that one too.

"I won the girls' middle school state title in my eighth-grade year," she remembers, "but I'd lost in the boys' district finals the week before. I was thinking, 'OK, now I have to win this.' Right after that, I wrote down that I was going to win that tournament."

In the midst of her debut year at Coeur d'Alene High, Randles and the rest of the local newbie mat class headed to Mt. Spokane High School for the Joe Ridlington Freshman Invite. Coming in off a slew of middle school titles and a couple of early wins at Coeur d'Alene, Randles got the top seed and a bye at 122-pound competition.

She scored a first-period pin in her opening match. But all that did was convince North Central's Andrew Boniecki to take the gal seriously, taking her down in the first period to jump ahead 2–0.

"The kids I was competing against were like, 'Oh, I have to wrestle a girl!'" Randles says. "But once you're wrestling, they tend to forget you're a girl and just wrestle you."

Shortly into the second period, she all but exploded, taking Boniecki down for a near-fall to grab the lead. Another near-fall handed her her seventh point in less than 40 seconds.

Boniecki came right back, scoring a reversal to end the period and escaping from her early in the third to get to 7–5 with half the period to work with. But Randles notched one more takedown, and, with about 20 seconds to go, held Boniecki down for the pin.

"That was a fight for sure," she says. "We were scrambling back and forth, and I caught him. I remember getting him on his back. When I pinned him, I took a breath, and was like 'Awww!' It was a great feeling."

Now all that stood between her prophecy and reality was University High's Xavier Sanders.

"My mindset wasn't where I wanted," she admits. "I'm in the finals of a boys' tournament. Most of them, I get to the finals, and then I lose."

She scored a takedown early on, and Sanders tied it up with a reversal. Neither could put the other down for the second period

"He was pretty strong and aggressive," she says. "He was snapping me, banging on my head, pulling me. I had to move fast and use techniques, because he was strong. I went to my basics, like a fireman's carry, going off the situation, making sure I wasn't risking something."

Much of the third period went the same way. With a few precious seconds left, things stopped, and Randles re-started on the bottom.

Then she grabbed a reversal for the two deciding points.

"Both of us had been fighting for position for the whole match," Randles says. "I was exhausted afterwards. I finally had punched through my mental issue of losing against boys. It's my all-time favorite moment."

That may have been true at the time. It still may be, and could be for quite some time. But other candidates would arrive soon. Her first year ended with a state title in February 2020, and a three-tourney array the next month in the Washington State Wrestling Association's Columbia Cup in Richland, with Randles notching golds in women's folk and freestyle and a silver in Greco, all in one day.

Early in 2021, she became the first female to compete and win a match at the Ter Hark Cup wrestling dual, helping her squad to victory. Valentine's Day brought her an extra gift the next month: her second straight state title.

"Boys or girls, it's a fight either way," she says. "There's a lot more pressure against boys; you know it's not going to be fair. You don't have testosterone. They have the natural upper hand. I just try to keep my mindset the same: just give it your all and have fun."

Over the past few seasons, female wrestling numbers had gone up and up, and certain people noticed. In September 2020, the Idaho High School Activities Association announced that Randles and her colleagues had won sanctioning in their state, beginning in 2021–2.

"The mindset is to do your best and have fun," she says. "I even attack when I'm ahead. Sometimes I want to see how many fireman's carries I can get. I never look at the score during a match to keep my mind in right place."

Between matches, between rounds, sometimes right in the midst of mat battle, wrestlers may need a bit of motivation from the inside.

Even after her voice had been heard across arenas for years, once in a while, Gigi Bragg just needed to hear from herself; like every wrestler once in a while, she had to be her own pep talker.

Before combat, or even when a match isn't going the greatest, explains the Michi mat woman, "Self-talk really helps me keep my mind straight. I listen to music, in pretty good shape." That's when she's not making her own; Bragg's a common sight and sound at the Carver-Hawkeye Arena, her methodical melodic version of the national anthem starting off wrestling matches of an older crowd.

"Whenever I'm not wrestling, I'm not as happy as when I am," says Bragg, who took up the sport in kindergarten. "It's such a weird sport. It's so amazing. I work out every single day, and I wrestle almost every day. It's hard when you get to the end."

Over the past few years, her ends tend not to occur until the final tournament match, whether winning at the World Team Trials U15 division a few years ago, taking 40-kilogram Cadet gold at the June 2021 Pan-Ams in Mexico City, or even finishing second at Greensboro's Super 32 competition the following October.

Just after finishing her junior year of co-ed competition at Anoka High (in, shockingly, *Anoka!*), Bragg charged to the Great Wrestling State of Colorado and the city of Colorado Springs, to Broadmoor World Arena in March for 2002's USA Girls Wrestling Folkstyle Nationals. Before the first day was done, she'd held down four opponents for the 16U 100-pound title.

And she wasn't even close to being finished.

"I'd been preparing for this tournament all year," Bragg asserts. "I knew I could do it in my mind. I was happy I won, but I can't get too high, because I knew I had to stay focused and not get too excited, because I knew I had to compete the next day. I knew it would be harder, with older girls and a bigger bracket, and I remembered I had to stay focused and prepare for next day."

That would be the Junior event, filled with women who, despite sharing Bragg's weight class, were often well ahead in experience and success. We're talking state champs and national titlists here.

And not all of her opposition came on the mats, Bragg sadly claims.

"I had a low rank," says Bragg, seeded 26th in a field of 32. "I think a lot of that is political. People talk, and I get a reputation. I don't really know why I'm not liked; I've never really done anything bad. I've done what I needed to do, and I should have been ranked first, or at least in top five."

Iowa champion Jillian Worthen took her nearly to the end of the second round before Bragg managed to pin her. After a similar result against California's Brenda Nuñez, Bragg managed to outlast fellow Minnesota rep Aspen Blasko, 6–0 (despite living in Minnesota, Bragg was representing Michigan at the event, as her family's ownership of property in the Great Lake State makes her carded to compete for it).

Not long after winning the national 100-pound title in Fargo, Makenzie Smith had pinned her first three Junior opponents in just over two minutes combined.

Bragg nearly scored a takedown in the first minute, but the wrestlers fell out of bounds. About 20 seconds later, she lifted Bragg, only to have the Indiana native power her way to the ground and slam her back, almost getting her own takedown before falling out again. Bragg flipped Smith over her back and nearly got her shoulders down, but time ran out.

About midway through the second period, Smith began a re-start on top. Bragg managed to slip under her and power her way around for a reversal and 2–0 lead. She started the third period on top, and Smith nearly turned her over or escaped a few times, but time ran out, and Bragg was on to the semis.

Olivia DeGeorgio, fresh off a Texas state title, took control early in the final, slamming Bragg down for a 2–0 lead in the first 30 seconds. Bragg tossed her off with a leg-scissor, then managed behind DeGeorgio to tie things up before a hand-locking penalty gave DeGeorgio a 3–2 lead to end the period. But with seconds left in the second, Bragg managed DeGeorgio just far enough onto her shoulders to jump ahead 4–3, and an escape point in the third iced the win for her.

Two days, eight wins, two titles. More than enough for most. But some little voices on the inside reminded Bragg that even more was possible.

"I was pretty tired," she says. "My arms were sore, my legs were sore, and I didn't want to lose on the last day after already winning, but that's what I train for." She went right back out and scored four more wins (12–0 for the event) in the team event, in which Michigan took third.

But despite all of that, and scoring a winning record against guys in the previous season back in Anoka, Bragg's still a distance from her own personal finish line.

"There's a lot more work to do," says Bragg, who hopes to place at boys' state competition before leaving high school. "I'm a long way from being where I want to be."

Over the past few years of a wrestling career that's been running for nearly four-fifths of her life, Maggie Smith's opponent has become less and less the guy or gal on the other side of the mat.

Sometimes it's her own mind. Sometimes it's her body.

When she first strapped on the headguard at about age four, remembers the Wyoming native, "it was just fun, not as competitive as it is now. If I won, cool; if I didn't, that was OK too."

Then things started getting tougher. The enjoyment became secondary, the losing and mistakes less and less acceptable.

"As I got stronger and started to see that I could have a future, I began taking things a lot more seriously," she says. "My techniques have become much more of a priority over the past few years. Wrestling is

Very few of Maggie Smith's opponents have been able to take her down, in her Wyoming homeland or beyond— and in early 2021, neither could a near-fatal bout with diabetes. Photograph provided by Birch Smith.

hard and challenging, and it makes me feel like I'm doing something to make myself a better person in general."

Yes, none of that was so tough that she couldn't handle it, even embrace it. Not easily, but doable.

"I love intense stuff, and I like to challenge myself," Smith asserts. "As a freshman, I wrestled at 160. I was eating lots of fish, lots of veggies, and smaller meals, being smarter than the average 15-year-old about what I'm eating." Other issues, she'd find, don't just get wiped away so quickly.

A few months after sweeping a national competition in Utah in March 2021, Smith was gearing up for her next event.

"I was at practice, wrestling one of my coaches," she remembers. "He threw me, and I resisted, landing on my shoulder funny." Not worrying or even considering it all that much, Smith strolled into her next event ready to dominate some more unlucky draws. But per unusual, that didn't happen.

"I was wrestling so bad that my dad pulled me out and took me to the doctor," Smith says. Her summer was shot; just after the school year ended, she was under the knife for a torn labrum.

"It was weird for me to be out of the wrestling room for as much as I am," she admits. Weird is an interesting word there. She didn't say it was heartbreaking or earth-shattering or discuss plunging into a depression. Others may have. But it might not have seemed too bad, considering where she'd already been.

Not long after scoring the Most Outstanding Wrestler honor at Utah's Beehive Brawl event in January 2018, Smith got ready to jump across the pond to battle the best from the Far East. She'd gotten one hell of a Christmas present in an invitation to compete with other women from Montana and California in an international competition in Japan. But as February arrived, something else did as well.

Smith started feeling a bit under the weather. Tireder and tireder. OK, it happens to us humans, especially those always on the go. Then her back started hurting. Again, nothing especially new for your everyday mat warrior.

But things got worse. Her dad noticed that her vertebrae looked swollen—and if an injury like that is *visible from the outside*, something's going on.

A hospital trip didn't find a quick fix. Instead, Smith learned she'd be flown to Salt Lake City for treatment. Not the news a patient wants to hear.

Even there, no answers popped up. Doctors were sure she had a bad case of the flu, but the signs didn't match. Then someone decided to look elsewhere.

Like at her sugars. Diabetes had never been a concern, but a doctor figured it was worth a look.

Now listen to this. Not only was Smith diabetic, but she was in ketoacidosis—meaning that the body is so lacking in insulin that it starts producing excess blood acids.

Even for a seasoned diabetic, blood sugar levels of around 200 are worrisome. A 400 mark is grounds for an ER trip.

Smith's measurement? *800.*

Doctors were shocked. Patients have *died* from less than that. How Smith was not comatose, let alone walking and talking, was everything but a medical miracle. Her sight could have vanished. Her kidneys could suddenly die. The smallest flesh wound could lead straight to neuropathy.

Treating her frightened them. One small mistake could be catastrophic. She and they would be hanging from a cliff for days at a time.

But less than a week later, she walked out, vowing that her wrestling career would be re-starting soon. That sort of drive can make a champ, as it had for her on several levels before. Or it can lead the other way, and way too far.

"I was excited about wrestling internationally," Smith says. "My parents, not so much." Less than a month after nearly losing it all, she made that Japanese tournament.

"I was still weakened, so I lost fast," she remembers. "But I was *back*." A few weeks later, she won two free- and folkstyle Wyoming titles in the same weekend (by 2021, she'd won 10 such championships). The next year, she competed in Germany and Austria.

"My dad always says [that] if I make it to the third period or overtime, he knows I'm going to win," Smith says. "I don't care if I'm down eight points—I'm going to wrestle to the end. [Because of diabetes,] it's a lot harder to maintain and lose weight, but I still practice like I normally do. Sometimes I have to stop, but I get back as soon as I can. I'm not the type to let it control me. I control it."

Who would get the first shot? And when she got it, would the bullseye be gleefully elusive or unlucky?

These were questions dancing all over the Tony's Pizza Events Center as 170-pound action rolled forth at the second Kansas State High School Athletic Association championships in February 2021.

If gambling were allowed, the odds-on favorite for many would probably be Council Grove High's Jolie Ziegler. Winning Kansas's first-ever state title event the year before, a season she'd finished with a 27–0 record, had gotten her there.

But unbeaten and unbeatable had crashed into one another with the strength and tenacity of a mat battle earlier in 2020–1 competition; Ziegler had stepped onto the mat with Baldwin High freshman Hayleigh Wempe—and the younger gal had come away with the win. That victory, one of 31 that Wempe had racked up over the season (17 more than Ziegler) had made Wempe the top seed.

But her own opponent had a personal issue here herself; Wempe was opening things against Abilene High's Lyndsey Buechman. Buechman had reached the tournament finals the year before, only to fall to Ziegler: in *31 measly seconds*. Nothing would be better than a shot at revenge.

The previous week, Ziegler had secured the regional championship with a win over Larned's Ava Mull. An overtime win, it was Mull's first loss of the season. She was here at states too.

Growing up, Ziegler hadn't had all that much trouble against the opposite gender on the mats, scoring second in the state in a co-ed middle school competition.

"Parents would always say, 'Oh, she's *just* a girl,'" Ziegler remembers. "It always felt like I had something to prove. The older I got, the more difficult it became. I had boys that would try to hurt me."

Luckily, she arrived at Council Grove just as the state decided to sanction all-female competition.

"Everyone was super excited," she says. "It gave more girls the opportunity to wrestle and not get hurt by boys. Girls weren't as physical, so I dominated."

Except, of course, that one blemish at Wempe's strong hands. She certainly hadn't forgotten it, and was hoping to avenge it—but one way or another, it wasn't happening for a while.

After finishing sixth in the 191-pound games the year before, Burlington High's Bryleigh Isch had shed about an eighth of her body weight in a year to whittle down to Ziegler's class. And after notching last season's state crown with three wins in less than two minutes combined, Ziegler had her toughest state game year, barely escaping with a 3–1 victory. But she rebounded in the semis with a 21-second pin of Douglass High's Jewella Cokeley, and now it was time to wait.

Buechman had defeated Wempe 6–2 to open things, while Mull pinned Fort Scott's Jade Russell in the second period. A determined Mull didn't lose a step in the semis, rolling past Buechman, 7–2. A regional rematch would end the state event.

Ziegler got a quick 2–0 lead, but Mull kept coming. A takedown, an escape, and a takedown later, Ziegler clung to a 4–3 advantage as time ran down.

And then out. Two years at Council Grove, two state titles for Ziegler.

"I was very proud," she says. "My hard work had paid off. I hope I'll be able to be a four-time state champion, so I can encourage other girls to wrestle."

As unpredictable as a great wrestling match can be, sometimes that lack of control goes spinning right the hell off the mat.

Like, say, having to do battle in a weight class that a mat woman just happens to be, well, *sufficiently* short of? Rules-wise, it shouldn't happen. But when the numbers are low, as they still often are for female wrestling, sometimes it's just making the best of a rough situation.

If there aren't enough participants to fill a particular tournament weight group, one option might be to just cancel it. But then you let down the ones who showed up. So as tough—and, to be fair, as dangerous—as this can be, another, usually more preferable solution is to expand the class. Maybe five pounds, maybe an extra 10, maybe anything.

Females still have this happen far too often, especially in states, or at least areas, where their sport hasn't really taken off. And female numbers tend to drop off fast once one gets into the higher classes (which, to be fair, for women means about 140 or 152) by nature anyway.

Near the end of her rookie season at Kansas's Buhler High, Emilie Schweizer had done pretty well.

"I was wrestling at 191, and nobody in that weight class could beat me except one girl," she claims. "We went at it all season, and by the fourth time I wrestled her, I had her on her back when time ran out, and she had more points." Before she could grab one more potential shot at revenge, however, fate darkly came for Schweizer's knee, it blowing out in practice in early 2020.

Five long and painful months later, she, almost literally, came crawling and limping back.

"It was really hard to get all of my muscle memory back," Schweizer says. "In wrestling, my body usually just knows what to do without having to really think about it, but I'd been out for so long that I was moving really slow. But after a while, it all came back."

Between co-ed battles as the only lady on Buhler's squad, Schweizer managed to slip all over the state for whatever few all-woman events were happening. Here's where that weight "discrepancy" we mentioned came around.

A few pounds shy of two bills for the most part, she'd have to face ladies potentially dozens of pounds up. It's all you can do when a handful of people (or fewer) are available to face.

In the last few tournaments of the season, the heaviest weight class ranged from 191 to 235; in other words, someone could walk in with a pound advantage roughly the size of a second-grader.

"I wrestled 235, but I wasn't 235," Schweizer says. "When your opponent is much heavier than you, you just have to play it smart." She fell to a heavier gal early in the season—but heading into Division II district competition in early February 2021, it had been her only loss of the season.

She defeated Ell-Saline High's Jennifer Calzada for the 191–235 title. The next week at regionals, Calzada fell to Averie Burns of Wellington, who Schweizer held down in 25 seconds.

And as impressive as that had been, six days later, Schweizer defeated both at the sub-state tourney, this time needing just 21 seconds to pin Burns for the title.

Six days later, that state title shot that injury had stolen away was a few matches in front of her at Salina.

She started off by pinning Prairie View's Whitley Cox-Halliburton in about 90 seconds.

"I was nervous for all of them," Schweizer says of her matches. "I don't like to go in super confident. I watch their matches before mine to see what they like, and then go into our matches knowing what to do."

Sabetha's Kylie Meredith gave her one of her toughest matches all season, as the two fought it out for nearly four minutes before Schweizer took her all the way down.

Now it was Schweizer and Chelsey Armbruster of Chapman, herself walking in with a first round bye, a former state title, and a significant weight advantage (Burns was at the event, but fell in the first round). Schweizer went low, but Armbruster yanked her back up. Armbruster went for a throw, but Schweizer planted her feet and stopped it.

Then Armbruster went for a takedown, and Schweizer got her to her knees. She stood, but Schweizer got her back down and slipped behind her for a takedown with moments left in the period.

Schweizer started the second period up top, and couldn't turn Armbruster over. But about a minute in, she wrenched over Armbruster's left arm and rolled her. Moments later, her shoulders were on the mat for just long enough.

"There were a couple scary parts," Schweizer says. "She tried running around me, then I got out of it and I pinned her. I stood up, took a deep breath, and started crying. It's a big accomplishment. It was so hard to reach, and now I got it."

It's just how life works sometimes for female wrestlers.

Having to bump up in weight class battle—sometimes *way* up—because there's simply no one around to face.

Driving all night and all over the place for a competition … and then getting the honor of facing a local opponent. Sometimes even a teammate.

Women get used to maneuvering through situations like this, especially those in the upper weight classes, where the numbers start to dwindle fast about halfway up the poundage charts.

"I started out in middle school at 170 and 182 pounds," remembers North Carolina's Ella Beam. "In eighth grade, I was 185 or 190, but I had to wrestle 220. I still won most of my matches. The guys would take it easier, or think I would lay down on the mat. I went 10–4 that year, all against boys."

She'd actually started off hoping to battle boys outside on the grass.

"I really wanted to play football in middle school, but my mom wouldn't let me,"

Beam remembers. "So I thought I'd pick the closest, most contacting sport there is. I was talking to my cousin from Michigan, who was really into it. I told him I really wanted to punch somebody, but I can't. I got really involved from there. My friends showed me moves all summer. Whenever I first started, my mom thought it would backfire on me, but it fueled me to want to do it even more. I like to throw somebody around on that mat. It's what I'm made of."

She and two other ladies broke some mat ground at Burns Middle School of the small town of Lawndale, the entirecity, not area itself populated with fewer people than many individual schools.

"When you beat somebody, it's pure strength," she explains. "Not just physical strength, but mental strength. You've got to be able to stay in it. You have to go six minutes in a match, and then go more if it's tied. It's a physically demanding sport. You give it all, practicing two hours every day, 95 degrees in that mat room, all for a six-minute match. You get what you give. I love to throw guys around and show them that not all girls want to sit there and look pretty. Just because I'm a woman doesn't mean I'm weak."

But as her opponents began to expand as she stepped into Burns High two years later, she almost decided to switch to softball or volleyball or one of those other sports that people had informed her was "for the girls."

"My old coaches told my mom about these huge, buff, 190-, 200-pound guys," she says. "You could see their muscles, and it scared me. Do I really want to do this? I could get hurt really bad! Then I took a dehydration test and got right back on the mat. I'm really glad I didn't quit, because I made so many new friends. Guys in middle school treated me like a girl, not as a wrestler. Guys in high school, they treated me like one of the guys. They knew that I liked to win, and they didn't want to get beat by a girl. They threw me around constantly."

Near the end of her freshman year, Burns's athletic director called her to his office to inform her of a new opportunity for ladies in the area. The state High School Athletic Association was holding its first wrestling tournament in Greensboro—for women only, that is.

"He told me and my mom, 'OK, you don't *have* to go. It's about your skill level and how good you are,'" she says. "I talked to my coach, and I was like, 'Why not go to it? Why not go to the first time this has ever happened?'"

Numbers went high for the debuting tourney; about 100 women showed up for the event. But, per usual, participants in the upper weight classes were few. So little so, in fact, that the 220- and 285-pound groups had to be combined. Well below even the two-bill mark herself, Beam was already at a high size disadvantage.

"I was freaking out," she says. "One girl I wrestled weighed 250; the other girl was 285. If she'd gotten me down, I would have been done."

"You can be state champion," her coach encouraged. "It's something no other girl has ever done. You can get in the school trophy case. Who cares if you have to wrestle 220? Get out there and prove yourself!"

Beam started things off giving away "just" 60 pounds.

"I got her with a cradle, and she came up and bearhugged me," she says. "I pushed her, and it didn't help. That made me mad, so I got her into a standing cradle, and rocked back. When you're wrestling, you have to see things in a millisecond; am I going to take the chance or not? I did it: I brought her back with me, and she was down. I threw her down, and her head bounced. Most of the time, you can break girls' grips, and she couldn't break mine." The ref smacked the mat, and Beam almost didn't need her hands and arms to get off the mat.

And she'd need even more adrenalin for her next match, against an even larger opponent.

"Sometimes with guys, I watch their stance for three to five seconds," she explains. "I can tell what they're going to do. She had bopped me in the nose and it made me mad. I got her and snapped her down and spun her around. My coach was like, 'Top, top, top!' It was hard to move her around, because I couldn't get my arms around her." A faked cradle got the lady down, and Beam put her away.

"Everybody at church, at school, at the store," she says, "everybody was like, 'Did you really win a state championship?' I was like, 'Yes!'"

Spurred on by her success, Beam started to make more of her presence in season two back at Burns.

"I got to face all the guys in my conference," she says. "They're all just standing around, these huge guys. Not a lot of girls around my weight class. These guys would go full-on against other guys. Against me, they'd be shaking their head. I go out there to win, to make my points known. I'm not here to lollygag. It was funny to see other people's reaction; they won't take the first shot. When I make the first move and throw them on the mat, it's clear that I'm not going to take it easy."

After spending her pre-sophomore summer buffing up by tossing haybales around the family farm for months at a time, Beam prepped to fire off opponents.

"I got down to 185, and I wanted to build muscle from there," she says. "Once I practiced with a guy 40 pounds bigger than me, and my coach asked me to buff up. I was really nervous, and lost my first five matches. Then my coach was like, 'Just drop the nerves and go out and wrestle.' That fire overtook my nerves. From then on, I wanted to win, I was going to win, and I went out there and just whopped tail. Some of the guys I wrestled were so much bigger and stronger than me, and I just waited for them to make a mistake. I finished the season 13–11 or 15–12 or something."

Good enough to send her right back to the state games in February 2020, this time in Concord. This time, her event had glued the 185- and 195-pound classes together.

"I wanted to be the first one to be a two-state champion," she says. "I really wanted people to know, this is who I am."

Walking in with the best regular season record (it was, in fact, 13–11) got Beam a bye for the first round. Then she slipped past Josie Sell of R. J. Reynolds High, 5–2.

"I had more problems than I expected from the first girl," she says. "When I wrestle girls, I'm very offensive, to when I wrestle guys, I'm defensive."

She escaped from Rosewood's Julissa Jaramillo, 7–4. Now Beam had to battle Sage Cook for the title.

And who could give her a better battle than someone whom she'd been working out with and had been observing with others throughout the past two years?

Yes, Cook just happened to be Beam's fellow Burns gal.

But familiarity goes both ways; as much as Cook was ready for Beam, Beam was on alert as well. Charging to a 4–1 lead, she started the final period on top, and Cook couldn't escape.

It sends a chill down the spine and ties the stomach into a bowline.

Somonauk. The moniker itself just calls up the fighting spirit of Native Americans.

You hear the name, you think of the type of fellow who'd be right there next to Sitting Bull, Geronimo, Crazy Horse, and everyone else who took arguably the world's strongest, proudest heritage and turned it into hardcore weaponry, kicking ass on some evil invader who'd stepped into their land. You imagine someone with the (admittedly a little stereotypical) focused strength and stoicism seen in about every artistic depiction of such a warrior.

Native Americans were wrestling long before anyone knew what the hell an America even was, and just going by a name as cool, as intimidating, as strong as something that you feel just by saying it and thinking it, like Somonauk, might score some intimidation points before the battle even commenced.

Well, not really. Not in this case. Not if you knew the background. Sorry to let anyone down after that buildup, but Somonauk is actually a Native American term (from the Potawatomi tribe of both the Great Plains and Great Lakes) for "pawpaw grove," after the fruit trees that used to fill the area. Kind of takes the impact down a few decibels, doesn't it? Can you imagine being named after a glorified garden?

It's also a small town in northern Illinois. And the town's title might not stand for warfare, but the name on the welcoming sign on its outskirts certainly does.

Soccer's certainly an aggressive sport, but scoring takedowns and leg sweeps in kicking combat gets a person penalized and yellow-carded, not points. After dishing out as much punishment to her opponents as to the poor checkered ball (and costing her team a few free shots in the bargain) in grade school competition, Shea Reisel decided to switch over to handing out purposeful pain for points.

"Wrestling was so intimidating, so difficult for me to understand," she remembers. "I was drawn to it because of how

Shea Reisel shows the sign her small Illinois homeland made in tribute to her national title. Photograph provided by Jennifer Reisel.

difficult it was. When I went into a wrestling club, I wasn't intimidated by the boys themselves; I was intimidated by the fact that it was something they could do and I couldn't."

And along the way, she started to feel something else. More and more and more. It's something that every athlete faces, and wrestlers maybe more so than any other.

You can't avoid it. That's simply not realistic. So the best you can do is turn it around and make it work for you. See it as a sign of accomplishment, not of suffering. Make it something of a goal, rather than an avoidance.

"I fell in love with mental and physical pain," Reisel asserts. "I had never experienced the pain that wrestling showed me. Wanting to give up and having no choice but to continue to push through, and feeling that exhilaration was a high for me. One of the things that was exhilarating was that in this room with coaches and boys, I was excelling past them. I was mentally tougher than some of the boys."

Bouncing (literally and figuratively) all over the Illinois Kids Wrestling Federation for the rest of elementary and middle school, she recalls, "I won quite a few girls' state titles, but one of my most memorable was in my eighth-grade year. I qualified for the boys' state events and made it to third at sectionals."

The next year, she debuted at Somonauk High as few women had before. In her very first event in December 2018, Reisel rocked the Seneca Fighting Irish Invitational, tearing through three guys on the way to the 106-pound title match.

"People loved it," she remembers. "There were older guys in that weight class. That was something people had never seen. They had never had a girl place so high in tourney, but that's what set me apart from other girls in that area. In the opposing coaches' mind, it was *not* possible for their wrestlers to lose to this girl, so there was a little bit of hatred because I was beating boys I wasn't supposed to beat."

When she jumped out ahead of Eureka High's Brayden Peiffer in the finals, it appeared that the audience's collective psyche was ready to blow. But Peiffer managed to tie things up in the final seconds and slipped past her in the extra period.

"That was a tough loss," Reisel says. "All I could do was pick my head up. I was very angry that I lost. I worked harder. I didn't win at Plano, and kept working harder."

"Didn't win" is a bit misleading; she actually took third at the Plano Reaper Invite later that month. Doing as well at the Byron Individual Wrestling Sectional the following February would have pushed her all the way into state competition, rare for any first-year matster. But that didn't happen, as winning one of three matches didn't make it.

By the end of the next summer, she'd won four tournaments—state titles in both Iowa and Illinois, a tournament at University of Illinois Armory in Champaign, and another in Oklahoma—scored sixth at a national event in Texas, and won a silver at the U.S. Marine Corps Cadet and Junior National Championships in Fargo, North Dakota, falling to near–Olympian Sage Mortimer in the finals.

"Winning a state title in Iowa was memorable because I knew I was good for Illinois," Reisel says. "Winning Iowa showed that I was a good wrestler, not just in Illinois. I don't think there was a huge change in my mindset. I just continued to wrestle the way I know."

Covid kept her (and every other mat lady in Illinois) from a new state title the next year. Back in Iowa in February 2021 with a few pounds added, Reisel warmed up by scoring a 112-pound AAU state title, just as she had two years before.

A few weeks later, she went back for the USA Wrestling Girls Folkstyle National Championships. Soon, it was Reisel and Michigan's Kendra Ryan for the title.

Reisel had a slight height advantage over the 61-inch Ryan, but that was about all; the Fenton High senior was strolling in on the strength of two state titles of her own, and had notched her 100th career win a few weeks before.

The pair went back and forth for the first two periods, with Ryan clinging to a 5–4 lead as the final section began. Then things went absolutely haywire.

One gal scored, then the other, then back again. As the seconds wound down, Reisel held down Ryan and an 11–10 lead. When Ryan escaped, it looked like things would go to an extra period. But Reisel managed one more takedown to reach tops in the nation.

As her state sanctioned her sport for the first time for the 2021–2 season, Reisel started making up for lost time early. Back in Plano action in December 2021, she swept through three opponents for the 113-pound title and the event's Most Outstanding Wrestler honor. A month later, both accomplishments came back around at the Seneca Invitational.

Then, in the last days of February 2022, she and the rest of Illinois's top mat women poured into Bloomington's Grossinger Motors Arena for the state tournament. For the first time, the Illinois High School Association had backed them with sanctioning.

She started 110-pound competition by pinning both Richwoods's Baya Perez and Cha-Anna Kassim of Hillcrest in less than two minutes combined. Reisel held off Lawrenceville's Shaina Hyre 4–2 in the semis.

Reisel and Jacksonville's Brooklyn Murphy blasted into each other early on, twisting each other all over the mat. A topple out of bounds slowed things down a bit, and Reisel grabbed a takedown with about 20 seconds left in the period. She stayed atop Murphy for the second period, but couldn't turn her over.

Early in the third, Reisel fought her way away from Murphy, but Murphy grabbed her in a headlock and slammed her to the ground, within a few seconds of a pin. Reisel managed to yank her head out and climbed on Murphy's back for a 5–0 lead. A pause put her on top of Murphy, and she managed to stay there for the remainder.

"I don't feel that I wrestled to the best of my abilities in that match," Reisel admits. "I do feel like it was a good match to come out on top. It didn't feel real. I was over the moon, but it honestly didn't feel quite real. It really felt like I won a state championship. When I won, it felt very different [from the first], more glamorized with [the sanctioning], and it made me feel really special that I was a part of that."

A few years from now, she might just have a longer, larger story to discuss.

"The Paris Olympics is still a major goal," Reisel says. "There's nothing negative about setting goals. I do my best to have a positive outlook on everything. The Olympics is a major goal I set when I was young, along with making it to state championships with the boys."

> "My sister went three years ago to a practice. I tried it out, and I just got better and better. I want to be the best. Wrestling boys makes me better, because when I go and wrestle girls, I'm tougher than they are. Boys have a lot of testosterone, so they're stronger.
>
> I won states in Indiana. It was an accomplishment, because I put in the work and effort. Then we moved to Ohio. There are more girls here, and I think the girls are tougher."
>
> —McKinzee Mills, 10, state champ
> in Indiana (2019) and Ohio (2021)

From the summer of 2020 to the summer of 2021, Madison Healey won more than 200 matches and a slew of titles. Photograph provided by Rich Vitale.

Most wrestlers will tell you that speed's a bigger advantage than strength, particularly those without much time or space (as in, especially at the beginning, five or less feet of height and nowhere near triple-digits of poundage!) to develop much of either. It's definitely the most common weapon in grade school mat battles, kids jumping all over the place, flipping each other around, one matster scoring a takedown only to find herself toppled over and right back on the defense.

Breaking the speed limit has been commonplace for Madison Healey since long before she hauled onto Pennsylvania elementary league mats right after her second-grade year started in late 2017. Nothing new about why—an older brother and uncle had, not necessarily intentionally, left some grappling footsteps for her to follow in.

When, however, was a different matter. One day, sort of out of nowhere, Madison strode right up to her mom and informed her of a slight monkey wrench in family weekend plans. There was a meet that weekend, and the local team was a part. Without any experience except from the stands, she wanted to participate.

Madison wondered what about wrestling made her brother want to do it. "Will I like it like he likes it? You just go out there and do your thing early, and you have coaches and your teammates by your side."

Her mom called the coach to inquire about adding a space to the lineup. Four days and two practices later, the eight-year-old was exchanging takedowns—and came out second overall.

The next March, the Pennsylvania Junior Wrestling Youth State Championships held a division for the ladies. Right off winning an area title, Madison roared right into the Mohegan Sun Arena in Wilkes-Barre and became one of the first female winners in tourney history, holding down her first three opponents (no one said that strength was out and out non-existent here!) in less than a minute and a half in totality before falling in the final.

If the snowball that Madison's career began as had just been nudged down the hill, it soon took off in a way that made Indiana Jones's natural enemy look like a marble. After a win here and a victory there for the first year or so, the local wrestling community might have thought she'd been cloned in the summer of 2020; from July to November, Madison stepped out for 126 matches and won 106 of them in 10U and 12U competitions. By the summer of 2021, her win total was well above 200 and brought her a state title from Pennsylvania, a victory at a World event in Reno, and state wins in both boy and girl events in national competition.

"I stay hydrated," Madison explains of her longevity. "Sometimes I don't get to hydrate that much, so I get nervous, but I have to keep food in my body to keep my energy up. Usually, we have to wake up super-early, like five or six in the morning, for most tournaments, and wrestling starts at eight or nine or ten. You just warm up with a partner, taking shots. You get your drink, you watch your team, you get warmed up, and then you get warmed up again."

But her Flash-level nature extends beyond the mats; the would-be doctor had burned through nearly half the public library system before finishing elementary school, once turning out hundreds of books in a single year, enough to score a pizza party for her entire class.

The medical career, however, would come after college and Olympic titlehood if Madison stays at the edge of sound barrier breakage. Nearly two digits' worth of matches in a single day, she predicts, "could get me ready for the NCAA. If I could wrestle a short amount of matches with everything I had, then why not start double- and triple-bracketing to get ready for the future? It's about aggression—just not being afraid to go out there. If I just go out there and wrestle my heart out, I earn something from that. [My opponents] may be stronger, because they're older and may lift more weights, but I don't care who I'm wrestling. Many kids may get a little nervous, because they're wrestling someone a few times bigger, heavier, stronger, or older, but for me, I'll just go out there and do what I have to do."

Crossing the border from eastern Georgia to the panhandling part of Florida's woods, you haven't really left. Stepping into the bottom of Alabama, you're still in the same spot.

That place is called Wiregrass. To those who live at the joint named for its native tall grass, it's everything but the fifty-first state.

When someone from that area makes a big athletic mark, the state in which he or she lives isn't all that important, not the top thing to them. It's that one of *Wiregrass*'s own (rather than Georgia's or Florida's) that made the homeland proud.

Technically, Evelyn Holmes-Smith would be considered an Alabama native by those of the geographically inexperienced. But the eighth-grader's victory in the January 2021 Alabama High School Athletic Association was more than just a state accomplishment; it marked the first time that *any* wrestler, not just of her gender, had brought a title home to Wiregrass.

"I like that it's me against one other person," says Holmes-Smith, who started wrestling around the time she began middle school. "It makes me a stronger wrestler and a stronger woman. I learn a lot on and off the mat. Wrestling takes mental ability, and that helps me in school."

Taking a quick breather between rounds at her first national event in Oklahoma, Holmes-Smith happened to stroll by a display, a visual incentive even, for those embroiled in mat battle.

"I saw the belts that the girls win at tournaments," she remembers. "I thought, 'I'm going to win one of those.'"

It didn't take too long. She soon took a national freestyle tournament in Myrtle Beach, and helped her squad to a victory in a folkstyle event soon after. Soon she won a Super 32 event in Florida.

"In wrestling, if I lose, it's a learning ability just for me," she says. "I know what I need to do to make me a better wrestler."

Her season started with a resounding win at the USA Girls Preseason Folkstyle Nationals in October 2020 in Illinois; ironically, Holmes-Smith won the 16U division, but only got second in the 14U event, falling to Missouri's Jayci Shelton.

Alabama's Evelyn Holmes-Smith shows off the physical sacrifice our national champ wrestlers make for success. Photograph provided by Evelyn Holmes.

It would be one of just two losses she'd suffer between then and the state games the next January at Hoover High.

"We trained hard at my gym," Holmes-Smith explains. "We'll go two hours non-stop. If I can go two hours nonstop, I can go six or seven matches pretty well."

Conditioning didn't appear a necessity early on, as she held down Kaylan Brown in just 15 seconds. Emily Hill, however, gave her a hardcore brawl, as it took Smith-Holmes nearly five minutes to put her away, albeit after building a 9–0 advantage.

Holmes-Smith had never even heard of finals opponent Mariah Jones, let alone competed against her. But she scored a takedown in 20 seconds, then got a few near-falls to end the first period with a 7–0 lead. She maneuvered Jones to her back early in the second, and Jones battled back, but Holmes-Smith managed to pin her with moments left. She'd finished the event unscored upon.

As she almost always was through most of the first few tournaments of her wrestling career, Trinity Gottler was one of the only, if not the only, female in that junior varsity tournament that winter afternoon in Kentucky.

And as she so often did before and since, Gottler came out on top of the guys in every sense, rocking and pinning her way to the title.

Off the mat, two hormone machines in training gave a frank appraisal and discussion of her looks. Suffice to say, they wouldn't have minded wrestling her outside of official competition … and maybe letting her win.

A fellow in front of them slowly turned around. He didn't seem to see the humor in their words, but maybe he was recalling his own testosterone-infused days.

Or maybe not. If he'd stared any harder, rays might have blasted through his irises.

"That's my granddaughter," he asserted, fire nearly blasting off every word.

A wrestling match suddenly became a track meet. The pubescent playboys were outside at three or four times the speed of light.

Yes, this is still a thing that happens all the time for female wrestlers, far more often behind them than before them. Still, as much grief as female wrestlers get from all angles, another rough moment became one of Gottler's earliest strongest accelerators.

In 2014 Louisville for one of her first events, the 10-year-old was battling against a boy three years her elder, one of many older, larger, stronger opponents she'd taken on in those long days.

Audiences might have thought the matsters' lives—or maybe tickets to a meet-and-greet with the times' biggest boy band—were on the line. The two hurled each other and themselves all over the mat, bouncing off the mat and right back up to warfare.

Time and again, the match was stopped for blood timeouts. Plugs held Gottler's plasma inside as she attempted desperately to focus on her opponent, not her bloodshed. The brawl rushed through regulation and into extra time.

But it just wasn't enough. Per usual in a wrestling match, the win went to the person who scored last, and her opponent did that here.

A roaring ovation nearly washed away her disappointment. As her family and coaches consoled her, a stranger walked over.

His son had been in the event, and she and everyone else figured he was just there to rub it in with this loss, just to remind her that losses should be all the proof she needed to admit.

But he didn't.

"That," the man informed Gottler, "was amazing."

That's when she, and everyone else, knew that it truly was amazing. That she was amazing. That this wrestling thing was worth sticking to.

About five years later, her third consecutive Kentucky Wrestling Coaches Association girls state title solidified her mark well past diamond levels.

And not the ones on which her athletic career began. As she finished up the latest softball season one Halloween, Gottler's dad basically told her she'd be trying out a different sport. Ten-year-olds can only run so far without stumbling across some sort of trouble, intentionally or otherwise, and he'd found something new for women throughout Kentucky. It was worth taking a shot.

Not surprisingly, she picked up the takedowns pretty quickly. Not surprisingly, her male teammates had a tough time having a lady on the team.

Which isn't exactly to crow that Gottler was too comfortable herself. The drills weren't all that bad, and the fitness was a gift she'd carried over from other sports. But squaring all the way off with a guy, especially in front of everyone? That can't be too easy for any lady newbie in the sport.

But her coach helped out. Just as her father had, he *told* her that it was time for conditioning and that she'd have no choice but to accept this mission.

As word jumped all over the gym that co-ed competition was commencing, a nearby basketball practice emptied into the room. It was Gottler against a 12-year-old guy.

OK, so she'd probably lose. But he wasn't going to push, or toss, her around.

She started off on the defensive, her opponent backing her around the mat. But she wouldn't go down, no matter how hard he pulled and pushed. That's not how this was supposed to go—and guys his age aren't known for being especially patient or deep in the thinking process.

Let's get this over with. He got a little more aggressive with her than the rules allowed. Grabbing, twisting, yanking, ready, if not outwardly *needing* to win.

Now this was personal. Both wrestlers had expected him to win, but Gottler had lasted this long. Why *not* go for it? It didn't look like this tough guy could beat her the legit way. Who said that upsets couldn't happen here?

Not her.

She fired him to the ground. Then she pinned him. Yes, it had happened. And it would occur again.

However, Gottler's all-gal debut soon after wasn't exactly smooth sailing itself. Uncomfortable in her uniform, combined with the new tights, she had to take on a lady of driving age.

Another huge audience. More hollering. An even longer match.

Same result. The younger gal pinned her opponent in the final period.

"I almost cried, I was so excited," Gottler remembers.

Over the next few years, she got used to being in the extreme gender minority.

"In eighth grade, I won a youth state event in Louisville," Gottler remembers. I was always the only girl. I was the only female at 168 pounds. I won four matches in one day, finishing against a guy who'd beaten me earlier." From fifth through ninth grade, she took home four regional titles. In March 2021, she scored her third consecutive Kentucky Wrestling Coaches Association girls' state tournament. By the time she finished high school in 2023, she'd score five state titles.

And even when she lost, Gottler could feel herself making a difference in Kentucky female sports. Over and over, a guy would get his hand raised against her, only to go storming off the mat and fire his headgear against the wall or a bench, or maybe even a teammate. He may have won, but he couldn't pin a girl. She, like so many others there and everywhere, was a hell of a lot tougher than the boys could have guessed.

> "I got into wrestling because my dad wrestled, and my brother wrestles now. I started when I was eight, but just as practice on our youth team. I am 10 now. I like the adrenaline I get, and the excitement. Wrestling, we have learned in practice, is discipline and hard work, both of which my parents have taught me. And in the end, the arm raised as a win is a thrill.
>
> My most memorable moment, there are two. My very first ever match was a win. I pinned the other girl in the second round, and my dad got to raise my hand. The other was when I made it to the youth state competition in my weight class; sadly because of Covid, I didn't get to compete."
>
> —Laycee Watson, 10, Ohio, multiple co-ed tournament champ at 131-pound competition

Jackie Joyner-Kersee did it on the track. Greg Louganis did it off the diving board. Justine Henin did it on the tennis court. Amy Van Dyken did it in the pools.

Someday, Maddie Hayden might do it on the mats.

It, in this case, refers to making Olympic medal-hood—and overcoming asthma while doing so.

Laycee Watson's dad congratulates her on another Ohio tournament win. Photograph provided by Daphne Watson.

Gifted with an early growth spurt that would quickly put her in the upper classes of wrestling, Hayden started her hardcore athletic career at the ripe old age of a second-grader, chasing down unsuspecting boy after boy on the Caledonia (near Grand Rapids), Michigan flag and tackle football gridirons. Watching from the sidelines, her coach could see her sports future.

Actually, theirs: he just happened to run a nearby wrestling squad. She might be the next puzzle piece to add.

Not many in the area could conceive much of a lady on the mat, but Hayden, as would become usual for her for a very long time, went all in at full speed. Just as quickly (well, maybe not, but pretty soon!), she started winning.

Often without female opponents her size, Hayden was all but forced into co-ed competition. Just as she'd done for football yardage, she went straight ahead and basically dared anyone to so much as set a toe in her way. Before she hit double-digit years, she was a national champ.

Around then, the phones started ringing. And not just from all-female squads; travel coaches didn't care about her gender, as long as she could win. She'd often find herself her gender's sole representative on the teams.

The wins kept coming. In late March 2019, Hayden rolled to the Michigan Youth Wrestling Association state events in Kalamazoo. In less than a minute and a half, she'd pinned three opponents for the 10U girls' heavyweight title.

And why settle for so little mat time in such an important event? She turned right around, went to the mat with four guys, and didn't allow a single one to get her out of the first period!

A week later, in Lansing, she did it again, pinning every male and female on the way to a pair of National United Wrestling Association for Youth heavyweight titles.

By that point, however, a lifelong health issue started to emerge for Hayden. It became common for her to feel wobbly in the midst of the match. Sometimes she'd hit her inhaler during period breaks. Once in a while, she'd need a mid-match time-out to get her breath back. As she fought for the 2019 U.S. Marine Corps Girls Folkstyle National title in Oklahoma City, a prematch asthma attack almost ended her tournament early. First she came close to forfeiting, then nearly was pinned early in the match.

But she persevered, and ended up with another title.

"I wasn't going to do that match," Hayden admits. "Once I pinned her, I felt like I was on top of the world!"

Stress and anxiety can trigger the hell out of an asthma attack, and it's tough to imagine a more stressful situation than having to go at your finest in front of even dozens of people, let alone hundreds, thousands, etc.

But Hayden keeps going; in August 2020, she scored the NUWAY Summer National Folkstyle title in Atlantic City and helped the Steel Valley Vixen squad to the girls duals title at the same event, a win that included her pinning an 18-year-old competitor.

You can't shake off, stretch off, or walk off asthma. You just hope that it has the common courtesy not to work its hurtfulness at the worst of times. Hayden's just doing all she can.

"Wrestling pushes my body as hard as it can go," she says. "Everyone can wrestle, but not everyone can get to the top of it. It has more of a mental aspect; if I gave up points, my mind used to tell me that I couldn't win. Now that my techniques have gotten better, if I lose some points, I think, 'OK, I'll get the next point, and then the next one.'"

> "Sometimes I get scared, but I know I can get better. I've lost to high school girls by a point or two, and then come back and dominated them. It feels good to beat the older girls, so when I get to their age, I know I'll be successful.
>
> I won a 97-pound title last year, so I knew I had to maintain that title. [Repeating] felt awesome.
>
> I have to go harder when I'm wrestling boys. Sometimes they cry because it hurts. The boys cry a lot! You can hear the dads saying, 'You better not let that girl beat you!' But I hear a lot of the men talking about how fabulous I am."
>
> —Delialah Betances, Georgia (multiple state champ before high school, winner of 15U national event at age 12)

Watching a bunch of huge muscular guys grapple it out yanked Kennedy Wheeler into wrestling. About a decade from now, she might be emulating a certain group of powerful women.

Critiquing the 2019 Big Ten wrestling championships (Penn State won it going away), the preschooler turned to her dad.

"I want to try that!" she blurted.

Georgia's Delialah Betances took several state titles throughout Georgia and a 15U national title when she was 12. Photograph provided by Jacklyn Limardo.

A stereotypical dad might have winced and refused. But Chris had been there in high school, as had his own father.

"I said, 'Hell yeah!'" he remembers.

Not long after, she was squaring with those curmudgeons on the elementary school squad.

"It was cool, wrestling boys," Kennedy remembers. Like most newbies to the mat game, she lost most of her first few battles.

Then she made it to the finals of a tournament. And hasn't stopped winning since.

Along with her Indiana homeland, she and her national squad Supreme Women of Wrestling have been all over Iowa, West Virginia, Kansas, Wisconsin, and elsewhere.

"I like pinning a kid," she says. "It's fun."

As her role models Sarah Hildebrandt and Jacarra Winchester, along with the rest of their squad, scrambled towards the Olympics in the team trials, Chris remembers, "She told me, 'Daddy, that is going to be me! I'm gonna go across the world and win an Olympic gold medal!'" If things go as planned, Kennedy could score a spot at the 2036 Games (she'll be 21).

In April, Kennedy scored the Indiana freestyle title. That, along with other tourney wins, won her a spot in June's NUWAY Nationals in Tennessee.

Per usual, she kept training three days a week at the nearby Contenders Wrestling Academy, facing contenders from both genders.

"What keeps her in it is mainly the fact that she has a blast with her friends," Chris says. "Well, there is no such thing as friends in wrestling. We're all family."

In practice, one can be choosy about her workout partners. When competitions arrive, however, that luxury goes away. When Kennedy walked into the Nationals, she found herself at a double disadvantage.

At six, she was in the 8U competition. Gifted with early growth spurts, many of her opponents were looking down at her. Others had a few extra years of experience, probably against opponents their own size and maybe larger.

Along with that, the 46- and 52-pound classes had been combined. Starting off at just over 44 pounds, height wasn't Kennedy's only physical obstacle.

"They were all taller than me," she says. "I thought I was going to lose."

A few quick wins started to change her mind and raise her confidence. Then her last opponent took over—fast.

The girl took her down, again and again. With less than a minute left, Kennedy was on the wrong side of an 8–0 score.

Then the shots she'd been sharpening in practice lately came shooting through. She jumped down and in, took her lanky opponent down, and, with just over 20 seconds left, scored the pin and the national title.

"She ran over and jumped into my arms," Chris says. "She said, 'Daddy, I did it! I'm the best in the country!'"

> "I saw that many girls never (wrestled), and I wanted to see if I could be one of the girls that would stand out to people, and it really worked. I started when I was six or seven. At a tournament in 2020, I beat two of the top kids, and I thought, if I beat the top kids, I could become one of the top kids. I sometimes wrestle in a lot of tournaments at once so I can practice for getting to the Olympics and hopefully being a gold medalist. My mom tells me that I'm the greatest and that I can beat all those people.

I stick to my funky self and my techniques; I've very creative on the mat. My coach shows me a new move, and I go on the mat and try it, even if it's a very weird position."

—Lyric Hetzer, 11, multiple national and Ohio state titlist, both all-female and co-ed.

Gail Sullivan couldn't breathe.

Not because her singlet was too tight, or because her opponent was squashing her too hard, or because Atlantic City can get heated in the summer.

She just didn't have time.

The nine-year-old stepped off the mat at the 2020 Summer Nationals, wiped off her face, guzzled a sip of water (maybe!), then ran back out into action. And we're not talking about breaks between periods, either. This is about match after match after match. And even repeating that a few more times.

In less than an hour, the young New Yorker powered her way through eight matches, winning all of them. Against women up to five years older and often a few pounds heavier (Covid-caused low turnout forced the competition to combine age and weight classes), she finished off an overall 12–0 to take the title. Almost all of her opponents wallowed off the mat in tears.

It wasn't the first time she'd caused such a reaction.

A few years before, swimming in the Dominican Republic, she'd been accosted by a guy trying to toss his weight around. She didn't respond favorably.

He slapped her in the face. She launched a right cross to his jaw. Revealing just who the weaker gender was in this encounter, he fled to the deep end. She stood on the side, roaring at him to climb on out and resume the brawl.

But back to the Nationals. As if wrestling under tents in 90-degree heat that day in August 2020 wasn't enough, competitors kept getting shoved in and outdoors to avoid a certain virus.

"I just tried to keep breathing good," Gail recalls. "The refs were asking me if I wanted more breaks or water, and I kept saying no. But I could have done more. I wanted to keep wrestling after it was over. I wrestled at another event the next day. My dad said he would get me a kitten if I won all three, and he did. I named it Snowflake."

And the very next year, she came right back and did it again, winning the 10U and 12U titles on the same day back at Nationals.

Certain things in wrestling, a wrestler can only feel.

That burst of adrenalin that comes rushing through when you hit a great move, when you find yourself in the midst of a major comeback. That relief, the satisfaction that comes with finally hitting a move that stubbornly didn't work for so long, or when your hand gets raised, particularly over an opponent that's come out on top of you before. The weariness, even the pain from a match when you gave it your all. And, yes, the depression that might come from that same match, where giving it your all wasn't enough.

Physical touch may be one of our five senses, but this sort of feeling can overtake them all. Sometimes those of us who fully or partially lack some of the other senses are the ones who truly experience this.

After all of one week of wrestling practice, all of which took place in the Anthony living room, Adalynn Anthony stepped onto the mat for the first time. The second-grader finished third. In her next tourney, she notched first.

Adalynn Anthony overcame a severe lifelong hearing problem to win titles in her native Ohio and up and down the Midwest before she was through with elementary school. Photograph provided by Leanne Anthony.

"I am aggressive and relentless," bluntly states the Ohio gal. "I have no fear of losing or making a mistake."

Losing, she's taught, as all young wrestlers should be, doesn't exist. There's winning and learning, but not losing. And even braving her way through nearly 400 matches in her first two years of competition—and this was while Covid was working so hard to cripple wrestling seasons across the globe—she's had plenty to learn in matches, practices with coaches and teammates, practices at home with the brother whose own career enticed her to start hers and the parents who were a bit iffy about it way back when, everywhere.

She can hold down and throw around people with double-digit weight advantages on the 40-pounder. Her former gymnastics career molded her spine into a form of tough rubber, allowing her to stretch and bend her way away from and out from under opponents.

"What has made her successful is her coaches and friends that have become family," says her mom, Leanne. "Her wrestling friends have become family, even when she's lost in finals matches, like when she took runner-up at a national tournament. Her best friend was there to pick her right back up."

Not surprisingly, not everyone has been so welcoming or helpful. In the summer of 2021, Adalynn showed up at a wrestling camp. Sadly but not shockingly, she was the only female.

A chauvinist piglet (these are kids we're talking about, remember!) gallantly stepped forward.

"It's a girl!" he blared, like anyone couldn't guess. "You don't belong here!"

She didn't flinch, hardly blinked. Just looked him in his narrow-seeing eyes and laid it down.

"Try to keep up," she calmly challenged. Both of them learned quickly that he couldn't.

Those months would prove quite eventful for her. On July 9, she won both the 9U folkstyle and 8U freestyle and took second in the 8U folkstyle at Wisconsin's Grand River Rumble.

Two *days* later, in Indiana for the Midwest Nationals, Adalynn pinned her way to the top of the Girls First/Second Grade division, then came within a win of the boys' title in the same division, pinning two fellows along the way.

The next month, she arrived in Michigan for the Midwest Summer States event. On August 7 alone, Adalynn won *five titles* in freestyle and folkstyle competition and got second or third in three other events.

"My favorite memory is winning girls states and nationals, the pure excitement when I realized I did the unimaginable being a year into wrestling," Adalynn says. "Another great memory was I would always lose against one person and finally I won and I ran to my mom afterward and was crying happy tears because I believed in myself and finally did it!"

In all these accomplishments, everything that she's shown, including all that promise for the future, it's easy to miss something about Adalynn. It's not like people stand around looking for this stuff. No one walks around saying, "Hey, just for the heck of it, let's see if we can notice anyone with a hearing issue in the general public!"

With all the fans and teammates roaring from the sidelines, along with an opponent trying to make us a permanent part of the mat, it can be tough to hear our coaches barking out orders. Adalynn and her coaches found a way around that issue.

They had to. Chronic ear infections stole half of the hearing from one of her ears in toddlerhood, and a quarter disappeared from the other. Before putting on a singlet, she spent years methodically counting out one gymnastic routine after another.

Now she and the coaches use a special kind of sign language to communicate. She can't hear and doesn't have to. Their hand signals inform and encourage her through moves and matches.

And it's working. For too long, her hearing loss, and everyone's inability to approach it, caused her to stumble out of the top ranks of far too many tournaments. In one match that could have propelled her to a state title, she had an opponent on her back. Her coaches and family yelled for her to cradle the girl, to get her head off the mat. Unfortunately, Adalynn didn't hear, and time ran out. Then she lost in a sudden-death overtime.

Then came changes in clubs and coaches. Together, she and they learned the new system of communication.

And Adalynn turned right around and won a state title.

"It's honestly scary and amazing at the same time," says her mom, Leanne. "They still yell at her mat side and she does her own thing. Sometimes she has completely stopped wrestling and looked up for a sign or hand movement of what her coaches want her to do. Prior to this she would get upset because she would lose a match because she couldn't hear what we were telling her to do until it was too late. The hardest thing was not for Adalynn to learn to deal with not hearing what is being said, because she's used to that, but it was us as parents and her coaches to learn what to do to communicate with her to keep her moving. Now with her going into her second season she flows more in her movements, so it helps."

Chloe Dearwester: "One person's hand's going to get raised and one isn't. I have to get my hand raised, and I'm thinking about what strategy I need to get my hand raised."

Stepping in front of a camera can have a few separate effects, not all of them all that special.

A moving motion picture shoot, that's one thing. For wrestlers, it's usually a benefit. Cameras can capture your greatest triumph, the highlights of your career, something you don't really mind putting on display, even with others present, sometimes when things are down elsewhere. They can also be learning tools; we can use them to measure our weaknesses and mistakes and fix or avoid them the next time. Or we can look for these things in others, and make for sure to exploit them like crazy in next weekend's tournament.

Still photos, though, they can mean a different story. Stepping in front of a camera like that, getting turned into an impromptu model, it can be tough. Even tougher if people all over social media might see them, people we don't know. Especially for kids, particularly for young women, for whom self-esteem is a pretty common issue to begin with, this can be problematic. Even if it shows a huge trophy and a relieved smile, beaming down from the top of an awards plateau.

Both have happened to Chloe Dearwester. And they just keep happening.

"When you're just starting, you can feel like wrestling has something for you," says the Ohioan. "I do a lot of surprise tournaments, but it's my job."

She's been hard at it since elementary school. Before eighth grade, she was finishing at the top, or at least near it, in high school tourneys all over Ohio, and then the nation.

"Everyone needs to lose," she explains. "I don't get upset when I lose [a rarity of epic proportions!]. I watch my videos, go over what I did wrong, and then work on it the next day. I have to lose so I know what to work on. I have a good two or three backups, so if my first one doesn't work, I have a Plan B and a Plan C."

It was commonplace for Dearwester to battle her way through a group of women her own age, then hold down a line of older ladies at the same event, winning some 18U events in middle school.

"In eighth grade, I broke my hand," she remembers. "I snapped my knuckle in half, like at a 40-degree angle. Two days later, I won a male tournament. Then I was out for six months, but when I came back, I won a state and national title not even a week later."

In the fall of 2020, she swept through the World of Wrestling, a three-way event in Oklahoma and Las Vegas. That September, she was named the World's top lady. Soon after, her face beamed across the organization's web site.

"I thought I looked goofy," she admits, "but I was really happy, because it's what I worked for from the beginning. I had worked for it since I was 10."

Not long after, she became the first female to compete at William Henry Harrison High, and then the first to win. Switching back and forth between intra- and co-ed competition, she pulled out a 32–1 record, all but one win by pinfall. Ironically, Dearwester's only loss was a sad Christmas present at the hands of fellow lady titlist Olivia Shore.

That February, she and a few hundred ladies from all over the Buckeye State arrived at Hilliard Davidson High for the Ohio High School Wrestling Coaches Association's first ever women's event. Dearwester was seeded tops in 106-pound competition.

"I felt like I was expected to win," she says. "Everyone expects more from me because I've wrestled for longer than the other girls." In less than two minutes of collective action, she'd held down her first three opponents.

"I'm nervous going into any match," she says, "but I was excited, because that was one more step toward finals." Dearwester jogged. She stretched. She listened to rap music. Then she headed out to take on Bellefontaine's Chelsea Horsley, herself a previous state champ.

Dearwester scored a takedown in about 15 seconds, then twisted Horsley toward her back. It took about a minute, but she managed to hold Horsley down for the pin.

"It was just another match, and I needed to focus and do what I do," she says. "I tried doing a cradle, but it was in a weird position, so I did a low elbow, and I got her pinned in that position. I felt like there should have been more competition, but I just gave it my all."

She took the Cincinnati Female Wrestler of the Year honor, part of *USA Today*'s High School Sports Award program. Just as with the World event, Dearwester's photo jumped all over the American wrestling community, and probably outside Old Glory as well. In December 2021, she became the first woman to place at Ohio's Coaches Classic.

And the following February, her state title helped bring Harrison an Ohio High School Wrestling Coaches Association girls' state title—the school's first-ever state championship!

"I'm hoping to be a four-time champ," she says Dearwester, who won her third state title in March 2023. "I want to win all four years of high school, win nationals, and get on a world team."

Grace Montierth, Utah, state champ: "I started wrestling because of my mom. My mom, Melanie Montierth, wrestled in high school and continued her career in college, winning multiple national championships, and was the Senior Women's Freestyle Pan American Champion in 2000. She is now Ridgeline High's women's head wrestling coach. She's been my biggest inspiration, and she helps me strive to be my best. I was the first and only female wrestler on Ridgeline's wrestling team for two years. I was the first person from my high school to win the Dollamur All Star Duals. To explain what the All Star Duals are, it's essentially where they take the top two or three people from each weight class and have them wrestle off in the middle of the season to improve rankings. It's a very big honor and a big deal in Utah to be picked and win.

Honestly, I stayed in wrestling, even though I was the only girl, to prove a point. My wrestling career began with me wanting to show the world that I could make it; I wanted to show that no matter what happened in the season or how hard it got, I would stick with it and I would be the girl who didn't give up. I have now developed a love for the sport that grew much deeper than I thought it would. I love how wrestling teaches the importance of hard work, dedication, delayed gratification, and so many other qualities. Wrestling helped me realize how to work hard and that you can achieve anything if you put your mind to it and are willing to put it the work.

My most memorable moments in my wrestling career were primarily in my 2019–2020 season. Entering the season, I was a state champ and had gone undefeated in girls wrestling from my second tournament to state.

My main opponent that year was Kathleen Janis. Janis was a national champion and was a two-time state champion. I had previously lost to Janis in my first season, 2018–2019, but felt confident that I could beat her since I had been undefeated after that first tournament. I faced Janis at the All Star Duals in 2020, and I lost 5–0. That was a really hard time for me, but ultimately I'm grateful that she beat me then. After the All Star

Duals, I would work harder in practice and strive to do and be my best. Something my original high school coach would always tell us would be that when you feel like giving up during a workout or feel that something is too hard, imagine your opponent working out next to you and make yourself work harder than them. I took this mentality with me for years, but I will say that was my mantra for that year: I will outwork Kathleen.

The rest of the season went on and finally it was Utah High School Girls State. I met Kathleen again in the finals match, and I ended up beating her 5–0. I have to be honest: that was one of the best experiences of my life. That experience showed me that if I put my mind to it and if I worked hard, I really could do anything I put my mind to.

I'm the first person from my high school to be committed to a college and wrestle at a collegiate level. I'll be continuing my wrestling career at Hastings College with an amazing coach and team. While I don't entirely know what my future will hold, I hope to be the best person I can be, on and off the mat, and to remember these lessons from my high school years and take it to heart."

Arriving in Arkansas and ready for middle school, Archer Jones was a bit disappointed. She'd been working her way through the basics of cagefighting for a few years, but her new homeland didn't have that game, at least not for preteens (Arkansas native Bryce Mitchell had had to wait until near adulthood to become a UFC contender!).

Her new school, however, offered a different club sport. No girl had ever been a member, but this mattered not the least.

"I enjoyed that you can't stop wrestling in mid-match," Archer explains, "because that's when you get to be independent. It can turn around at any time." Before she finished middle school, she'd reached the top five rankings in the state.

But not long after her wrestling career started, something else did as well.

It started with some involuntary movement. She'd be sitting in class or home watching TV, and suddenly her neck would spin her head to the side. Then her fingers suddenly began to spasm around.

Had she pulled or strained certain muscles too hard out on the mat? Maybe some nerve pinchings or other similar damage? It's legitimate to imagine a wrestler suffering that kind of inadvertent self-harm.

But then things got worse. The ticking went from her fingers to her entire hand. Then her arm began to suddenly smash into her chest.

Soon her vocals were affected. Blasting out random, and not always G-rated, statements in public embarrassed her.

Her health started to become a dark domino effect. Suddenly being encompassed by all these strange, frightening symptoms, not surprisingly, fired up her anxiety, which started triggering asthma attacks. The depression that had been coming and going for years suddenly started visiting more and more.

She attempted to avoid walking near people, in fear that she'd start throwing involuntary kicks and punches. She broke her eyeglasses over and over.

"It really destroyed my entire social life," Archer sadly remembers. "It happened so suddenly, everyone thought I was faking it. I had a lot of depersonalization my entire life, out-of-body experiences where I didn't feel like myself. It was like watching myself do stuff. I felt myself be triggered by things that shouldn't bother me."

The general public assumption for these symptoms, especially the vocals, is Tourette syndrome, and three separate doctors decided to label it the culprit. But

Archer Jones (left) overcame Pediatric Acute-Onset Neuropsychiatric Syndrome to reach All American honors in Arkansas. Photo provided by Archer Jones.

nothing helped, nothing changed much at all, and now Archer and her family were faced with some sad realities.

Wrestling was done. Maybe forever. Being grabbed or held down sounded like some far too effective ways to trigger her spasms. She was left to sit and watch while her teammates and opponents stayed in the fight. Archer missed tournament after tournament that she knew she could have won. Some mental midget classmates started calling her "Tourette Freak."

Not surprisingly, the depression got worse. Losing her favorite sport, losing her independence, so many mysteries without anyone seemingly near a solution ... the future just looked even more ominous. Archer's family even started to wonder if she'd decide not to be around for it. Her physical symptoms might not have been life-threatening themselves (though they could certainly speed things up in that sense), but the effect on her mind definitely could be.

Then a silver sliver—not even big enough to qualify as a lining—sliced through the dark clouds.

A doctor in Texas had found just one more (maybe!) solution. Archer might just have Pediatric Acute-Onset Neuropsychiatric Syndrome (hereafter, PANS). It's doubtful that a brain disorder diagnosis is ever good news, but *an* answer was something.

PANS is still not fully accepted by the medical community; it's a longtime work in progress, unlike Tourette syndrome, which has been diagnosed and treated for years. The two have much in common, but PANS tends to hit one in the moods harder than Tourette, which could account for Archer's anxiety and depression overloads. Tourette also comes and goes on its own, while PANS victims tend to inadvertently relapse because of specific triggers.

Archer, her family, and the doctors turned inward to some homeopathic treatment, one relying on natural substance healing, rather than scientific medicine. It worked, as well as any such treatment of PANS can.

"It took me like one session for me to not tic the rest of the day," Jones remembers, "but it took months for my tics to stop happening on a daily basis, or even two or three times a week." The treatment managed to focus on the areas of her brain that caused her seizures.

Slowly, she made her way to high school at Springdale's Har-Ber, and back to the mat.

"Most of the year, I did not do quite as well, for medical issues," she says. "I didn't click much. I started to realize that I was slacking in practice, because of all the medical issues. I started to look at how long I'd been wrestling, and I couldn't stop halfway through. I hadn't wrestled girls much. It's a bit more pressure, but it's more exciting. I realized how different girls are to wrestle. They don't use strength hardly at all. They work on their techniques."

She did as well. And she started making her way up the state ranks. "I had more experience that most of the girls, because I'd been wrestling boys before [girls wrestling] was sanctioned in 2019," Jones says. "Most girls started wrestling then, but I'd been wrestling since 2016."

In early March, she arrived at the Jack Stephens Center in Little Rock for the girls state wrestling championship.

A few victories later, her final match gave Jones a bit of a double-whammy; not only could she become a 165-pound state champion as a freshman, always a cap feather for the youngsters, but she could avenge an earlier loss to Little Rock Southwest senior Leelah McKenzie.

"I had watched the footage of the last time we wrestled," Jones says. "I knew I could beat her." Things went back and forth for the first period, then for much of the second. But just before the six-minute mark, Jones scored a takedown for the pinfall and the title.

Then her coach informed her of a *slightly* larger scale.

"I got to go to the Junior Nationals in Fargo that July," Jones says. "I had an asthma attack when I got there, and I finished with two wins and three losses. I got eighth place and made All-American. It was cool and surreal to get up there. I think I'll get higher on the podium next year."

And yes, that opponent that she's can't tech fall away is still there. Probably always will be, barring some medical miracle.

"Sometimes, my mental state is really on and off," Jones admits. "I had a bad episode around winter and a few last year. It felt like I was in a mental state for about a month. Sometimes I'll do really well for a day, then come back and mentally not there. Blue lighting, certain textures and noises, or if someone else is ticking, it triggers me. One of my symptoms is that I can't regulate temperature, so I overheat easily. My feet and hands burn all the time."

Catherine Mullis is a liar.

You don't have to know her personally to find that out fast. You just have to see her.

"I am a horrible athlete," asserts the Georgia gal.

Uh-huh. The 100-plus wrestling wins, the state titles, and the scholarship to Life University are just a few reasons to question that theory.

But let's let her elaborate a bit.

"I'm not coordinated," she says. "I'm not good at sprinting. I'm not super strong, but the great thing about jiu-jitsu and wrestling is that if you have great technique, you don't have to be."

OK, maybe we can work with that for the time being.

"I'm the type of person that likes to be busy all the time," Mullis explains. "I was wrestling, and I was in an eco club at my school, and I was in Girl Scouts, and I was still doing jiu-jitsu." She'd actually picked up the martial arts before kindergarten, and as common as it is for youth to dream of a career in pro sports, a lady aiming for the Ultimate Fighting Championships was still only slightly less rare than Loch Ness Monster sightings.

Catherine Mullis scored state titles, more than 100 wins, and a scholarship to Life University during her high school years in Georgia. Photograph provided by Frank Mullis.

"I wanted to be in UFC before they were letting women into it," says Mullis (Ronda Rousey would break the mold during Mullis's elementary school years). "I had seen my dad do jiu-jitsu, and I saw it as a way to connect with him [her dad, Frank, has been teaching mixed martial arts since before she was born]. I ended up falling in love with it. My dad told me that if I wanted to go to UFC, I needed to learn how to wrestle."

The price you pay, huh? As good a reason as any.

Nearby Baldwin High, Mullis recalls, "let upcoming eighth graders wrestle in high school. I was 100 pounds. The second-lightest person was 130, and he beat the crap out of me every day. But wrestling makes you tough. When somebody beats the crap out of me, I'm not the type to run away. I'm the type to try to get better, so I can beat the crap out of them." By the end of her freshman year, she'd taken home a USA Wrestling state title.

"I had a ref try to explain to me how to wrestle," she sighs. "You know he'd never do that to a male wrestler. I had one team get mad at me; they put their freshman out there when I was a junior. They stole my shoes, and I had to go get my coach to get their coach to give them back. In my 10th-grade year, I figured out I'm not going to have any control over a guy in upper body strength, so I do this thing called 'running legs,' when I use my lower body to help me. It helps balance the playing field."

Battling guys, she fought to the top of the region in both her junior and senior years at Baldwin.

"I knew I needed to do it again," she says, "and let everyone know that I'm still here."

Before her farewell tour, she'd been voted the Baldwin captain. Even in a season handicapped by the Covid virus, she got an extra present for Christmas 2020 with her 100th high school win (at least 80 of which, she estimates, were over guys). But certain other people needed to be reminded as well—like the one who'd seen her make it near the top of the Georgia High School Association state finals for the past two years, and now had another shot.

"I was wrestling at 132 this year," she says. "I was 112 and 122 in previous years. I was 5'2" when I started high school, and now I'm like 5'9", so it was an easier weight cut. I cut 13 pounds in my freshman year and 10 last year. This year, I just had to eat clean for a couple of days."

As she walked into the Macon Centreplex in February 2021, a few years of work could finish paying off.

"I won four matches the first day," says Mullis, who dislocated an opponent's shoulder in the first outing. "Thank God I got to go home and sleep, and let my stomach settle a bit."

Warming up with some oranges and granola bars the next day, she could feel herself on the brink of history. Just Kennesaw Mountain's Genevieve An in the way. And here's where a few more bricks were added to the mental bridge between wrestling and the cage brawls she couldn't wait to enter.

"I need to absolutely dominate," she said. "It's what my coaches expected of me, and what I expected of myself." But that didn't happen first; less than 10 seconds in, she was on her hands and knees, with An on her back. Mullis nearly wrenched her opponent's knee, and time was called.

The second started off the same, with An turning a headlock into a takedown and 4–0 lead. Then Mullis escaped to get on the board, and soon turned An over for a near-pin and 5–4 lead to end the period.

"You get in the match, you feel it out a little bit," Mullis explains. "She was a little more technical that the others girls I'd wrestled, but she still had some things wrong, so I exploited that. I wrestled very aggressively."

An started the last period on Mullis's back, but Mullis soon turned her over for another takedown, then upped her lead to 9–4. An kept fighting, but Mullis inched up on her chest and head, and, with just two seconds left in regulation, pinned her.

"I got called for unnecessary roughness for clubbing her head," she says. "I ended up on top, cranking her shoulder. She started screaming, but they didn't stop it, and I pinned her." Now it was time for her Life to begin … well, not yet.

"I was crying in my car," she says. "It wasn't really sadness or happiness. It hit me that my season was over. It was just having put in as much work and time and effort, and made the relationships I've had, and knowing that I worked so hard for something and finally got it. It was over and on to the next thing, and start a new life."

See that? Cute play on words, right? But it was finally time for that other combat-based dream of hers to start coming true.

And guess what? It's not just her statements that fall on the wrong side of credible either. Even her moniker leads us the wrong way. Calling someone the "Gentle Savage," as Mullis goes by in the mat and cage communities, is right there next to "open secret," "living dead," and maybe even "political ethics" in the Oxymoron Queen department!

But it worked; on August 21, 2021, Mullis debuted at the Valor Fighting Challenge in Chattanooga, Tennessee (her high-volume red hair even won her a spot on the event's poster!) scoring a striking stoppage against Greta Mars.

Her wrestling career was closer to the end than to the beginning. OK, that happens to everyone.

Her career might very well end with a loss. That's fine—it usually goes that way.

What Kaden Campbell *wasn't* going to accept, however, was her career ending early because of bad luck and tentative body parts.

Her hip had broken, and plunged that neck of her body into a degenerative nerve condition. Not enough. Her ACL and most of her MCL had torn, and then her MCL had the audacity to tear again, and didn't even have the common courtesy to do so on the wrestling mat! Yeah, no way was she going to end things that way.

Campbell's career had started off quite differently.

Attending a school focusing as much on takedowns and back rolls as trigonometry and chemical formulae? Talk about a dream educational environment for anyone, let alone someone about to enter the ring of hell known as middle school! After Campbell hit the young Colorado wrestling world hard, her family decided that the public schools didn't share her career priorities.

She should become the next addition to Sons of Thunder's wrestling school, which put, shall we say, *extensive* importance on physical education. It was in a small town called Castle Rock, a full nation from the same-named fictional Maine land that Stephen King put through all sorts of hell and finally ruined in *Needful Things*!

"I think I've wrestled in all 50 states," says Campbell. "I've been to Germany, Sweden, Mexico, Japan, everywhere." In 2015, she took a national cadet championship and a world title at the Reno events.

But that December, something appeared to go permanently wrong.

As was typically the case for her, Campbell was up against a guy; Colorado didn't sanction women's wrestling until 2019. As her opponent attempted to flip her into a spladle, her hip popped out of place.

She got a quick stoppage, shoved it back into place, and finished the match. The next day, much of her leg in wrappings, she won an all-female tourney. Prepping for a trip to compete in Canada a few weeks later, she was practicing for hours at a time.

Then, at a camp, "one of the counselors was feeling around," Campbell remembers. "She told me, 'You do *not* need to be competing on this.'"

She finally turned to the medical field. Amputation might have been about the only way the news could have been worse.

Her labrum was torn. Her ball joint was fractured. They'd found a nerve condition in her hip that was going to get worse as time went on, though no one could know how fast.

Doctors were amazed that she'd even lumbered into the hospital, let alone competed for so long.

What little remained of 2015 was gone. Much of 2016 would be as well. After that? Well, that might be an unrealized vision as well.

"I was out for about a year," Campbell recalls. "There were, of course, ups and downs. Was the risk worth it? At the end of the day, I still had to be in the wrestling room. I still helped with the coaching. I still watched it. I just wanted to be a part of the sport. More and more girls were starting to pop up, and I could help with that if I came back."

Things got back together just below her midsection. The pain would never completely leave, but her mindset and adrenalin could push it backward, enough for a few matches. As the anniversary of her injury date drew near, Campbell finally stepped back onto the mat, this time for a Sweden tourney.

She didn't win. She lost a few times, and pretty fast, actually. But she was back—and the next year, she took another world title home from Reno, a state high school title (she competed against public schoolers in these), and some other national titles.

The next year started off the same way, titles rolling in. Now post-secondary school was looming—and, unfortunately, Sons of Thunder wasn't accredited for college courses!

Her namesake school of Campbellsville held out a wrestling scholarship, and she accepted it, ready to cross America to Kentucky. But mere days after signing her moniker to her future's bottom line, tragedy came right back.

She'd torn up in North Carolina's Super 32 event the year before, and couldn't wait to get back.

At the University of North Carolina a few days before the event, Campbell and her coach were warming up. She went for a shot, and he doubled back behind her and rolled through. The two came down on the same leg she'd injured before.

A little too hard. But, again, she didn't quit right away.

"I was on crutches around the tournament," she says. "Everybody was asking me what had happened, and I told them I didn't even know yet." Back home, though, she found out: a full-torn ACL and 80 percent rip in her MCL. No Campbellsville debut this year.

Campbell still went back to work, rehabbing it as hard as she ever had. But later that winter, a fall re-tore her MCL, sending her back under the knife.

And just as she came back from *that*, something else happened. But this one was way out of her control and affected many more people than just her.

Days away from a national tournament, word came down; the pandemic was postponing this event, and many more after it.

"The bike and pool have been my best friends," she explains. "Mentally, I still know all my techniques, but I'm more worried about trying to 're-teach' my leg."

Easy? Hell no. Not ever. Not what you get into if you're going to get anywhere in this sport. But winning state, national, and world championships hadn't been no crystal stair either. And in late 2021, Campbell announced she was heading back into Campbellsville competition at high speed. That year, she'd finish with an 11-1 record.

"I got a great scholarship," Campbell vows, "but even with this injury, I refuse to go out the way I did. If I'm going to go out due to an injury, it's not going to be from practicing."

Epilogue

"If you look at women's wrestling, it's just blowing up. Just women's wrestling in general is so impressive, what it's been able to do. Even in the year of Covid, we've added programs. We've added talent. We've had coaches jump on board. It's really been a positive step. But just for being a little girl in the United States, in this world, I didn't dream big enough and I didn't know that there were these things out here. I didn't know I could be a professional athlete into my thirties. I didn't know that I had a husband and a career and be able to balance those two things at this stage, and I held myself back at a young age because I didn't know these things are possible. So I hope all the little girls really understand that they can go and get their master's degrees. They can go and win Olympic medals. They can have balance in their lives, and focus on very big things. It sounds cliché to dream big, but I really hope that they see these groups of women who are doing these amazing things, and they're inspired to take their goals and set those goals, and make them even bigger."

—Adeline Gray

"Wow, it's a good thing. It's pretty fantastic, actually."

—Hall-of-Famer Dan Gable on female wrestling

"It's not that every woman has to wrestle, or that every girl should. It's that every girl in America can know she can."

—Patricia Miranda

Man, was this book tough to finish.

No, really, I mean that literally—one of the hardest parts was just deciding when enough was enough.

I had intended to make the Olympics the final piece, in the hopes that our women would create a happy ending, an inspirational sendoff for my readers.

Well, they did. And then they, like the rest of the wrestling community, turned right around and kept going.

Can you imagine walking up to a guy who just helped his team to a Super Bowl title and saying, "Great job! But when you try that again in, I don't know … *a few weeks*, will you do as well?"

He'd think you were crazy. He'd be thinking, "I just played one of the most important games of my life, and you expect me to already be getting ready for another? Jeez, at least give me a few weeks to lay around and heal!"

Wrestlers don't do that. Maybe they *could*, but they don't. They're too worried about rusting out and falling behind. When you're not working on the mat, someone else is, and people are going to be talking about her and asking you about her. It's bust your ass to the best of your abilities so you can bust someone else's, and then go right back out and bust someone new. Off-season? What's that?

A few days after our women rocked Tokyo—Godzilla might have skittered away from them if he'd happened to show!—the ones who *almost* made it there were in Russia at the Junior World Championships. Kennedy Blades and Kylie Welker, who'd made it to the finals at the Olympic trials, came back with golds, as did fellow trials competitor Emily Shilson.

Get this—had she been born a few *hours* earlier, Amit Elor would probably have been at the trials with them. But Elor didn't show up until the first day of 2004, making her *just* too young to qualify. But she also won gold in Russia to help America to the team title.

Expect these names to show up when the 2024 Games come about.

And the ones that did make it to the Olympics, well, they got home from there, took a deep breath and maybe a nap, and then right back to the padded battlefield, this time for the Worlds in Norway for the 2021 Senior World Championships. Just a few short months after tangling with the world's finest in Asia, Adeline Gray, Sarah Hildebrandt, Kayla Miracle, Helen Maroulis, and Tamyra Mensah-Stock were now ready to do it again. It was like re-starting the NFL playoffs in March!

And look what happened! Miracle and Hildebrandt took silvers. Mensah-Stock recovered from an upset loss to Japan's Rin Miyaji to destroy Adéla Hanzlíčková of the Czech Republic 10–1 in the bronze match. Gray pinned all of her opponents, the first time she'd ever done so in six World title victories. And Maroulis, robbed of a chance to train by a battle with the Covid virus, rebounded with her strongest performance since her 2017 World gold, scoring the 57-kilogram championship. Overall, our ladies' final score of 147 was second only to Japan's 196.

Helen Maroulis: This is the worst I'd ever felt. I had no idea what to expect, just kind of praying. Just to be able to compete, I'm very proud of that. I did all the prep work, so I felt really good during my matches. I was telling myself, you've felt crappy before, you've felt out of it, and you just find a way.

After I won in 2017, I walked off the mat and turned to my coach and said, 'I don't know if that was worth it.' I don't know if it was worth the work we put in. Not the hard work that wrestling takes, but the external things. There's a lot of extra burdens that I wasn't managing well, and I had to step away and be able to separate. What does wrestling require? I know I love it; that's never going to change. So what are the other things that I need to change to make this enjoyable? I'm so proud of the way I compete. That's what I wanted out of the sport: to like the person that I am and be proud of the things I have inside. The reward is the experience, the journey. I don't think that winning is the highest objective. I think when you have a reason that's bigger than yourself, that's better. That's where I find success. I went to a daycare in Greece after the Olympics, and the kids were so excited, and it was really eye-opening. The kids were like, 'Why are you visiting us? Our president doesn't visit us or care about our country!' These kids have been through so much. I didn't think they would like wrestling, but they were like, 'Teach us wrestling! Please come back! We'll do anything you say!' I couldn't get them to stop wrestling.

I was so excited about the World Championships. After Japan, I was thinking, we've already peaked. We've already put in all this hard work! Why would we take a break and get out of shape? I'm definitely planning on [the 2024 Games] in Paris, unless life changes."

Tamyra Mensah-Stock: "[The bronze] isn't what I wanted, but at the same time, through all this adversity that I've had since the Olympics, I just thank God that I was able to pull through. I wanted to give up, and my support staff was like, 'No, you don't want to.'

It's been really tough since the Olympics, and I haven't had a chance to sit back and enjoy the fruits of my labor. I proved that I am strong enough and that I am enough.

Back-to-back tournaments, the Olympics, and being on an incredible high and barely being able to enjoy the moment, and then having to come back. I was under the guise of, 'Yeah, I'm happy and ready to be here!' but right now, I feel like I have a target on my back. I feel like the underdog." The very next year, she came back at the 2022 World in Serbia, roaring to the 68-kg gold. Fellow countrywomen Dominique Parrish was tops at 53-kg and Amit Elor the 72-kg champ. Maroulis fell in the 57-kg gold match to Tsugumi Sakurai of Japan, whose 62-kg colleague edged Kayla Miracle for the 62-kg crowd. Mallory Velte tied for the 65-kg bronze, as did Sarah Hildebrandt in 50-kg action. Overall, Japan scored the gold with 190 points, slipping past America's 157.

That's a wrestler's life. Wrestle here, wrestle there, come home to wrestle, go elsewhere, win a state title here, an international event somewhere else, and then a school district championship around the corner. No letup. Always a new trek to take, a new challenge and opponent to face and face down.

Therefore, by the time you read this, our women might have racked up a few more great achievements that we just didn't have time to include! Can't update a book like you can a website article! We'll just write what we can and hope it's enough for the right people.

We've heard story after story about female wrestlers following their brothers—even their dads and uncles—into the sport. Over the next few years, more and more might just take after their sisters, their aunts, even their moms.

Kent Bailo: "There are probably some second-generation high school wrestlers. Moms are sitting in the stands saying, 'I could have kicked her mother's ass 20 years ago!' Soon they'll be saying, 'Yeah, my grandma kicked your grandma's ass!'"

Tamyra Mensah-Stock: "When I first started wrestling, I wanted to be an emblem, a light to show younger women that you can be silly, you can be fun, and you can be strong, you can be tough, and you can be a wrestler. You don't have to be this tough 'Grrrr, I'm going to be mean to you.' I wanted to be that light.

When I do retire, there are so many wonderful wrestlers that are going to come behind me and follow the example that I set. It means so much to me, just to show the God-given talent that I have and to show it to these young girls."

Someday, and probably not too long in the future, Mensah-Stock hopes, young women might look at her and the rest of the champs and say, "'Mommy, that girl looks like me. I could do that too?' 'Of course, baby! Of course you could do that!' When you can see yourself in something, you most likely can achieve it…. They see someone like themselves on that podium, someone like Helen [Maroulis] on that podium, and they see that just because you're a female doesn't mean you can't accomplish the biggest goals."

Ironically, it didn't take long for Mensah-Stock's hopes to come to life.

As Stockton, Illinois, residents strolled through their city middle school in April 2022, an array of celebrities were there to greet them. Inventors. Actors. Musicians. Even a president or two.

And, yes, some athletes showed up as well. Stepping down the hallway, visitors were stunned to bump straight into Maroulis herself— clad in her singlet and displaying her 2016 Olympic medal in the living color of gold!

She detailed the start of her wrestling career in elementary school half a nation away in Maryland, and how the sport had taken her to college titlehood and to that medal around her neck.

Well, sort of. It may not quite have been Maroulis herself, but the resemblance was there, give or take a year or so.

Career-wise, the two women had a pretty similar past. Time will tell on the future.

Like Maroulis, Piper Sandell had gotten started early, winning her first co-ed tournament before first grade. By the fall of 2021, she was second in an Illinois tournament. Also like Maroulis, and many still today in Illinois middle school competition, Sandell was often alone in her gender in team mat wars.

As her career commenced, Sandell, like most young ladies of the area, found a role model in Kennedy Blades, who'd emerged from Chicago and rolled to national titlehood, a Pan-Am medal, and within a win of the 2021 Olympic squad before being stopped short by Mensah-Stock.

One night, shortly before the Stockton event, Sandell perused the Internet, looking for someone to become for one night; her school was about to put on a wax museum event, in which she and her classmates got to become living exhibitions of the people they'd like to be one day.

A short film on Maroulis made up her mind. Sandell put pen to paper to detail just where Maroulis had been and where she wished to go.

"A lot of people don't expect girls to go out on the mat and be successful and I like to prove people wrong," she said. "I like Helen Maroulis because she inspires me, and I think it's cool that she was the first American woman to win an Olympic gold medal in wrestling."

A Final Farewell!

Aren't women just amazing?

American society, almost by its very makeup, handicaps them, and we're not even going to cop out with chauvinism. That's there, but it's also the quick way to pass the blame. There's much more to it than that.

Think about it.

Any woman who expresses the slightest bit of self-confidence or assertion or leadership automatically gets labeled with the eternal chauvinism cop-out that rhymes with *snitch*. Many of the women we've met throughout this piece have heard it to their faces, and probably *all* have had gotten it behind their backs. So many qualities that win praise in a man are criticized in women.

Women who choose to be of the career sort, to be their own independent, often bread-winning, people are accused of ruining the family unit. Those who decide to raise children and keep houses get badmouthed for holding their gender back.

If a man had to go through even one time a certain health issue that women tough out every single month, he'd be hospitalized, bawling for weeks at a time. There isn't a male in world history who would be strong enough to pull off pregnancy, labor, and childbirth. Again, though, we don't think about that because it's just what women are *supposed* to do.

Women get laughed at and held back from making headway in some of our most important fields, like law enforcement, firefighting, and medicine (doctors if not nursing). It took America over 200 years to get a woman on a major political ticket, and even today, that whole number doesn't fill an entire hand. Women are underpaid, undercredited, mistreated, and basically told to just sit down and accept—lest, again, they run the b-word label risk!

Sports have never been any different. They still aren't, not nearly enough.

Wrestling, explains 2008 Canadian gold medalist Carol Huynh, "provides not only a way to be in control of our bodies, but to feel powerful because of it. To feel strong, confident, and able, rather than meek and subservient, is very empowering as a female in a patriarchal society."

The richest players in the WNBA make just over $200,000 a year, which sounds great until you consider that the *low*est-paid guys in the NBA bring in over *four times that*. Not only that, but an NBA player who wins a title can get a single bonus that's more than a WNBA player makes,, not gets in an entire season!

Basically, a guy can be a fourth-string benchwarmer who's lucky enough to play a supporting role on the best team in the league (and not even play in the finals!), and he'll still outearn a lady who tore it up all year, all game, every game, to get her squad to her respective title!

Role models welcome the next generation! Senior National team member Lauren Louive (left) and World champ Jacarra Winchester show multiple state and national champ Kennedy Wheeler some mat pointers. Photograph provided by Allykan Wheeler.

Our men have never so much as sniffed the World Cup or Olympic gold in soccer; our women have been there repeatedly. But gender-wise, the losers constantly get more credit than the winners.

But there's nothing better than seeing an athlete, regardless of gender or sport, who goes all out for the love of the contest. We've met dozens of such people throughout. What a story it all makes. What a difference. The tales of some young women who had a goal, had a dream, and did what they could—everything they could—to make it real. For some, it came truer than others. Some finished higher. That's just how it goes in sports, especially individual sports, in which one ends up at the top and so many others stand in line. But being a winner in a sport like wrestling shouldn't be determined, especially not by those who didn't finish first, by who ends up scoring highest. What matters is having the guts to give it your all. Doing that is so much more than many of us have. Doing that makes a lady wrestler someone many of us should try to emulate.

Tristan-Paige Folkner, Missouri: "I would encourage every student to try wrestling, just one season. Because you will be amazed at what you will find within yourself. The bonds you will make will go and grow far beyond the mat. If you just stop saying 'I can't' and start saying 'I can try,' your world will explode to levels you'd never imagine."

Women's wrestling numbers have been blowing up since the start of the millennium, tripling from about 6,100 in 2009 to past 21,000 in 2019 alone. The Covid epidemic put a huge dent in wrestling, as it did in all sports at every level, but women came right back and went right back up, moving past the 52,000 mark in 2023.

Because they keep finding strength in one another. All over sports, a hell of a lot more so than their male colleagues, women matsters don't have trouble stepping back and forth across the line between not so much friend and foe, but colleague and opponent.

Evelyn Holmes-Smith, Alabama: "Girls make friends very easily. Whether you beat them, or they beat you, every girls' team I've been on, you make friends instantly. We hang out with each other. We're having a blast. The boys' duals teams I've been on, no one talked to each other. They're just sitting on the bench, not getting excited or anything. Us girls, we're on the mat, screaming for each other. The ref has to tell us to get back on the bench. On the mat, you're enemies. During the match, I'm serious, but after the match, I'll be your friend."

Leanne Anthony, mother of Adalynn, Ohio: "Addy has made many wrestling friends in the community that we follow and keep up with and whenever we can meet up with them. They are not friends but family. I can honestly say that girl wrestlers stick together a lot because our community is smaller than the boys' community.

At [a recent tournament], Adalynn lost to a little girl she beat the day before. She was bigger than Addy and wrestling longer. Addy was very upset because she made a rookie mistake which cost the match. Her best friend, she met at wrestling just a few months prior. They became friends very quickly.

Addy walked over to Kennedy and Kennedy gave her a giant hug. Addy said, 'Well, I guess you are better than me since you won the eagle.'

Kennedy looked at her and said, "No way! We are equal. You have beat me. You deserve it too." She told Addy to go get the next national championship, which she did at the Midwest national championship."

Loralei Smith, West Virginia: "In eighth grade, my best friend, who is on another team, had just lost a tough match at a dual meet against somebody from my team. Usually at a dual meet, we aren't allowed to talk to the other team, but here, everyone split and my friend and I met in the middle with a big hug. After the meet, several people came up to us with tears, saying it was one of the sweetest things they had ever seen. There were big men in the stands crying."

Chloe Dearwester, Ohio: "With girls, there's more communication. With boys, you wrestle and you're done. With girls, they all know who each other are, so they talk to each other. It's not like 'You're my opponent and I hate you!' It's more like, 'You beat me, so I'll have to go back to training and get better.' Girls come from a different perspective. We're trying to grow the sport together, since it's not at the point where the boys' is. We work together."

But before we leave, let's look at the less obvious gifts of the sport. When people think of a wrestler's gifts, they of course go straight to physicality. And believe it all, those assets are there. But as we say goodbye, let's look at a few more reasons to get and stay on the mat, those that require a few closer, deeper looks. Those that can help a lady wrestler in those few precious moments when she's elsewhere. Wrestling careers may not last more than a few years, but certain things we learn might, and hopefully should, stay with us forever. What else does wrestling teach us?

How about thinking on one's feet?

Operating under extreme pressure?

Formulating up a way to win in what looks to be a no-win situation?

And of course, standing up to those who get off on shutting down females.

All these skills and so many more come in handy for our ladies of the mat. So much they learn, so much that helps them, so much more than just being able to overpower someone in the physical sense.

How about focusing? What about multitasking? Balancing one duty with another, and eventually adding a few more.

Standing there, watching her beloved aunt slowly pass away, Cheyenne Atwater made her a promise.

"We made a deal with my aunt before she passed that nobody could miss a day of school," she recalls. "Then we did it." From kindergarten through elementary and middle school and then on to Bauxite High, the Arizonan *never missed a day of school*. That, along with keeping her grades high enough to captain her wrestling team, as well as other non-classroom activities.

Wrestling, she explains, "has helped me show leadership, to show respect no matter what's going on, like sportsmanship. It's helped me make good decisions. I knew I had to make good grades, or I couldn't stay on the team."

Making her way through five years of mat wars with guys in Ohio, Sairra Tapp learned about not allowing one's emotions to get too far out of hand. A little anger, some frustration that heads to aggression is OK, but a wrestler who loses her fortitude typically loses her match.

"It's definitely a mental thing," says Tapp, the runner-up in 131-pound competition in the Ohio High School Wrestling Coaches Association's girls state tournament in February 2021. "A lot of times, kids get sad if they lose and super happy if they win, but I'm kind of neutral: what happens, happens."

Once finished up at Tiffin University, she hoped to step into a new career that requires extreme concealment of emotions.

"It's always been a dream of mine to be a police officer," Tapp claims. "If something happens, I can stay in control of it, rather than getting upset or happy. It'll show that I'm really strong, to help me qualify for the police academy."

> "My coach told me to do my best, and that's what I'm going to do. I'm not an aggressive person to begin with. [Wrestling] taught me to be more firm with people."
>
> —Kristi McDonald (1991, Mariner High, one of Florida's first high school female wrestlers)

Daelynn Torbert, Indiana: "I was getting expelled from school for drugs and fighting. Going to juvie was really bad for my health. I was hanging out with the wrong people and didn't really care what I did. I didn't have somebody to tell me no. I got sent to community service because I threatened to beat somebody up on multiple occasions. I was really disrespectful to my teachers. I wanted to stop getting in trouble, and I thought wrestling would be a good way to help. After school, instead of getting in trouble, I was at wrestling practice. After wrestling practice, I would be too tired to do anything.

I fell in love with the sport, and it pushed me to be a better person so I could keep going. It's fun, because I get to beat people up in a good way. My grades are still bad, but I'm working on it. I'm learning hard work and dedication, and being in a group of people. Instead of being loud and the center of attention, I'm learning self-control. It teaches you sportsmanship, because you're going to lose. Now, if I lose, it's because they're better wrestlers. You're going to lose or win, but if you're not going to put up a fight, there's no point. A year ago, I probably would have thrown hands and fought the people I lost to."

Marina Doi, California (2014 Tricia Saunders award winner): "Wrestling's 90 percent mental, and 10 percent physical, especially in women's wrestling. I carry the lessons I learned in everything I do. In school, I just have this drive that pushes me to try to be better—not better than anyone else, but better than I was yesterday—by staying disciplined, doing things that I don't want to do when I don't want to do them. If I wasn't training, my opponent was, so I should get up and go train. Same with studying; instead of sitting down watching TV, I should be studying."

Mady Gray, four-time Kansas state champion: "I like the working aspects, the discipline. You work on things in practice, and then you put them to work in tournaments. You get better with a diet and a routine. I have to take care of my schoolwork when I wrestle. You learn perseverance. You take a break for a moment, then you go back and keep going. Wrestling is a harder sport, because there's the physically demanding side of practice and the mental side of how well you can complete. You go from, 'I'm going to lose!' to 'I'm going to go in and try and compete, and keep going!' When I started wrestling, I'd be so upset when I lost. Now I focus on what I did wrong and what I can do to get better."

Naomi Bullis, Virginia: "Once you step on the mat, nothing else matters. You can focus on one thing, and nothing else matters.

I have bad social anxiety, so wrestling is my outlet. For anything I don't want to express, I express on the mat. I always lived in a really strict household and never traveled a lot, so going to other places makes me really nervous. I haven't been away for long amounts of time, so wrestling is a tie to something familiar. I'm not judged in the wrestling room. I'll even go to the wrestling room to study sometimes if I'm stressed out."

Tiare Ikei, Hawaii, state champ: "The continuous challenges of being in this sport, there's a lot of adversity. If you talk to high school wrestlers, middle school wrestlers, senior national wrestlers, adversity is a common term used. The number-one wrestlers are number one for a reason, and knowing that is a challenge. What can I do? What changes can I make to achieve the best of myself? It translates a lot to regular life. Ever since I started wrestling, I've had a whole new perspective. A lot of people say that once you wrestle, it makes a lot of things in your life easier. That makes a lot of sense. You have that mental gain over a lot of other people. Wrestling is a sport, but if your journey is made with intention, there's a lot more you can gain from it. That's what keeps me going: how much it applies to everyday life."

Grace Montierth, Utah: "I have now developed a love for the sport that grew much deeper than I thought it would. I love how wrestling teaches the importance of hard work, dedication, delayed gratification, and so many other qualities. Wrestling helped me realize how to work hard and that you can achieve anything if you put your mind to it and are willing to put it the work."

Tristan Paige Folkner, Missouri: "Wrestling has taught me discipline, tolerance, patience, and courage. Discipline is probably the biggest part of wrestling that has changed my life. Kids can make some bad choices. Discipline taught me that things are not handed to you; you have to earn them. Discipline taught me time management, how to balance homework, practice, and social time, in that order. Discipline taught me how to make choices that would better me and my goals versus going with the flow set forth by peer pressure. And through discipline, I learned tolerance, because everyone has his or her own starting point. Through tolerance, I learned patience, with myself foremost, but also to get to know people and meet them where they are. Through patience, I learned courage, courage to be ME and celebrate who I am—as a wrestler, as a leader, and a person with learning disabilities."

Catie Campbell, Indiana: "It teaches you a lot of life's lessons, like discipline and how to be a better person. The outcome of your matches shows how much you've put into it, because there's really no cheating. If you put in the time, you'll win. With learning your moves, it helps you be better at being coachable and learning new things in general. When you're in a match, you're trying to think fast of moves to beat the other person. It's critical thinking. When you're conditioning, you're pushing yourself to get better, instead of giving up."

Jessica Philippus, Nebraska: "For girls, the number one thing that they love about wrestling chokes me up. They always say about how confident it makes them feel. They don't really care about winning and losing; they care about each other, and they care about how good it makes them feel. You don't always hear that from boys, but that is the number one thing I hear from girls."

Shania Villalba, two-time Texas state champion: "Wrestling can be very physically and mentally exhausting. Having that mental state, that discipline, that all helps when it comes to anything in life that I work towards now. Just having that discipline and being mentally strong, I've carried it on in relationships, knowing what's best for me and my life. You have to be mentally strong to know if you deserve more, if your life is pointing you in the wrong direction. Even if you want something so bad, you have to know when to say no and when to let go of certain things. Like when you're getting ready for wrestling, you have to know when to stop eating, or when you can't do other things. Nobody wants to get up at five or six in the morning to go to practice. Sacrifice was really big in wrestling, and sometimes in your career, you have to make sacrifices, and know how to hustle. When I'm at work, I'm struggling at times, but at the end of the night, just like at the end of the match, it's going to be worth it."

Sarah Torbert Tellechea, Indiana: "Wrestling changed my life for the better. There is no way I could have gone through a war, gone through a divorce. I had a child die. I could never have gone through these things if I had not wrestled because there is a fortitude that happens when you're wrestling. Your brain tells your body, 'You can quit! You can quit!' and you have to continuously tell yourself you cannot. You work on that when you're a child or you're a young adult, and it builds up to where you can take on anything."

Jillian Worthen, Iowa, state champion: "I wrestle because I love it. I wrestle because it melts my anger away. I wrestle to grow the sport for women's wrestling. I wrestle to show little girls that it can be done. I wrestle for myself. I wrestle for my town. I wrestle for my state. I wrestle for my country. I wrestle because it puts me in my own little world. I wrestle to escape reality. I wrestle to make new friends. I wrestle so it is not just a boys' sport. I wrestle to be part of a team. I wrestle so I can also be independent. I wrestle because it makes me a better person. I wrestle because I want big goals. I wrestle when I am mad. I wrestle when I am happy. I wrestle when I want. I wrestle, hoping a little girl looks up to me. I wrestle for a chance to wrestle in college. I wrestle for a chance to wrestle in the Olympics. I wrestle because I don't win every match. I wrestle because I don't lose every match. I wrestle to make myself better. I wrestle to become more disciplined, tough, and determined. I wrestle because I said I was. I wrestle because I want to be great at it. I wrestle to make my own path. I wrestle because others said a girl can't wrestle."

Bibliography

Abbott, Gary. 2021. "Tokyo Blog (August 8): Historic USA Wrestling Performance at Tokyo Games is Something to be Proud Of." *USA Wrestling*, July 27, 2021. https://www.teamusa.org/USA-Wrestling/Features/2021/July/27/Tokyo-Blog-Heading-off-the-Tokyo.

Abbott, Gary. 2021. "Maroulis Wins 57 KG Bronze Medal, Her Second Career Olympic Medal; Winchester Is Pulled Into Repechage." *USA Wrestling*, August 5, 2021. https://www.teamusa.org/USA-Wrestling/Features/2021/August/05/Helen-Maroulis-wins-Olympic-bronze-medal.

Abbott, Gary. 2021. "USA Wrestling to Pay a Record $950,000 in 'Living the Dream' Medal Fund Bonuses to its 2020 Olympic Medalists." *USA Wrestling*, August 12, 2021. https://www.teamusa.org/USA-Wrestling/Features/2021/August/12/LTDMF-record-Olympic-payout.

Aberman, Maddie. 2019. "The Lipstick 'Marvelous Mrs. Maisel' Star Rachel Brosnahan Swears By." *Women's Health*, September 22, 2019. https://www.womenshealthmag.com/beauty/a29132245/rachel-brosnahan-skin-beauty-routine/.

"Adeline Gray (76 kg) after making the 2021 Olympic team." 2021. *FloWrestling*, April 4, 2021. https://www.flowrestling.org/events/6921883-2021-usa-wrestling-olympic-team-trials-watch-party/videos?playing=6956165.

"Adeline Gray and Alejandro Sancho Pre-Olympic Team Trials Press Conference." 2020. *USA Wrestling*. Retrieved May 24, 2021. https://themat.tv/all_videos/237138-adeline-gray-and-alejandro-sancho-pre-olympic-team-trials-press-conference.

"Adeline Gray Discusses Thrilling Semi Victory To Make Olympic Final." 2021. *FloWrestling*, August 1, 2021. https://www.flowrestling.org/events/7089234-olympic-games-watch-party/videos?playing=7127290.

Archdeacon, Tom. 2004. "Bruises Badges of Honor for Grappler." *Dayton Daily News*, May 25, 2004.

Azzoni, Tales. 2013. "Role of Women Key for '20 Spot." *The Atlanta Constitution*, September 7, 2013.

Bader, Mark. 2021. "Jenna Burkert: 'It's a Lot to See Yourself Bawling on NBC.'" *FloGrappling*, April 15, 2021. https://www.flograppling.com/video/6967749-jenna-burker-its-a-lot-to-see-yourself-bawling-on-nbc.

Bader, Mark. 2021. "Jenna Burkert's Mom's Dying Wish." *FloGrappling*, April 15, 2021. https://www.flowrestling.org/video/6967750-jenna-burkerts-moms-dying-wish.

Barnas, Jo-Ann. 2004. "Gardner Wrestlers Onto Olympics Team." *Detroit Free Press*, May 24, 2004.

Binner, Andrew. 2019. "Exclusive: Adeline Gray Bodyslams Sexism in Wrestling." *Olympics*, September 19, 2019. https://olympics.com/en/featured-news/adeline-gray-sexism-equality-wrestling.

Bosserman, Ken. 2008. "Young Grapplers Form Cougar Core." *The Daily News Leader*, December 13, 2008.

Bosserman, Ken. 2010. "Gap Wins Leader Tourney." *The Daily News Leader*, January 17, 2010.

Bosserman, Ken. 2010. "Lee Defends SVD Crown." *The Daily News Leader*, February 6, 2010.

Boylan, Esther R. 1944. "Women Wrestler Normal with all Feminine Frailties." *The News Journal*, May 24, 1944.

Brown, Obrey. 2011. "Beaumont High School's Hendey is Folkstyle Champion." *Record-Gazette*, April 1, 2011.

Brunt, Cliff. 2021. "Mensah-Stock First Black U.S. Woman Wrestler to Win Gold." *AP News*, August 3, 2021. https://apnews.com/article/2020-tokyo-olympics-wrestling-tamyra-mensah-stock-4ea820d803cd834cb8d60cd4b0359b86.

Brunt, Cliff. 2021. "USA's Gray Seeks Olympics Gold to Go with Her 5 World Titles." *AP News*, July 28, 2021. https://apnews.com/article/2020-tokyo-olympics-sports-canada-olympic-team-belarus-olympic-team-russia-olympic-team-0f12c669c24dbdb1d6693412e1b3fed2.

Bruntil, Emma. 2021. "Body Dysmorphia: The Reality of Elite Wrestling." February 26, 2021. https://emma9629.wordpress.com/2021/02/26/body-dysmorphia-the-reality-of-elite-wrestling/.

Buganski, Patrick. 2006. "She's Just One of the Guys." *The Central New Jersey Home News*, February 18, 2006.

Bumbaca, Chris. 2021. "Helen Maroulis Didn't Need History-Making Bronze to Prove Olympic Success Isn't Measured in Medals." *USA Today*, August 5, 2021. https://www.usatoday.com/story/sports/olympics/2021/08/05/helen-maroulis-womens-57-kg-freestyle-bronze-olympic-medal/5497891001/.

Byrne, Ed. 2007. "Ebert Wrestles to First Place in Pan Am." *Green Bay Press-Gazette*, July 20, 2007.

Cannon, Jane Glenn. 2005. "Police Seek Answers in Student's Death." *The Daily Oklahoman*, March 15, 2005.

Chappell, Bill. 2020. "Tokyo 2020 Olympics Have a New Start Date: July of 2021." *National Public Radio*, March 30, 2020. https://www.npr.org/sections/coronavirus-live-updates/2020/03/30/823780370/tokyo-2020-olympics-have-a-new-start-date-july-of-2021.

Cherian, Dona. 2017. "4 things to know about how actors trained for Dangal." *Gulf News*, January 5, 2017. https://gulfnews.com/entertainment/tv/4-things-to-know-about-how-actors-trained-for-dangal-1.1956748.

Child, Joi. 2018. "Elvire Emanuelle and Olivia Newman Speak On Netflix's 'First Match,' Gentrifying Brooklyn and Wrestling [Interview]." Okay Player. Retrieved January 9, 2021. https://www.okayplayer.com/originals/elvire-emanuelle-olivia-newman-first-match-interview.html.

Christie, Kelly. 2020. "Beth Phoenix Age, Net Worth, Bio, Personal Life, Career." *Latest Bolly Holly*. Retrieved January 10, 2021. latestbollyholly.com/beth-phoenix-age-net-worth-bio-personal-life-career/.

"Clarissa Chun Uses Judo Move to Clinch America's First Medal in London." 2021. *Wrestling Insider Magazine*. Retrieved October 19, 2021. https://www.win-magazine.com/2012-olympics-coverage/womens-freestyle-tournament/clarissa-chun-uses-judo-move-to-clinch-americas-first-medal-in-london/.

Clarke, Liz. 2013. "Wrestling Put on International Olympics Committee Short List for 2020 Games." *Washington Post*, May 29, 2013. https://www.washingtonpost.com/sports/olympics/wrestling-put-on-international-olympics-committee-short-list-for-2020-games/2013/05/29/e6c1dd5c-c87f-11e2-9245-773c0123c027_story.html.

"Cortez Third in National Girls Wrestling." 2003. *Hanford Sentinel*, April 1, 2003.

Costa, Brian. 2008. "A Born Fighter." *The Atlanta Constitution*, January 13, 2008.

Creason, Tim. 2021. "Dream Within Reach: Granger's Sarah Hildebrandt to Wrestle for Spot on Olympic Team." *South Bend Tribune*, March 31, 2021. https://www.southbendtribune.com/story/sports/2021/03/31/dream-within-reach-grangers-sarah-hildebrandt-to-wrestle-for-spot-on-olympic-team/116619142/.

"Decision Day Coming." 2013. *The Gazette*, September 8, 2013.

Dheensaw, Cleve. 2013. "Tokyo Victory Welcomed by Swim Coach." *Times Colonist*, September 8, 2013.

Dobie, Michael. 2004. "No Holds Barred as Women Arrive." *Newsday*, August 8, 2004.

Dougherty, Denis. 2005. "Appleton Man is Speeding Toward Olympics." *The Post-Crescent*, March 29, 2005.

Eck, Frank. 1949. "Girl Rassler has 50G Profession." *Argus-Leader*, May 9, 1949.

Elston, Kyle. 2000. "A Guiding Light." *Star-Gazette*, April 20, 2000.

Emert, Rich. 2000. "This Female Champ is Just One of the Guys." *Pittsburgh Post-Gazette*, February 16, 2000.

"Family Doubts Ruling on Daughter's Death." 2005. *The Billings Gazette*, November 18, 2005.

"Female Wrestler Makes State Prep Sports History." 2009. *St. Cloud Times*, March 21, 2009.

FloWrestling. 2021. "The Bader Show–Helen Maroulis." Streamed live on January 20, 2021. YouTube video, 39:25. https://www.youtube.com/watch?v=CLvL69YRC6o.

Frantz, Eric. 2005. "Northeastern Girls Have Lock on Wrestling Spirit." *Springfield News-Sun*, December 29, 2005.

Frauenheim, Norm. 1996. "Women's Wrestling Champ is Sport's Advocate." *Arizona Republic*, July 2, 1996.

Giannandrea, Nick. 2008. "Corona Captures 146 Crown." *The Fresno Bee*, February 1, 2008.

Giannandrea, Nick. 2008. "Growing and Grappling." *The Fresno Bee*, February 1, 2008.

"Girl Wrestler Seeks Michigan Title." 2000. *Argus-Leader*, March 10, 2000.

"Gold Medalist Hurdler Banned for Positive Test." 2008. *Arizona Daily Star*, August 17, 2008.

Gonzales, Randy. 2008. "Cheerleaders Wait; Wrestler Wins." *The Hays Daily News*, February 24, 2008.

Good Morning America. 2019. "How Rachel Brosnahan discovered her love of wrestling." December 13, 2019. YouTube video, 1:21. https://www.youtube.com/watch?v=9CIL6QInF_Q.

Goodwin, Cody. 2019. "Wrestling: Kayla Miracle defeats reigning world bronze medalist, makes 2019 world team." *Hawk Central*, June 15, 2019. https://www.hawkcentral.com/story/sports/college/iowa/wrestling/2019/06/15/2019-final-x-lincoln-hawkeye-wrestling-club-kayla-miracle-2019-world-team-thomas-gilman-joe-colon/1466070001/.

Grohmann, Karolos. 2013. "Wrestling Wins Vote and Will Be Part of 2020 Tokyo Olympics." *Reuters*, September 8, 2013. https://archive.ph/20130908181738/http://www.theglobeandmail.com/sports/more-sports/wrestling-wins-vote-and-will-be-part-of-2020-tokyo-olympics/article14179694/.

Hall, Mike. 2001. "Girls Succeed in a Boys' World." *Albuquerque Journal*, July 6, 2001.

Hambleton, Ken. 2005. "Maslowsky Takes Her Place in History." *Lincoln Journal Star*, February 19, 2005.

Hansen, Marc. 2012. "Girl Wrestler Exceeds Expectations, Not Yet Satisfied." *Visalia Times-Delta*, February 12, 2012.

Hansen, Tony. 2000. "Making Her Mark on the Mat." *Battle Creek Enquirer*, March 4, 2000.

Hassan, Carma, and Scottie Andrew. 2021. "At Least 20 People Tested Positive for Covid-19 After Attending a High School Wrestling Tournament." *CNN*, January 25, 2021. https://www.cnn.com/2021/01/25/us/covid-wrestling-tournament-outbreak-trnd/index.html.

Henderson, Joe. 2004. "She Knows No Limits." *The Tampa Tribune*, August 1, 2004.

Herwees, Tasbeeh. 2018. "How Netflix's Newest Star Is Subverting the Coming-of-Age Genre." *Vice*, March 30, 2018. https://www.vice.com/en/article/paxka8/netflix-first-match-elvire-emanuelle-interview.

Hine, Tommy. 2004. "Miranda Wins 'Consolation Prize.'" *Hartford Courant*, August 24, 2004.

"How Jaimie Alexander's High School Wrestling Helped with 'Blindspot' Role." 2017. *Extra*, January 11, 2017. https://extratv.com/2017/01/11/how-jaimie-alexanders-high-school-wrestling-helped-with-blindspot-role/.

Hughes, Mike. 2015. "Tough Star of 'Blindspot' Started Girls Wrestling Team." *Lansing State Journal*, September 20, 2015. https://www.lansingstatejournal.com/story/entertainment/television/2015/09/20/tough-star-blindspot-started-girls-wrestling-team/72392956/.

"Jacarra Winchester qualifies USA for Tokyo Olympics at 53 kg in women's freestyle." 2020. Retrieved July 20, 2021. https://themat.tv/athletes/jacarra-winchester/video/9-jacarra-winchester-qualifies-usa-for-tokyo-olympics-at-53-kg-in-womens-freestyle.

Karges, Crystal. 2021. "Male Wrestlers and Bulimia—How Does it Happen? What Do Coaches and Parents Need to Know?" *Eating Disorders Hope*. Retrieved March 16, 2021. https://www.eatingdisorderhope.com/-treatment-for-eating-disorders/special-issues/teen-adolescent-children/male-wrestlers-and-bulimia-how-does-it-happen-what-do-coaches-and-parents-need-to-know.

Keeler, Sean. 2019. "A Colorado Springs wrestler made history when he knocked himself out of the state tournament rather than wrestle a girl." *Denver Post*, February 23, 2019. https://www.denverpost.com/2019/02/23/colorado-state-wrestling-tournament-colorado-springs-wrestler-girl-forfeit/.

Kiszla, Mark. 2021. "Kiszla: Colorado wrestler Adeline Gray defers dream of mother-hood to chase Olympic gold." *Greeley Tribune*, April 23, 2021. https://www.greeleytribune.com/2021/04/23/adeline-gray-colorado-wrestler-defers-motherhood-dream-olympic-gold/.

Klee, Paul. 2002. "A Headlock on History." *Casper Star-Tribune*, June 21, 2002.

Klingman, Kyle. 2021. "American Women's Wrestling Took a Leap Forward After 2020 Olympics." *FloWrestling*, August 14, 2021. https://www.flowrestling.org/articles/7134849-american-womens-wrestling-took-a-leap-forward-after-2020-olympics.

Koman, Stuart, and Gail Hanson-Mayer. n.d. "Which Athletes Are Most Likely to Develop Eating Dis-orders?" *Walden Eating Disorders*. Retrieved March 15, 2021. https://www.waldeneatingdisorders.com/blog/which-athletes-are-most-likely-to-develop-eating-disorders/.

Kosek, Koy. 2005. "Ebert Stars at Nationals." *Manitowoc Herald-Times*, August 3, 2005.

Krah, Steve. 2021. "Sarah Hildebrandt and Olympic Wrestling Training Tour Come to South Bend." *South Bend Tribune*, June 29, 2021. https://www.southbendtribune.com/story/sports/2021/06/29/2021-tokyo-olympics-saint-marys-college-hosts-usa-wrestling/7794906002/.

Kudialis, Chris. 2021. "Sarah Hildebrandt is all business as she prepares to live her Olympics dream in Tokyo." *South Bend Tribune*, July 24, 2021. https://www.southbendtribune.com/story/sports/2021/07/24/wreslter-sarah-hildebrandt-is-all-business-subdued-olympics-japan/8080277002/.

Lance, David. 1997. "Judge Turns Down Request to Allow Girls' Wrestling." *Fort Worth Star*, January 3, 1997.

"Lancer, Jet Wrestlers Advance." 2004. *Manitowoc Herald-Times*, February 15, 2004.

Lee, Sonia. 1998. "Wyoming High School Activities Association Oks Waivers." *Casper Star-Tribune*, November 25, 1998.

Levendusky, Derek. 2021. "Maroulis Dominates Bronze Match, Winchester Will Wrestle Again." *American Women's Wrestling*, August 5, 2021. https://www.americanwomenswrestling.com/news-2/maroulis-dominates-bronze-match-winchester-will-wrestle-again.

Levendusky, Derek. 2021. "Hildebrandt & Winchester Both Fall in Morning Session, Hildebrandt will Wres-tle for Bronze." *American Women's Wrestling*, August 6, 2021. https://www.americanwomenswrestling.com/news-2/winchester-hildebrandt.

Levendusky, Derek. 2021. "Hildebrandt Bronze, Team USA Women Finish with 4 Medals." *American Wom-en's Wrestling*, August 7, 2021. https://www.americanwomenswrestling.com/news-2/hildebrandt-silver-team-usa-women-finish-with-4-medals.

The Lily News. 2017. "After Coping With Tragedy, Sara McMann Puts Up a Fight." July 25, 2017. https://medium.com/the-lily/after-coping-with-tragedy-sara-mcmann-puts-up-a-fight-d8e35115c1f.

Luchau, Jeremy. 2008. "Hanford West Wrestler Wins Title at State Invitational." *Hanford Sentinel*, Febru-ary 2, 2008. https://hanfordsentinel.com/sports/hanford-west-wrestler-wins-title-at-state-invitational/-article_9c5947f2-7895-554c-97d9-be66c258ea7d.html.

MacLean, Heather. 1993. "New Brave Coach Sets Goal of Title." *Daily Sitka Sentinel*, February 5, 1993.

MacLean, Heather. 1993. "MEHS Teacher Quits as Wrestling Coach." *Daily Sitka Sentinel*, February 9, 1993.

MacLean, Heather. 1994. "Edgecumbe Coach Returns to Position." *Daily Sitka Sentinel*, January 14, 1994.

MacLean, Heather. 1994. "Tenacious Wrestler Competes in Nevada." *Daily Sitka Sentinel*, May 3, 1994.

Maroulis, Helen. 2016. "Olympic Wrestler Helen Maroulis: My Darkest Secret That's Greater Than Gold." *Sports Illustrated*, November 11, 2016. https://www.si.com/the-cauldron/2016/11/11/helen-maroulis-olympic-gold-medalist-fear-darkest-secret.

"Mat Club Competitors Earn Medals at Wrestling Classic." 1997. *The Lebanon Express*, January 15, 1997.

Mathur, Yashika. 2017. "Dangal casting: How Nitesh Tiwari finalised Fatima Sana Shaikh and Sanya Malhotra." *Hindustan Times*, August 20, 2017. https://www.hindustantimes.com/bollywood/-dangal-casting-how-nitesh-tiwari-finalised-fatima-sana-shaikh-and-sanya-malhotra/story-m7XyEe2grzzlh8N5hVDP4J.html.

Mayeda, David. 2013. "A Blow for Women's Sport." *Aljazeera*, March 8, 2013. https://www.aljazeera.com/sports/2013/3/8/a-blow-for-womens-sport.

Mercer, Kevin. 2021. "Magazine: U.S. Wrestler Helen Maroulis Praises God Through Hills and Valleys." *Sports Spectrum*, August 3, 2021. https://sportsspectrum.com/sports-spectrum/2021/08/03/magazine-wrestler-helen-maroulis-praises-god/.

Merda, Mallory. 2020. "HS Wrestling: Trojan Wars, Multiple Large Tournaments Cancelled due to Covid-19 Pandemic." *The Sentinel*, September 30, 2020. https://cumberlink.com/sports/high-school/wrestling/-hs-wrestling-trojan-wars-multiple-large-tournaments-canceled-due-to-covid-19-pandemic/article_c40d5ba8-25eb-5a87-ad52-ef921170ea9a.html.

Meredith, Luke. 2013. "Women Are Crucial to Wrestling's Olympic Future." *Casper Star-Tribune*, August 17, 2013.

Meredith, Luke. 2013. "Wrestling Reinstated for 2020 Games." *The Record*, September 9, 2013.

"Mildred Burke Finds Outlet in Wrestling." 1941. *St. Joseph News-Press*, August 30, 1941.

Miller, Bruce. 2015. "Iowa Wrestlers Helped Give Jaimie Alexander All the Right Moves for 'Blindspot,' 'Thor.'" *Sioux City Journal*, September 27, 2015. https://siouxcityjournal.com/entertainment/television/-iowa-wrestlers-helped-give-jaimie-alexander-all-the-right-moves-for-blindspot-thor/article_12e5a472-8060-58f9-91c3-c2de94bbf7ca.html.

Mink, Joe. 2015. "From Glamazon to Glamamom." *Star-Gazette*, January 11, 2015.

Monahan, Melony. 1997. "Editorial: Whenever I Wrestle, I Wrestle To Win." *Fort Worth Star*, January 19, 1997.

Morton, Tom. 2005. "Police Await Tolin Report." *Casper Star-Tribune*, April 8, 2005.

Morton, Tom. 2005. "Police Still Investigating Tolin's Death." *Casper Star-Tribune*, July 17, 2005.

NBC Sports. 2021. "Tamyra Mensah-Stock clinches Olympic spot with trials win | NBC Sports." April 3, 2021. YouTube video, 13:25. https://www.youtube.com/watch?v=xwLh4FrOLEI.

Niyo, Jordan. 2004. "Women Grapple for Attention as They Make Debut on Wrestling Mat." *Detroit Free Press*, August 22, 2004.

Nuckton, Gerri. 1990. "Pittsburg Wrestler Finds a Silver Lining." *Martinez News-Gazette*, July 14, 1990.

O'Brien, Pam. 2019. "Rachel Brosnahan On Why She's All About Pushing Herself Out of Her Comfort Zone." *Shape*, February 10, 2019. https://www.shape.com/celebrities/interviews/rachel-brosnahan.

Oliver, Greg. 2011. "Phoenix has Risen Again and Again." *Slam Wrestling*, February 3, 2011. https://slamwrestling.net/index.php/2011/02/03/phoenix-has-risen-again-and-again/.

OlympicTalk. 2019. "Jacarra Winchester, after foe bites her, wins first wrestling world title." *NBC Sports*, September 18, 2019. https://olympics.nbcsports.com/2019/09/18/jacarra-winchester-wrestling-world-championships/.

OpenArc Support. 2017. "Wrestler Olivia Rondeau Makes History." *Montgomery County Sentinel*, August 3, 2017. https://www.thesentinel.com/communities/montgomery/sports/wrestler-olivia-rondeau-makes-history/article_d01491ad-3169-56b6-9c07-95d1b037fba1.html.

Oyeleke, Sodiq. 2021. "Blessing Oborududu: Meet Nigeria's first wrestler to win silver in Olympics." *Punch*, August 4, 2021. https://punchng.com/blessing-oborududu-meet-nigerias-first-wrestler-to-win-silver-in-olympics/.

Pederson, Heidi. 2004. "Coll. Heritage Senior Caps Perfect Season." *Star Telegram*, February 29, 2004.

Pellegrino, Nick. 2001. "Silvia Cortez Breaks Ground in the Sport of Wrestling." *Hanford Sentinel*, May 22, 2001.

Peters, Caroline. 2021. "Tamyra Mensah-Stock is Thrilled to be Making Her Olympic Debut." *KOAA News*, July 24, 2021. https://www.koaa.com/community/brand-spotlight/team-usa-in-our-community/-tamyra-mensah-stock-is-thrilled-to-be-making-her-olympic-debut.

Piecoro, Nick. 2004. "Olympics Gives Validity to Women's Wrestling." *Arizona Republic*, September 8, 2004.

Pinkston, Buddy. 2006. "Proving She Belongs." *The Atlanta Constitution*, February 11, 2006.

Price, Karen. 2021. "Jacarra Winchester Fights Her Way to Olympic Wrestling Team." *Team USA*, April 9, 2021. https://www.teamusa.org/News/2021/April/09/Jacarra-Winchester-Fights-Her-Way-To-Olympic-Wrestling-Team.

Proia, Olivia. 2019. "Lancaster Wrestler Meets WWE Role Model." *WKBW*, November 29, 2019. https://www.wkbw.com/news/local-news/lancaster-wrestler-meets-wwe-role-model.

Quintanilla, Milton. 2021. "'Never Lose Faith': U.S. Wrestler Helen Maroulis Glorifies God Following Olympic Return." *Christian Headlines*, August 6, 2021. https://www.christianheadlines.com/contributors/milton-quintanilla/never-lose-faith-us-wrestler-helen-maroulis-glorifies-god-following-olympic-return.html.

Reed, Jess. 1997. "Wrestling is a Family Affair for Plagmanns." *The Lebanon Express*, April 2, 1997.

"Reedsville's Ebert Wins USGWA Title." 2006. *Manitowoc Herald-Times*, April 15, 2006.

Reilly, Rick. 2011. "Wrestling With Conviction." *ESPN*, February 18, 2011. https://www.espn.com/espn/news/story?id=6136707.

Rendell, Rick. 2018. "A fighter's mentality suits Framingham's Bella Ricchiazzi well on the wrestling mat." *Metro West Daily News*, April 1, 2018. https://www.metrowestdailynews.com/sports/20180331/fighters-mentality-suits-framinghams-bella-ricchiazzi-well-on-wrestling-mat.

Robbins, Julie R. 1992. "Okemos Girl Invited to Olympic Session." *Lansing State Journal*, May 22, 1992.

Roose, Bill L. 2000. "Battle of the Sexes." *Detroit Free Press*, March 9, 2000.

Rose, Shannon. 1999. "Haritan Closes With a Clean Slate." *The Orlando Sentinel*, March 20, 1999.

Rosen, Karen. 2004. "Women Wrestlers Grapple for Acceptance." *The Atlantic Constitution*, May 23, 2004.

Rudis. 2021. "My Journey Through Wrestling: Kayla Miracle." July 1, 2021. YouTube video, 1:28. https://www.youtube.com/watch?v=aeGI7R7JX74&t=3s.

"Rulon Rallies for Another Improbable Olympic Spot." 2004. *Great Falls Tribune*, May 24, 2004.

"The Rush: Olympic wrestler Maroulis on breaking barriers, mental health and making a difference." 2021. *Yahoo Sports*, August 7, 2021. https://sports.yahoo.com/the-rush-olympic-wrestler-maroulis-on-breaking-barriers-mental-health-and-making-a-difference-044810564.html.

Saliong, Sarah Mae. 2021. "Olympic Wrestling Thanks God For Winning Gold Medal, Says She's Happy to Represent Her Beloved America." *Christianity Daily*, August 4, 2021. https://www.christianitydaily.com/articles/12797/20210804/olympic-wrestler-thanks-god-for-winning-gold-medal-says-she-s-happy-to-represent-her-beloved-america.htm.

"Sarah Hildebrandt Medals After Lifelong Olympic Dream." 2021. *FloWrestling*, August 7, 2021. https://www.flowrestling.org/collections/6751866-interviews/video?playing=7130573.

Schultz, Ted. 2021. "Scoring an Eagle." *The Republic*, June 10, 2021. http://www.therepublic.com/2021/06/10/scoring_an_eagle__6yearold_wrestler_wins_national_championship-2/.

Schwartz, Tim. 2021. "Tokyo Olympics: Rockville Native Helen Maroulis Earns Bronze, Becomes First American Woman to Win Two Medals in Wrestling." *The Baltimore Sun*, August 5, 2021. https://www.baltimoresun.com/sports/olympics/bs-sp-helen-maroulis-wins-bronze-wrestling-tokyo-olympics-20210805-lbhnimfrx5eapcpraozrcjqkxe-story.html.

Shai, Katherine. 2020. "Six Feet Apart: Covid-19 Stories." *LuchaFit*, June 20, 2020. https://www.luchafit.com/blog/tag/Katherine+Shai.

Shinn, Peggy. 2021. "Tamyra Mensah-Stock: Why the Olympic Gold-Medal-Winning Wrestler Likes Karaoke." *Team USA*, August 14, 2021. https://www.teamusa.org/News/2021/August/14/Tamyra-Mensah-Stock-Why-the-Olympic-GoldMedal-Winning-Wrestler-Likes-Karaoke.

Simon, Scott, and Amanda Morris. 2019. "Instead Of Wrestling A Girl, High Schooler Chooses To Forfeit State Wrestling Match." *WGBH News*, March 10, 2019. https://www.wgbh.org/news/lifestyle/2019/03/10/-instead-of-wrestling-a-girl-high-schooler-chooses-to-forfeit-state-wrestling-match.

Skol, Mark. 2021. "Sarah Hildebrandt Returns Home, Prepares for Dream to Compete at Olympics." *WNDU*, June 29, 2021. https://www.wndu.com/2021/06/29/sarah-hildebrandt-returns-home-prepares-dream-compete-olympics/.

Spaulding, Anthony. 2015. "College Wrestling: Former Brave, 3-time All-American Ashley Iliff shares tips with youth." *New Jersey Herald*, June 11, 2015. https://www.njherald.com/article/20150607/SPORTS/909014791.

Spencer, Jon. 1997. "Girl Wrestler's Debut Swift." *News-Journal*, December 11, 1997.

Spencer, Jon. 1999. "Whippets Live Up to Lofty Goals." *News-Journal*, December 15, 1999.

Spencer, Jon. 2001. "Future Bright for Girl Wrestler." *News-Journal*, June 8, 2001.

Spencer, Jon. 2011. "Girls Deserve Equal Treatment." *News-Journal*, February 25, 2011.

"Ten Local Wrestlers Earn Freestyle State Titles." 1997. *The Marion Star*, May 18, 1997.

"Texas Wrestles Sexism." 1997. *Press Democrat*, January 5, 1997.

Thurmond, Neathery. 2021. "Laxative Abuse in Bulimia: Physical Consequences, Complications, and Ramifications." *Eating Disorder Hope*. Retrieved March 15, 2021. https://www.eatingdisorderhope.com/information/bulimia/laxative-abuse-in-bulimia-physical-consequences-complications-and-ramifications.

Tierney, Mike. 2004. "Silver No Solace for U.S. Wrestler." *Longview News-Journal*, August 24, 2004.

Troy, Jack. 1943. "All in the Game." *The Atlanta Constitution*, December 23, 1943.

Troy, Jack. 1945. "All in the Game." *The Atlanta Constitution*, January 12, 1945.

Tufaro, Greg. 2006. "Just One of the Guys." *The Central New Jersey Home News*, December 14, 2006.

USA Wrestling. 2020. "Helen Maroulis After Winning the Pan Am Olympic Qualifier Wrestle-Off." February 8, 2020. YouTube video, 9:22. https://www.youtube.com/watch?v=Uz6OUHaFfLM.

USA Wrestling. 2020. "Catching up with Macey Kilty after her double title performance." November 17, 2020. YouTube video, 20:57. https://www.youtube.com/watch?v=hPdtozUruOs&t=737s.

USA Wrestling. 2021. "Kyle Dake and Sarah Hildebrandt Pre-Olympic Team Trials Press Conference." March 23, 2021. YouTube video, 31:28. https://www.youtube.com/watch?v=WsbYJM7SPDI.

USA Wrestling. 2021. "2020 Olympic Team Trials WFS 53KG Ronna Heaton After Challenge Tournament Finals." April 1, 2021. YouTube video, 3:03. https://www.youtube.com/watch?v=JvtPaZlx31Y.

USA Wrestling. 2021. "2020 Olympic Team Trials WFS 76KS Kylie Welker after challenge tournament finals." April 2, 2021. YouTube video, 3:32. https://www.youtube.com/watch?v=XKoHA_BnrHI.

USA Wrestling. 2021. "National Women's Coach Terry Steiner Prior to Olympic Games in Tokyo." July 30, 2021. YouTube video, 5:52. https://www.youtube.com/watch?v=vZdezVuoRs0.

USA Wrestling. 2021. "Six-Time World Champion Adeline Gray After Winning 2021 World Gold at 76 KG." October 6, 2021. YouTube video, 8:27. https://www.youtube.com/watch?v=kk_v7Dk3BeU&t=5s.

USA Wrestling. 2021. "Helen Maroulis (USA), 2021 57-kg World Champion." October 7, 2021. YouTube video, 10:36. https://www.youtube.com/watch?v=i5L_i938Wj0&t=2s.

USA Wrestling. 2021. "Tamyra Mensah-Stock (USA), 2021 World Bronze Medal at 68-kg." October 7, 2021. YouTube video, 7:09. https://www.youtube.com/watch?v=ABCdHS01c_I&t=3s.

Vikayakar, R. M. 2016. "Exclusive: 'Dangal' Girls Talk About Their Dreamy Debuts with Aamir Khan." *India West*, December 19, 2016. https://www.indiawest.com/entertainment/bollywood/exclusive-dangal-girls-talk-about-their-dreamy-debuts-with-aamir-khan/article_ba629c84-c5b4-11e6-8f63-479cf9da8282.html.

Walker, Esther. 1944. "Lady's Slant on Lady Wrestlers." *Santa Cruz Sentinel*, February 25, 1944.

Wellens, Matt. 2008. "Queen of the Mat." *Manitowoc Herald-Times*, April 12, 2008.

Williams, Kari. 2019. "Tragos/Thesz Hall of Fame Inductee Beth Phoenix 'Revels in the Magic' of Wrestling." *Slam Wrestling*, July 28, 2019. https://slamwrestling.net/index.php/2019/07/28/tragos-thesz-hall-of-fame-inductee-beth-phoenix-revels-in-the-magic-of-wrestling/.

"Woman Wednesday: With the Limitless Maya Nelson, Q&A." 2020. *American Wrestler Blog*, November 4, 2020. https://americanwrestlerblog.com/f/woman-wednesday-with-the-limitless-maya-nelson-qa?.

Worthen, Joshua. 2021. Facebook, August 25, 2021.

"Wrestler Mensah Stock taking Olympics postponement in stride." 2020. Wayland Baptist University, April 1, 2020. https://wbaathletics.com/news/2020/4/1/-7-womens-wrestling-wrestler-mensah-stock-taking-olympics-postponement-in-stride.aspx.

"Wrestling Dropped From 2020 Games." 2013. *ESPN*, February 12, 2013. https://www.espn.com/olympics/wrestling/story/_/id/8939185/ioc-drops-wrestling-2020-olympics.

"Wrestling Federation President Quits." 2013. *ESPN*, February 16, 2013. https://www.espn.com/olympics/wrestling/story/_/id/8954047/wrestling-federation-president-raphael-martinetti-resigns-omission.

Yost, Aaron. 2001. "Plagmann Makes a Name for Herself." *Albany Democrat-Herald*, February 18, 2001.

Zaccardi, Nick. 2018. "Helen Maroulis Wrestled in the Dark With Concussion." *NBC Sports*, May 16, 2018. https://olympics.nbcsports.com/2018/05/16/helen-maroulis-wrestling-concussion/.

Zaccardi, Nick. 2021. "Helen Maroulis, Trailblazing Olympic Wrestling Champion, Back at Trials After Briefly Retiring." *NBC Sports*, March 30, 2021. https://olympics.nbcsports.com/2021/03/30/helen-maroulis-wrestling-olympic-trials/.

Zopf, Jonathan. 2008. "Girl Among Boys: Buford's Female Wrestler to be Honored Tonight by Atlanta Sports Hall of Fame." *Gainesville Times*, June 11, 2008. https://www.gainesvilletimes.com/sports/high-schools/girl-among-boys-bufords-female-wrestler-to-be-honored-tonight-by-atlanta-sports-hall-of-fame/.

Index